This book is unique
in that it is bound
upside down.
                    RCD

TO DANIEL BRETT,

Many thanks for your help with

the 1991 Campaign.

May you go on to make your own

mark in Tory Party politics.

                    Ron Dean (Cllr.)

The Making of Conservative Party Policy

The Making of Conservative Party Policy

The Conservative Research Department
Since 1929

John Ramsden

Longman
London and New York

Longman Group Limited London

Associated companies, branches and representatives
throughout the world

Published in the United States of America
by Longman Inc., New York

First published 1980

British Library Cataloguing in Publication Data

Ramsden, John, *b.1947*
   The making of Conservative Party policy
   1. Conservative and Unionist Party
   I. Title
   329.9'41   JN1129.C72   79–41309

   ISBN 0-582-29508-4

Printed and bound in Great Britain by
William Clowes (Beccles) Limited, Beccles and London

Contents

Introduction

The Conservative Research Department is now half a century old, and it seems appropriate that its largely unsung exploits over that time should be given an academic exposition. For, while studies of civil service procedures, the opinions and habits of back-benchers, and the role of pressure groups have proliferated, and while the thought processes of front-benchers can at least be inferred from their utterances while, and after, they hold office, there has been very little systematic work on the parties' professional machinery for policy making. Michael Hatfield's important study of the making of Labour's policy of 1974, *The House the Left Built*, repairs this omission on the Labour side but on the right the gap remains. The information side of the Conservative Research Department's work was studied by Michael Rush and Anthony Barker for *The Member of Parliament and his Information*; there have been frequent biographical references to salad days spent in Old Queen Street, especially when Iain Macleod, Enoch Powell and Reginald Maudling were (allegedly) 'Rab Butler's backroom boys'; and there have been frequent references to work done on Party propaganda in the series of Nuffield College election studies, and in other works on electioneering. But all of this has been fragmentary, largely because the parties have tended to regard research as a domestic matter which might occasionally be discussed off the record, but which was not a proper subject for close scrutiny. The short time that research organisations have existed has also militated against their close investigation. Half of the members of the Conservative Research Department's staff of the 1930s are still alive and active, and many of its staff of the 1940s and 1950s are now leading party politicians in their own right; embarrassment to the party present might result from the investigation of the Research Department past.

For my own part, I had frequently visited the Research Department while studying the history of the party, and as an observer of British politics I had come to admire it from afar. I was therefore particularly pleased that the fiftieth anniversary was deemed to be an appropriate opportunity to fill this important gap in the literature of modern British politics. I have received encouragement both active and passive in my task, and I should perhaps explain at the outset what my relationship with the department has been. Without the enthusiastic support of the then Chairman (Rt Hon Angus Maude, MP), Director (Chris Patten) and Associate Director (James Douglas), the whole project would not have got off the ground, and it was they who laid down my terms of access to the Department, with the approval of the Leader of the Party. I was given free access to all departmental papers up to 1964, to the bulk of papers for the period 1964–70, and to selected papers for the period 1970–74. I have therefore spent a great deal of time in Old Queen Street and at the University of Newcastle (where some of the papers are now deposited) reading through old, and in some cases not-so-old files. It was stipulated that I should be free to quote whatever I liked for the period up to 1964, but that restrictions might have to be imposed for the last few years. In the event, nothing that I wished to include in my text had to be removed. Nevertheless, there is an inevitable shift in the course of the narrative from material that is entirely based on archives to a final chapter that is basically observational and anecdotal. It is to be hoped that the change of gear has not been too abrupt. The problem has been eased by the availability to me of several of the department's key members from the whole of the fifty year period, both as direct sources of information and as critical readers of various drafts of the text. I have talked to about fifty past and present members of the department's staff, and I regret that time alone has prevented me from taking up many more offers of such help. As experienced draftsmen of party manifestoes, David Clarke, Lord Fraser of Kilmorack, Brendon Sewill, and Chris Patten, have all made helpful comments on the text, though of course the responsibility for what remains there is entirely my own. I should also like to thank Dr Philip Williamson and Mr Michael Bilton (for reading parts of the text over a critical weekend in March 1979 when a General Election was to be called within days, and all of us had much else on our minds) and Mrs Angela Ellis for help with typing.

J. A. Ramsden

Chapter 1

Research and Conservative policy

A visitor to Westminster in the 1970s would be unlikely to have felt that the Conservative Research Department was one of the places that he should not miss; and if he happened to wander down Old Queen Street, near St James' Park, it is unlikely that he would have noticed anything very striking about number twenty-four. He might appreciate the unpretentious Georgian architecture of the building, but he would certainly not have guessed that it housed one of the dozen or so offices from which the trends and tides of British party politics were directed. Nor indeed would the name 'Conservative Research Department' have enlightened him much if he had seen it on the door – actually he couldn't have seen it, for the brass plate was removed for some long forgotten street demonstration and only blue shutters at the windows would have hinted at what lay within. To judge from recent evidence, the British press is equally uncertain about what took place behind those blue shutters. Most unusually, the Research Department figured in news stories in its own right on two occasions during 1978, and it was clear that even the correspondents of the serious newspapers had only a hazy understanding of the department's work.

To a great extent, this is the result of a conscious decision to keep the Department out of the limelight and so avoid the difficulties that might follow any over-exposure of its activities. Almost all that is said, published or broadcast in the name of the Conservative Party is affected by the Department's work, and much of it is actually written there, but this material is rarely given any imprint or acknowledgement to indicate its origin. Within the Department, this principle goes further. Departmental work is highly decentralised. As is the case in many Government departments there is a single officer manning the desk which deals with one area of policy, but his name will be unknown to all but a few party people and those outsiders who are directly involved with his work; his name does not appear on press releases or policy documents. The analogy of a Government department is informative, for the Research Department is the

Party's civil servant on policy matters. At election times, the Department is involved in most of the policy initiatives with which the Party hopes to win newspaper support, but press enquiries are not taken there directly, and officers do not liaise directly with journalists 'on the record'. As Lord Fraser of Kilmorack, the Department's longest-serving Director, has put it, 'the correct place for back-room boys is in the back room.'[1]

In order to understand how the Department operates in the context of Conservative policy making, it is necessary to understand what exactly Conservative policy *is* and how it is made. That such a question can even be asked is due to the real difficulty of defining where power lies in the Party and from the fact that the Conservatives alone of British parties do not have a constitution. Various sections of the Party have very detailed rules (for example, the National Union, or the Party in Parliament when electing a new Leader), but there are no binding rules on the central question of the Leader's authority and the making of policy. Traditionally, this led commentators to accept unquestioningly the official Party line, which is to say that all policy decisions are made by the Leader. In the policy field, this view is still sometimes expressed, most recently by Michael Wolff, who was one of Edward Heath's closest advisers when he led the Party:[2]

> Policy-making in the Conservative Party lies entirely in the preserve of the Leader of the Party and through him or her of the Cabinet or Shadow Cabinet. This is no mere formal statement of the constitutional position: it is what has been happening, certainly for the past 30 years. It applies to strategy as well as tactics, to broad principles as well as the minutiae of day to day action.

But is this really all that there is to say? It can certainly be agreed that the Party is more oriented towards leadership than other British parties, and that the Leader can usually get his way on an issue if determined to do so – as not only Edward Heath but his predecessors and successor have all demonstrated. And yet, the actual working of the system is more complex, more subtle than Wolff's statement of the overriding principle would suggest. Robert McKenzie demonstrated a quarter of a century ago that the real freedom of action of a Conservative Leader is much less than might appear from strict theory, and this is especially true of policy making. Christopher Patten (the Director of the Research Department, 1974 to 1979) accepts the theory, but argues that,[3]

> in practice, the Leader carries out this work in consultation with her or his chosen colleagues in the Cabinet or Shadow Cabinet, and with

members of the parliamentary party. The Leader must also take account of the views of the party outside parliament, as expressed for example at the Party Conference.

To a great extent, the reasons for this are obvious. The Party can only avoid the public embarrassment of policy splits if decisions are taken after wide-ranging consultations; then at least the followers are convinced that their views have been weighed before the leadership decides. This is especially important to Conservatives for both the press and opponents expect a greater degree of cohesion from the Conservative Party than from Labour. What Lord Kilmuir used to call the Tories' secret weapon, loyalty, is no longer such a clear advantage; expectations of unity are raised so high that a minor policy debate among Conservatives occasions as much interest as a public row in the Labour Party. A Conservative Leader who did not try to offset this in advance would be foolish indeed, and he can at least make sure that the policies that he expounds command the support of a broad cross-section of the Party. Within such consultations, there are opportunities actually to change policies in detail or in principle, either by changing the mind of the leaders on the merits of an idea, or by making it clear that the policy would not justify the political trouble that it would involve. The Leader thus 'makes' policy with his colleagues, but it is not necessarily the same policy that either he or they would have made before taking advice.

There is a second factor which reduces the Leader's role from that of a dictator to something more like an executive managing director. The sheer complexity of issues in modern politics, and the technical difficulty of many of them, makes it impracticable for any individual to exert total, personal control, and this in turn endows the Party's professional advisers with a greater importance. Policy ideas cannot be started only at the top, and as a result some influence accrues to those whose initiatives are taken up and developed, for it is they who draft the first statement of the case, they who shape its initial direction. Whatever constitutional theory may say, the making of Conservative policy must be a collegiate activity, and there are both organisations to promote policy initiatives and machinery to consult opinion throughout the Party. For all that, Conservative policy making remains a grey area, partly because it is not easy to say what that policy is at any one time. When in office, it is certainly correct to say that Conservative policy is to be found in whatever the then Conservative Government is doing, for there is no concept of a Party policy distinct from the work of Conservative Ministers, as there is on the Labour side. In opposition, it is not quite so simple, for though the main lines of policy may be set out in the periodic manifestoes and policy statements, the rest has to be deduced from the speeches, writings and interviews of the Leader and his colleagues.[4] Only in the Queen's Speech of the next Conservative Government will the Party's real policy position be made clear again.

The most central of the policy organs of the Party is the Cabinet or Shadow Cabinet; Leaders do not commit the Party to major policy proposals without securing the advance approval of their colleagues. Most of the election manifestoes in the last half century have been vetted both in outline and in detail by the full Cabinet/Shadow Cabinet, and it is only with their express approval that even a manifesto pledge can become an actual proposal through the Queen's Speech, and then a Bill. The back-benchers of both Houses are also involved in making both long- and short-term policy. Parliamentary Committees which meet regularly during sittings are open to all back-benchers interested in the subject, and the leadership is kept in close touch with their views. In opposition, the party's chief spokesman usually chairs the appropriate Parliamentary Committee, but other contacts are kept open when in office, and the other officers of the committees are elected by the MPs rather than nominated by the Leader. When more specific policy work is being undertaken on a subject, MPs are always included in the policy committees and there is usually an overlap of membership with the Parliamentary Committees so that long- and short-term influences on policy are kept in step.

The National Union has a more limited involvement, though policy can be, and is, discussed at every level from the local ward to the annual conference. Any effect of these discussions has to be generalised and cumulative, even in the case of the public debates of the conference. Writers on the Conservative Party usually cite the housing debate of 1950, when the conference wrung a pledge from an unwilling platform, as evidence that the conference *can* determine policy, but as Michael Wolff has pointed out, the fact that no other case can be found weakens the argument. As this book shows, the party leaders were perturbed by what took place in 1950 and took steps to prevent it from recurring.[5] In any case, the National Union's real influence on policy is not intended to be exercised through the Conference, but by its taking part in the Advisory Committee on Policy (ACP), which brings together representatives of the party's voluntary workers (through the National Union), MPs (through the 1922 Committee), peers, and the chief party managers. This committee reports directly to the Leader and is thus an overall liaison group. The ACP meets about once a month during parliamentary sittings. It sees policy proposals at about the same time as the Shadow Cabinet (rather later when in office), and is given an early sight of any election manifesto or equivalent policy statement. It has no formal powers, except the right to advise the Leader on how the Party at large will react to a proposal; it can therefore act as a useful sounding board but little more, and even by 1963–64, Lord Windlesham felt that it had joined the 'dignified' sections of the party organisation rather than the 'efficient' ones (taking Bagehot's distinction). Its standing clearly depends on the character of its Chairman and the way in which he uses it, so that when Edward Heath himself took the chair at its meetings when Leader, its role was thereby enlarged.[6] In general though, that role is rather limited.

The final areas in which policy is influenced lie within the Party organisation as such, for the presentation of policy through electioneering and publicity material may come to affect the policy itself – at least by re-ordering priorities; the results of opinion polls and reports from agents in the constituencies certainly have a similar effect. But this area of influence may be considered as the most marginal.

The Research Department stands at the centre of this network, and it plays a part in all the policy mechanisms described above. It provides for the Leader his main policy advisers when in opposition and a major source of policy advice when in power. It works directly for the Leader and to his instructions, with its senior staff appointed only with the Leader's approval; in practice though, some of this authority has usually been delegated, for the Department has had as Chairman a man of Cabinet rank (also appointed by the Leader), and the Department's responsibility to the Leader has been through its Chairman. The Parliamentary Committees are serviced by research officers who act as secretaries, draft reports, take minutes, and write letters for the committees; special policy groups are handled in the same way when they exist. The Director sits in on meetings of the Shadow Cabinet and the ACP, and other officers also attend on occasion, one of them acting as secretary. Manifestoes and other policy documents are drafted by the Director and/or the senior research officers, and the publicity material put out by Central Office is vetted by the Department for accuracy in matters of policy. In particular, the Department itself publishes the weightier and more policy-based Party documents, especially the fortnightly *Politics Today* and the several-hundred page *Campaign Guide* produced for each election. In much the same way, the Department services individual MPs, with briefs for general circulation on matters of current debate, and, in some cases, with tailor-made briefs for MPs. Over a hundred briefs a year are written for general release and countless others are produced in response to special requests. A study undertaken by Anthony Barker and Michael Rush ten years ago found that Conservative MPs were very satisfied with the service they received; eighty per cent of Conservatives agreed that the Party offices constituted for them 'a major source of information' (compared with only eighteen per cent of Labour MPs who had the same confidence in Transport House). Over ninety per cent of Conservatives expressed general satisfaction with the service, and eighty-four per cent felt that they could always get an individual brief if they should ask for one. (This last published figure caused some consternation in Old Queen Street, lest eighty-four per cent should actually try to put their beliefs into practice by all demanding a brief at one!) The then Director of the Research Department, Brendon Sewill, estimated that about a quarter of his officers' time was taken up with actual policy research for the future, with the rest of the time being devoted to advising Shadow Ministers, to briefing MPs and servicing committees.[7]

In assessing the actual significance of the Research Department, Wolff placed it squarely with the Leader and the Cabinet among the 'effective' Party organs, ahead of the Parliamentary Committees, the National Union, and the ACP, and this ranking seems about right. But any assessment of relative influence in the Conservative Party must beware of giving a picture that is more definite than is the reality, for we can give only a still rather than a moving picture. So much always depends on circumstances and personalities.

The Department that is thus employed consists of about thirty research officers, rather more when in opposition and sometimes less when in power, and about the same number of secretaries. The desk officers, almost all of whom are graduates, are grouped into five 'sections' which cover respectively, home affairs, economics, foreign and defence policy, constitution, and general political matters. There is a substantial research library, and until recently the Department was also responsible for the Party's press cuttings library too, though this is now run entirely by Central Office. The Heads of Section, together with the Director and his Deputy and Assistant make up the small hierarchy of the Department, but internal relations are informal and every desk officer may expect to be in close touch with MPs and front-benchers from the day of his arrival. This has made the Department a valuable training ground for future politicians; the old boys of Old Queen Street in Cabinets have included Henry Brooke, Lord Longford, Iain Macleod, Enoch Powell and Reginald Maudling, while the Parliament elected in May 1979 included twenty-five ex-research officers as Conservative MPs. Out of a total Party expenditure of about six million pounds, the Department's budget accounts for only about a third of a million pounds – about six per cent of the total. It is, therefore, a small organisation, and one that has a tight and cohesive nature resulting from its size; when Michael Fraser was appointed Director in 1951, he was told by R. A. Butler that 'it is a beautiful little destroyer, and you will enjoy commanding it.'

The role of the CRD can perhaps be presented in sharper relief by a comparison with its main rival, the Labour Party Research Department. (The 'Labour Research Department' is an entirely separate body, mainly financed by trades unions, and well to the left of the Labour Party. The Liberals' research organisation is too small to make any real comparison possible.) The chief difference lies on the chain of command, for Labour allots to its research organisation a specific place in the Party's constitution, a role that brings it out into the open and involves it in the clash of opinions. The LPRD is formally a part of the headquarters at Transport House, with its Director coming under the General Secretary, but it works on policy matters for the National Executive Committee and its sub-committees. When there is a Labour government, there is a clear separation between Government and Party policy, and the LPRD is clearly ranged on the Party side. It takes its instruction from the Party organisation, accepting the rule which says that a proposal that achieves a two-thirds majority at a conference becomes Party policy, rather than from the reality which suggests something rather different. Hence, the LPRD has been involved in conflicts between the Labour Party and recent Labour Governments; for example, in 1969 the LPRD was briefing Labour MPs with arguments to use in opposition to the Government's proposals for the reform of industrial relations. A more general separation of policy took place after 1974, with the LPRD working towards the left-wing policies of *Labour's Programme 1976* rather than to the more moderate ideas of the Government which emerged in the 1979 Party manifesto. As a result, most of the drafting of the 1979 manifesto had to be done not in Transport House but in Downing Street; there has indeed been a steady movement away from the use of the LPRD by Labour Governments since 1964. Individual ministers still work very closely with Transport House, as Tony Benn did between 1974 and 1979, but he was involved with the LPRD as Chairman of the Party's Home Policy Sub-committee, not as a Minister. When in opposition, these problems are less severe, partly because the Party's leaders are deprived of civil service advice and so have to fall back on the LPRD, partly because the leaders have more time for party business anyway. However, the fact that Labour's policy making is so open, and so much played by the Party's rules (with either faction ready to cry foul when the rules are breached), can lead the LPRD into great difficulties. Both parties have experienced a greater degree of factionalism in the 1970s than in other recent years, but this has seemed particularly acute for the Party that has to conduct its debates in public. Michael Hatfield has shown how the Labour left mounted a determined and ultimately a successful campaign to win over the Party in the years of opposition after 1970; the main vehicles for this advance were the NEC which the left controlled, and the work of the LPRD which had to work for the NEC whatever its own views. In these circumstances, even the appointment of research staff became a matter of some debate in the Party, as with other appointments to Transport House. In practice though, much important work was also done by the LPRD for the Liaison Committee of the TUC, NEC and Parliamentary Party, a sign that for Labour too the rules are not the only determinants.

The LPRD is hampered by its Party standing from becoming a very effective research apparatus, and the more ideological tenor of debate in the Party often leads to rather more heat than light being created from the prolonged bargaining on policy. The 1963 policy document which made such an impression at the Scarborough conference had to go through seventeen drafts before agreement could be reached (about twice the par for the same course on the Conservative side) and the end result was not very satisfactory even then. Terry Pitt, who became Director of the LPRD in 1964, recalled that *Labour and the Scientific Revolution* 'was a superb slogan, but was not even precise enough to be called a comprehensive policy document on science and technology, let alone industry in general.' This largely follows from the fact that the LPRD has a smaller, less well-paid, less educationally qualified staff than the CRD, more demands on its time and less resources with which to meet them. The LPRD has only about a third of the number of research officers of the CRD, and a smaller proportion of them are graduates. As the servant of the NEC, it has to spend more time servicing the Party outside Parliament rather than in briefing MPs and their committees; hence the rather poor view of the LPRD given by Labour MPs when interviewed for Barker and Rush.[8]

In one way though the LPRD and CRD share a common feature, for both train leaders for the future; several research officers have gone on to become Labour MPs and one ex-Director is Peter Shore.

By comparison, the CRD is saved from a conflict of loyalties by the anonymity in which its work is done and by its direct, uncluttered, responsibility to the Leader who is elected and sustained in office by the Parliamentary Party. It has sufficient resources to carry out its task to the satisfaction of most of those for whom it works, though with the increasing demands on its time since 1964 its resources have had to rise sharply to keep up that level of service.

The final point to be made by way of introduction is the influence given to the Department by its position in the network of Party communications, for as Lord Windlesham demonstrated, political power in the British party system is closely related to the control of communications. In that sense, the central position is vital, for it is only in the Department and in the Leader's private office that all the threads of Party advice on policy can be tied together; as Michael Wolff puts it, the Research Department thus 'does for the political side of cabinet policy-making what the Cabinet Office does for the government.'[9] This is according the Department a high but far from exaggerated importance; in opposition, when there is no Cabinet Office or Central Policy Review Staff available to the Party, it rates even higher. Actual influence naturally ebbs and flows with changing circumstances and with the interplay of personalities. The Department's role is indeed constantly changing, affected by whether the Party is the Government or the Opposition, by the character of the Leader and the methods he employs, by the nature of policy being made (whether in detail as after 1965 or in broad terms as after 1975), by the different stages in the life of a single Parliament, by the balance of issues between the material and the more philosophic, and by the new tasks that are constantly being added through such novel events as the advent of an elected European Parliament. In these conditions, flexibility is of the essence, but it has been equally important that continuity has been maintained as well.

One such continuous feature has been the high standard insisted on by a succession of Directors from Joseph Ball onwards, and another has been the determination to demonstrate the same professionalism in the clear-headed separation of politics from policy. On the one hand, the Department seeks to advise the Party about policies on their merits, taking the national interest as its criterion – though naturally seeing the national interest from the viewpoint of a group of Conservatives; on the other hand, officers have to swallow their own views on policy when the decisions have been made, in order to advise the Party effectively on the best way to present those policies that have been agreed. Something else that has not changed, under a succession of very different Directors, is the atmosphere inside the Department itself, perhaps because its Directors have been appointed from the inside, and because they have all been recruiting the same sort of research officers, at about the same age, and on the same basic criteria for half a century. Most research officers have been recent graduates; over the period from 1929, the median age at entry has been twenty-eight and about seventy per cent have moved on within five years. The preponderance of young graduates has meant that something of the intellectual high-spiritedness of student politics at its best has always pervaded the place; John Wyndham has described this atmosphere as it was at the end of the 1940s, and an observer can see the same features today.[10] There is a heady excitement in the office, natural enough for an institution full of men who may well have been undergraduates in the Spring and who are then required to draft a policy for the Party or a speech for a Shadow Minister in the Autumn. This atmosphere has also helped the Department to retain its political flexibility and to remain fast on its feet. When the pound was unexpectedly devalued in 1949, every research officer turned up for work on the Sunday when the announcement was made without any summons being sent out; two days of intensive work culminated with the posting to MPs on the following Tuesday of a fifty-page brief on the economic and political consequences of devaluation, in time for them to read before the Parliamentary Finance Committee met on Wednesday and before the Party launched its attack on the Labour Government. That story must stand for many others which would demonstrate a similar flexibility, but it also shows the degree of commitment exhibited by the Department's staff. Few have left the Department without at least some regret, even when moving on to Parliament, and the old boys of the Department feel much the same loyalty as its current employees. It is difficult to disagree with the characteristically-restrained verdict of one of the Department's most distinguished former officers, Reginald Maudling, that 'taken all in all, its been a pretty good organisation, and its served the Party pretty well all these years.'[11]

Notes

1   Quoted by Christopher Patten in 'Policy making in the Conservative Party', in Z. Layton-Henry (ed), *Conservative Party Politics*. This introductory chapter also draws on the following published works, as well as interviews and observation: Arnold Beichman, 'The Conservative Research Department: How an elite subsystem within the British Conservative Party participates in the policy-making process'; Anthony King, 'How the Conservatives evolve policies', *New Society*, 20 July 1972; R. M. Punnett, *Front-Bench Opposition;* Anthony Barker and Michael Rush, *The Member of Parliament and his Information*; Michael Wolff, 'Policy-making in the Conservative Party' in John Mackintosh (ed), *People and Parliament*; Michael Hatfield, *The House the Left Built: inside Labour policy-making, 1970–1975.*
2   Wolff, 'Policy Making' op. cit., 112.
3   Robert McKenzie, *British Political Parties*; Patten, 'Policy making' op. cit.
4   Wolff, 'Policy Making' op. cit., 112–13.
5   See p. 160; Wolff, 'Policy Making', op. cit., 116.
6   Wolff, 'Policy Making', op. cit., 115; Lord Windlesham, *Communication and Political Power*, especially chapter 3.
7   Barker and Rush, *Member of Parliament*, 248–53, 420; Punnett, *Front-Bench Opposition*, 272–5.
8   Terry Pitt, 'Labour Policy Making' in John Mackintosh (ed), *People and Parliament*, 125–6; Barker and Rush, *Member of Parliament*, 234–5; Punnett, *Front-Bench Opposition*, 276–8.
9   Wolff, 'Policy Making', op. cit., 114.
10 Beichman, 'The Conservative Research Department'; John Wyndham (Lord Egremont), *Wyndham and Children First*, 141.
11 Interview with the author, July 1978.

Chapter 2

The origins of the Conservative Research Department

The historic Conservative Party was never notably policy-orientated, and any work done on policy was the consequence of the backstairs maneouvring of Conservative Governments rather than of any conscious involvement of the Party as a whole. Conservatives discussed policy matters at the annual conferences of the National Union after its foundation in 1867, and at equivalent local gatherings, but there was no supposition that the results of these discussions had more than a superficial relevance to the decisions that Conservative Ministers might take in the actual circumstances of office. There is no nineteenth-century equivalent on the Conservative side of the commitment to electoral reform forced on Gladstone by the Liberal rank and file at their conference of 1884; there is no equivalent of the package of programmes imposed on the Liberal leaders at Newcastle in 1891, nor even of the 'unauthorised programme' proclaimed by Joseph Chamberlain for the 1885 General Election.[1]

Nor, rather more peripherally, were there Conservative equivalents of the cornucopia of pressure groups which sailed under the Gladstonian flag, each with its good cause to promote, each with a paid staff of publicists, each with its political patrons and its sprinkling of MPs.[2] The few exceptions to this pattern, like the Agricultural Protectionists in the 1850s or their descendants in the Fair Trade Movement of the 1880s, show the ineffectiveness of such methods on the Conservative side. By the end of the century, with the development of the concept of the electoral mandate, a Party programme of sorts could be discerned in the personal manifesto issued by the Party leaders, but it remained a singularly unrevealing one. Party leaders sought the support of the electorate in order to retain and preserve – in a word to 'conserve' – rather than to propose new measures or to promote change. And even when the demands of electoral politics forced the Party into the market place in the search for votes, it preferred to explain 'What the Conservatives (had) *done* for the British people' rather than to explain what it would do if re-elected.[3] In part this was an understandable trait in a party of resistance, but in part it also demonstrated a genuine reluctance to enmesh the Party in the difficult, time-consuming and contentious business of constructing detailed programmes – a reluctance that the Party rank and file shared with their leaders. Conservative Governments of the late nineteenth century were not 'do-nothing' Governments, and indeed their capacity for administrative and legislative activity was not much less than that of Liberal Governments, but there was much less talk about policy by Conservatives, less hard work on policy, far fewer promises.

Against this dominant strain should be set a persistent under-current of dissatisfaction, an unsuccessful but continuous demand for a more positive Conservative attitude. The Tory radicals and humanitarians, the Young England movement, the Fourth Party, Lord Randolph Churchill's Tory Democrats, (and other exponents of reform in every generation) criticised the Party's leaders as supine and negative. The few successes that these critics achieved were the result of problems that the leaders faced in opposition (except for Peel's rather special, and self-imposed difficulties of 1846); when the difficulties subsided, so did support for programme politics. The long years of Salisbury's rule before the turn of the century demonstrated how far the collective party leadership could play politics 'off the pitch', living from month to month on their past record and making little attempt to survey their bridges in advance. For the Party these were relatively-harmonious years, but harmony could scarcely have been maintained in such a broad-church grouping if each issue of policy had been researched and debated from first principles. The lack of detailed and consistent policy chimed in well enough with a Party whose dominant characteristic remained that of the gentleman amateur. It was indeed a source of pride to Conservatives that they did not engage in full-time politics and that they exhibited both loyalty and unity – features that were enhanced by the aristocratic aloofness of the leaders and by the political inexperience of the rank and file.

For all this, Salisbury's Government was drawn into areas of policy that would scarcely have been dreamed of in Disraeli's time, drawn not by inclination but by the demands of an increasingly professional civil service, by a burgeoning Government involvement in economic matters, and by a deteriorating social and international situation. In part they were also pressed into action by the Ministers who had come over when the Liberal Party split in 1886, and especially by Joseph Chamberlain. In his Liberal days, Chamberlain had been one of the foremost exponents of programme politics, and he and his sons

were to play the major role in imposing their approach onto an
unwilling Conservative Party in the twentieth century. Chamberlain
was able to pursue a forward policy on his own account at the
Colonial Office after 1895, but he made little impact on his colleagues
in his regular attempts to make the Government as a whole more
active. His opportunity came with the aftermath of the Boer War,
which demonstrated the need to adopt rather more businesslike
methods. The Committee of Imperial Defence was set up to provide,
for the first time, professional backing for Ministers in defence
matters. The armed forces were reorganised and Royal Commissions
investigated the problems thrown up by the War.[4] Chamberlain was
never again to hold office after 1903, but he developed from the back
benches the first real party research organisation on the Conservative
side. He had resigned on the tariff issue, believing quite correctly that
the majority of the Conservative Party, leadership as well as rank and
file, backed his policy, and he therefore set out to convert the
minority to his views.

As Chamberlain's campaign got under way, it became apparent
that the practical case for tariffs was not easy to promote in a country
where free trade had been the ruling orthodoxy for half a century.
The tariff reformers also began to fear that, even if they succeeded in
taking the country by storm, they would then get bogged down by
Treasury and Whitehall opposition to their ideas; unless the
practicality of the tariff could be established *before* taking power, then
the whole impetus of the campaign might well be lost. At the
suggestion of Professor W. A. S. Hewins, Chamberlain set up the
Tariff Commission in December 1903, explaining his purpose in a
public announcement:

> We are told that we cannot make a scientific tariff. . . . Now we are
> going to try to do it. . . . We are going to form . . . a commission – not a
> political commission, but a non-political commission – of experts – to
> consider the conditions of our trade and the remedies which are to be
> found for it. The commission will comprise leading representatives of
> every principal industry. . . .[5]

The Commission included representatives of some industries and
called witnesses to gather the opinions of others; it also included a
few outside experts like Charles Booth. Indeed, Beatrice Webb took
the inclusion of Booth as a sign of how important such experts had
become in British politics, as showing 'what power, nowadays, is
wielded by a non-party expert who is free to throw himself on one
side or the other'.[6] A great deal of money was raised by the leaders of

the Tariff Reform League (TRL) and the Tariff Commission began work at the beginning of 1904. Hewins, former Director of the LSE and an academic economist, was its Secretary and Percy Hurd his assistant; both were subsequently to be Conservative MPs. The Commission was of course only a 'non-political' body in the sense that it took evidence from both sides and that it sought to persuade everyone equally. Its real work was in laying the practical, professional groundwork for the more overtly political campaign run by Chamberlain and the Tariff Reform League. This was clear from the outset, as the hostility of Chamberlain's opponents indicated; Liberals attacked the Tariff Commission as both unreliable and constitutionally dangerous. The Commission remained in existence for several years, keeping the tariff plans up to date, as in 1910 when Chamberlain set it to work to consider the implications of the Reciprocity Treaty which Canada had signed with the United States.[7]

One reason for Chamberlain's crusade for tariffs was his fear of the rising Labour movement. The opposition to Labour could only compete with a working-class party if it too could offer advanced programmes of social reform and the means to pay for them. The Conservative side had to do this without upsetting the Party's supporters by increased taxation; tariffs provided a short cut to old age pensions, using the ingenious slogan 'make the foreigner pay'. Chamberlain appreciated the political wisdom of linking the evolution of policy, the education of his Party and the preparation of propaganda to convert the nation; they are the three links of the chain of policy making that can most easily be forged together. The effect of the tariff agitation was to liberate the Party from its previously negative attitude to policy making; the Free Traders in the Party came together and formed organisations to combat the TRL, organisations that could never mobilise equivalent resources or support but which at least tried to work along similar lines. And the younger men in the Party (more upset than most by the national humiliation of the Boer War) took to policy discussion with great enthusiasm under Chamberlainite auspices. One result of their efforts was *The New Order*, published in 1908, and another was F. E. Smith's book of speeches, *Unionist Policy*, published in 1910.[8]

It was also F. E. Smith who took the lead in the next experiment in policy making, with the Unionist Social Reform Committee (USRC), founded in April 1910. This was a body that consisted mainly of tariff reformers (though by then the Party as a whole also consisted mainly of tariff reformers) and it set out to disprove the

Liberal charge that the Conservatives were the 'stupid party', by elaborating a series of detailed policies that a Unionist Government could implement on returning to office. It worked on Chamberlainite lines, and included Neville Chamberlain (then a Birmingham councillor) among its active workers, but it also drew directly on the traditions of Tory Democracy. Its organising secretary, Maurice Woods, an apostle of the creed of Richard Oastler and Lord Randolph Churchill, was later the author of a classic little book on the subject, *Toryism and the People.* As he explained to Lord Willoughby in August 1911, Woods was still,[9]

> absolutely convinced as I have always been that unless you can put yourself straight with the people on Social Questions all your Tariff, Home Rule or Constitutional thunderbolts will be discharged in vain. You have to establish your bona fides before you can be listened to. Therefore I want you to promise to speak in the autumn at three or four meetings got up by our members in the House of Commons for Social Reform purposes. I have arranged about fifteen meetings so far but I intend to get forty. May I say that you will speak at a few of them? I have got F. E. for Plymouth, Falmouth, Hull and Birmingham and am going to Bath and Durham myself.

The purpose for which the USRC had been founded was explained by F. E. Smith to party activists in May 1911:

> It had been felt for some time past that, while the Unionist policy with regard to small ownerships in land was well understood in the country, there were many other urgent social problems, vitally affecting the welfare of the people, upon which the policy of our party should be crystallised and laid before the electorate with the least possible delay. Among such problems I may particularise reform of the Poor Law, Insurance, Housing, Decasualisation of Labour, Technical Education, Emigration, Sweating, and the Aliens question. All progress with Social Reform is stayed, of course, for the moment, by the prosecution of the Radical–Socialist–Nationalist attack upon our ancient Constitution. But it must be recognised that all the great problems which I have enumerated will come sooner or later within the purview of the practical politician. It is the belief of the Unionist Social Reform Committee that they may be solved upon (the) traditional principles of our party.[10]

From the start then, the USRC aimed to shape policy as well as to expound it, though Smith was quick to add that 'Construction is our purpose – not obstruction, still less destruction'. For this purpose, the Committee had secured the services of 'some of the best experts available' and was spending time and money in sending commissioners to study social experiments abroad as well as collecting evidence at home. A year later, reporting back on what had already been done, he argued that the Committee would 'in a short time have covered most of the ground of a possible Unionist social policy in the future'.[11]

By the time that the work of the Committee had been completed in 1914, Maurice Woods recalled that 'the task which we set ourselves in 1911 was . . . to supply the Unionist Party with the groundwork of a social policy to be carried into effect when the Party returned to power. Schemes of this kind on the part of an Opposition are rare. I cannot, indeed, think of any precedent'. The justification given, more defensive than that given by Smith at the outset, was that over 'the last eight years the attention of those who take a real interest in national affairs has been turned more and more towards the discussion of social problems'. He suggested that Joseph Chamberlain had been responsible for this new focus of interest through the tariff campaign, but that, 'whatever the original causes are, we have entered on an economic age, and this fact must be recognised by any great Party which calls itself a national one. The recognition of this truth produced the Unionist Social Reform Committee'.[12]

The USRC was always an unofficial body, not least because the Party leaders did not wish to be committed by its more controversial proposals, but it was given help by the Party Organisation. It shared premises with Central Office in St Stephen's House, it was given publicity in Party literature, and its paid staff and research programmes were almost certainly subsidised from the funds of the Party. This contact became even closer when Arthur Steel-Maitland, a member of the USRC, became Chairman of the Party Organisation in July 1911. The Committee itself was made up of back-benchers, of whom about seventy (not far off a quarter of back-benchers) eventually joined, but non-MPs like Neville Chamberlain were encouraged to take part in the detailed work of its sub-committees. A great deal was done over the following three years, and the Committee made some real impact on the long-term evolution of Conservative policy in such fields as Housing and the Poor Law, if only by educating those who were to be Ministers in the next generation. But this was its real weakness; it saw itself mainly as a ginger group within the party. It therefore created antagonisms and forced the official Party to keep its distance, as, for example, over rural labourers' wages in 1913.[13]

The normal pattern of work was for a committee of about twenty MPs to work on each topic, dividing into sub-committees as necessary (the Poor Law committee, for example, divided to cover public health, children, unemployment, and mental deficiency), with each group free to recruit its own interested outsiders and experts. Reports were then submitted to the Committee as a whole at a series of dinners at the House of Commons, and most were subsequently published in book form. The education report was written up by Samuel Hoare, Poor Law by Jack Hills, insurance by Laming Worthington-Evans and industrial unrest by Jack Hills and Professor W. J. Ashley. The final stage involved an attempt to press the policy in question on the Government, either by framing suitable amendments to Government Bills – Maurice Woods claimed that the government's Mental Deficiency Bill 'is certainly more Mr Leslie Scott's Bill than Mr McKenna's' – or even by the drafting of Private Members' Bills, as Arthur Griffith–Boscawen did on housing and Edward Goulding on the aliens question. The success of amendments to Government legislation and the lack of sympathy shown by the Government for Bills such as Griffith–Boscawen's were both features that could be exploited to good propaganda effect.

Thus, Woods was able to claim in 1914 that 'the manifest interest taken by the Unionist Party in social evils and the sane and practical nature of the remedies put forward, should go far to convince the electorate, now growing tired of the Chancellor and his quick nostrums, that the best friends of the people are to be found in the Unionist ranks'. But he was also able to assert with justice that

> a very wide area has been covered; that on no point of grave importance which is likely to be raised during the tenure of office of the next Unionist administration will the government be lacking in the support of a great number of members of Parliament, who are well qualified for the shaping of social policy, or for defending it and explaining it to the country and the Commons.[14]

Bonar Law certainly took little direct interest in the Committee's work but had he become peacetime Prime Minister as expected in 1914–15, he would have been unable to ignore its achievements.

Developments in the official Party machine had also helped to sharpen the definition of policy, assisted partly by chance and partly by the activities of Steel-Maitland at Central Office. From the beginning, Steel-Maitland tried to organise the approach to policy in a more businesslike way, in keeping with his approach to Party management. He fostered cooperation between Central Office and the Parliamentary Party by allocating a staff man to each political issue as it arose, to 'shepherd' its progress. He was immediately accused of unwarranted interference in a sphere that should be left to

MPs.[15] When Bonar Law became Leader in November 1911, Steel-Maitland sent him a lengthy briefing memorandum on Party affairs which included an ambitious proposal for a standing research organisation.

> The manner in which at present we coquet with certain questions, or indeed commit ourselves to policies, is most unbusinesslike. As a party we preach agricultural small-ownership, though we really do not know if it is possible or not. There are several questions of this kind, upon some of which at any rate we ought to be at work. It is possible to get sufficient information upon some of them in order to see what general lines are feasible and what are not, even though it may not be possible to frame an actual Treasury estimate or draft a Bill. Such questions are:-
>
> 1 Plural Voting.
> 2 Small Ownership.
> 3 Poor Law.
> 4 Co-ownership or profit-sharing in (a) distributive (b) factory (c) agriculture.
> 5 Housing in (a) slums (b) developing suburbs.
> 6 Minimum wage.
> 7 Arbitration in trade disputes.
> 8 Commercial questions, e.g. simplification of Private Bill legislation.
> 9 The nexus of Imperial questions.
>
> What agency can tackle any of these? The questions indicated are of different kinds. But even of those connected with Social matters, I am now sure that the Social Reform Committee cannot do the work. It is useful in creating an atmosphere, not in working out a policy for which you could take responsibility. Such work, if done, must be done by a small committee, appointed by you, with a paid secretary expert in that subject. The committee must also have a forum, so as to ventilate their views without fixing responsibility on you, and so as to get the corrective against one-sidedness and inadequacy which is afforded by the publicity of a Committee or Commission. I have done a little already on these lines, and have talked with Mr Balfour about a small-ownership committee – which would be the largest and most costly, and which should if possible be started soonest.[16]

In this document, Steel-Maitland posited all the bases on which successful policy reviews were to be made thirty and fifty years later, but the list of controversial issues requiring further definition must have caused consternation to the new Leader.

There are few signs that Steel-Maitland's advice was taken to heart, and fewer still that Bonar Law was prepared to back his policy-makers when they ran into the inevitable storms. In July 1912,

Walter Long, writing on behalf of 'Mr. Bonar Law and I', invited
Charles Bathurst to join a small committee under Basil Peto to
consider the position of the agricultural labourers and to devise a
policy with which the party could counter Lloyd George's land
campaign. When this committee began interviewing landowners at
Central Office, and actually asked their views on the introduction of
a minimum wage in agriculture, there was an outcry and Bonar Law
was quick to disown the Committee and point out that their work
was 'quite unauthorised'.[17] Steel-Maitland was thus left to do what he
could on his own, working from Central Office but with little more
official backing than the USRC could get. Central Office worked on
the National Insurance Bill of 1911 in collaboration with the USRC,
and provided briefs for the task-force of MPs who were fighting the
Bill in the Commons. The Party's social reformers, including Steel-
Maitland, were anxious to resist the Bill in detail while avoiding
giving the impression that they opposed its good intentions; their
efforts were largely nullified when Bonar Law told the House that
the Conservative Party would repeal the Bill – a tactical error that
was not repaired by a subsequent change of front.

To prevent such slips, Steel-Maitland bombarded Law with
briefing material from Central Office on areas as diverse as Home
Rule and Poor Law, and he offered Law the services of a member of
the Central Office staff 'to devil for your speeches'.* He also engaged
in private enterprise policy-making of a different type under the
guise of Party publicity. In order to get full coverage of the Leader's
speeches in the national press, he persuaded Law to submit his major
speeches for distribution through Central Office, thus getting
advance warning of what Law would say. He also commissioned a
series of books on policy through Lord Selborne, using ghost writers
supplied by Central Office and issuing the books over the names of
Party leaders, as Selborne reported to Law;

> Now he wants to get out a small handbook on our Trade Policy, as
> distinct from and as a larger thing than Tariff Reform, and he has asked
> me to ask you whether you could name anyone you could trust to write
> this and whether you would be prepared to look over it when it is written
> and possibly give your name to it. In the same way that Mr. Chamberlain
> is giving his name to a similar work written by Hewins on Tariff Reform
> and as I am doing in the case of the navy to a little work written by Mr.
> Hurd.

---

*Steel-Maitland was also involved in getting up a group to devise 'a rural life policy'
for the Party, and he offered Milner and Plunkett the services of a secretary and a
thousand a year from Party funds.[18]

In much the same way Steel-Maitland himself recruited Lord Robert
Cecil's assistance (and his name) for a book on constitutional issues by
G. Lowes Dickinson.[19] Books on critical policy issues that appeared
over the names of Party leaders naturally came to be interpreted as
statements of official policy, but they were at the same time rather
more detailed than any policy outlined in speeches could have been.

The Edwardian period thus saw the first signs of an awareness in
the Party that it needed to modernise its policy machinery; it also saw
the first halting experiments, all more or less unsuccessful. By the
time that the Party next returned to opposition in 1924, the influences
that had encouraged experiments before 1914 had become greatly
strengthened. The business of government was transformed by the
First World War, in scale and in complexity. While the overall level
of retail prices in the 1920s in Britain was not far from its level in the
Edwardian period, the scale of government expenditure had
increased fivefold (with massive effects on personal taxation); many
Government departments had developed into far larger organisations
with much-enhanced duties and responsibilities; Government had
been drawn into areas of the economy and society, such as the
organisation of industry, where neither Liberals nor Conservatives
would have ventured before 1914 and from which no Government
could subsequently retreat. The rise of Labour to the position of
second party had underlined the extent to which Governments had to
concern themselves with social and economic problems. By 1924, few
could have resisted Maurice Woods' earlier assertion that 'we have
entered on an economic age'. The Conservative ministers who sought
to deal with these problems in the 1920s were for the most part the
younger generation of MPs who had striven for a more active
attitude to politics in Edwardian times, and who were therefore more
open-minded than their predecessors. But they were also the same
type of men as their elders, most of them part-time politicians with
little expert knowledge of the problems they were called upon to
solve. The Conservative benches in the 1920s were filled with hard-
headed businessmen, but few of those who had personal experience of
business ever actually sat in Conservative Governments.[20]

Government remained predominantly an amateur art for the
politicians, even though administration had become a much more
professional operation. This contrast was made painfully clear by the
experience of the first wholly-Conservative Government after the
War, the Bonar Law/Baldwin ministry of 1922–3. Law had been
anxious to avoid unseemly wrangling over policy when he succeeded
Lloyd George as Prime Minister, and he had therefore gone to the

country in 1922 with no definite policy. He campaigned on the need for tranquillity, and his most specific commitment was the entirely negative pledge not to introduce food taxes without a special general election. This non-policy proved irresistible at the election, but it was a poor basis for administration after the election had been won. The Government made a pretty poor fist of its single year of office and had spectacular difficulties over such complex issues as the settlement of war debts and the decontrol of rents. The two greatest successes were both in areas where Ministers could be considered to be experts in their field; Curzon was by this stage of his career as well-informed about foreign policy as any professional diplomat, and the municipal experience of Neville Chamberlain certainly helped him to be a successful Minister of Health.[21] The rest of the team – and Baldwin himself – showed far less grasp.

The Government's difficulties were compounded, in the Autumn of 1923, by the strategy that Baldwin picked on to rid his team of the image of men who fiddled while the dole queues lengthened. Baldwin announced that he had personally reached the conclusion that the country must have tariffs in order to fight unemployment, and he was then forced willy nilly into an election that he had probably not wanted and had no time to prepare for. The Government fought what could only be a one-issue election without ever defining what its policy was to be on that one issue. The broad lines of the tariff policy were not agreed until after Parliament had been dissolved, and the detailed ramifications were never worked out at all; candidates therefore gave their own interpretations and the Party's opponents had no difficulty in presenting the Conservatives in a most unflattering light.[22] In part, the policy difficulties involved with the tariff election of 1923 were simply personal failings of Party management, but in part they also represented the death of a whole style of Conservative politics. From the defeat, Baldwin himself drew the moral that policies were dangerous things that should be talked about only in the most extreme emergencies, but many of his colleagues reached the opposite conclusion, that a party could neither fight an election nor govern in modern conditions without a clear idea of what it intended to do and how it meant to do it. The tension between these two views framed the making of policy until the Second World War.

The priorities after the election defeat of 1923 were to sort out what was to occur in a parliament where no party had an overall majority, and to reconsider Baldwin's position. Once Baldwin's leadership had been re-established and Labour installed in office, the Party settled down to make use of its time in opposition constructively. Since his survival as Leader had been only narrowly confirmed, Baldwin had to go along with the views of his colleagues. When the party was reunited and the ex-coalition Ministers received back into the fold, in January 1924, Austen Chamberlain and his colleagues were invited into the Shadow Cabinet by formal letters, as if they were being invited to join a real Cabinet rather than an informal consultative group.[23] At the first meeting, Baldwin took a self-effacing back seat and allowed Austen Chamberlain almost to chair the meeting. Thereafter, the Shadow Cabinet met regularly – if not quite as often as the Chamberlains might have wished – and Austen made it clear that he expected to be given the chance to offer his advice on any policy view that the Leader might wish to put forward. There was also a weekly meeting of ex-ministers from the Commons to co-ordinate short-term tactics, and a series of policy committees consisting of back-benchers and outsiders, each chaired by a Shadow Minister. The policy committees were to report directly to Baldwin and Austen Chamberlain, and they were provided with a professional backing by a Secretariat created specially for the purpose by Leo Amery and Neville Chamberlain.[24]

The Secretariat was housed with Central Office at Palace Chambers and shared rooms with the Leader's personal staff. At its head was Colonel Lancelot Storr, a highly experienced staff officer, an Assistant Secretary to the War Cabinet and recently an assistant to Baldwin's friend J. C. C. Davidson. He recruited a team of bright young men, including Geoffrey Lloyd and Robert Boothby, then aged twenty-two and twenty-four respectively but both of whom were to be candidates in the election later that year, and both of whom were later to be ministers. Nevertheless, the driving force behind all this activity was Neville Chamberlain, content to remain behind the scenes if he could get what he wanted. In March, he provided Baldwin with a detailed draft for a major speech in Edinburgh which laid down the Party's policy on insurance. A Committee under Neville was already hard at work providing details of how it might be implemented.[25] In July it was Neville who pulled these disparate threads together and drafted a document that was published as *Looking Ahead*. This was a statement of policy in every field, a document that had no comparable predecessor but many descendants; the published text made no reference to its authorship, and Neville Chamberlain was amused when the *Daily Herald* believed that it could detect the handiwork of Curzon. He had thus stage-managed an operation which had provided the Party with a comprehensive and practicable statement of its policies for the first time ever, and made the provision of an election manifesto a few months later an easy task. But this did not satisfy him. In August he told a correspondent what he would do if he had a free hand to run the Party:

> Every one of my colleagues who was worth anything should have some special question assigned to him . . . I should try to be prepared with information which would enable me to formulate a policy about everything. In particular I should begin to pick out particular industries and work out the case for McKenna–dutying them, and I should try to get out a new policy for agriculture,

details of which he then set out.[26] Denied the opportunity to go as far as he wished with Party policy in general, he could nevertheless make sure that he was fully prepared to go back to the Ministry of Health. With the help of Samuel Hoare he prepared himself so thoroughly that a week after he was appointed he was able to set the Ministry to work on a new four-year plan; less than a fortnight later he presented the Cabinet with a list of twenty-five Bills that he would want to introduce during the Parliament, twenty-one of which became law over the next five years.

There is no doubt that the policy exercise of 1924 played a part in the Conservative recovery of that year, if only by helping the Conservative leaders to recover their belief in their own ability to govern effectively. Chamberlain was not the only Minister who was more effective in power because of preparations undertaken in opposition. But for all that, the careful management of policy that he evolved in 1924 was allowed to disintegrate as soon as the Party returned to office. Departmental rivalry probably played some part, and the Party Chairman proved to be the Secretariat's main critic, ostensibly on grounds of cost. Lancelot Storr went with the Party back into government, becoming secretary to the Lord Chancellor with responsibility for ecclesiastical patronage, Robert Boothby entered the House of Commons and most of the rest of the Secretariat was dispersed to the winds. The members of the Secretariat protested against this decision, and the case for retaining it as a permanent organisation was put to the Cabinet in November 1924 in a memorandum sent by Amery to Baldwin.

Baldwin was reminded that the policy Secretariat was founded not only to assist with co-ordination but also 'to arrange for such research or inquiry as might be required by the Leaders of the Party for the purposes of formulating the policy of the Party'. This task had been

satisfactorily performed, but would be needed even more in power
than it had been in opposition:

> In opposition a Party naturally tends to think of the next election, of
> framing programmes, or winning public support, and its leaders are
> naturally kept in touch with the Party machinery. In Office a
> Government rapidly becomes so immersed in the . . . administrative
> point of view as to lose sight both of the electoral aspect of its actions and
> of the need for continuous and effective propaganda. This, the greatest
> danger to any Party in office, can only be overcome if there is the closest
> *liaison* and inter-communication, both upwards and downwards, between
> the Leaders of the Party on the one hand, the Party Organisation, the rank
> and file, and the Press on the other. It is no less essential that the Party
> should be preparing a programme for the future, not based on
> departmental ideas, but on political considerations. The idea that the
> Party in office can rely for its materials for preparing the political
> campaign upon departmental officials or upon the Cabinet Secretariat is,
> we think, wholly erroneous.

It was therefore suggested that Storr should become one of the Prime
Minister's secretaries at Downing Street, on the Government
payroll, and that most of the rest of the staff should be kept on at
Central Office to service back-bench committees and 'such
Committees of Ministers for the study of new aspects of policy as
cannot be dealt with departmentally', and to keep open communications with the Party and the press. Amery's paper concluded with
the reminder that he had invited people to join the Secretariat when it
had been intended to be a permanent organisation, and that to close it
down summarily would be a breach of faith with those who had come
to work for it.[27] This appeal certainly had some effect, in that the
Party committees remained in being, sixteen in all at the beginning of
the 1924 Parliament, and some staff members of the Secretariat were
absorbed onto the Central Office staff in order to service them. But
Storr was not given access to the Prime Minister and the other vital
elements of Amery's scheme were not met either. Baldwin was a
major public figure in his own right after the triumph of 1924 and he
no longer needed to accept the advice of his colleagues when he did
not wish to do so. In Cabinet, Baldwin did not oppose Amery's view,
but his silence was sufficient.

Some policy work did continue during the 1924–9 Government,
though on a rather random basis. Pembroke Wicks and Claude Davis
were absorbed into the Chairman's personal office at Central Office,
while John Green and others were transferred to the publicity
department to work on 'policy' and especially on agriculture; the

total cost of these operations fell from £1,452 in 1925 to a mere £331 in 1929 and the remnants of the 1924 Secretariat seem to have faded away rather than to have been wound up. Two staff members were sent to Geneva in 1927 to keep an eye, on behalf of the Party, on the Disarmament Conference, and in the same year an expert was put at the disposal of the Party's India Committee – a man carefully chosen for his moderate views. Policy certainly had little priority at this time; the Central Office press cutting department occupied six rooms on the main floor of Central Office, while John Green's work for all the Parliamentary Committees was carried on from a desk in the registry.[28] The folly of this approach was recognised by some at the time, and demands for action were made by (amongst others) Lancelot Storr, by Harold Macmillan and by John Buchan.

Storr wrote to Davidson (shortly to become Party Chairman) in September 1926, pointing out that two years had already passed since the Party's triumph, that the need for another election might arise at any time, and that the party should emulate its successful exercise of 1924, for 'an elementary measure of self-preservation and forethought is the timely preparation of a sane and popular programme, upon which a General Election can be contested with confidence'. He repeated Amery's earlier view that ministers were too absorbed in their departmental work to give sufficient thought to preparing for the Party's future.

> It may be urged that the natural place for the procreation of a programme is the Central Office; but party officials, however able, cannot proceed usefully in the dark. They must have the direct guidance and authority of the Leader and his colleagues. In brief, what is required is that the Cabinet should meet occasionally as a 'Shadow'; that is to say, for purposes of party politics only, for discussing plans and for preparing a programme. It would be undesirable and irregular for the services of the Secretariat at 2 Whitehall Gardens [the Cabinet Secretariat] to be utilised for purely party business, and other provision would have to be made. The nucleus of the 'Shadow' Secretariat still survives in Palace Chambers, however, and should be made available.

He suggested that a small group of Ministers, assisted by the Chief Whip and the Party Chairman, should meet to discuss a programme, that departmental Ministers should give advance notice of their plans and attend meetings when relevant business was to be discussed, and that the Secretariat should work for this group. He stressed the need for flexibility and the need to delegate: 'the direct guidance and authority of the Leader of the Party are indispensable. But the Prime Minister has already more labour and responsibility than it is right that any human being should be burdened with'. This whole plan reflected Storr's previous work with Lloyd George's War Cabinet, which had worked along very similar lines; in its recognition of the need to remove the initiative from Baldwin, it also came very close to Lloyd George's own plans when fretting under Asquith in 1916.[29]

It would appear that a further attempt to consider future policy was made at Cabinet level in 1927, following the Conservative defeat at the Bosworth by-election. A committee was set up under the chairmanship of Worthington-Evans after discussions in Cabinet and ten other Cabinet Ministers were invited to join; the secretary was to be Pembroke Wicks, previously of the Secretariat and still on the Central Office staff. The exact status of the Committee remained shadowy, and some Ministers clearly did not understand it themselves, as evidenced by a letter from Joynson-Hicks to the chairman, but it seems that it was intended as an opportunity for senior Ministers to meet informally without civil servants in attendance. However, there is little sign that it made much impression, and it may have faded away during the squabble over de-rating and the other internal disagreements that occurred in 1928–9.

Harold Macmillan, a very junior back-bencher but one who was greatly concerned with the development of a positive social and economic policy for the Party and a man who was well aware of the need for professionalism in policy making (as his later involvement with the Party was to show), also submitted a paper calling for a new organisation for research.[30] There is no sign that either Storr or Macmillan made any impact with their views on a Prime Minister who was anxious to avoid damaging disagreements in his Government. John Buchan was a little more successful in 1928, probably because he took care to enlist powerful support before offering his views and because he circulated them widely. He also took care to link the need for work on policy with the need for political education, a case that was accepted throughout the Party as it struggled to resist the real threat of another Labour Government. A Party College had been in existence for several years and an Education Department had existed within the Central Office, but these efforts were thought to be 'hopelessly insufficient' by Buchan and his friends.

Buchan was a lifelong Conservative with a national standing of his own as a novelist, who had recently entered the House of Commons at a by-election; he represented a strand of Party thinking close to Baldwin's own and had already assisted Baldwin greatly in the debate on the future of the House of Lords. Nevertheless, it was to Neville Chamberlain that he took his ideas and only when Baldwin had failed to act did Buchan follow it up himself, in a letter that was quietly insistent.

> I am loth to worry you in the middle of your holiday but I wonder if you have ever had time to look at our educational scheme, which Neville Chamberlain told me he had put before you? The fact is, before we can get on much further we want your approval. For the scheme has two parts – (1) Adult Education, work which we have been doing successfully for two years, and (2) Political Research work, for which we have the machinery sketched out, and which badly needs undertaking. In case you have not had time to look at the memorandum, and cannot lay your hand on it, I enclose another copy. The trouble is that we want your approval before we can take any practical steps in the latter work, and the Head Office also wants to know that you approve before it can assist us. We are working in the closest touch at present but in order to simplify the working we have our own separate organisation.

The accompanying document was a printed pamphlet called *Political Research and Adult Education*, and set down the cumulative case made by all the advocates of a new style in party policymaking over the past few years. It established the need for research in modern politics because of the greatly increased involvement of Government in industry and society, and it pointed out that a Labour Research Department had existed since 1912, a Liberal Industrial Enquiry since 1927, and it described the methods and achievements of each of these. It then proceeded to ask for the creation of a 'Conservative Research Department' with three distinct objectives: it should consider the scientific use of organisation and publicity, so that Party money would be more effectively spent, it should liaise with outside bodies in order to attract academics and other outside experts to the Party's service, and it should undertake detailed research on social and economic policies that were listed. The pamphlet also called for a far more active approach to education work, once again making unfavourable comparisons with the work of the Labour Party, the WEA, Ruskin College, the Co-operative Union and so on.[31]

Buchan's tactic of writing to Baldwin directly was probably intended to by-pass the disagreement with the 'Head Office' to which he referred in his letter. A few days later, when Central Office heard what was being done, Joseph Ball (Director of Publicity of Central Office) wrote to Baldwin's secretary to express his concern: 'an important issue of principle is involved, viz whether the political research of the Conservative Party should continue to be done as heretofore in this Office, or whether it should be carried on by an outside, if a closely allied body such as John Buchan's Education

Department. I do not suppose you will have heard that we have recently decided to transfer the whole of the educational work of the Party to a committee under the chairmanship of John Buchan. This committee will work in the closest possible touch with and under the control of the Chairman of the Party, and will be housed in St Stephen's House adjoining us here. But, so far as I am aware, no agreement has been arrived at whereby this Committee is authorised to undertake at the same time our political research'.[32] Baldwin was urged not to make any promises to Buchan until after the Party Chairman had been able to express the views of Central Office. Thus, departmental rivalries again entered into what was already a contentious matter, and the result seems to have been another decision not to decide. Buchan got his new educational institute, with Baldwin as President and Harold Macmillan, Nancy Astor and Walter Elliott among its Council.[33] But research, such as it was, remained at Central Office and disputes between the two organisations continued, for it was scarcely feasible to separate Party publicity from political education.

Hence, little was done to prepare for the next election, and by the time that it came in 1929 there was no Secretariat that could be used. As Amery had predicted in 1924, Ministers tried to prepare for the election as a Government rather than as a Party, and made a poor job of it. When Central Office tried to begin preparations in the Summer of 1927, they could only use the Prime Minister's personal office to co-ordinate a Government position. Letters were sent out to each Minister by Baldwin's staff asking for a review of the work done in the departments since 1924 and for future proposals; since Ministers were too busy to give their personal attention, most of the replies were sent in by Civil Servants, and correspondence continued at this level over the next two years. The same method was adopted when the Opposition published *Labour and the Nation* in 1928, with civil servants again asked to produce a critique of Labour's plans, for the use of the Conservative Party.[34] Central Office then played no great part in the framing of the Conservative manifesto for the 1929 election. Ministers, after four active years in Government, came up with few positive proposals and the Party had to fight the election on its record and on the proposals of their opponents. Since both Labour and the Liberals produced a great deal of policy for the election, the Government fared rather badly during the campaign; once again a more detailed Conservative policy was ruled out not only by the lack of appropriate machinery but also by Baldwin's desire not to disturb sleeping dogs by reopening for general discussion such issues as the tariff question. An election campaign was fought on 'Safety First' because of the lack of any real alternative.

The experience of the 1929 election campaign underlined the need for changes. On the advice of R. B. Howorth of the Cabinet Office, the Government created an Emergency Business Committee of the Cabinet to deal with affairs during the election; this was set up by a minute of the Cabinet on 24 April 1929, a few days before Parliament was dissolved, and it met for the first time on 2 May 1929. The Chairman was the Lord Chancellor, Hailsham, and the other members were the Ministers who had constituencies in the London area. Howorth himself acted as secretary, but Davidson and Pembroke Wicks from Central Office were both invited to attend meetings in order to improve liaison with the Party. The first task was to produce a manifesto and this was farmed out for drafting rather haphazardly; Chamberlain was asked to write a paragraph on Colonial policy although he had never so far specialised in it. These efforts were pulled together by Hailsham and Davidson and then presented to the Committee for scrutiny, the whole of this process being carried out in under twenty-four hours. The Committee did not much like what they saw and decided to ask Ministers to re-work various sections; Worthington-Evans, Amery and Elliott were asked to recast the agriculture section, Neville Chamberlain was asked to remedy the fact that housing was missed out of the social services section, and (presumably on the principle of horses for courses) Hailsham and Churchill were invited to draft an introduction and a peroration respectively. Within four days of the first ideas being put down on paper, the manifesto had been through several drafts, had been accepted by the full Cabinet and issued over Baldwin's signature – though he had not attended any of the drafting meetings. The final product, not surprisingly, bore all the signs of haste and of having been cobbled together by several hands; it demonstrated a total lack of preparation for the election during five years of power.

The second and more time-consuming task of the Emergency Business Committee was to sit at regular intervals during the campaign and work out appropriate answers to unexpected questions about Party policy and especially to questionnaires sent in by local and national pressure groups. This had to be integrated into the normal process of Government decision-making, since the Conservatives remained in power until the election was over and so civil servants would need to act on their decisions; so for example, it was decided that the British pavilion at the Antwerp International Exhibition should not be built with Belgian steel (this had been criticised during the election) but should instead be built of timber, Empire timber if this could be managed without too much delay, and orders were given to put this into effect at once. Questionnaires were collected by Central Office and passed on to Howorth, sometimes with a suggested draft reply; he then sent copies to the various departments involved and asked them to draft replies for the Committee to consider. As the campaign progressed and as the politicians became increasingly busy, more and more civil servants attended the meetings and fewer and fewer Ministers. By the last meeting, there were only four politicians and ten civil servants to produce answers to ten questions of policy. Nor could Central Office prevent control of policy from slipping into the hands of the civil service, for the questions were too technical for their advice to carry much weight; all they could do was to send vague exhortations about the political effects, exhortations that rarely did more than state the obvious. So for example, they passed on a question about pensions for widows and orphans, commenting that 'Central Office are unable to make suggestions on a technical matter of this kind' but pointing out that 'if a sympathetic reply is possible, it would be a great advantage'. The idea that the National Insurance scheme should be opened up to voluntary members was 'a matter of future Government policy upon which Central Office can offer no suggestions. If actuarially possible, the extension of Health Insurance will of course be popular among the people with limited incomes'. When a department took a strong line, or when two or more departments agreed a policy amongst themselves (as for example the Treasury and the Ministry of Transport on lorry taxation, or the War Office, the Air Ministry and the Admiralty on policy towards the British Legion), there was little room for any political dimension.[35]

The defeat of 1929 administered the final impetus towards reorganisation, not by helping to produce any new ideas but by removing opposition to old ones. Defeat renewed the calls that had been made with increasing urgency in the past years, but it also made it quite impossible for Baldwin to resist any longer. Geoffrey Ellis, who was Chairman of the Yorkshire Area and who had lost his own seat at the election, wrote to Baldwin to bewail the lack of contact between leaders and followers in the Party, but he also urged the creation of 'a proper educational system, well linked up with the Provincial as well as the older Universities, not only for political training but for industrial inquiry and research'.[36] Harold Macmillan, more bluntly wrote that 'the fundamental weakness of the Unionist Party today lies in its present confusion of thought. It has no clear policy on immediate problems; it has no clear goal towards which it feels itself to be striving. It has too many "open questions" and too many closed minds'.[37] In order to meet these criticisms, Baldwin now accepted the need for a research organisation and discussed the form that it should take with the Party Chairman, Davidson, over the Summer of 1929. Davidson during his time at Central Office, had been anxious to promote schemes for political education and had already achieved a great deal; he later recalled that he had regarded the creation of a Research Department as one of his main aims, but if so he had had no more success than others in persuading Baldwin of the need for urgency – 'perhaps I delayed too long'.[38] Now that a new agency was to be created, Baldwin and Davidson agreed the need to keep it firmly under the control of the Leader and Party Chairman. Other ex-Ministers were more dubious, partly because they felt that Davidson was too close to Baldwin to make a real go of it. The one man that might have taken control of the situation, Neville Chamberlain, was affected throughout 1929 by a curious lassitude following the disappointment of defeat. He noted in June that Austen quite looked forward to a period of rest in opposition, and reflected that he himself could never settle to inactivity now that he had become fascinated by the problems of administration and policy. Through the Autumn of 1929 he fretted at the frustrations of opposition, and only a prolonged visit to East Africa in the following Winter restored his drive and his morale. In October he wrote to his sister Ida that 'everywhere and from all sides I hear of depression, distrust and despair in my Party'. Four days later, after describing the Shadow Cabinet meeting on the Irwin Declaration on India's future, he told Hilda Chamberlain that 'we discussed Foreign Affairs at some length but Home Affairs and in particular the position of our own Party not at all. Nor do I know when we are to meet again nor what measures are to be taken to decide on policy. . . . It is all very depressing'.[39]

Difficulties with Beaverbrook on the tariff question forced Baldwin's hand and provided Chamberlain with an opening to press for detailed research:

> What we have got to do now is to stimulate S. B. to get going with the enquiry. He is like a top. You have got to keep whipping him or he falls over! . . . If I were he, I would get into touch with the leading agriculturalists, industrialists, economists, and financiers and talk with them till I could get my own mind clear as to the lines to be followed and then I would set Philip and Sam [Cunliffe-Lister and Hoare] to work out

details with them. But I doubt if he will do it that way for I have never yet
been able to persuade him to take any subject under his own wing.[40]

However, another fortnight of pressure did yield results, and on the
eve of his departure for Africa, Chamberlain could report that Hoare
had established contact with F. L. Engledow, the Professor of
Agriculture at Cambridge, and Chamberlain had himself talked to
the Canadian Prime Minister. Baldwin had agreed to see both of
these and to commission Engledow to conduct an inquiry into
Imperial agricultural problems.

> On the industrial side the idea is really the same. An inter-Imperial cartel
> in each industry and then a duty against the foreigner. Sam and I
> suggested to S. B. that he should begin by seeing certain leading
> industrialists and financiers to find out whether they would take up the
> idea and to get their views, and that he should then get Philip C-L to take
> on the chairmanship of a committee to work out plans. Accordingly he
> (generally in company with Philip) has seen W. Weir, Peacock of the
> Bank of England, and Arthur Duckham, and is to see Stewart (cotton),
> McGowan (ICI) and others. It is useless to let S. B. see these people alone.
> He never seems to know what to ask them and at the end of the interview
> he doesn't know what they've said and they don't know why they were
> sent for. Really, he can only deal with very general ideas, on details he is
> completely at sea. However, I am very well satisfied with our beginning
> both on the industrial and agricultural side. But I don't disguise from
> myself the difficulties . . .[41]

Chamberlain was recovering his determination and his interest in
politics, and coming to recognise that policy making in opposition
could be as interesting as in power. But his lack of interest in the
proposed new department remained, in part because Baldwin had
won the argument as to the form it should take and because
Chamberlain had a particularly low opinion of Central Office.

The decision to set up a Conservative Research Department was
formally taken at the Shadow Cabinet meeting on 23 October 1929
and announced in a statement to the press in mid-November:

> In view of the growing complexity of the political aspect of modern
> industrial, Imperial and social problems, Mr. Stanley Baldwin has
> decided to set up a special department charged with the task of organising
> and conducting research into these matters. The department will be
> under the direct control of the Leader of the Party, who has entrusted the
> task of organizing it to Lord Eustace Percy and to Mr. Joseph Ball, who
> has been appointed director of the new department. It is understood that
> it is Mr. Neville Chamberlain's intention, on his return from South
> Africa, to associate himself actively with the work of the department. In

the conduct of its operations the department will be independent of, but will work in close liaison with, party headquarters.[42]

Baldwin and Davidson had won their point in the terms of reference given to the new department, and also in its first organisers. As ex-Director of Publicity at Central Office and a close confidant of Davidson, Ball could be expected to work with rather than against the Leader. Percy was the most academic of Baldwin's colleagues in the Shadow Cabinet, but he was also one of the most junior and one of those closest to Baldwin himself in outlook. It is not altogether surprising that Percy was Baldwin's personal choice for the task or that Ball was suggested by Davidson. But it was only in the absence of Chamberlain that these dispositions had been possible; he could have had control of the Research Department from the beginning had he wanted it, and several colleagues urged him to accept the Chairmanship. The curious form of words in the press announcement may reflect this fact, but Chamberlain himself had given no assurances to justify such a statement: 'I have refused to commit myself till I come back and see what the conditions are then.'[43] The effect of this was to delay the *real* foundation of the Conservative Research Department for another four months.

Notes

1   This was the general view of M. I. Ostrogorski whose *Democracy and the Organisation of Political Parties*, published in 1902, was based on research done mainly in the 1880s.
2   See Hamer, *Politics of Electoral Pressure*.
3   McKenzie and Silver, *Angels in Marble*, 44.
4   Searle, *Quest for National Efficiency*.
5   Amery, *Joseph Chamberlain*, vi, 529.
6   *Ibid*, vi, 532.
7   *Ibid*, vi, 962.
8   Ramsden, *Age of Balfour and Baldwin*, 30.
9   Woods to Willoughby de Broke, 16 August 1911, Willoughby de Broke MSS.
10 *Our Flag*, July 1911, 73–4.
11 *Ibid*, July 1912, 103–4.
12 *Ibid*, June 1914, 86.
13 Ramsden, *Age of Balfour and Baldwin*, 76–7.
14 *Our Flag*, June 1914, 86.
15 Ramsden, 'Organisation', 86.
16 Steel-Maitland's memorandum for Law, Novemeber 1911, Steel-Maitland MSS, GD193/108/3.
17 Long to Bathurst, 4 July 1912, Bledisloe MSS; Sanders Diary, 13 October 1912.
18 Steel-Maitland to Law, 17 February 1912, Bonar Law MSS, 25/2/30. I am grateful to Mr Matthew Fforde for the Plunkett reference taken from the Plunkett diary, 1 May 1912.
19 Selborne to Law, 15 October 1912, Bonar Law MSS, 27/3/35; Steel-Maitland to Lord Robert Cecil, Cecil of Chelwood MSS, BM Add MSS, 51071.
20 Guttsman, *British Political Elite*.
21 Ramsden, *Age of Balfour and Baldwin*, 169–77.
22 *Ibid*, 179–81.
23 Middlemas and Barnes, *Baldwin*, 264.
24 Amery, *My Political Life*, ii, 291–2.
25 Macleod, *Chamberlain*, 106.
26 Feiling, *Chamberlain*, 115.
27 Memorandum on the Policy Secretariat, Baldwin MSS, vol. 48, file 1. I am grateful to Mr David Nicholson for information from his

forthcoming edition of the L. S. Amery Diaries, on which this account of the Secretariat is partly based.

28 Ramsden, 'Organisation', 258.
29 Storr to Davidson, 14 September 1926, Davidson MSS.
30 I am grateful to Mr Philip Williamson and Mr John Barnes for this information.
31 Baldwin MSS, vol. 53, file 7.
32 *Ibid.*
33 Smith, *John Buchan*, 311.
34 Baldwin MSS, vol. 53, files 12 and 14.
35 CRD file, 'EBC Papers, 1929'.
36 Ellis to Baldwin, 10 June 1929, Baldwin MSS, vol. 36; see also Ellis to Neville Chamberlain, 10 June 1929, Neville Chamberlain MSS, 7/11/22/7.
37 Macmillan, *Winds of Change*, 249–50.
38 Davidson, *Memoirs of a Conservative*, 275.
39 Neville to Ida Chamberlain, 22 October 1929 and Neville to Hilda Chamberlain, 26 October 1929, Neville Chamberlain MSS, 18/1/673 and 674.
40 Neville to Hilda Chamberlain, 24 November 1929, Neville Chamberlain MSS, 18/1/677.
41 Neville Chamberlain's diary, 8 December 1929, Neville Chamberlain MSS, 2/22.
42 *Gleanings and Memoranda*, December 1929.
43 Neville to Hilda Chamberlain, 24 November 1929, Neville Chamberlain MSS, 18/1/677.

Chapter 3

The new Department
established (1929–31)

There has been a lively little debate among Conservative Party historians as to who actually 'founded' the Conservative Research Department, with cases being made out for Baldwin, for Davidson, for Lord Eustace Percy and for Neville Chamberlain. The case for Baldwin does not amount to very much; it is simply that the Department was set up under his authority at the time when he was Party Leader and that it was thus his responsibility.[1] The formal decision was indeed set down in a minute from Baldwin's private office, but it can scarcely be regarded as a personal initiative. He had wound up the Secretariat in 1924, he had resisted suggestions that a new standing organisation be set up in the intervening years, and he had only agreed to act in 1929 because pressure from his colleagues had become irresistible. The fact was that Baldwin was not a politician who took the making of policy seriously – he was far more interested in the creation of atmosphere; he remained Leader for eight years after the Department came into being in 1929, but there is no evidence of him referring policy matters to the Department for investigation and report, a few occasions only when he was forced into accepting their advice by Chamberlain's strong-arm methods. Indeed, the Research Department rapidly despaired of making any impact on Baldwin. Ball even found ways of making use of Baldwin's lethargy, as when he needed to borrow Government papers of restricted circulation for the Department's use: 'I could probably obtain the loan of them without difficulty. . . . I do not imagine that the Leader's secretariat are busily engaged upon them preparing criticisms of them for the information of Mr. Baldwin'.[2] Baldwin had many creditable political features, not the least of which was his readiness to leave the making of policy to others who were better informed, but it is surely misleading to see him as the author of the new departure of 1929–30.

J. C. C. Davidson certainly has a better claim to be the Department's founder, in that he had been a supporter of the idea that lay behind it. As Party Chairman in 1929 he took the responsibility for translating Baldwin's decision into an effective organisation. It was

Davidson who selected Ball as the first Director, Davidson who raised money to get the Department off the ground, and Davidson who found premises; in November 1929 the Department opened its doors in Victoria Street and a few months later it moved into a permanent home in Old Queen Street, Davidson having acted with his usual acumen to negotiate a long lease from which the Department was still benefiting in the 1970s. And yet, to regard Davidson as the Department's founder, as Rhodes James suggests, is misguided, and is to claim more than Davidson himself ever did; in a memorandum dictated just before he ceased to be Party Chairman, he recalled that he had regarded the foundation of a Research Department as a prime aim of his time at Central Office, and that he was glad that this had been done before his departure.[3] His commitment to the idea is not in doubt, but he had not been successful in persuading Baldwin of its urgency and, in any case, he was too close to Baldwin to establish the Department as a body that could be independent. Only a few months after the Department began work, Davidson was unceremoniously hustled out of the Party Chairman-ship and he did not have much to do with its work thereafter; he had little connection with the Department during the years in which its character was established.

Lord Eustace Percy had an even more tenuous link with the foundation, as his autobiography makes clear:

> My next unfinished venture in 1929 was the formation of a research department for the Conservative Party. I did this at Baldwin's rather half-hearted request as a preliminary job of survey and organization, on the understanding that the department would be taken over by Neville Chamberlain on his return from abroad. On his return, I left almost immediately on a visit to Canada and the United States and, when I came back, he gave me clearly to understand that he did not want me to have any more to do with it.[4]

The original press release had merely given Percy 'the task of organizing it' along with Ball and he clearly saw himself as no more than a *locum tenens* for Chamberlain. When the negotiations about the new Department were taking place, Chamberlain was being talked about as its possible 'chairman' as he duly became in March 1930, but Percy was not given (and does not seem to have sought) that title. In the four months during which he was temporarily in charge, and while the Department was only beginning to find its feet, he could not make a real impact. Nor indeed did he ever try to make a personal impact or to stamp his personality on the new organisation.

The fact that underlies this whole paternity suit over the foundation of the Department is that the need for a new research organisation had been widely recognised in the Party over the previous decade. The cumulative pressure applied by Davidson, Amery, the Chamberlains, Macmillan, Buchan and many others had created a situation where the formation of a new body in 1929 was inevitable, and the decision was in that sense a collective one by the Party hierarchy as a whole. Confusion arose because those who had a clear idea how such an organisation might actually function were either out of favour in the Autumn of 1929, like Amery and Macmillan, too concerned with other Party problems like Davidson, or standing aloof like Chamberlain. The Party leaders thus took a general decision to set up a Conservative Research Department, but did not resolve the far more difficult question of how the new body would operate, what would be its relationship to Central Office and the Shadow Cabinet, or how it would relate to a Leader who would have authority over it but who would take no interest in its activities.

The new Department was small in size and strictly limited in its objectives. Apart from Ball as Director, its staff consisted of Henry Brooke and Frank Pakenham (both of whom were young men in their twenties with a keen interest in politics and with political ambitions of their own), Harold Stannard and Major Fosbrooke-Hobbes, together with three secretaries. Its work was entirely on the domestic side of politics (though taking in tariffs and Empire trade as 'domestic' rather than 'foreign' problems) and in the early years it was sometimes referred to as the 'Conservative Economic Research Department'. Brooke's first task was to collect information on the problems of British industry for work on industrial policy; starting from the report of the Balfour Committee on industry, appointed by Baldwin's Government, he concentrated on steel and cotton as the industries most in need of reorganisation. He was soon writing to Ball about the huge volume of material with which he was having to familiarise himself and asking if the Department could secure the services of a statistical adviser who had access to a good library, such as that of the LSE. Brooke also arranged an early meeting between Percy and industrial organisations, such as the National Federation of Iron and Steel Manufacturers who met Percy on 6 January 1930 and afterwards sent Brooke detailed evidence on the future of their industries.[5] Similarly, Fosbrooke-Hobbes was collecting, digesting and summarising copies of all the legislation and reports on National Insurance since 1911; scarcely had he completed this mammoth task when the Government passed a new National Insurance Act and thus

required him to re-work all his material.[6] This dry assembling of facts
and opinion was necessary before the Department could ever hope to
offer any advice of its own, and it was precisely because it was a new
organisation that it was bound to begin with a period of drudgery.
Morale in those early months was not high, and the situation was not
helped by the lack of clear direction from the top.

The Party was already beginning its struggle with the Beaverbrook and Rothermere newspapers over British trading policy, a
struggle that revolved around exactly those areas of detailed policy
with which a Research Department ought to have been able to assist,
but in fact the Department played no part. The programme of work
that Chamberlain had sketched out before his departure wilted when
left to Baldwin to sustain, and the Party as a whole staggered under
Beaverbrook's attack. What response there was tended to be
unofficial, and Percy exercised no overall control. Hence, when
Beaverbrook explained his ideas to the Conservative Imperial Affairs
Committee in November 1929, it was left to loyalist MPs to provide a
reply, concentrating entirely on the policy issue. Waldron Smithers
reported that:

> We took it that our terms of reference were to point out the economic
> and practical aspect (such as the advisability of obtaining the support of
> the *Daily Express* for the Party, the amount of importance to be given to
> Mr Baldwin's reference to Lord Beaverbrook at the Albert Hall, or the
> extent to which political ambitions affect the whole matter).

The MPs therefore commissioned a critique of Beaverbrook's plans
from the *Financial News* and the *Statist*, which duly convinced them
that 'the more one looks into it the worse the policy appears and the
more dishonest the arguments'. This critique was privately circulated
to a number of key MPs and editors and only then was it even shown
to the Research Department. Smithers then asked that the Party
should pay the cost of the operation, and Davidson authorised this
from the Research Department's funds. The cost involved was only
£29, but the Research Department was supposed to be independent of
Central Office and there is no sign that the Department was
consulted.[7]

Percy saw his own role as strictly limited, not as the impresario of
policy but as a consultant, and he ran the Department along these
lines. Nor did he wish to involve the research that he was doing in the
rough and tumble of day to day politics, a separation that was quite
unrealistic in view of the Party's position on tariffs and its battle with
Beaverbrook. Nevertheless, the early months of the new Depart

ment's life were bound to be difficult ones and Percy certainly felt that they had not been wasted. When Chamberlain sarcastically remarked to Percy that 'the Leaders of the Party did not seem to know what I was after', Percy

> felt inclined to reply that, after two or three months preliminary work, I hardly yet knew what I was after myself, except that I had convinced myself, at least provisionally, that the problem of unemployment insurance finance was soluble and that the protection of the home market was as essential to the restoration of the steel industry as it was useless as a basis for any system of imperial preference.[8]

Chamberlain, unlike Percy, recognised that the practicality of a policy could only be assessed in the light of political as well as economic factors. He recognised not only the need to convince himself of a policy, but also the need to establish means to convince his colleagues.

Things therefore changed with dramatic suddenness when Chamberlain returned from Africa in March 1930, refreshed and full of determination. His position was also inherently strengthened by the weak showing that the Party had made in his absence and by the increasing criticism of both Baldwin and Davidson. Within a week of his return Chamberlain had set about consolidating his position, and within a fortnight he had things firmly under his control, as he told Ida:

> Though I have not been in the public eye I have done a good deal of work for the Party behind the scenes. I have now definitely taken over the Research Department which will next month be housed at 24 Old Queen Street with the principal rooms overlooking Bird Cage Walk. The Leader and his staff will share the building with us and I expect there will be a lot of colloquing there between us. . . . With immense difficulty we have got S.B. to set up a sort of inner Shadow Cabinet called the Committee of Business which is to meet regularly and I am arranging to take my instructions from and report to them.[9]

By this stage he had also talked frankly to Davidson and told him that he should resign; it was to take several weeks before this bore fruit, but in due course Davidson was forced out and, since the Party would not accept his nomination of Geoffrey Ellis as Party Chairman, Chamberlain took over the job himself. The new broom was felt quickly at Central Office, and a wholesale reorganisation was effected during the year in which Chamberlain was in charge. There was a general recognition that the Party was now under a firmer control, and not only from Conservatives; Warren Fisher wrote to

Chamberlain, explaining that he could not as a civil servant express any partiality, but warmly approving 'the terribly overdue recognition of the need for you in a controlling position if realities are to be faced'.[10] Chamberlain himself noted the effect that his arrival had had on the Research Department:

> I found things in rather a mess, for Eustace, who always said that he was not the man for the job, had started a number of hares without any clear idea of where he was going, and the office was evidently dispirited and uneasy. But there is a different atmosphere now and they are all rather excited and feeling that they are going to be an important body. I am getting very much interested myself and it seems to me that through my new Department I shall have my finger on the springs of policy.[11]

As soon as he became involved in its work, there was no further doubt of Chamberlain's commitment to the Research Department. A week after he took over he noted that:

> I have been going to my Research Committee every day and have got my Agricultural Committee going and various other activities, including West Indian Sugar on which the Committee of Business suddenly discovered we had no policy. I think they felt it an improvement to have some definite body to refer to.[12]

When he became Party Chairman he decided to retain the Chairmanship of the Research Department too, although this meant committing much of his time to Party activities when most Shadow Ministers were using the period of opposition to make money; when he gave up the Party Chairmanship in 1931, he did not offer his resignation as Chairman of the Research Department. The original understanding, that he would have to give up his Research Department work if he returned to Government, gradually faded as he became more involved in the work. In May 1931, Ball told him that 'the prospect of your giving up the Department when the Party gets back to office is one that fills me with dismay. I am not without hope that when the time comes, some plan for avoiding that calamity may be devised'. Chamberlain noted on this letter the substance of his reply: 'As for future, does not look as if either of us need worry about such changes are likely take me away from Research Department' (sic).[13] When the National Government was formed, there was no talk of Chamberlain giving up his position as Chairman, and he therefore remained in charge until his death in 1940. Direction by a senior Party figure has brought immense benefits to the Conservative Research Department over the years, placing it at the centre of the

Party's policy making activities, and ensuring that its views would be heard at the highest level.

In view of the change of direction that took place in March 1930, it will be as well to establish exactly what Chamberlain's aims were when he took over. Lord Eustace Percy saw the change as a simple contrast between open-minded research conducted along academic lines and political hatchet jobs run by a politician:

> My impression is that we approached the project from two diametrically opposed points of view. He wanted a group of men who would 'devil' for him personally, or would at least work out the application of measures which would be given them as the Party's policy. . . . My conception was the more academic one of a group ranging more at large over the whole field of unsolved probelms, and suggesting conclusions out of which a Party policy might be constructed.[14]

Chamberlain, who more than once referred to Percy as 'hopelessly academic', would have recognised the distinction, though he would doubtless have described it differently. As a senior politician he certainly intended to use the Department to devil for his speeches. What are not true are the suggestions that Chamberlain wanted the Department to be only a secretariat, or that it should not conduct real research work for the Party as well as mere devilling. The point is quite clear in Chamberlain's own description of the role that he saw for the Research Department in the Party, and in the first tasks that he set for it:

> We shall be at once an Information Bureau providing data and briefs for leaders, and a long term Research body, and the results of our work will be supplied not to the public but to the Committees of Business, the Central Office and Ashridge College. As a start I am setting up a Research into Unemployment Insurance and outrelief to work out the proper method of dealing with able-bodied unemployed who are not really insurable and weight down the Fund but are at present excluded from outrelief. I shall have another committee on overproduction, which is the new world phenomenon, another on social and industrial problems, including thrift and co-partnership, and finally another on agriculture. I am particularly pleased with the latter, because hitherto all our investigations have simply endeavoured to find some vote-catching device with the result that we bring forward a series of disconnected proposals which have no relation to one another or to any coherent scheme. I have persuaded my friends that what we want is a survey of the whole position which shall establish the proper proportions of the different kinds of farming – arable, dairy, stock etc. in the light of our soil, climate and economic conditions, and then a consideration of the

means necessary to establish each kind in its proportion. On this plan we shall be able to rule out many of the really childish suggestions which our agricultural committees have been wasting their time over, and such measures as we propose will fall into their proper place as necessary for the purpose at which we are aiming. It will take time but if done in the way I want it should give us for the first time a solid groundwork of principles and a strong (policy) which we can make intelligible in the towns as well as in the country.[15]

It is indeed arguable that the Department was *more* open-minded in its research programmes in Chamberlain's time than it has been since.

Chamberlain's advent helped to regularise procedures, since he insisted on businesslike methods being applied by the Department itself and by all its research programmes. Each committee that he set up was chaired by a front-bencher, or some Party figure of equivalent standing, was made up mainly of younger back-benchers, and had specific terms of reference laid down by Chamberlain himself. The committees were small bodies, with their members appointed directly by letter from Chamberlain and without power to add to their number – 'so as to sharpen the individual sense of responsibility in each member, though they are allowed to bring in any one they like to help them' as witnesses or advisers.[16] A staff member from the Department serviced each committee; acted as secretary, provided any necessary briefs for the members, and usually drafted the report. The reports were then submitted through Ball to Chamberlain; only after his approval did they go on to 'my colleagues on the Business Committee'. The formalisation of this last stage was taken rather too far; reports from the Department were numbered in series, from CRD1 (Agriculture) and CRD2 (Iron and Steel) through to less pressing matters like CRD7 (London Traffic). All the copies of each individual report were numbered, all were marked 'most secret', and a receipt was provided (together with a stamped, addressed envelope) for the Shadow Ministers involved to signify the safe arrival of their copies. The last process involved the Director's secretary in a great deal of extra work, since Chamberlain's errant colleagues often failed to return the receipts, and she was then required to chase them up. It was not easy to persuade such men as Winston Churchill of the need for security in matters like the future of the pigmeat industry or the case for centralised slaughterhouses; there were many ironic replies in which the Department was informed that the report in question was safely locked away in a safe. Baldwin proved especially difficult to break in to these routine methods, and after a year the system was abandoned. Nevertheless, high security did pay off on at least one occasion, over a memorandum on Indian policy. It is not clear what sensitive and potentially embarrassing material was contained in this document; Robert Stopford, Secretary to the Indian Round Table Conference, wrote to Ball in December 1930 to tell him that 'Sir Samuel Hoare tells me that it was decided at the Business Committee on Monday that *all* the copies of Sir Samuel's memorandum CRD8 should be destroyed. He asked me to ask you if you would be kind enough to have any copies which may still be in your office destroyed, and that not even a file copy should be kept!'. Conscious of the need for security, Ball compiled with the request and thus left an intriguing gap in the departmental files.[17] In another, less obvious way, Chamberlain found Ball's methods helpful in the early days of the Department. In the leadership crisis of February 1931, when Chamberlain was in the embarrassing position of having lost Baldwin's confidence but being unable to persuade him to resign, he turned to Ball for information. It was Ball, still with his ear to the ground in Parliament and the Party, who told him exactly what Baldwin was thinking when Baldwin himself was ostentatiously silent.[18]

The value of policy research began to appear in public from the Autumn of 1930. The Party was calling for a more definite statement of policy from Baldwin to head off a renewed attack from Beaverbrook, and the climate of opinion had shifted sharply in favour of the tariff and against intermediary policies like a referendum. Chamberlain drew on the findings of his research committees to suggest the bones of a policy before Baldwin returned from his holiday; this was Chamberlain's 'unauthorised programme' – although based on the work of official Party committees. Chamberlain returned from his own holiday early in October and 'settled down to daily attendance at the Central Office and Research Department'; Baldwin himself 'came back in high spirits and great physical health, but apparently without an idea in his head about politics'.[19] He was persuaded to call a meeting of the Business Committee to discuss Chamberlain's ideas; after a week's adjournment to meet Churchill's objections to a wheat quota, the Business Committee agreed on the proposals, which were then published as a letter from Baldwin to the Party Chairman (Chamberlain). Even Chamberlain's sisters were fooled by this little subterfuge, as Neville's letter to Hilda Chamberlain relates:

I am so glad to hear that 'Mr. Baldwin's letter' made such a good impression on you and Ida. It has been a very interesting week and once again it shows that as we thought the chairmanship of the party does enable one to direct the policy though nominally he has nothing to do with it. As a matter of fact S.B. *never saw* the letter till a few minutes before the Business Committee when he read it out as 'the result of our meditations'. Except for a few minor alterations, therefore, made at the Committee, it was drafted by me from beginning to end.[20]

But it was the Chairmanship of the Research Department, combined with a seat in the Business Committee, that had enabled Chamberlain to get his way – as he was to do on many later occasions when he had ceased to be Chairman of the Party.

The first research projects to yield political dividends were those on unemployment insurance and on tariffs. Chamberlain set up the Unemployment Committee in March 1930, under Sir Henry Betterton and with Walter Elliott, William Ormsby-Gore and Robert Hudson as members. Brooke acted as secretary and the terms of reference invited the Committee to range widely as well as concentrating on the need to restore the insurance principle of the original fund and to find a way of dealing with unemployed adults excluded both from the existing scheme and from outrelief. The Committee's report, submitted to Chamberlain at the end of July, made recommendations for a reorganisation of the system; the scheme should 'on principle' be extended to industries like agriculture that had previously been excluded; the principle of insurance should be restored by a strict enforcement of the rules relating benefits to contributions; those who were thus deprived of benefit should be maintained by local authorities, with the Exchequer meeting three-quarters of the cost; the Unemployment Insurance Fund's existing debts should be written off to allow a fresh start. The Committee recognised the need for far more information than was readily available to them and called for investigations into the possible refund of contributions on retirement, into earnings-related benefits and contributions, and into the local causes of unemployment. Finally, they emphasised the extent to which changes could relate only to methods:

> Centuries ago, the national conscience decided that it would not tolerate starvation in the community. The question with which we have been dealing is not a question of whether to spend more or less. It is entirely a question of how to spend more carefully and usefully what has to be spent in any circumstances, and on what system to divide the cost.

This point was emphasised by Betterton in his letter to Chamberlain; it had not been intended to devise a system that would deal with the existing crisis situation, but rather to establish what an ideal structure would be when things had returned to normal.[21] It is in that light that the work should be viewed and it was when the level of unemployment had begun to recede in 1933 that the findings of the report began to be implemented – by which time Betterton himself was Minister of Labour and Hudson his Parliamentary Secretary. All the same, the Party now had a useful corpus of information and a number of experts in the field.

When the Government set up a three-party committee on the Fund, Betterton and Elliott were nominated as the two Conservative representatives, and Brooke continued to work for them. The Committee had indeed expressed fulsome thanks to Brooke in its report: 'We wish to express our deep sense of appreciation of the invaluable assistance we have received from our Secretary, Mr Brooke. The care which he has bestowed in tracing the various ramifications of the complicated story of Unemployment Insurance has greatly facilitated the task imposed on us.'[22]

Over the following Winter, a complex ritual dance was performed over the insurance issue, with the Government, the Liberals, the Conservative leaders, the Conservative representives on the three-party committee, and the Research Department playing interlocking roles. All the Conservatives involved reached the conclusion that the Government had little to offer and that it was playing for time. Ministers argued that there would be little chance of turning the matter over to Public Assistance Committees run by local authorities since it would take at least two years to bring these into operation. The Conservatives were not convinced by this argument, for which little evidence was produced, and they stepped up the pressure by threatening to withdraw all cooperation. All this manoeuvring was handled by Ball and Brooke, and Chamberlain's views were conveyed to the Party representatives through the Department. Ball was also at work undermining the Government's position from within; he had talks with Sir Frederick Leith Ross of the Treasury and afterwards sent him a copy of the Conservative report together with a short covering note that set forth they way in which Public Assistance Committees *could* come into use quickly. By September 1930, the Government rather than the Opposition argued that it was suffering from the lack of information and suggested the appointment of a Royal Commission. To counter this delaying tactic, the Conservative representatives put forward their own report, amended to meet the political circumstances; for example, the suggestion that the accumulated debts of the Insurance Fund should be written off was now removed because this would give the Government a breathing space. This final submission was prepared in the Research Department in October, signed by Betterton and Elliott and sent off direct to the Government. Chamberlain was informed of its contents and approved the general principles, but did not see the final draft since he wished it to go forward as a personal rather than a Party submission – 'it will now be possible for him to say he did not see the Memorandum'. An additional copy was prepared for Baldwin but Chamberlain decided that this should not be sent off at all.

As Robert Skidelsky has shown, the appointment of a Royal Commission *was* a delaying measure by the Government at the end of October, forced on them because the other Parties would not support further subventions into the Fund without some sign of action; a Royal Commission was the least that they could do if they were not prepared to accept the Conservatives' more far-reaching proposals, and Ball was probably right in his guess that MacDonald's hope was to put the whole issue on ice until after the next election. If this was the aim, then Chamberlain did not give it much chance of success, for at the end of November, 'anxious that the Government should be well badgered by questions on the subject of Unemployment Insurance', he suggested to Ball that 'draft questions should be drawn up, in consultation with Sir H. Betterton, and submitted to Mr Chamberlain, with a view to their being asked by a team of questioners to be recruited for the purpose'. These draft questions were duly worked out by Brooke and sent off to Betterton for use by his Parliamentary colleagues. A few days later, Chamberlain considered the final version of the Unemployment Insurance Committee's report, as amended during the Autumn and submitted it for the first time to the Business Committee: 'it is proposed that the policy set forth in the Memorandum, if approved by my colleagues, shall be definitely included in the Party programme'. The Business Committee did approve, and Brooke was commissioned to write a pamphlet setting forth the new policy.[23]

Even this was not the end of the road, for other political considerations intervened before the policy could be published, and several Conservatives began to have cold feet about a commitment to a hard line on umemployment benefits. In the first place, Brooke was too busy working on the tariff question to produce his pamphlet in the Winter, and by the Spring the mood had changed. By then, the Royal Commission had been at work for several months and was expected to produce at least interim proposals in the near future. Brooke therefore wrote to Ball in April 1931 to put the case for publishing no

Conservative proposals until after the Royal Commission had reported: 'It is not only that the Royal Commission may eventually produce a better scheme, at any rate in some points', but also that to scorn the Royal Commission by ignoring it 'might leave a bad taste in the mouth of many of the sort of people who read the Times'. He suggested delay, but pointed out that pressure of work would make it very difficult for him to find a clear fortnight to go through the hundreds of pages of evidence submitted to the Commission; 'whereas most of this will be familiar, it is essential not to miss any critical point'. This last problem was dealt with by enlisting the help of Robert Hudson, who went through all the evidence submitted and produced summaries for the Research Department to use. The justification for delay became more apparent when the Royal Commission produced its interim proposals at the beginning of June. Brooke sent Ball a summary of these proposals on the day after publication, noting that in some ways they were more limited but in some ways 'more drastic than our previous ideas'. 'I feel strongly that there is more to be gained by a clear-cut acceptance of the Commission's present proposals in their entirety, *as an interim measure*, than by complaining that in some directions they do not go far enough.' (Ball marked this, 'I agree'.) Conservative acceptance 'forces the acutest issue on the Government, and should an appeal to the country result, the Conservatives have the chance of obtaining the whole benefit of the authority which the views of a Royal Commission always carry'.[24]

Others however were not so keen on identifying the Party with a potentially unpopular cause. Sir Patrick Gower wrote to Ball on the following day to urge restraint, since the evidence coming to Central Office from by-elections suggested that the dole question was having a great effect:

from the political point of view there is more danger in the Social Services and Unemployment Benefit cry than there is in the food tax cry. While there may be in many quarters a general agreement that the numerous cases of abuse ought to be abolished, the cutting down of benefit would seem to be regarded with genuine anxiety.

The same anxieties were expressed by Hudson on behalf of Conservative candidates in marginal seats. The Business Committee thus referred the decision to a sub-committee under Betterton which, although not a Research Department Committee, met at Old Queen Street and continued to draw on the advice of Brooke and Ball. This group recommended general acceptance of the Royal Commission's proposals, but hedged this around with a number of qualifications which Brooke disapproved of strongly. He told Ball that 'I think that the time is past for trying to conceal the fact that the Conservative Party intends that those who fall out of benefit should receive payments in relation to their needs, and not at a flat rate'. He was still anxious not to offend the Royal Commission, and argued that the best way would be to show them that the Conservatives were not afraid of the issue, 'for we want the strongest Final Report from them that we can get'. The Business Committee, however, made amendments which toned down the proposals even further and moved Brooke to further criticism: he assumed that the

> introduction of the words 'to maintain existing benefits, which is our aim' has been very carefully weighed. Economically, there is no doubt at all in my mind that for the national good this is a wrong policy. Politically, it is an admission by the Conservative Party that it now approves of the quite unjustified increase in benefits of 2/- a week which the Socialist Government enacted in the face of Conservative opposition sixteen months ago, in spite of a fall of 19 points in the cost of living since then.

The Report was adopted by the Business Committee with the pledge to maintain existing benefits still included. Even this decision could only be maintained with an effort, for further backsliding occurred before Baldwin was due to publicise the policy in his speech at Hull on 17 July.

Hudson was commissioned to draft the Hull speech for Baldwin, and chose to take a line more in accord with his own previous views, as he told Ball. 'It is perhaps my business to carry out instructions, not to make suggestions', but nonetheless he was still opposed to any definite statement of policy. 'May I very diffidently put forward an alternative type of declaration, more of the "elder statesman" nature such as I have sketched out?' Ball merely noted that 'Mr Chamberlain agreed this was unsuitable' and asked Hudson to try again. Two days later, Ball sent Hudson's second efforts on to Chamberlain, still not close to 'the line you had in mind, but I expect you will want us to revise them in the Department'. The final version, amended by Ball and by Chamberlain, was sent off to Baldwin only two days before the speech was due to be delivered; there is no sign that Baldwin or his staff had been asked for their views before the speech reached this final form. Ball wrote to thank Hudson for his efforts on the policy and the speech: 'It has ended as a composite production', but Baldwin would not say anything 'to cause heart-burnings among our candidates'.[25]

This prolonged exercise in shaping policy on the Unemployment Insurance Fund shows the Department finding its feet, but it also illustrates some of the recurring problems of making policy. The first stage, in which an ideal policy was worked out by a small committee was by far the most straightforward, but it was only after the Betterton Committee had reported to Chamberlain that the real policy making began. The gradual amendment of these proposals under the cross-pressures of Party politics resulted in a weaker policy, but one that had a greater chance of implementation in actual political circumstances. It was perhaps unusual at this time to be looking for a long-term solution to something which was politically immediate – a consequence of starting from scratch in 1929.

If unemployment insurance illustrated the evolution of policy from the ideal to the practicable, then tariffs demonstrated the opposite case of the Party riding a swell-tide of opinion in order to get nearer to the ideal. During 1930, Party policy moved towards a full policy of tariffs with imperial preference, and the Research Department was engaged in a fairly open-ended programme of investigation into the possible expansion of inter-Imperial trade. This investigation was done entirely within the Research Department, rather than through a committee of MPs, as Brooke explained to Ball:

> Broadly, I have taken the Imperial side of the ground . . . and Mr. Pakenham has taken the home trade and safeguarding side. Those notes were tentative and probably neither of us found himself working on the exact lines laid down there, because when one gets to work on matters like this, one always modifies one's programme slightly as one proceeds, new and important lines of enquiry emerging and demanding to be followed out.

Their work was completed by August 1930 and summarised in a bulky report by Brooke which made out a strong case for Government action to promote Imperial trade; much could be done, especially in Canada, if British industry could be modernised, rationalised and persuaded to adopt more modern methods of salesmanship. The level at which the Research Department was aiming in such research projects was neatly summarised by Brooke in the covering letter which accompanied the report:

> I have aimed at producing something slightly less abstract and more definitely linked on to Conservative policy than the Imperial Economic Committee's recent 'Memorandum on the Trade of the British Empire', and rather more searching than the Central Office's new production, 'A United Empire' (which seems to me very well done so far as it goes, seeing that it is not its business to be critical).[26]

The Research Department's middle position was to be more political than independent bodies but less blindly partisan than the rest of the Party organisation. The timing of the report was also significant, since it was intended to provide background for talks that the Party leaders intended to have with Dominion politicians while they were in London for the Imperial Economic Conference; it was also available for Chamberlain's 'unauthorised programme' and the subsequent modifications of Party policy. So, during November, Chamberlain attended a luncheon given by Lord Camrose 'but arranged by the Research Department' to put J. H. Scullin, the Australian Prime Minister in touch with Conservatives: 'I sat between Scullin and Parker Molony, his Minister of Trade and Commerce and I had a good talk with them both about what they wanted and what they were prepared to give us'. After similar talks with R. B. Bennett of Canada, Chamberlain recorded that 'we have made good use of our opportunities of making contacts with the Dominions, and I hope to get the results embodied in a report which will remain on record among our files. It is an immense comfort to my orderly mind to have the Research Department in existence. I wish I knew a rich man who would give it a whacking big sum to endow it'.[27]

By the end of 1930, there was no further doubt that the Conservatives were committed to the full tariff policy or that they had little to fear from its traditional unpopularity with the electorate; Chamberlain told a correspondent in Australia that 'our electorate here is, at the present time, more interested in the question of a Tariff than in anything else; and if only we could get the opportunity of going to the country, I have little doubt that we should obtain a majority large enough to enable us to put it into operation'. Most reports from the constituencies confirmed this view, and there were even signs that traditional Free Traders in the Liberal and Labour Parties were on the point of abandoning their resistance to tariffs. The problem was no longer to establish the desirability of tariffs but to work out the best means of implementing them. Chamberlain was also anxious to establish the tariff in such a way that it should be permanent, so utilising the current disillusion with free trade to make a lasting change of fiscal policy.

A committee was thus set up under Sir Philip Cunliffe-Lister, with Leo Amery, Sir Basil Blackett, George Lloyd and Herbert Williams, all men with a great interest in Imperial trade policy, among its members; Henry Brooke was again secretary. The committee met twenty-five times in the first half of 1931 and consulted a large number of expert advisers. In particular, advice was sought from James Hope and two other Deputy-Speakers on the best way to frame tariff resolutions and tariff legislation in order to waste the minimum of parliamentary time in getting the tariff into effect. It was decided that an emergency tariff should be introduced by special resolution and that the permanent tariff should be embodied in a special Tariff Act, so as to avoid the embarrassment of an annual debate on tariffs taking place if rates were fixed through the Finance Bill; a Tariff Commission should be set up to protect the Minister from the responsibility of fixing different rates for different industries, and to supervise the transition from the emergency tariff to the final 'scientific tariff'. The committee report, a document of over a hundred pages was submitted to Chamberlain on 24 June 1931; Ball noted that 'the main burden has fallen on the shoulders of Sir Philip Cunliffe-Lister and Mr Brooke'. (Henry Brooke has recalled that none of the other members seemed really to understand what it was all about!) Ball also supported the Committee's recommendation that when the Party got back into office it should make sure that more adequate statistics were collected by the Board of Trade; significantly, Chamberlain noted 'Yes' on his copy of the report. The report was circulated to the Business Committee on 17 July; perhaps Chamberlain had little hope of commanding his colleagues attention for so weighty a volume, for he also included a short summary of its proposals and offered to 'store' all the copies of the main report at Old Queen Street should his colleagues wish to be relieved of them. Five days later, he told a correspondent that 'the Research Department (of which I have retained the Chairmanship) has now worked out pretty completely the arrangements for an early imposition of an emergency tariff; the procedure for getting it through Parliament as quickly as possible; and the setting up of a Tariff Commission or Board, to administer it, and to carry out subsequent adjustments'. Thanking James Hope for drafting the model resolutions, he told him that 'we shall be able, if and when we are returned to office, to bring the Tariff into operation with the minimum of delay'. The formation of the National Government in August put the tariff debate out of court for a few months, but once the General Election had been won in October, the prepared plans could be put into effect. Ball sent Chamberlain a summary of the proposals just before the election campaign ended, to 'provide you with material for defeating Free Traders who suggest that the Conservative Party has given no real thought to the Tariff problem!' And in the following year, when Ball accompanied Chamberlain to

Ottawa, he took the Research Department files with him.[28]

Other research took second place to tariffs and unemployment during 1930 and 1931, but there was still a lot to be done. The Agricultural Research Committee in particular was pressing on with the work that Chamberlain had set it when he took over, and there was a close relationship between the agricultural and tariff policies. Chamberlain noted at the end of 1930 that:

> my studies at the Research Department have shown clearly enough that the future of British farming is not in wheat but in livestock, dairying, pigs and poultry. To build up these industries, so vital to the general prosperity of the country, a tariff seems indispensible, though it must of course be combined with other measures.

A few months later, the Party's agricultural advisers were involved with the refinement of the tariff policy and at least one joint meeting was held between the Agricultural Committee and Cunliffe-Lister's Tariff Committee to co-ordinate their approach. The end product of this policy review was 'a new agricultural order', implemented through the legislation of 1933 and 1934 which, as Sir Keith Feiling noted, 'reversed the whole of nineteenth century thought'.[29]

A major investigation into possible economies in public expenditure was less successful, for reasons that were as instructive as those which had made other projects effective. The committee was set up in February 1931 and reported in the following June. It was probably created to find answers to those Conservatives who were calling for draconian cuts in expenditure, but it does not seem to have enjoyed Chamberlain's active support. Nor was it composed of men who had any great experience of public expenditure, for its chairman was Vivian Henderson MP who had merely served for two years as Under Secretary at the Home Office; the other four members did not include any ex or future Ministers, though one had been City Treasurer of Birmingham. Their report, drafted by Frank Pakenham, underlined the difficulties inherent in such an operation: the lack of access to civil service advice had severely hampered the reliability of the figures available to them; local authorities, jealous of their autonomy had not been keen to co-operate; and their main finding was that cuts could only be symbolic, since there were no obvious areas where substantial savings could be made. Their recommendations were made in great detail, concentrating on areas where departmental expenditure had risen sharply since 1929, or since the Geddes Committee had reported on expenditure in 1921, but in almost every field they could recommend only hypothetical savings of stationery and manpower. There is no sign that their report made much impact on Chamberlain or that it was circulated at all to his colleagues; and there is certainly no sign that the Conservative Ministers of the National Government were interested in this sort of approach to economy.[30]

Another traditional blind alley was the research done on the possible reconstruction of the House of Lords. Chamberlain was well aware of the difficulties that beset constitutional reformers and he suggested the investigation to Hailsham in July 1930, 'not to drag into the limelight immediately this somewhat thorny problem, but to ensure that if and when it is dragged into the limelight (probably by others), we shall be ready with a clear-cut policy of our own'. Over the following six months, time-consuming negotiations were held with the Peers and with other Conservatives interested in the issue, not least because of the extreme difficulty of finding a Chairman who was prepared to take on the job and who would command confidence. These negotiations were scarcely helped when the ever-touchy Lord Midleton went to the wrong address for a meeting with Chamberlain because he had been inadvertently invited to the Research Department on note-paper that bore the old (Victoria Street) address. Chamberlain was trying to persuade Hailsham himself to take the chair, but Hailsham insisted that only a chairman from the House of Commons would endow the committee with sufficient standing to give its proposals any chance of being implemented. Chamberlain thus asked Ball to provide a list of suggested names – a document tersely marked by Ball 'Get Vacher'. In January 1931 Chamberlain invited William Ormsby-Gore to take the chair, pointing out that the Labour Government might take up the issue at any time: 'apart from the urgency, it does seem to me dangerous to have a question of this kind in the offing when our Party has no decided views about it, and no plans which could enable it to take up with any confidence a definite attitude at any moment'.

Ormsby-Gore was an obvious compromise choice between Lords and Commons since he was an MP but also the heir to a peerage, but he was not so central in political terms. He replied to Chamberlain that he was always ready to help the Party, 'and your Research Department in particular', but that his views on the House of Lords were too 'advanced' to allow him to be Chairman; somewhat unhelpfully, he volunteered to serve on the Committee as its 'left-wing' member. Further soundings left Chamberlain with no alternative but Lord Linlithgow, suggested by Hailsham months earlier, but it was not until April 1931 that he was persuaded to accept. Further time was spent on agreeing exact terms reference with Linlithgow and getting his approval to the names of the other members, so that a year had passed in talk before the Committee began its work in June 1931. It was a large group for such a controversial task, containing six Peers and five Commoners, and many of its members had fixed ideas of the sort of Upper House that they would wish to see. There were thus inevitable disagreements between such men as Lord Midleton who wished to restore power to the hereditary Peerage and others like Duff Cooper who would have liked to remove the hereditary Peers altogether. A consensus eventually emerged and a draft scheme proposed by Linlithgow himself was approved by all the members except Cooper, but the commitment of other House of Commons members was no more than lukewarm. Even these unpromising proposals did not get any further; by the time that the committee reported in September 1931, there was clearly no room in the Party programme for a restoration of the House of Lords, and so Chamberlain gave orders that the report was to be neither published nor circulated. Being a persistent man, he bided his time and waited his opportunity.[31]

All this will demonstrate how wide a range of topics the policy exercise covered in the first two years; in the Summer of 1931, apart from the House of Lords, economies, tariffs, agriculture and unemployment, there were six more committees at work. These covered over-production (under Hilton Young), Imperial affairs (Tryon), industrial foundations of society (W. S. Morrison), clean milk (Lord Iveagh), Post Office (Gilmour), and sugar (Ormsby-Gore).[32] It was an ambitious and far-reaching programme to undertake with a Department that still had only five members of staff, and in addition to these long-term commitments were the demands on the Department for political briefs and speeches. It was in this context that the Department played its part in the more historic events of 1931, the political crisis and the election.

The political crisis turned on the failure of the Labour Government to agree on means to balance the budget sufficiently to reassure foreign financial opinion and the consequent need to find an alternative Government which could do so. The budget had become acutely unbalanced largely because of the constant drain of unemployment payments, and the only way to restore balance by economies (rather than by *increasing* taxes) was to cut the level of dole payments. Much therefore turned on the questions that Betterton's committee had been working on for Chamberlain over the previous sixteen months. Their first report had urged the restoration of balance by a rigid adherence to the insurance principle and, though they had deprecated any cuts in dole payments, they had plumped for cuts if no other way could be found of restoring balance. Despite the haverings of the intervening year, the Party had stuck more or less to that view, and the report of its own Economies Committee must have removed any lingering ideas that there were major cuts that could be made in other areas of expenditure. When the crisis finally broke in August 1931, it was handled for the Conservative Party by Chamberlain; Ball was out of London. Several crucial meetings on the Conservative side took place at Old Queen Street though, and other members of the Department gave their advice. So for example, Henry Brooke passed on useful information to Chamberlain on 20 August. The Royal Commission on Unemployment Insurance had commissioned enquiries into the effects of 'striking off' which showed them to be far less serious than was being alleged, but the Government had never published these findings; if Chamberlain wished to step up the pressure on MacDonald, he could demand that these findings be published. Ball also sent to Chamberlain from Cornwall on 17 August a long memorandum on the tactics to pursue in the current situation; this proved remarkably accurate in predicting the way in which the crisis talks would develop, and Ball's recommended line was very close to that which Chamberlain took, though it is impossible to say whether the advice.did more than confirm his own views.[33]

Once the National Government had been formed, the Department was busy with the political tasks of explaining what had taken place and justifying it. Brooke was set to demonstrate that recent events had not been a capitalist conspiracy against a Labour Government and produced comprehensive figures on recent trends in industrial profits. He was then put to writing a simple statement, 'in haste, at Neville Chamberlain's request', of 'What the ordinary man stands to lose'. This set of notes explained the reasons for backing currency with gold, the lessons of the German inflation of 1923, the risk to savings and pensions of a loss of confidence, and the threat to the poor. After a number of revisions, this received the approval of Chamberlain and was passed to Central Office for publication by Ball: 'personally I have no doubt that the readers of the *Daily Herald* would be able to understand it'. This and other drafts that originated in the Department provided the backbone of the Party's public relations response to the crisis. Joseph Ball, who was particularly skilled in this form of political warfare, also made a number of initiatives of his own: he commissioned reports on Germany in 1923 from two of his friends who had been there at the time, and he placed these in various newspapers; he persuaded Lord D'Abernon to broadcast on the same subject on the BBC; and he provided Chamberlain with voluminous briefs for his Commons speeches, showing for example that teachers' pay after the salary cuts just imposed would still be higher in real terms than in 1914 or 1918.[34]

Ball remains (as usual) a shadowy figure in the critical decision to fight an election as a National Government, but he certainly gave advice in favour of an election. More definitely, he intervened to influence the shape of the election with suggestions made to Chamberlain on 16 September. He pointed out that the National Government had saved Sterling but that Conservatives believed that only tariffs would restore the balance of trade – and that tariffs could not be achieved without an election. Conservative MPs were beginning to demand an election and would not be satisfied until they had got one, but an election campaign would involve renewed risks to Sterling (during the campaign) and to tariffs (since there might not be a majority for them afterwards). 'The question therefore arises whether it is possible or not so to arrange matters in advance of the General Election that there is no danger of the Election itself or its possible results having any adverse results whatever upon the pound sterling'. He therefore suggested an electoral pact, built around 'a seats arrangement' with Liberals who would commit themselves in favour of tariffs; every Liberal MP who supported tariffs would get a free run, in return for which Liberals would support Conservative sitting members; the full weight of the attack would be concentrated on Labour, with the strongest anti-Labour candidate having a free run in each Labour seat. Ball calculated that this would *guarantee*, without any swing, at least ninety-four Conservative gains and fifteen Liberal gains. In other words, it would guarantee, before the election was even called, that it would result in a large majority against Labour and a majority in favour of tariffs. He predicted quite correctly that the inducement of office would be sufficient to persuade Liberals to go along with this arrangement, but it might be necessary to offer them electoral reform.

> Our own right wing in the House might be vocal, but once they realise that by means of a plan of this kind we should secure certain victory for our tariff policy and a continuity of policy for a period of years not otherwise obtainable, I think their opposition would die away. Most important of all, the pound sterling would not again be placed in jeopardy, and socialism would be forced to take a back seat for the best part of a generation.

This prophetic memorandum contains all the basic features that underpinned the National Government's appeal to the country, and when the election had been won, Ball wrote again to Chamberlain to say 'I told you so'. He pointed out that half of the 190 seats gained from Labour had previously been held on a minority vote: 'You will perhaps remember that in my memorandum to you of the 16th September last, when recommending the conclusion of an arrangement with the Liberals, I put our Conservative gains in these seats as likely to number 106'. The effect of Ball's advice can be gauged from the fact that in the whole country only one constituency was held by Labour on a minority vote – ironically this was Attlee's seat in Walthamstow.[35]

Two policy committees including Conservatives were set up for the purpose of the election, one purely on the Conservative side under Hailsham and one including all the parties in the Government under Sankey. The first dealt with most of the routine business and all of the questions of a purely Party nature; at its first meeting, the committee accepted Neville Chamberlain's suggestion to deal with as much as possible of the business itself, and to refer questions to three-Party meetings only when absolutely necessary. 'Petty matters' were to be dealt with by Central Office and the Research Department summarily; Ball was a full member of the Committee, along with four Cabinet Ministers, and Brooke was secretary. It was resolved that Brooke would send copies of the Committee's decisions to Baldwin only 'where necessary'. It was also this committee that supervised the deal with the Liberals and sent a stiff protest to Liberal headquarters when it heard of a policy questionnaire being sent to a Conservative candidate in a constituency where the Liberals had offered to support him; the Liberals apologised and Ball successfully demanded that the apology should appear in the *News Chronicle*.

The all-Party Committee was much like the Emergency Business Committees (EBCs) run by one-Party Governments in previous elections; it was serviced by the Cabinet Office and worked in close liaison with Government departments, especially with the Treasury. Ball was the link with the Conservative organisation, as Wicks had been in 1929, but the existence of party committees rather devalued the work of the EBC. It was useful for co-ordinating Government response to questions on disarmament and economies, but it answered only twenty-two enquiries during the campaign – compared with fifty-eight in 1929. The Conservatives intended to retain their autonomy on matters of policy.[36]

The value of a real research organisation was first demonstrated in electioneering in 1931, for the Conservative Research Department was now drawn directly into the campaign. Ball and his staff collected information for candidates, drafted speeches and leaflets, and provided advice on tactics. A wide net for information could be especially valuable; Pakenham was used to collect and monitor Liberal publications, with findings that were both positive (Sir John Simon's election address was given wide publicity in the Conservative press) and negative (notes published by the Liberal National Office proved to be a gold-mine of useful quotations about the past careers of such Liberals as Lloyd George and Sir Herbert Samuel). The Research Department also administered for the first time a restraining hand on the publications of the Conservative Party itself, always likely to get carried away in the excitement of a campaign – and never more so than in the crisis atmosphere of 1931. So Fosbrooke-Hobbes' response when asked to read the agricultural section of the Central Office *Speakers Handbook* was extremely hostile: 'I am unable to recommend the publication of this material in its present form'. After much redrafting and with the election campaign due to begin, he was 'unable to find any authority other than that of bare statements in Central Office literature' for most of the facts and figures cited on agriculture, and on conditions in Soviet Russia. The whole thing was toned down and amendments were inserted at proof stage to provide a more solid factual base for what was being said. The final arbitrator on what was and what was not Party policy was the 'Pledge Book' that the Department had been keeping since its foundation and which had been updated for each speech by Baldwin and each decision of the Business Committee.[37] Thus, the election campaign of 1931 enabled the Research Department to find an additional role; as well as a briefing group for the Party leaders and a thinking machine for long-term research, it had also become an integral part of the Party's publicity operations, checking, and on occasion, drafting the literature which the Party put out to the public. It was this tri-partite role that was to remain the Department's function.

Notes

1 Middlemas and Barnes, *Baldwin*, 551.
2 Ball to Chamberlain, 12 December 1934, CRD file 'C.C.C. Correspondence'.
3 Davidson, *Memoirs of a Conservative*, 275, 338.
4 Percy, *Some Memories*, 149.
5 CRD (N) file D/1/b/1 'Steel'.
6 CRD (N) files, 'Unemployment 1929–31'.
7 CRD file E/1/b/1 'Lord Beaverbrook'.
8 Percy, *Some Memories*, 149–50.
9 Neville to Ida Chamberlain, 22 March 1930, Neville Chamberlain MSS, 18/1/686.
10 Fisher to Chamberlain, 24 June 1930, Neville Chamberlain MSS, 7/11/23/5.
11 Neville to Ida Chamberlain, 22 March 1930, Neville Chamberlain MSS, 18/1/686.
12 Neville to Ida Chamberlain, 29 March 1930, Neville Chamberlain MSS, 18/1/687.
13 Ball to Chamberlain, 19 May 1931, Neville Chamberlain MSS, 7/11/24/5.
14 Percy, *Some Memories*, 149.
15 Neville to Ida Chamberlain, 22 March 1930, Neville Chamberlain MSS, 18/1/686.
16 *Ibid.*
17 Signed receipts and correspondence in CRD file B/2/B/1.
18 Neville Chamberlain diary, 11 and 21 March 1931, Neville Chamberlain MSS 2/22.
19 Neville Chamberlain diary, 11 October 1930, Neville Chamberlain MSS 2/22.
20 Neville to Hilda Chamberlain, 18 October 1930, Neville Chamberlain MSS 18/1/713.
21 CRD (N) file, 'Unemployment', folder 2.
22 *Ibid.*
23 CRD (N) file, 'Unemployment', folder 4; Skidelsky, *Politicians and the Slump* (Penguin) 293–5.
24 CRD (N) file, 'Unemployment', folder 3.
25 *Ibid*, folders 3 and 7.
26 CRD file, 'Empire Trade – General I'.

27   Neville to Hilda Chamberlain, 15 November 1930, Neville Chamberlain MSS, 18/1/717.
28   CRD file D/2/C/5, 'Tariff Committee, 1930–31'.
29   Neville Chamberlain Diary, 6 December 1930, Neville Chamberlain MSS 2/22; Feiling, *Chamberlain*, 229.
30   CRD file, 'Report of Economy Committee, 24 June 1931'.
31   CRD files, H/1/a/1 'House of Lords Reform Committee' and 'House of Lords: Mr. Chamberlain's personal file'.
32   CRD file, 'Conservative Research Department Committees'.
33   CRD file F/1/A/1, 'Crisis of August 1931'.
34   *Ibid.*
35   CRD file B/2/b/3, 'Election results'.
36   CRD file B/2/a/4, 'General Election, 1931'.
37   *Ibid.*

Chapter 4

'Neville Chamberlain's private army' (1931–1939)

From the Autumn of 1931, the Conservative Research Department had to cope for the first time with the fact that the Party was in power; although there remained a substantial minority of non-Conservatives in Government positions right up to 1945, the Conservative leaders had regained direct touch with the Civil Service from the August of 1931. The work of the Research Department did not change in principle, since a staff of the same size continued to work on the same operations, but there was a change. Ball remained Director throughout the 1930s but widened his interests, industrially and internationally, so that he was able to devote less of his attention to the Department. Henry Brooke eventually became Deputy Director and he was undoubtedly the pivotal figure in the Department at this time. In 1932, Frank Pakenham left the Department to return to academic life at Christ Church and he was replaced (in 1935) by David Clarke; Pakenham had gradually drawn away from Conservatism and he was soon to be an active member of the Labour Party, later a Labour Minister. Stannard (resigned) and Fosbrooke-Hobbes (tragically killed in an air crash) were replaced in due course by W. F. Wentworth-Shields and P. Hanrott; when Brooke became a parliamentary candidate in 1937, he left the Department and in 1938 Clarke became General Secretary as Brooke had been before becoming Deputy Director. The general appearance of the Department, a Director and only three or four officers, were thus the same in power as in opposition, but the real position was changed.

During the 1930s, the Department still played an important part in the framing of policy, but its role was now intermittent and partial; with the full force of the Civil Service available to Conservative Ministers and their allies, the Department was no longer the only source of ideas, no longer the only place in which proposals could be checked out or facts unearthed. Perhaps the main difference was the changed position of the Department in relation to its Chairman; in 1932 there was a Cabinet which did not include only Conservatives, and with which a Party organisation could not therefore work directly, but before 1934 there was no equivalent of the Shadow Cabinet or Business Committee which had acted as the focus of the Department's work when in opposition. Neville Chamberlain was ready to listen to ideas on policy matters, but as Chancellor of the Exchequer in a time of crisis he had little time for anything except the business of the Treasury. Above all, the fact that Chamberlain no longer came into the office regularly and could only be reached by letter or by appointment devalued the role that the Department could play. This change can be seen in the correspondence between Ball and Chamberlain; Ball wrote in June 1933 to offer the help of the Department for anything that Chamberlain might need doing during the Imperial Conference that Summer. Chamberlain's secretary replied to say that the Chancellor was far too heavily occupied with Treasury business and did not see how he could make real use of the Department. Ball did not let the matter drop, but renewed his offer of help and also offered to call and see Chamberlain in Eaton Square if this would make things any easier; there is no sign that this produced any better response.[1] It may be that the Treasury saw the Research Department as a possible rival for the ear of their political chief; there was certainly no very close connection between the two. So for example in 1933 when the Department was considering Government policy on industrial assurance and motor insurance, they had to divine the line along which policy was developing from the public pronouncements of Ministers; after his investigations, Brooke could only report that there was 'probably' no Bill being prepared.[2]

Through all this time, the Department went on working directly for Chamberlain on more overtly political matters, especially helping with his main speeches. So he had earlier reported to Ida Chamberlain from Birmingham: 'I had come here to address a League of Nations Union meeting last night. I know mighty little about the subject but, with the help of the Research Department, I produced a lot of stuff that was new to the audience and I think practically it was a very helpful meeting'.[3] Chamberlain was a satisfying politician to work for, since he made it clear exactly what work he wanted done for a speech and then reworked the material that was submitted into a form that could be truly said to be his own; other colleagues, less scrupulous and less comprehending, all too often sent in vague requests for material for a speech and then delivered verbatim whatever was sent to them. In the 1935 election, a speech draft that had been prepared for Baldwin but never used was sent instead to the National Labour Minister, Lord de la Warr, and used in its entirety.

Chamberlain's very different approach was exemplified by the preparations for a speech delivered at Gloucester at the end of June 1934. The Department received from Chamberlain's secretary a dictated note asking Ball to provide information by five o'clock on the same day:

> I want him to show (if the figures warrant it) that our loss of export trade is due, not so much to the trade barriers that we hear so much of, but to the loss of purchasing power in the agricultural countries, due to the fall in prices. For this purpose, I should take our three largest agricultural customers (I suppose Australia, Canada and ?) and give values of their purchases from us, say in 1929 and 1933. It would be useful to know the figures of total exports in the same years, though that would not necessarily be mentioned. Then I should take the principal agricultural products of the said countries (wheat, wool, maize or cotton etc.) and give the average prices for the same years. I should perhaps have the total value of exports of these commodities from the three countries in question. If the figures come out right, they should show the relation between our exports and the prices of agricultural products, and lead to the conclusion that we are vitally interested in the maintenance of these prices.

All this information was collected by the Department and sent off the same day in the form of raw data, notes and critical apparatus for interpretation (explaining, for example, the difficulties of comparing prices that were not all expressed in gold equivalents). Two days later, Chamberlain sent Ball the draft of his speech and the figures that he had worked up to use. Ball was quick to urge care: Chamberlain should be careful to specify that the fall was from the highest prices of 1929 to the lowest of 1933 'or we shall have the *Economist* on our track next week'; he also suggested a slightly less specific use of figures on cheese, since the most recent figures were only estimates.[4] This care in detail was a common feature of the work that the Department did for Chamberlain and indicates one of the aims that Ball had set his staff. Just as Brooke had been anxious about the views of those who read *The Times* in 1931, so Ball in 1934 was anxious not to offend readers of the *Economist*; the Conservative Research Department would ensure that Party spokesmen did not use unreliable material in their speeches, not because Ball was unaware of the political value of occasional exaggeration, but because he was anxious to foster the impression that the Party and its leaders were reliable and competent men of business. It may also reflect the fact that both Ball and Brooke believed in a high standard of accuracy for its own sake, and it became a matter of departmental pride. It was the same basic intentions that had led to the Department vetting for Chamberlain publicity material put out by Central Office for the use of Conservative candidates. The charge that the Conservatives were the 'stupid Party' was as common in the inter-war years as in the previous century, and the work of the Department might help to rebut such claims. Chamberlain was good to work for in other ways too; David Clarke recalls that 'he was very prompt at reading our reports and sending back comments and queries. You really felt that it had his full attention.'

Ball and his staff were especially keen to help Chamberlain not only because they were working to his instructions, but because he represented their link with the top of the Party hierarchy; the enhancement of Chamberlain's influence on policy was also the enhancement of their own. Equally important perhaps, was the real admiration that was felt for Chamberlain as a politician by almost everyone who worked for him – the same loyalty was generated in both the Ministry of Health and the Treasury when he was in charge. Thus, in 1936, the Research Department took especial care over the preparations for Chamberlain's speech to the Party Conference; this would be the last that he would deliver before he took over the Party Leadership and so he should take especial care to make sure that nothing went astray or that no wrong impressions were created. Brooke wrote to Ball to suggest a way in which the situation could be turned to advantage though:

> For his own personal benefit I suggest that he would be wise to say something, aimed in this case beyond the walls of the Conference room, about his belief in democracy. There is a widespread feeling among people that Mr. Chamberlain is an autocrat at heart, and that if he were to take Mr. Baldwin's place as P.M. we should be taking a step away from democracy. Hitler and Mussolini have seen to it that democracy is enjoying in our country at the moment a popularity which none of us would have prophesied for it five years ago. If Mr. Chamberlain should say something at Margate to diminish the popular impression that he is an authoritarian at heart, I think he would be striking a shrewd blow in his own cause.[5]

This idea was duly incorporated in the various drafts of the speech worked over in Old Queen Street and Chamberlain had a considerable personal triumph at the Conference. Relations became even closer after that, partly no doubt because Chamberlain's accession to the premiership placed the Department more at the centre of things, partly perhaps because Chamberlain no longer had the Treasury staff directly available for his use. It may also have relied to some extent on an increasingly close personal sympathy between Chamberlain and Ball; apart from an increasing use of Ball as a personal political agent, Chamberlain visited Ball on occasion for holidays, since they shared a passion for fly-fishing.

The relations of the Department with Baldwin were always distant and indirect. It was decided in 1931 that Baldwin's public speeches on Party matters should be handled through Central Office and Sir Patrick Gower. Gower did not have the resources to do this properly and the Research Department were therefore called on to provide factual material over the following years, but only when asked. There were occasional exceptions to this rule, as, for example, Baldwin's 'Peace and War' speech at Glasgow in November 1934 which contained a long critique of the Peace Ballot prepared by Ball, but these occasions were few and far between.[6] Other Conservative Ministers drew on the help of the Research Department in an equally rare and haphazard manner. Assistance was available but was rarely used, no doubt because the other Ministers thought of the Research Department as Chamberlain's private office. In one sense they were right; when working for other Ministers, copies of drafts were often sent to Chamberlain for his information too.

Relations with the different Government departments varied but gradually developed during the early 1930s into an attitude of greater trust. It was not an easy liaison to establish for, as the Cabinet Office was told by Brooke, 'co-operation with any of the political organisations must be nothing but a curse to everyone in the Civil Service'. Things probably depended on the attitude of the Minister in charge; the India Office, under Hoare, was especially helpful, not only in itself but also for the way in which it could be used against other departments. In 1932, Hoare asked Ball to undertake research on a possible economic agreement to be made between Britain and India, suggesting a Research Department committee under Douglas Hacking. This was duly done by the Department, arranged not only through the Department's own contacts (such as Sir Geoffrey Corbett, recently Secretary to the British delegation to the Indian Round Table Conference and now Reader in Indian history at Oxford), but also with information given by the Indian Office itself. When documents on the British side of the question could not be got out of the Board of Trade, Hoare dealt with the matter by requisitioning them direct from the President, Runciman, and passing them on to Ball. In May 1932, Hoare wrote to thank Ball for his report and sent at the same time a further batch of documents on the question.[7] Over the years, other departments learned to live with the

Research Department and it therefore became easier to get information. In 1934, the Department had correspondence with the Air Ministry about the air estimates and only a part of the information supplied was ever cleared for publication. In 1935, Fosbrooke-Hobbes wrote to Ball to ask for another batch of Government papers which he needed for his work, papers that Ball would 'doubtless' get through his departmental or ministerial contacts; in this case, as in some others, the failure of ordinary approaches could be followed by the provision of the relevant papers for the Department through the Leader's private office. Sometimes, help could be even more positive, as with the investigation into Social Credit in 1935. This topic was taken up at the request of the Party Chairman, who was anxious about the political impact that Social Credit was making, and who therefore wanted an investigation of Major Douglas's schemes as a basis for Party propaganda. Criticisms of his ideas were prepared by Brooke and Clarke, but they were submitted to the Treasury for comment before being given wide circulation. Donald Fergusson gave the response of the Treasury experts, which was that the Research Department had expressed 'a rather crude version of the theories of Keynes', and he feared that the document 'might be quoted as showing that the Conservative Party is out of sympathy with thrift as a virtue'. The Research Department in 1935 was clearly up to date in its economic thinking, perhaps more up to date than the Treasury.[8] Ball passed on to Clarke Chamberlain's thanks and the news that the Chancellor now felt that he actually understood what Social Credit was about.

Most of the detailed research work done by the Department between 1931 and 1933 had been carried over from the period of opposition. For the most part, this involved monitoring the extent to which the National Government was implementing plans that the Conservative Party had prepared, keeping those plans adjusted to contemporary circumstances, and occasionally giving Ministers a sharp reminder of what had been decided. It is hardly surprising in the circumstances of the time that unemployment and tariffs continued to occupy much of the Department's effort. Work was done to prepare for the Ottawa Conference and background papers were taken out with Ball when he went to Ottawa to advise Chamberlain (his very presence there was a testament to the standing which the Department already enjoyed); work for Hoare on India had been linked in with these preparations. Once the tariff had been implemented in 1932, the Department tried to monitor its effects and to suggest improvements. At the end of 1933, Chamberlain asked for a review of the work of the Empire Marketing Board, which was about to be wound up, and for suggestions as to how its work could best be continued. A few months later he was supplied at his request with a massive review of the tariff position throughout the world, listing each trading nation and its tariff legislation.[9]

On unemployment insurance, attention was still concentrated on the Royal Commission; Ball wrote to Chamberlain in November 1932 to draw attention to the increased deficit on the Fund, due to the increase in the numbers of unemployed, and urged that the Royal Commission should be pressed to produce their final report. When this came out, later in the month, Brooke was extremely critical of its financial provisions: 'the secretary of the Commission, Mr. Emmerson, must have an unparalleled grasp of every side of the problem, but I do not think he can be very much at home in matters of finance'. It is an interesting reflection on the role that Brooke himself had already played in a large number of research committees that he attributed any shortcomings in the report to the failings of the secretary. The Department turned an equally-critical eye on many of the schemes that were put forward to alleviate some of the miserable consequences of mass unemployment. Ball told Euan Wallace in 1934 that he would not need to investigate 'Broad's scheme', since it had been looked at in 1930 and found to be unworkable. 'More recently, however, we examined for the Chancellor a pamphlet produced by Ernest Bevin, in which proposals were made for retarding the age of entry into employment by the extension of the school leaving age and accelerating the exit of the worker by granting "optional" pensions at 60'; this was impracticable since it would cost £100 million a year to save less than a quarter of a million jobs.[10] The same scepticism applied to the ideas of the Ministry of Agriculture on job creation in 1934; the Ministry estimated the creation of 100,000 jobs but the Department only a little over half of that number.

Even when unemployment was falling later in the decade, there was research to be done on it; in February 1935, Ball asked Brooke to draw the Minister of Labour's attention to the recent trend of juvenile unemployment figures and to ask pointedly if any new proposals were under consideration. The rates at which unemployment was falling in the different parts of the country were tabulated at intervals, and the frequent changes made in methods of calculation were also noted. The last task of the Department on unemployment insurance before the Second World War was a rather unexpected request from the Prime Minister to consider his own legal position in relation to his employees: Ball told Chamberlain that 'if, through the failure of the employer to pay contributions, the employee has lost benefit to which he would have been entitled, he can recover a sum equal to the benefit so lost as a civil debt from the employer. But I think you will escape imprisonment successfully'. It is not clear which employees had not been kept in benefit by Chamberlain as their employer, but the reference of Ball to 'grooms, gamekeepers, water-bailiffs and chauffeurs' – and the ironical tone of the letter – suggests that it might relate to their common interest in fishing.[11] In any event, it would have been a somewhat embarrassing question for the Prime Minister to put to his civil servants.

A third theme that carried over from opposition was the agricultural policy that Chamberlain had initiated in 1930. Here the Research Department played a more direct part, for the Ministry involved was unsure about both the wisdom of making any substantial change of policy and of many of the details of what was proposed. Little could be done to implement these ideas during the worst depression years, but the Research Department and Chamberlain himself began to look for action at the end of 1933. The Minister, Walter Elliot, told Ball that he himself was quite keen on the Party proposals, especially as they related to the pig industry, but that his advisers did not like any of them. He therefore drew on the advice and assistance of Ball and his staff during 1934, in order to provide him with arguments to counter those of his own Ministry; when the issue reached the Cabinet, the Minister pressed forward the views that he had agreed with the Research Department, and he made sure that all the relevant Cabinet papers should be circulated to Ball too. Similar pressure was mounted in order to get the Party policy on centralised slaughtering implemented despite the resistance of the Ministry of Health. This originated in work done by the Research Department during 1933 and approved by Chamberlain, but it proved difficult to convince the Minister of Health, Hilton Young, who was a Conservative Minister but one who was much influenced by his advisers. A test case arose over a new abattoir at Leicester and Baldwin's personal intervention had to be sought in order to bring the Ministry of Health into line.[12]

Chamberlain had the same experience with Hilton Young in 1934 in connection with housing proposals, but with less immediate success. In the first place, he was impressed by Young, who seemed 'receptive and anxious to learn all I could tell him'; in January 1934 Chamberlain noted that Young's housing policy was likely to be based on 'a memo I gave him a year ago', but when Young suggested changes in the plan Chamberlain merely referred them back to him for further consideration. Chamberlain and Ball were anxious to embark on a major programme of 'reconditioning' houses and slum clearance, but further talks with Young convinced them that they would not get very far so long as he was in charge:

> As to housing, Hilton Young finally adopted most of my ideas and we worked them out into a series of proposals which he brought to the Cabinet a little while ago. He is so bad at getting his ideas across that I suggested his paper should be referred to a committee in order to try and get a nucleus of the Cabinet to understand what they meant and approve them. This was done, I was made chairman and secured provisional approval without much difficulty. If this is confirmed by the Cabinet next Wednesday he is then to begin negotiations on finance with the L(ocal) A(uthorities). Meanwhile, Ball suggested to me that it would help very much to show the country that we were in earnest if we were to set up a Housing Department with a minister under the M/Health – and this would have the additional advantage of relieving Hilton Young of the direct responsibility and of the task of exposition. Accordingly, I mentioned the idea to both Sam Hoare and S.B. yesterday and they both warmly, the latter enthusiastically, approved.[13]

The idea was endorsed by a meeting of Ministers from all three Government Parties two days later, and Chamberlain began canvassing the name of Geoffrey Lloyd for the new post – a man well known to himself (as a Birmingham MP) and closely linked with the Research Department too. It was at this point that things began to go wrong, for a leak to the press (which originated from J. H. Thomas, according to Chamberlain) scotched the idea of appointing a Minister as young as Lloyd. Chamberlain had therefore to fall back on a more wide-ranging reconstruction of the Government, which would have brought his protégé Sir Kingsley Wood to the Ministry of Health, but this was prevented by the refusal of Lord Sankey to retire with a good grace; everything therefore waited a year, but Wood duly became Minister of Health in 1935 and proceeded to put the required drive into the new housing programme.[14]

However, the subject which most clearly illustrates the role of the Department in the early 1930s is coal. Between the failure of the miners' strike in 1926 and the industry's nationalisation in 1947, the coal industry was never at the head of the political agenda, but it was always a problem of which Governments were aware, and the intractable problems of the industry remained much as they had been in the 1920s. The Conservative attitude to coal was similar to the Party's attitude to other depressed industries: that it was mainly up to the industry to reorganise itself, but that Treasury assistance should be made available if the industry's rationalisation promised a permanent improvement in the national interest. It was on this basis that steel was reorganised under the influence of meetings between Brooke and the industry's leaders. Coal was different only in that the Government had more specific legal and administrative commitments – there was a Department of Mines – and that the industry's leaders evinced no greater readiness to reorganise themselves than they had done in 1926. So, when a Coal Mines Reorganisation Commission (CMRC) was set up by the Mines Department to investigate the problems, the leaders of the industry refused to work with it and indeed never formally recognised its existence.

Chamberlain asked the Research Department for a full report on the industry in the Summer of 1933, and he asked especially for recommendations on the vexed question of the future of mining royalties. Chamberlain was sympathetic to state acquisition of mining royalties and of using this as a lever to force the mine-owners into reorganisation, but he feared that it might make it too easy for a future Labour Government to subsidise the mines by exacting no charge for the royalties. Ball reported that Chamberlain had 'a moderately good opinion of Ernest Brown, the Minister, and after reading our report, proposes to see him in order to get his views generally and to persuade him to stir up the various moribund committees with which the industry is at present cursed'. The initial report went to Chamberlain early in October 1934, written by Brooke, and Chamberlain replied a fortnight later that he had 'now carefully read Brooke's report, which is extremely interesting, and I have made an abstract of it, for the purpose of my conversation with Ernest Brown. I have arranged for an interview with him before long'. Ball then warned Chamberlain that the Department was likely to recommend the purchase of the mining royalties, 'if not by the state, by some ad hoc body'; they had discovered that a Bill had been drafted during the Labour Government of 1929–31, but never published, and it was hoped to get hold of a copy of this through departmental channels. The Department did indeed recommend purchase of royalties by the state, suggesting that a future Labour Government could be restricted by setting up a body analogous to the Central Electricity Board, 'and safeguarding its position adequately by Act of Parliament'.

Early in November, the Research Department got directly in touch with the Coal Mines Reorganisation Commission by meeting its chairman and secretary, Sir Ernest Gowers and C. S. Hurst. Gowers had been the senior civil servant at the Mines Department before going to this special commission and he reported that the real source of obstruction, apart from the mine-owners, was the Mines Department itself. Brooke reported that Gowers had a very low opinion of both his old Department and of its present Minister, that a unification of royalties was essential to foster amalgamations in the industry and to prevent the reopening of uneconomic pits, and that a 'big push' was desperately needed if the rationalisation of the industry was ever to get started. Chamberlain thanked Ball for all this information: 'I am glad you are in touch with (Gowers). I should imagine that progress on the lines he suggests will not be very easy, in view of the condition of affairs at the Ministry of Mines, but it is possible I may be able to help later on, when I know a little more how it is suggested that matters can be worked out'. An alliance was thus formed between the Coal Mines Reorganisation Commission, the Conservative Research Department and the Chancellor of the Exchequer to force a policy on the Government and the industry. The affair took on a rather more political flavour since both the President of the Board of Trade and the Secretary of the Mines Department were Liberals. Ball urged Chamberlain 'not to remain a spectator for too long'.

When the Mines Department resisted the unification of royalties, it was agreed that an inter-departmental committee should study the question, and a Cabinet sub-committee was also appointed. After consultations with the Treasury, Brooke was convinced that the Mines Department was so negative in its attitude that it would have to be overawed. When a meeting of the Cabinet Sub-committee on Coal was due in March 1934, he suggested to Ball 'that it might be well to have a word with Mr. Baldwin, who is a member of the Sub-Committee, on the advisability of demanding an early report from the Inter-Departmental Committee, and strongly suggesting that it should be constructive and not negative'. Regular talks with Gowers and Hurst, who were rather more *officially* involved in all of this than was the Research Department, made sure that Ball and Brooke were kept abreast of what was being decided. In January 1935, Hurst told Brooke 'that there seemed to be no one in the Cabinet more keen on the unification of royalties than the Chancellor' and that Runciman had at last withdrawn the opposition of the Board of Trade. The inter-departmental committee was thus drawing up a moderate scheme, which would vest ownership of royalties in the Coal Mines Reorganisation Commission itself, but would include no powers for compulsory amalgamations so as not to further antagonise the owners. Brooke immediately set down the case for pressing ahead with the full scheme, for creating a special body (since using the CMRC to hold royalties would in effect make this a substitution for reorganisation of the industry), and for compulsory powers. But he was also conscious of the deep waters into which the policy was running, for press and industrial opinion was already heavily critical of the very idea of Conservatives going in for nationalisation. He wrote to Ball at the end of 1934 to exonerate himself from these charges. 'When I first dictated these notes I see that I was rather careless about the use of the phrase "*nationalisation* of royalties". That phrase rather obscures the issue. The real point is whether the ownership of the royalties should be *unified*'. There were in fact several ways of administering the royalties after their purchase by the state, but Brooke felt that handing them over to a Government department direct would be the worst. 'The word "nationalisation" creeps in because it was the word commonly used in 1926. The word "unification" is a much truer and a much safer one'.

It was indeed to the unification of royalties that the Conservative Party committed itself through the 1935 manifesto, but this was not quite the end of the argument. With the apparent approval of the Government, the CMRC introduced its first compulsory amalgamation scheme in May 1935, only to see it rejected by the Canal and Railway Commission on legal grounds. The Government therefore had no alternative but to give the CMRC effective overall powers, announced in February 1936 and subsequently embodied in a Coal Mines Bill. Not surprisingly, this was greeted with howls of rage from the coal-owners and from the Federation of British Industry, reflected too on the Conservative benches in the Commons. The Bill received no special preparations for publicity and so the field was left clear for its critics; the coal-owners who approved the idea of reorganisation were silent, while the Bill's critics were loud in their hostility and both the FBI and the Mining Association organised lobbies. The Bill had a difficult, confused and controversial time in the Commons, during which the Government first hesitated and then lost their nerve and withdrew it. Brooke was extremely critical of the way in which things had been handled, and especially of the ministerial leadership involved. He urged, not for the first time, the need for a Minister who was prepared 'to think out what he wants to do and to stick to it. Government policy for a long time past has suffered from month to month shiftings, like playing a game of chess with no constructive plan, but simply moving to counter the threat in the opponents' last move'. The Bill had been badly thought out, even though it had been intended to fulfil a desirable object, and the

Ministers had shown no real judgement, no capacity for concentrated work, while it was under discussion. At the critical time, when the Government had introduced amendments intended to save the Bill from its critics, Runciman had botched his speech. Notes for this speech had been provided when it had been intended that Crookshank (Secretary for Mines) was to speak, but Runciman had decided to wind up the debate himself:

> It is understood that they were notes only – descriptive and informative material, with no attempt to polish them into persuasive form. Mr. Runciman was supplied with a copy, and instead of working on them he read them out verbatim to form the main portion of his speech in the House . . . . In connection with the Government's proposed amendments, it had been suggested in the brief prepared by his officials that Mr. Runciman should use a form of word which should so precisely cover the argument used by the F.B.I. in its criticism of the Bill that it would be prevented from returning to the charge; but they warned him to avoid explaining what he was doing, and to be careful not to mention the F.B.I. openly. Mr. Runciman ignored the warning, and thereby let loose for the rest of the debate the standard charge that the Government took its orders from the F.B.I.

There was no disguising the fact that the Government had suffered a setback, on a policy where they could have scored a triumph. Brooke urged that the granting of powers (which was likely to be unpopular) should be taken along with the unification of royalties (which had many supporters) and that the question of public relations should be dealt with in advance. But above all, it could only be done if Ministers had 'the heart for it. If they have not it may be better to revert to a policy of "Safety First" and give up hope of making coal one of the Government's successes. The recent Bill had better not be reintroduced at all, unless its sponsors are to be more purposeful than on the last occasion'. The upshot was much as Brooke advised: after a pause, the Government decided to take amalgamations and unification of royalties together, pressed on under a more purposeful President of the Board of Trade (Oliver Stanley), and braved the criticism of its supports. After a stiff fight in the Commons and an even stiffer one in the Lords, the Bill passed into law in the Summer of 1938, along lines that the Research Department had recommended in 1934.[15]

The House of Lords issue was as frustrating as ever, another case where policy debate carried over from the opposition years. It surfaced again in 1933 for two reasons, because Conservatives were increasingly critical of a Government with a huge Conservative majority not redeeming its ancient and oft-renewed pledges to restore the powers of the Lords, and because some Conservatives including Ball were worried by Sir Stafford Cripps's published opinion that a future Labour Government would have to take 'emergency powers' in order to get its way. The issue was forced by Lord Salisbury when he introduced a reform bill into the House of Lords, but it was eagerly taken up by Chamberlain who had tried once before to settle the question in 1930; Chamberlain also saw reform of the House of Lords as a means of buying off the Conservative right, currently in a mutinous mood because of the Government of India Bill. He therefore asked Ball to produce a report on Salisbury's ideas, comparing them to those of the Linlithgow Committee of 1931; in fact the two sets of proposals were remarkably similar, probably because Salisbury was associated with many of the Peers who had served on Linlithgow's committee, and it may well be that he intended merely to introduce a Bill that Conservative Ministers could not oppose. Baldwin also asked for a copy of the Linlithgow report and Ball explained that 'we have pigeonholed the scheme because we felt that the subject was too thorny to touch unless and until we were absolutely obliged to deal with it'. Baldwin was not at all convinced that the moment had yet arrived and he led a resolute rearguard in the Cabinet, opposing the idea that *any* proposals should be introduced by the Government. By the Autumn of 1934, it was clear that nothing would be done during the current Parliament, a decision that almost led to Lord Hailsham's resignation since he had to explain it to the enraged Conservative Peers. Nor did the 1935 manifesto make any reference to the subject, and Baldwin turned aside the criticisms of such men as Salisbury with fair words but with no intention to take any action. In June 1936, Baldwin again asked to see a copy of the Linlithgow Report before meeting a deputation of Peers, but once again with no apparent intention of taking action.[16] The 1931 proposals thus occupied a curious policy position during the 1930s; they were widely regarded as being as good a scheme as Conservatives could hope for, but neither the Research Department nor Baldwin had any wish to make known even the fact of their existence. After two failures on the issue, Chamberlain seems to have learnt his lesson, for they were not brought out again when he was Prime Minister.

It will be clear from all of this that the role played by the Conservative Research Department in the 1930s related very closely to the extent to which it was able to convince Chamberlain to take its ideas up to Cabinet level. As he himself wrote in 1932, 'it amuses me to find a new policy for each of my colleagues in turn'.[17] It was thus a matter of great importance for the Department when in January 1934 its Chairman decided that the time had come for a comprehensive policy review for the next election and beyond. Chamberlain noted that 'I saw Ball this week and told him I wanted to set to work on a new programme to include Empire migration, maintenance and development of the Ottawa agreements, relations between industry and the state, improvement of the national physique by physical training and sharing out of work'. Ball's own notes on the same meeting gives a clear indication of Chamberlain's reasons:

> The Chancellor expressed the view that the National Government was now nearing the end of the work which it had been returned to do. Agricultural policy was well under way, the great conversion operation had been completed, the tariff had been introduced, and regulation schemes had been started in certain areas where a tariff was not likely to prove effective. The Government was now entering upon the most critical period of its existence, and must look around and decide what new policies should be undertaken. In these circumstances the Conservative Research Department must look forward to a very active existence, and Mr. Chamberlain desired me to consider carefully what subjects ought now to be investigated by it, bearing these observations in mind.

The topics suggested by Chamberlain himself at this meeting with Ball indicate how widely he intended the policy review to range, even from the start: the investigations should include 'creation of a Ministry of Defence, future relations of State and Industry, and worksharing schemes (Hitler and N.R.A.)'. This also disposes of the oft-quoted view that Chamberlain had a completely closed mind on the organisation of defence policy and on the question of whether Britain could learn anything from Roosevelt's New Deal.

On reflection, Chamberlain saw the value of giving the new programme 'a wider base' than merely instructions from himself to the Research Department. He therefore saw Baldwin and suggested that a meeting of the Conservative Cabinet Ministers should be called, with Ball present to take instructions; Baldwin agreed, but Chamberlain had 'no doubt that further pressure will be necessary to produce any result'. Kingsley Wood, Hoare and Hailsham were also consulted by Chamberlain and gave their enthusiastic support. Chamberlain noted on 17 February that 'no meeting has yet been called. I spoke to S.B. again a week ago, but he said he could not do anything until after his speech at Preston. The speech was made on the 14th but he has not mentioned the subject to me since'. The same impatience can be seen in Chamberlain's comment that 'the more I think about it the more anxious I am to get to work to map out our programme (1) up to the election, (2) to go to the country with'. Meanwhile, Ball had agreed to act as Secretary to the proposed committee and had decided that it would be as well to call it together at 10 am in Old Queen Street, 'bearing in mind that it is highly desirable not to arouse any suspicions in the minds of other people'. Ball also submitted to Chamberlain several drafts of the list of topics for discussion and revised them to suit Chamberlain's wishes. Further questioning from Chamberlain elicited a promise from Baldwin that he would see MacDonald: 'I never thought he would but he told me next day that he had done so, that the P.M. quite understood and raised no objection – we fixed Friday March 2nd at 24 Old Queen Street for the meeting'.[18]

Hence, after a month of patient pressure the first meeting of the Cabinet Conservative Committee (CCC) took place with ten of the fourteen Ministers present. Chamberlain's triumph should certainly be described in his own words:

> I had suggested to S.B. that he should make a few introductory remarks and then call on me. This he did and I gave an account of the origin and history of the Research Dept. I then related the circumstances under which I (or 'we' for I pretended this was a joint effort with S.B. who had in his remarks represented it as such) had felt that we ought to be thinking about the future. Finally I said I had prepared a skeleton outline of topics for discussion of which Ball had copies and asked if he might come in and distribute them. When this was done I went through the paper and discoursed upon the meaning underlying each of the items there set out. This paper created a profound impression. None of my colleagues, not even S.B., had any idea that I was going to produce so well prepared a scheme and they appeared to be equally astonished and delighted to find that so much thought had been given to the subject. Hailsham was particularly enthusiastic, saying that it was the most stimulating paper he had seen for 2½ years. Baldwin and Betterton were equally forthcoming in their expressions of approval and after a brief discussion the meeting agreed to my suggestion that Ball should report on item 7, viz. 'the future of British industry in relation to international trade' with five subheads showing what was wanted in the way of data and how it could be obtained. We are to meet again on Friday next at the same time.[19]

Hailsham's comment hit the nail on the head, for this meeting represented the beginning of a more intensive period of policy work than had been done since the summer of 1931, since the Party had been in opposition. A week later, the proposed scheme of research on trade was approved; Chamberlain said that 'he thought the Research

Department was well-qualified to undertake the investigation of the whole subject, and in addition to its own resources it was in a position to tap the opinions of leading industrialists and economists outside'. He suggested that the Department should now work out schemes for all the other topics and that the next meeting of the CCC should decide on priorities. 'It was essential, not only that we should have a new programme, but that we should have it well before the next election, in order that the necessary advance propaganda can be adequately conducted. He had in his mind that a programme should be ready within a year from now'.

The third meeting, at which 'Mr. Baldwin asked Mr. Chamberlain to open the proceedings' was on 19 March 1934, and received the full research programme for discussion. This proposed to build on past work, updated where necessary and integrated with entirely new projects; it was suggested that some ideas should be deferred, pending the work of Royal Commissions or departmental enquiries, and that no work should be done on foreign or defence problems – 'matters requiring accurate and detailed knowledge' which would not be made available to a Party organisation. There were three topics to be given priority, of which the most novel was the question of the national physique; Chamberlain noted that this 'is taking on considerable proportions as my colleagues realise the appeal that so novel a proposition would make'. He was also anxious 'not to overload the Research Department, which had a very small staff', and to press on with the consideration of trade problems – 'generally he wanted to know where Ottawa had gone wrong'. But the most pressing question was the enormous one of industry, which Chamberlain saw on very expansive lines:

> He personally preferred that the Department should now undertake an examination of a more general character as to the relations which should exist in future between the State and Industry, what limits should be set to the State's interference, and what were the dangers to be avoided. After receiving a report of this character, the CCC would then be in a position to come to some decision on general principles, and those principles should subsequently be applied to solving the problems of individual industries.

When Hailsham expressed doubts about the wisdom of such a rigidly theoretical approach, Ball was quick to explain that no Research Department industrial reports had ever been drawn up without establishing relations with the industry itself, seeing its leaders and usually visiting some of its plants. These three topics having been agreed the meeting left the Department to get on with the work along the lines that Chamberlain had wanted: he asked himself in some amusement 'I wonder if they realise how closely I am guiding every step?' If indeed they had any doubts they cannot have lasted long; Chamberlain was effectively the Chairman of the Committee, Baldwin was not always present and when he did come it was noted in the minutes that 'at Mr. Baldwin's request, Mr. Chamberlain opened the proceedings as usual'. This was not an unmitigated blessing for Chamberlain, since it was essential that Baldwin be kept involved in the policy work if he were to be committed to its results. After Baldwin had missed a number of meetings, Ball called on his office in order to fix the next one on a day when he could definitely attend; when this proved difficult, Ball told Chamberlain that he was going over to the House 'to put some pressure on' Baldwin. Baldwin could not escape two such experienced anglers and he was duly landed for the next meeting; this session did little more than confirm the findings of previous meetings for the benefit of the Leader who had missed them.[20]

The adoption of the 1934 research programme certainly meant an intensification of the Department's efforts; as always, routine work for Ministers went on, according to the rhythm of Parliamentary sessions, and longer-term research had to be done in addition. Stannard was instructed to produce a report on international efforts to control trade, Fosbrooke-Hobbes to look at Roosevelt's American policies and the aftermath of Ottawa, Brooke to investigate the real effects of the 'most-favoured-nation' system in trading. Ball himself worked on the collection of information and the opening up of contacts. Help from the Department of Overseas Trade was secured through the Minister (Colville), from Lazards through Guy Kindersley MP, from Boots through Lord Trent, and from the Treasury through personal friends of Ball; Hailsham provided information from the War Office on the physical condition of recruits, Elliott offered the assistance of the statistical branch of the Minister of Agriculture, and Kingsley Wood suggested several contacts in the insurance industry. Nevertheless, it was an abrupt change of gear for the Department; after a month, Brooke reported that he had been working up the subject of international trade by reading up all the available literature, statistics submitted to the League of Nations and so on; it was necessary to do this to catch up, 'for we have all been working in the past years on matters mostly concerned with home production'. Outside help was in any case needed in order to undertake the range of research required: John

Wheeler-Bennett in Berlin was asked to report on work-sharing schemes in Hitler's Germany, presumably drawing on the resources of Chatham House, and Gerald Palmer (a Conservative candidate) was invited to report on 'the evolution and working of the corporate state' in Italy.[21]

Of all this work, the topic that created the greatest interest was undoubtedly the future relations of industry and the State, a subject much in debate in the 1930s. When the Research Department had completed its report in October 1934, it was referred to a sub-committee of the CCC under Chamberlain for detailed consideration. But first, the sub-committee considered and rejected Harold Macmillan's far more radical proposals whereby considerable powers of intervention in industry should be given to the Government through a short and very general Enabling Bill. The Research Department considered this idea to be 'unsound' and the Minister of Labour, Oliver Stanley, said that it would be 'disastrous'; there was unanimous agreement that an Enabling Bill would be a dangerous precedent to set for a Labour Government and unsatisfactory on other grounds too. When summing up, Chamberlain saw that 'the committee seemed to be unanimously opposed to the Macmillan proposals, and he thought that it should be possible now to set out the arguments in favour of a middle course between laissez faire and state control'. In view of Harold Macmillan's public espousal of The Middle Way four years later, it is ironic that his Party's policy-makers should feel compelled to set aside his extreme views before going on to articulate their own 'middle course'. The sub-committee then approved the lengthy set of proposals put forward by the Research Department, making only drafting amendments, though they had doubtless been seen and amended by Chamberlain before they ever came before the Committee.[22] These decisions were then approved by the full meeting of the CCC on 8 February 1935, and again for Baldwin's benefit two months later. In view of the great significance that was attached to industrial policy in the next phase of the Research Department's existence, in the 1940s, it will be worth examining the policy agreed in 1935.

The basic rule that was agreed was that Governments should intervene only where the state of the industry was such as to demand reorganisation and where this could not be achieved by 'natural forces' within a reasonable time. Reorganisations should only be imposed with Government help if some properly representative central body could be set up in the industry to maintain goodwill; the minutes record that Ministers approved this 'with some show of enthusiasm' – no doubt because of recent experiences in the coal industry. Equally, there must be some machinery for consulting workers in the industry, such as the joint industrial councils, and any reorganisation plan must include provision for those who would become unemployed as a result of it. On all substantive matters, the Government should take the advice of impartial investigators and all valuations should be independent. Once the industry had been reorganised, there must be no remnant of political control, so that safeguards against political partisanship should be written into any system of appointment to boards of control. Safeguards must also ensure the prevention of monopolies and there must be a clear limitation of the extent to which the Exchequer was committed to future liabilities. The essential character of the proposals was that Government should come into the industry, secure a reconstruction that was acceptable to employers and workers, and then leave the industry to carry on with its work. This was exemplified in the strict provision that reorganisation schemes should not be a barrier to new firms coming into the industry or inhibit other such developments in the future.[23] This approach underlay much that the Baldwin and Chamberlain Governments did before 1939, especially in the coal and cotton industries, but it also came remarkably close to the policy that emerged from the Industrial Policy Committee after 1945.

Less satisfactory progress was made over international trade and national physique. A second sub-committee was set up under Hailsham to consider ways in which the home market could be divided between Empire and foreign products, but the discussions proved inconclusive. Baldwin lamented the failure of the hopes of Ottawa and warned that 'we might be driven to economic nationalism', but the general view was that defensive measures should not be forced on Britain by the lack of cooperation shown since Ottawa by the Dominion Governments. Walter Elliott struggled to defend his agricultural policy, arguing that it was in accord with Ottawa, 'but Mr. Chamberlain, Sir Philip Cunliffe-Lister and Lord Hailsham all dissented vigorously, Mr. Chamberlain pointing out that the contrary was in fact the case'. The lack of reliable and up-to-date information led the sub-committee to recommend the formation of an Imperial Statistical Bureau; Chamberlain secured the approval of R. B. Bennett of Canada to this idea and then talked it over with Geoffrey Dawson, one result of which was a favourable leading article in *The Times*. The issue was deferred in the end for Baldwin to conduct soundings among the Dominion leaders while they were in London for the King's Jubilee.

The question of national physique fell between two stools, for some of the Ministers saw this only as a matter of physical fitness while others also saw a political opening. A 'National Health Committee' included Patrick Gower of Central Office because of the wish to graft a new interest in physical fitness onto the Conservative Party organisation, a replacement for the old Junior Imperial League which was failing fast in the 1930s. Thus, Kingsley Wood urged that there should be a new organisation to take advantage of the popularity of physical training, open to those between twenty and forty. It should not be a Conservative group as such, but 'a national voluntary organisation with its objectives carefully drafted in such a way as to exclude the Socialists. It should be based not only on health and physique, but also on citizenship'. Hoare, more cynically, urged that there should be a Government body to make grants for physical training 'and then make sure that our own organisation was able to secure 95% of the grants'. Joseph Ball was a keen supporter of this idea, suggesting that the new body should be made up of natural leaders, men who were 'prominent athletes, social workers and other people of sound political views, but not normally associated in the minds of the public with politics'. Underlying all of this was a wish to draw on the enthusiasm for fitness which the Fascists were exploiting and to guide it into safer political channels.[24] With such conflicting aims, it is perhaps not surprising that little was achieved, but the issue remained on the Research Department agenda right up to the War.

The main purpose of the policy review of 1934–5 had of course been Chamberlain's view that the Party should prepare for the next election well in advance. Thus the Party's new industrial policy began to appear in speeches by Baldwin and Chamberlain early in 1935 and the more detailed policy preparations were worked on through 1935 with a view to the coming manifesto. Closely linked with these preparations was the opening of contacts with the other Government parties, suggested by Ball in February 1935 as a step towards the evolution of a joint policy for the election, and agreed by Chamberlain. In March, Ball met Alec Beechman of the Liberal National headquarters and agreed with him on eleven areas for joint research. The Liberals entered these talks with great suspicion, as Brooke recounted to Ball after another meeting with Beechman:

> He told me that he found among his Liberals a common opinion that the CRD had a cut-and-dried programme fully worked out which at a given moment they proposed to force down the throats of their Liberal National and National Labour allies at the point of the pistol. After his conversations with members of the CRD he personally was convinced

that this suspicion was entirely groundless . . . . He had approached the CRD originally with an expectation that we would attempt to blindfold him and lead him up the garden, whereas in fact he had found no sign of a desire to treat him anything but frankly. I think he is sincere in this; and that our methods have succeeded.

It is not entirely clear what is meant by the last sentence, but it seems most likely that the Department had adopted an open attitude as most likely to lead to good relations. So in April, Fosbrooke-Hobbes reported that the Liberal Nationals' plans for land settlement were unexceptionable and sent them in return a copy of the CRD's family farm proposals. Progress continued along these lines, with all three Government parties agreeing on a policy on unemployment, youth, land settlement, finance, and the organisation of industry, in March. This document was drafted by Beechman, but was clearly based on a great deal of work that had been done by Ball and his staff. If the Conservatives got most of what they wanted, then it was not because they forced it down the throats of their allies, but because they alone had a real research team and because they started the talks with much of their own work already done. The final act of this drama had a touch of comedy though; when the representatives of the three parties had agreed on policy, Runciman was asked to pass it on formally to Neville Chamberlain and Ball was commissioned to find our discreetly whether he would be prepared to accept such a document. Since he had been kept abreast of the talks throughout, it is not entirely surprising that he agreed to accept the document that . emerged at the end.[25] From this work, Henry Brooke produced the first draft of the manifesto at the end of September 1935, drawing heavily on preparatory notes by David Clarke. The draft was then passed up to Ministerial level, where it was taken in hand by Chamberlain himself.[26]

As in 1931, the Research Department took an active part in the 1935 campaign, both through the formal organisation set up to answer policy questions and in the more direct business of electioneering. As in 1931, there were two committees on policy, an all-party committee under Baldwin which met only three times to approve the manifesto and deal with questions of overriding importance, and a Conservative committee under Hailsham which provided advice to Conservative candidates on day to day business. This rather cumbersome procedure did not work well, because of the time taken up with consulting the Party's allies, and Brooke suggested after the election that on any future occasion it should be replaced with a simpler, unitary system. There was also a brisk little skirmish with Central Office, occasioned by a reply being given direct to a questioner without reference to either of the committees or to the Research Department. The Chairman of the Party was informed sharply that 'officers of the Party Organisation had no authority to speak for the Party on questions of policy' and an apology was extracted from him.[27] Substantive issues of policy were also involved in the preparation of Baldwin's major radio broadcast, which could be expected to get across to a higher proportion of the electorate than any other piece of publicity. Drafts for this broadcast were prepared by both Brooke and Clarke, deliberately written in a form that would need extensive cutting before use. On the instructions of Sir Kingsley Wood, this was then redrafted in the Department by Ball, playing down the issue of rearmament (which Baldwin, unlike Chamberlain, was not anxious to keep at the forefront of the campaign) and suggesting other reasons to justify dissolving Parliament. On 8 November, Ball attended a tactical conference at Chequers, when it was agreed that the Labour Party were concentrating on industrial issues and that it would therefore be as well for Baldwin to play down rearmament even further.[28] In much the same way, the Research Department acted, as in 1931, as a drafting and checking agency; the *Speakers' Handbook* was again vetted in the Department, several speeches and articles were written and published over a variety of signatures, and detailed critiques of the opposition Parties' programmes were produced by the Department and circulated to all ministers.

Party publicity efforts were aided in 1935 by the creation of a National Publicity Bureau (NPB) to co-ordinate the Government's work. Ball was its Deputy Chairman, and it is not at all clear when publicity work was being done directly for the Conservative Party and when for the NPB. What is certain is that by one means or the other the Research Department worked for all the parties in the Government and played an important part. A major speech on social policy by Sir Kingsley Wood was heavily revised by Ball; references to a possible future war with Italy were struck out altogether and references to the 'Socialist-Liberal opposition' were changed to 'the present Socialist opposition' since the Government wanted to draw attention to the Liberals who were on its side and not to those opposed to it. When on 4 November, the *Daily Herald* claimed that the unemployment figures had been rigged, Ball drew up an immediate reply, dictated it by telephone to the Press Association and got very good coverage for his reaction. A letter to all Conservative candidates from Runciman, giving them support on behalf of the

Liberal Nationals was actually drafted by Ball. A statement on foreign policy by Hoare was severely pruned by Ball, though in this case he took the precaution of clearing his amendments with the Foreign Office before publishing the text. Finally, the Department moved onto the offensive by organising a statement by Lord Essendon, a prominent Liberal industrialist, that he would be giving his support to the Government, and a scare statement from the leaders of the building societies about Labour's programme. This last initiative, headlined 'Your house to go! Your building society too! If socialism comes!', was regarded by Ball as a particular success: 'We gave them the shock of their lives, and, apart altogether from the votes which they lost over the episode, I learn that even within their own party there is a good deal of comment on the way in which the Tories managed to put them on the defensive right in the middle of the Election campaign, and even drove them to the abandonment of one of the main planks of their policy'. Sir Harold Bellman of the Abbey National and Sir Enoch Hill of the Halifax, the men whose statements on Labour's policy had started off this particular hare, were both men who had been in contact with the Research Department over the past few years in connection with the Party's housing policy, and it was the Research Department which drafted and corrected their public statement at the election.[29]

After the 1935 election, the Research Department returned for a time into a subordinate position, reliant once again on the help of Chamberlain to make its views known. Ball was more closely involved with Chamberlain, as with his private negotiations with Count Grandi on Chamberlain's behalf in 1938, if no less involved with the Department. It may well be that with the deteriorating European situation Ball was re-forming his links with the world of espionage, for during the war he was to become Deputy Director of the Security Executive. Some signs of these involvements survive in the Research Department's files, though very few. So in March 1938, Ball received a remarkably comprehensive report on recent labour troubles in Trinidad, a report which traced the involvement of the British Communist Party in the West Indies, the route by which money reached them through Prague, and the names of several of the agents involved. This was duly sent on by Ball to his old chums in MI5 and proved to contain only information that they had already. Rather less clandestine but equally unofficial were Ball's contacts with Senor Batista y Roca when he came to London in 1938 as representative of the Government of Catalonia. Ball was put in touch with Roca by his Research Department subordinate Wentworth-Shields, and he then acted as an intermediary between Roca and the British Government. Ball arranged for him to see Halifax and Cadogan at the Foreign Office and passed on quite a lot of information in the Summer of 1938. Nothing came of the Catalan's wish to drag Britain and France into the Spanish Civil War in order to save Catalonia from destruction; it was probably typical of many of Ball's interests, unusual only in that the papers have survived him.[30] Ball was also involved in domestic political intelligence work on behalf of the Prime Minister once Chamberlain moved from number eleven to number ten. The Research Department kept files of cuttings of 'speeches by Foreign Secretaries' and especially of those by Eden; when Eden finally resigned, Ball told Chamberlain after the debate that he had 'destroyed the cases made by Eden and Cranborne. I have been told that you dominated the assembly. I need hardly add that I have taken certain steps privately, with a view to getting this point of view over to the whole country'. These private steps presumably involved his personal contacts in the press, and it was certainly true that Chamberlain had a remarkably easy ride from the press over the resignation of his Foreign Secretary. The *Manchester Guardian* indeed commented on the 'curiously distorted' view that had been given by the Conservative papers: 'for the most part the Government press has preserved a unity of silence that could hardly be bettered in a totalitarian state'. Ball indeed filed this last quotation among his cuttings; did he take it as a tribute to his work?[31]

Just before Chamberlain became Prime Minister though, he differed sharply from Ball on the subject of the National Defence Contribution (NDC), a question that provided Chamberlain with his clearest defeat of the decade in the domestic sphere, and on this occasion Ball was certainly working against his Leader's policy. The Research Department had been working on various new ways of raising money to pay for rearmament, considering the imposition of a turnover tax such as existed in the United States and a sales tax like that used in Canada. When the idea of a National Defence Contribution was announced by Chamberlain in his last budget before becoming Prime Minister, the Department was very hostile to it. Clarke drafted a note showing how heavily the proposed tax would bear on new businesses, and several of the Department's industrial contacts turned to it for help in resisting the new tax. Lord Luke reported that his own firm, Bovril, would not oppose in public a tax that might be generally popular, but he also reported that the directors of Metal Box were organising city opinion against it. Frank Platt, who had assisted the Department with their research on cotton, wrote to object on behalf of the Lancashire Cotton Corporation, and D. H. Williams did much the same on behalf of the woollen trade. Williams was not only a friend of the Department, but a personal and fishing friend of Ball, so on this occasion Ball broke ranks; he advised Williams on the wording of a memorandum that he meant to send to Chamberlain – stipulating that his involvement must remain secret. Ball also seems to have worked on Chamberlain himself to try to get him to change his mind, and to work on some of Chamberlain's colleagues too. He told Chamberlain that 'I realise, of course, that the CRD speaks without access to the vast store of accumulated knowledge and experience of taxation matters possessed by the Treasury and the Inland Revenue authorities, and that our suggestions may be quite impracticable. Nevertheless, our work does bring us into close contact with Industry, and in this way we get to know where the shoe is likely to pinch'. This letter accompanied a powerful case against the NDC on economic and industrial grounds, drawn up by Clarke. Wentworth-Shields was also asked to draft the outline of a speech for Chamberlain, in which he reaffirmed his belief in the NDC but agreed that it needed major amendments before it could be implemented. Finally, Ball sent copies of this correspondence to Sir Kingsley Wood, together with a cutting that was extremely hostile to the NDC, taken from *Information*, the magazine of the Anti-Socialist and Anti-Communist Union. All 'this activity took place during May 1938, and on 1 June Chamberlain announced to the House of Commons that he would abandon the NDC. The reaction from industry had been spontaneous, and Chamberlain would certainly have come under strong attack in any case, but on this occasion Ball used the Research Department to support a campaign *against* its Chairman.[32] But Ball was genuinely convinced that Chamberlain had blundered into a serious mistake in announcing NDC, not least because of the views of industry, and his strategy may well have been intended to find his boss a way out.

Most of the Department's activities at this time were considerably less exciting, and far more characteristic was the research on population movements, on company law, national health and the voluntary organisations. The interest in population began in 1934, following claims in a recent book that falling birth-rates would lead to a rapid decline in the population of the United Kingdom in the 1940s and after; figures were submitted to the Cabinet Conservative Committee suggesting that the population would fall to about thirty-two millions by 1976. Thereafter, the Department was more critical, in part because of advice from the Registrar General's office, but confusion remained. Clarke noted in 1936 the confusion between the different predictions being used by different Ministries, and the Department regularly called for a Royal Commission on Population to establish reliable criteria for future planning. Such confusion prevented any serious work being done, but Wentworth-Shields was encouraged to write up the views of the Department in a book on 'Population and Government Policy', a project that Ball summarily dismissed as 'written for propaganda and educational purposes and does not really rank as a piece of research work'.[33] The work on health and national physique was much more serious and derived from the work of the CCC in 1934. At that time, the Department was keen on plans to improve health cover, but all except Ball were sceptical of the sort of organisations that were then discussed to carry out the policy: Brooke argued that such schemes would create 'the right atmosphere for "private armies", which would be a diabolical result'. The organisations with which the Department *was* entirely in sympathy were the Youth Hostels Association and the National Playing Fields Association, both new and immensely popular in the 1930s; Brooke kept in close touch with their progress and urged that they should get public support through the Ministry of Education. A commitment to improve the health of the nation was included in the 1935 manifesto, and reasserted a year later in Chamberlain's Party Conference speech, drafted in the Department; after the success of the Conference speech, Ball wrote to Chamberlain to argue the case for pressing on with policy on national health and sent him a Departmental memorandum listing 'Items of action required to implement a National Health policy'. Thereafter, the Department was constantly spurring the Government on to a more positive policy on nutrition and health-care. Brooke provided the expertise on nutrition, conscious always that these good intentions must be given a political edge: 'There is, of course, a great deal of general material available which one could put into a treatise if one were engaged on pure research, but on the principle that this is a political Department concerned with political research, I have concentrated my attention . . . on those parts of the field which seem to offer scope for practical action'. This evoked Chamberlain's interest, and Brooke was commissioned to provide more material; this was derived from the publications of the Economic Advisory Council (EAC), and Brooke asked plaintively why the EAC could not have been asked to write it up for Chamberlain. In 1938, Clarke urged the political value to the Party of extending medical benefit to the families of all insured persons; this should be included in the next election programme, as a counter to Labour's scheme, already published. In the following year, Hanrott was extremely critical of the Ministry of Education's policy on school meals; there was an opportunity to extend services without going so far as making the meals free, and in any case the 'milk dose' should be raised to half a pint on nutritional grounds. In the last days of peace, Hanrott wrote again to urge the inclusion of nutrition in the coming election manifesto, and to urge that it be linked with agricultural policy, the raising of wage levels, and family allowances as a complete social policy.[34]

A minor aspect of this interest in social policy that linked in well with the worsening foreign situation was the provision of recreation camps. The extension of holidays with pay by the National Government in 1938 had provided many workers with more leisure time than they had ever enjoyed before; Hanrott suggested the setting up of camps in rural settings to provide assistance for these 'new holiday-makers' – the camps would also then be available for war use if necessary. He wrote again to Ball, several times during December 1938, quoting support in Parliament and the press for his idea and even linked it with an argument that Ball himself had used four years earlier: 'probably the most effective aspect of Nazi technique is the close identification of the Party with the recreation and enjoyment not only of the workers but of the lower middle classes also, and this seems to me to be a leaf which might well be taken by the National Government out of the Nazi book'. The Research Department was by no means the only supporter of this idea, but its persuasion of the Prime Minister may well have smoothed the path for the Camps Bill, introduced in March 1939.[35]

Despite the apparent approach of war, plans went on for the election expected to take place in 1939 or 1940. Throughout the 1930s, Brooke and later Clarke had been assigned to provide Ball with assessments of the state of public opinion as shown by by-elections, and these were passed on to Chamberlain. A review in 1939 compared results with the last three general elections and showed the Government doing consistently better than 1929 (which was Labour's best ever year, used by the Department as its basic yardstick). There was every sign that the Government was retaining the overwhelming majority of the old Liberal vote, 'except for London, where there seems to be a case for a prolonged special effort to overcome apathy and counteract Herbert Morrison'; this last remark was an early sign of demands for reorganisation in London that finally bore fruit in 1939. In the Autumn of 1938, the Department was asked for an assessment of electoral prospects, maybe as a result of the discussions then taking place on the possibility of an election to capitalise on Government popularity after Munich. Hanrott sent to Ball a review of results up to the Summer which suggested 'that a General Election held then would have made very little difference to the Government's majority'; there was weakness in London, but in almost all the English boroughs and counties the Conservative position was well ahead of that in 1929. This rosy picture, derived from work previously done by Clarke, was soon contradicted by an urgent note from Clarke himself; this reviewed the 'Munich by-elections' and showed that the outlook was now considerably less promising, that the Government should on no account risk an election during the Winter of 1938–9.

Although the trend was again slightly better in the Spring of 1939, the Department was preparing for an election on the assumption that the Government would have a real fight on its hands, and this was often cited in support of the need for more positive commitments in the social field. The actual preparation of a manifesto was set in train in January 1939, when Clarke urged the necessity of constructing a programme that would raise 'faith' in the Government as well as belief in its competence; his main suggestion was an extension of pensions. Notes for use in the production of a manifesto had been gathered together by May, based in part on the Government's public statements and in part on the Department's own research. By August, Clarke had completed a rough draft of the manifesto and the main problem was finding out from the Board of Education what its National Labour Ministers intended to offer: De la Warr and Lindsay were keen to promise an extension of technical education, which 'would certainly make an admirable "plank" but it would be expensive as we are so backward'. By this time too, the Department had lost its battle for a very extended social programme, when the Government announced early in July that it could not meet the cost of increased pensions. Hanrott noted on 15 July that this statement had been a partial cause of poor performances in the most recent by-elections, and it was again cited as a cause when the Government lost Brecon and Radnor in August; another cause was 'the apathy induced by the early prospect of a general election'.[36] The election did not of course take place for six years, by which time the face of British politics had been transformed and the policy machinery of the Conservative Party had almost ceased to exist. Nevertheless, from work already done in the Research Department, it seems likely that a Conservative manifesto of 1940 would have included family allowances and the inclusion of dependants of insured persons in

health cover – about half of the advances that are usually traced to
Beveridge.

Notes

1   CRD file, 'Neville Chamberlain'.
2   CRD file, 'Industrial Assurance'.
3   Neville to Ida Chamberlain, 11 October 1930, Neville Chamberlain MSS 18/1/712.
4   CRD file, 'Neville Chamberlain'.
5   *Ibid.*
6   CRD file, 'Stanley Baldwin, speeches 1930–36'.
7   CRD file, 'India and Ottawa'.
8   CRD files, 'CCC, correspondence' and 'Social Credit'.
9   CRD files, 'India and Ottawa', 'Empire Marketing Board' and 'Tariffs'.
10   CRD (N) files, 'Unemployment Insurance'.
11   *Ibid.*
12   CRD files, 'CCC minutes', 'CCC sub-committee B' and 'CCC correspondence'.
13   Neville Chamberlain diary, January 1934, 17 February 1934, Neville Chamberlain MSS 2/23a.
14   Neville Chamberlain diary, 28 February 1934, Neville Chamberlain MSS 2/23a.
15   CRD (N) files, D/1/c/1 'Coal' and D/1/c/2 'Royalties'.
16   CRD file, 'House of Lords: Mr. Chamberlain's personal file', Neville Chamberlain diary, 27 January and 30 October 1934, Neville Chamberlain MSS 2/23a.
17   Macleod, *Chamberlain*, 164.
18   Neville Chamberlain diary, January and February 1934, Neville Chamberlain MSS 2/23a, CRD files, 'CCC correspondence'.
19   Neville Chamberlain diary, 3 March 1934, Neville Chamberlain MSS 2/23a.
20   CRD files, 'CCC minutes' and 'CCC correspondence'.
21   CRD file, 'CCC correspondence'.
22   CRD file, 'CCC sub-committee A'.
23   CRD file, 'CCC minute of meeting held on 8 February 1935'.
24   CRD file, 'CCC sub-committee B'.
25   CRD file, 'Co-operation with Liberal Nationals and National Labour'.
26   CRD file, 'General Election 1935, manifestoes'.
27   CRD file, 'General Election 1935, Questionnaire Committee'.
28   CRD file, 'General Election 1935, Mr Baldwin's broadcast'.

29 CRD files, 'General Election 1935, press publicity' and 'General Election 1935, miscellaneous'.
30 CRD files, 'Trinidad Labour Troubles' and 'Contact with Sr Batista y Roca'.
31 Ball to Chamberlain, 21 February 1938, Neville Chamberlain MSS 7/11/31/10; *Manchester Guardian*, 24 February 1938.
32 CRD file, 'National Defence Contribution'.
33 CRD file, 'Population'.
34 CRD files, 'Health and Physique of the Nation, 1–4'.
35 CRD file, 'Camps'.
36 CRD file, 'Election Results and Prospects'.

Chapter 5

Post-War problems (1939–1947)

On the outbreak of the Second World War, the Conservative Research Department was, like so many other institutions, closed for the duration. On 2 September 1939, Ball and part of his staff moved to the Senate House of London University to set up the Films Division of the Ministry of Information. However, also like many institutions (and like places of entertainment too), the Department was reopened when the immediate impact of war was found to be so much less than had been feared. The Department was open between January and June 1940, though in only a temporary sort of way. David Clarke, recalled from war work, was set to work on the implications of a sales tax as a special wartime means of raising money – though the Department had worked on this before the War; he also looked at the question of location of industry. The reopening was not very successful, mainly because conditions were so different: Clarke reported that it was difficult to estimate the scale of the problem while the size of defence spending remained a closely-guarded secret, and that it was in any case almost impossible to estimate the yield of a tax in war conditions.[1] Clarke's other task in those months was to close down the office properly, put the furniture in store, and take a selection of its secret and important files to his home for the duration.

Although Chamberlain fell from power in May 1940 and was replaced by Winston Churchill, Chamberlain remained Party Leader until the following October and Chairman of the Research Department until his death soon afterwards. Sir Kingsley Wood then succeeded as Chairman of the Research Department, an obvious choice since he was a protégé of Chamberlain and had already worked closely with the Department. But little could be done in wartime, and when Wood also died, in 1943, the position was not properly filled.

Winston Churchill had little reason from either the past or the present to make him advance the position of the Party organisation. In the past, the Research Department had worked with the rest of the Party to support his political opponents and to limit the effectiveness of his friends; in 1938 Churchill had admired Eden greatly, while Ball was working to run Eden down. Once in power, Churchill saw the premiership in a statesmanlike light that left little room for the Party. He revolutionised the Government's attitude to research and expert advice, but he carried out his revolution within the Government machine and not within the Party; with Lord Cherwell and a picked team of economists and other experts at his personal disposal in Downing Street, Churchill had in any case no need of the Party's research apparatus. As the years passed, Churchill was always anxious that the concentration of effort should be on the War itself, and not on elaborating policies to be followed after victory had been achieved. He therefore sought to keep the planning of post-war reconstruction within the all-party machinery of the Government's Reconstruction Committee, chaired by the Minister of Reconstruction, the non-party management expert Lord Woolton. He also resisted regular demands from Conservative MPs that the Party should become more active in the social field and that it should make its policies clearer. Some of Churchill's distrust of the Conservative Party organisation remained with him for the rest of his life, and so far as policy-planning took place at all before 1945, it was without the support of the Leader.

Nevertheless, the same year that saw Churchill take over the Conservative Party from Neville Chamberlain also saw the beginning of the trend that was to revitalise Conservative policy after the War and place the Research Department back in a pivotal position. In the anxious and emotional weeks after Dunkirk, a sea-change in British opinion began, a change that led on to the Labour victory of 1945 and to the very different political world of the 1950s. So noticeable was this shift, even at its beginning, that senior Party figures began to seek means of adapting the Party to accommodate it. Their failure to keep up with the trends of opinion during the War should not blind us to the importance that the War years had in preparing the Party for what was to follow.

In July 1940, Sir Douglas Hacking, then Party Chairman, asked R. A. Butler to undertake a programme of research into the currents of opinion in the country, 'with a view eventually to adjusting the Party's outlook to the radically different trends of thought which prevail at a time like this'. Butler explained to Chamberlain that he hoped to use the Party to improve morale on the Home Front and so prepare both the Party and the country for the problems of reconstruction. Nor was Hacking the only Conservative to see what was happening, for the Party postbags were full of letters urging the

Party to keep up with changing public moods and produce a new statement of policy.[2] The choice of Butler to oversee this difficult task was an appropriate one, and as it turned out a very important decision. He was still only thirty-eight in 1940, but he had been in the House of Commons since 1929 and a junior Minister since 1932. His ministerial experience had been mainly in fields where the Party research apparatus did not operate, India and the Foreign Office, but he had been given a spell at the Ministry of Labour by Chamberlain who had told him that 'it was time for me to understand the home front'. He had certainly been groomed by Chamberlain for high ministerial office, so it was fitting that he should emerge as Chamberlain's successor in control of the Party's thinking machine. Butler had spent some years as a don and come from a distinguished academic family, but he was in no sense 'hopelessly academic' as Chamberlain had found Lord Eustace Percy. Like Chamberlain, he recognised the need to give the Party's researchers clear directions and to keep the apparatus under his own control in order to get the best from it.

Little was actually done in the pressing circumstances of 1940, and Butler himself was fully occupied with his work at the Foreign Office, but the problem remained in view. In April 1941, Butler was suggesting that it would be useful to modernise the Party structure, especially in finding candidates and publicity; an independent 'intelligence centre' should be set up to monitor the broadcasts of the BBC and to watch over the Party's interests. At about this time, discussions were taking place which were to lead to action. On 26 May, Sir Robert Topping wrote to Butler from Central Office to outline the results of talks he had been having with Sir Eugene Ramsden (chairman of the National Union) and other Party dignitaries: a small, high-powered and representative committee would be set up to examine the whole question of post-war policy, and it would be suggested that Butler should be its chairman, with Topping as its honorary secretary. This proposal was put to the National Union Central Council by the Party managers the same day, and was enthusiastically received; thus was born the Post War Problems Central Committee (PWPCC).[3]

When the PWPCC met for the first time on 24 July 1941, Butler was duly elected chairman, with David Maxwell-Fyfe as his deputy and with Topping as secretary; apart from Henry Brooke and Lord Cranborne from the House of Commons, the other members were from Central Office and the National Union. A planning group was set up to map out a programme of research and commissioned to report back on how the work might be carried out by sub-committees. Butler then sent out a circular letter from his new office at the Board of Education, asking for help in the new venture and outlining its purpose as he saw it:

> I have been made chairman of the Conservative Policy Central Committee, and we are setting up a series of sub-committees on various aspects of national life. It will take a little time to constitute these sub-committees effectively. Meanwhile, I am anxious to associate with them figures who, though in general sympathy with the party faith are not of the machine. Thus I want to bring in new blood.

Among those who offered their help were George Kitson Clark, Douglas Jerrold, G. M. Young, Keith Feiling, Arthur Bryant, George Clark, Kenneth Pickthorn, Arnold Toynbee, Sir Charles Petrie and Geoffrey Dawson; for a body that was concerned with the future, the PWPCC had a remarkable number of historians among its advisers.

By September, a scheme had been prepared for an initial programme of eight sub-committees to work on agriculture, education, national security, finance and industry (with Brooke as chairman), forestry, reconstruction, electoral reform and the constitution. Additional ones were set up later to cover local government and social services, and by 1945 the total number had grown to sixteen, each with about a dozen members. However, some of the defects of this form of policy work were to be seen from the outset; when the proposal for a committee on agriculture was brought forward for approval by the PWPCC, it was severely criticised and the suggested membership was revised to include a representative of the Conservative MPs' House of Commons Agriculture Committee and a representative of small farmers. As an official Party body, the PWPCC had to make sure that its investigations reflected the balance of Party opinion, and this did not make for dynamic policy in a time of rapid change. At the other end of its life, in May 1945, the PWPCC was forced to stop the circulation and publication of its own sub-committee's report on constitutional reform because the members of the full committee would not take responsibility for what was proposed; not for the first time, the future of the House of Lords was the major stumbling-block. Most of the investigations produced results that were less controversial; most of them were also too unexciting to compete with much chance of success against such ideas as those of Beveridge. Reports had to be approved by the Central Committee, and were then sent to the Chief Whip, the Vice-Chairmen of the Party, and to Churchill's PPS.

Butler was later given discretionary authority to show them also to Conservative Ministers and to report their substance to the 1922 Committee.[4]

After initial enthusiasm, the PWPCC seems rather to have lost its way in the middle years of its life. This may well have been due to the demands that the War itself placed on its members; the difficulty of travel, firewatching duties and civil defence. In July 1943, Butler resigned as Chairman because of the pressure of work occasioned by his Education Bill, due for the coming session; Maxwell-Fyfe took his place as Chairman, with Henry Brooke as his deputy, but this change down-graded the Committee's work. Butler was still a junior Party figure in 1943, but he carried more guns than Maxwell-Fyfe, who had been in the Government for only a year, and in the peripheral office of Solicitor-General. The change was made all the more significant by the fact that Maxwell-Fyfe was more interested, at this stage, in propaganda than in policy as such. Under his chairmanship, the PWPCC inaugurated a regular publication called *Politics in Review* until it had to be suspended in May 1944 because of its cost and the difficulties of regular publication. The same financial problems beset the *Signpost* series of pamplets intended to publicise the committee's main work; the original programme of publications had to be reconsidered when the early issues failed to sell, and the whole idea had to be revised so as to sell a small number of copies at a high price, rather than the mass circulation that had been hoped for.[5]

It was at this time that the limelight was stolen from the PWPCC by the Tory Reform Group (TRG) of MPs led by Lord Hinching-brooke, Peter Thorneycroft and Hugh Molson. This group saw itself as a ginger group on the left of the Party, aiming to influence the Parliamentary Party, and was not constrained by any need to balance its proposals to meet all shades of Party opinion or by a desire not to embarrass the Government. The Tory Reform Group fused the old Tory tradition of state interventionism with the more recent ideas of Harold Macmillan and other radical Conservatives of the 1930s, producing an amalgam more in keeping with current ideas. It also adopted professional methods and had a paid research staff – which is more than the official Party could ever manage in wartime. There was a certain overlap between the PWPCC and the TRG, but not with any great success since their aims were so different. So, when Hugh Molson of the TRG served as a member of Butler's Housing Sub-committee, he insisted on submitting a minority report calling for far more radical changes than were contemplated by the other members. When he later asked if this could be returned to him for his own use, the PWPCC agreed only on the understanding that no reference should be made to its origin. Whereas the PWPCC was persuaded to wind up its work on the social services after the Beveridge Report, so as not to clash with the committee of Conservative MPs who were working on the subject, the TRG saw the Beveridge Report as an opportunity to intensify its efforts. Conversely, within the Party the PWPCC was in a better position; demands that the Conservative Party should take a more active role in local government were encouraged by the PWPCC, a local government reform group was set up in 1943, and when the National Union finally decided to set up a new Advisory Committee on Local Government it was presented by the PWPCC with a list of names of those who should be asked to serve on it. The end product in post-war Conservative thinking was to owe something to both the PWPCC and to the TRG, but only the TRG made much impact while the War lasted.[6]

There was a further attempt to gear up the Party as the War drew to a close and the post-war General Election came nearer. Suggestions were put forward for Party research in November 1943, but Ball (who had been looking after the interests of his old Department as Acting Honorary Chairman since the death of Wood) was not very helpful on the question of finance. However, a memorandum on 'Political Research' by David Clarke drew a more positive response from Henry Brooke when sent to him in June 1944, and this probably started the ball rolling when sent on by Brooke to Butler, Dugdale (Party Chairman) and Topping. With his Education Act safely negotiated through Parliament, Butler resumed the chairmanship of the PWPCC in August 1944, with Maxwell-Fyfe and Brooke as joint deputies. Butler realised that much remained to be done to carry out the committee's original intentions both of making policy and of making it known. For this task a permanent organisation was now essential, and at the first meeting at which Butler was in the chair it was decided to set up a Research Department under Brooke; the new Department would work for the Conservative Party on the whole range of Government plans for reconstruction, would overhaul and update reports already accepted by the PWPCC, and would pull together the work done by unofficial groups of Conservatives during the War. Brooke was commissioned to prepare an outline of how his Department should be organised and to submit it to the next meeting on 10 October 1944; this document, which may have been amended and was certainly approved by Butler before it was submitted, summarises Brooke's own experience of research in the decade before the War, but it also provides the foundation stone on which all later development has been based.

First of all, it was important to recognise the limitations on what could be done:

> No party research department can possibly possess the resources for extensive original work. What it can and must do is to keep a systematic watch on other people's ideas, analyse them, sift the good from the unsound, warn the policy makers of the Party against the latter (however attractively dressed up), and think out means of weaving the former into the texture of a programme. This kind of research work, if it is to be any use, must always be directed towards the building up of material that might form part of a future election programme. When an election approaches, the leaders of the party must decide, on political grounds, which bits they wish to use. But the business of the research department is to make sure that the bits are there, and that (at any rate from the administrative and economic standpoints) they are sound and will not 'come to pieces in the hand'. That is why a second-rate staff, however large, is useless. The staff may have to be small, but it must be first-rate in reliability and thoroughness.

Brooke therefore deprecated the use of these highly-qualified experts for the mundane task of answering routine questions, questions that would be answered far more efficiently by an information bureau. The urgent task was to watch the development of reconstruction policy with a view to the next election, and he laid down the criteria to be used in this work:

> In this sifting of ideas, there must be four criteria:
> (i) Is it in harmony with Conservative philosophy?
> (ii) Is it in practicable form?
> (iii) Will it be acceptable, or can it be rendered acceptable, to the Party?
> (iv) Does it meet a real want?

> It is regrettable that it should be necessary to include (iii) as well as (i), but unfortunately there seem to be numbers of people calling themselves Conservatives who have confused and sometimes conflicting views about the true nature of the Conservative attitude. That points to the paramount need for setting forth in modern language and with modern application, a statement of what the Conservative philosophy really is.

On 24 October, Butler reported that the new organisation had been approved by the National Union and that they could therefore set to work. However, it proved impossible to find staff, especially with Brooke's determination that they must not relax their standards, and the only immediate result was to provide Brooke himself with an office and a secretary for his Party work. With enormous problems, inadequate resources and a Leader indifferent to their work, it is hardly surprising that little was done in the Winter of 1944–5. When the election was imminent, in April 1945, David Clarke came back, but for the campaign the Department consisted only of Clarke, Brooke and their two secretaries (and Brooke was himself a candidate).

The Research Department was not actually revived until after the 1945 election, for nobody was appointed Chairman or Director and neither the furniture nor the files were removed from store. Ball advised Clarke not to bring back the files while he was working on Central Office premises, not only because this was a means of safeguarding the independence of the Research Department for the future, but also because the Departmental files contained a lot that was 'unflattering' about Central Office itself. Thus, Clarke and Brooke agreed to work with Central Office and worked for the election from a room in 34 Old Queen Street. The main effort was to pull the disparate strands of policy work done for the PWPCC into a single policy document which would then come out in book form. Further delays followed, so that it was impossible to publish the book before it was overtaken by the election itself. *Forty Years of Progress*, published late in 1945, therefore came out in the wrong circumstances and made little impact, though it was a useful compendium of all that the PWPCC had been doing.[7]

The 1945 election was probably not one in which the Party organisations could have made much impact, except in the negative sense that the Conservative organisation had become almost non-existent. Central Office had moved from its large premises in Palace Chambers into Old Queen Street in 1941. At the election, the Central Office staff was so small that the Research Department was diverted to help draft leaflets and to do other tasks normally done by publicity staff. The manifesto was drafted by Brooke and Clarke, so that in policy terms it drew on the work of the PWPCC.[8] Serious newspapers commented on the extent to which the programmes of the two major Parties were alike – not surprising, since each had drawn its policies from the same Cabinet experience since 1940. But the language and the style of the manifesto, like the rest of the campaign, were certainly influenced by the combative way in which Churchill intended to fight the election. For advice, Churchill relied not on the Party managers but on personal friends like Beaverbrook, Cherwell and Bracken, with disastrous consequences. The same personal control was shown in the Emergency Business Committee, which as before handled policy questions that arose during the campaign, originating either from the public or (on this occasion) from Ministers. This was set up by a personal minute from the Prime Minister, rather than by resolution of the Cabinet as had been customary, and there is no doubt that it included far too many senior Ministers; most of the members were usually away speaking in the country, so that the bulk of the work was done by the Chairman, Lord Swinton, with the help of David Clarke and the usual secretary from the Cabinet Office. This was even more important because so little work had been done on policy before the election began, and because an unusually high proportion of Conservative candidates were inexperienced. Clarke later reported that things had only gone reasonably well because of the special help provided by Murrie of the Cabinet Office, who had proved unusually adept at amending departmental drafts himself in order to give them a political edge without wasting time; this should not be relied on in future, and the answer was to do much more work before the election was called.[9]

The election results, however, came though as a profound shock. Among the Party's leaders, only Harold Macmillan and R. A. Butler seem to have anticipated defeat, and there were few on the organisational side of the Party who would have agreed with them. For a year, the Party organisation staggered, punch-drunk, before it began the long and painful process of re-building from the foundations. It was not until the Summer of 1946, with Woolton's appointment as Party Chairman, that the Party organisation began to revive and it was only at about the same time that the policy apparatus began to function properly again. Henry Brooke, who had lost his seat at the election, had been deputed to lead the Conservatives on the London County Council, in addition to becoming Deputy Chairman of the Southern Railway Company. David Maxwell-Fyfe had held his Liverpool seat but was fully occupied in the Nuremburg trials, and was to take on the investigation of the Party organisation that was to bear his name. Among experienced politicians then, R. A. Butler was the only one with previous knowledge of the Party's policy making machinery, and although he was made Chairman of the Research Department soon after the election defeat, it was a long time before there was a Department to take charge of. Butler was nevertheless an immediate asset, for through his 1944 Education Act he already symbolised a solid Conservative achievement on precisely the moderate reformist lines along which policy was to develop; he also symbolised in his person the blend of youth and experience, of tradition and open-mindedness, that the Party was looking for. In the year after the War, Butler was Chairman of the National Union and he made an effective *demarche* with his speech at the first post-war Party conference, calling for a review of 'fundamental issues'. The press reaction to this initiative was favourable and Butler's only regret later was that the speech had been issued verbatim in pamphlet form, instead of being worked up into a book, for 'it was the beginning of the whole approach which carried on over the next three years'.[10]

It was clear in the aftermath of defeat that the first priority must be to restore the effectiveness of the Parliamentary Party, decimated at the election and with scarcely enough front-benchers of experience to enable it to keep up a sustained opposition to the Labour Government. It was therefore decided to set up first a Parliamentary Secretariat to service parliamentary groups and committees, to write briefs for Members and generally to support the Party's efforts in the Commons. Equally important was the demand on the secretariat by front-benchers who were dependent on such advice after so long in office. David Clarke was given the task of creating this organisation and remained in charge during its formative months, handing over in May 1946 to Henry Hopkinson, a career diplomat who had retired to enter politics. The decision of 1944 that information and briefs were not an appropriate part of the work of a Research Department was adhered to: so the Secretariat became an entirely separate organisation even when sharing offices with the Research Department. The driving force behind its creation in 1945–6 was Ralph Assheton, then Party Chairman, who persuaded Clarke to set it up, found the money to launch it, and put it into temporary accommodation in Wilton Street.[11] By the Christmas of 1945, three officers were servicing twenty-three Parliamentary Committees.

Among Clarke's recruits were some destined for political fame in their own right, Reginald Maudling, Enoch Powell and Iain Macleod. Like Hopkinson, these three came to the Secretariat with the intention of entering Parliament and were soon looking for seats themselves. This was again in contrast to the Research Department, which had in the 1930s insisted on its staff *not* being candidates; when revived after 1945, the Department was still looking for 'backroom boys' to form a 'shadow civil service' rather than for a galaxy of future political stars. The distinction made a good deal of sense, for a Research Department would come under the greatest pressure just before and during an election campaign, when all the parliamentary candidates would be otherwise occupied, while the Secretariat functioned around the Parliamentary Party which was dissolved when the election was called. The benefit to the Party of gaining the services of such recruits was considerable, so much so that the tradition remained even when the Secretariat ceased to exist as a separate office; young men could be given an intensive full-time preparation for their careers in politics, and in the meantime the Party would make use of them too. Only in the Spring of 1946, with the Secretariat established, could Clarke be spared to get the Research Department going again, and only then could qualified recruits be spared to undertake longer term research. Because of the determination not to make appointments until people of the right calibre could be found, this was a slow process and it was not until late in 1946 that the Research Department was up to strength.

Among the earliest officers to be appointed were Michael Fraser, David Dear, Geoffrey Block and Peter Goldman. Butler later recalled that Fraser and Goldman 'were soon to establish a long-lived working partnership based on an empathy which ensured that, whatever crisis arose, they never flapped simultaneously'. Fraser, 'the best adjutant the party had ever had', and Goldman 'whose loss to the party would later be as important as the resignation of any Cabinet Minister' provided with Clarke, Block and Dear the Department's experience and continuity, the solid foundation of its research work over the next fifteen years and more. The lack of qualified staff at Central Office also placed unusual demands on the Research Department, and the Annual ACPPE Report for 1946 stated that 'the Department had assisted the Education Department by providing background material for the discussion books produced and to be produced, and is also responsible for writing the "Topics for Today" series'.[12]

Two further reforms in the aftermath of the election defeat also helped to shape later developments, the appointment of an Advisory Committee on Policy and Political Education (ACPPE), and the formation of the Conservative Political Centre (CPC). The Post War Problems Central Committee, having been set up by the National Union, continued to operate in the Autumn of 1945 pending a decision about its future. The meeting on 16 October was taken up with a general discussion of how the committee could best function in the new situation. Butler suggested that there should now be three aims: they should stimulate and foster constituency activity in political thinking, they should prosecute research through the new Research Department when staffing made this possible, and they should encourage political education through schools and colleges. Further discussions produced the conclusion that a reorganised committee would be needed to promote these aims on a permanent basis and a series of proposals were put to the National Union Central Council in November by Henry Brooke, on behalf of the PWPCC. The National Union therefore set up an Advisory Committee on Policy and Political Education, with Butler as its chairman and with political education as a primary aim. However, although the ACPPE was set up by the National Union, details were left to Butler to work out himself, including the membership. The way in which he saw the new committee working can be seen from the letters by which members were invited to serve. To Aubrey Jones, he wrote that 'I am authorised . . . to invite some of you who are interested in Politics and in our philosophy, but have not been condemned to follow the narrow Party track and would help us with a wider outlook. to join the Committee'. To Victor Raikes, who had served on the PWPCC, Butler stressed the continuity between the two bodies and pointed out that the new committee 'would not be a large one and would include some of the brighter people of the Party'. The ACPPE was thus set up as an informal organisation, much as the PWPCC had been, with the selection of members left to the Chairman and with no attempt exactly to balance opinions and interests in the Party. The first Annual Report sought to meet possible criticisms by saying of the ACPPE that it was 'not intended that this Committee should lay down Party policy but that it should help to provide the necessary material on which long term policy could be based. To achieve this end the Research Department has been revived with Mr R. A. Butler as chairman'. When asked to comment on the first draft of this report, Marjorie Maxse of Central Office observed succinctly that it was 'not so much a report to the Conference as an apologia for the life and purpose of the committee'.

The task of political education was entrusted to the new Conservative Political Centre, set up in December 1945, very much on Butler's initiative. Its task was to 'revive and extend the educational work which between the wars had been undertaken by the Central Education Department'. Although operating from within Central Office, the CPC quickly established an effective independence, even though it was financed from Central Office funds. Since it came under Butler's control as chairman of the ACPPE it was natural for it to work with his Research Department rather than with Woolton's staff at Central Office. In the early months indeed the CPC could not have operated at all without help from Clarke's staff and a close relationship remained thereafter. The CPC had the main function of political education, carried out mainly

by means of its 'two-way movement of ideas', a network of
constituency discussion groups linked through regular meetings into
a national framework for the explanation and testing of policy ideas
among the Party activists. Briefs for these discussion programmes
have almost always been written in the Research Department; as the
CPC developed into the Party's general publishing agency a further
area of joint action emerged, with the CPC publishing books under
its own imprint, though written by the Research Department. The
CPC's first Director was Cuthbert Alport, already a close friend of
Butler's and together they planned to turn it into 'a kind of
Conservative Fabian Society which would act as a mouthpiece for
our best modern thought and attract that section of the post-war
generation who required an intellectual basis for their political faith'.
The Research Department was called on regularly to help with the
provision of an intellectual basis for the CPC's publication, and
eventually it provided in Peter Goldman a Director of the CPC who
brought the two organisations even closer. The net effect of these
changes, as reported to the National Union in 1946, was that

> the Research Department reports on its work to the Advisory Committee
> and lends its assistance to the CPC's work for political education. It is
> available to assist all departments of the Party as far as lies within its
> proper sphere. The main duty of the Department is to undertake the
> preparation of material as a basis for future policy on all subjects referred
> to it'.[13]

By the end of 1946 the first stage of recovery was over, and the
Research Department, the Secretariat and the CPC were all firmly
established. Central Office had moved into new peacetime offices in
Abbey House (Victoria Street), leaving the Research Department in
its old home in Old Queen Street. It was at last possible to get on to
the real problems of policy, but the form that this took owed a great
deal to the attitude of Butler, and to the support given by Churchill.
Butler and Churchill were each reluctant to get involved in making
detailed policy for the Party, though for rather different reasons.
Butler was anxious that the Party should get over the immediate
shock of defeat before it set out its priorities for the future, and he
also wanted to get the fundamentals straight before giving any
detailed commitments which would bind the Party in future. Like
Baldwin, he placed great importance on atmosphere and principle
and gave the making of actual policy a rather lower priority. In 1949,
in a speech in Zurich, Butler paid an extravagant tribute to the
memory of Baldwin and called for the continuance of 'Baldwinism' –
a most unfashionable attitude for a Conservative leader of the time.

He described his own policy-making as 'impressionism', the painting of a picture with broad strokes of the brush rather than the taking of a series of detailed photographs. One of his first priorities, as set down for the PWPCC in 1944, was to get some works published on Conservative philosophy, linking contemporary ideas to the longer traditions of the Party. For this reason he asked David Clarke to write *The Conservative Faith in the Modern Age* published in April 1947, and he persuaded Quintin Hogg to write *The Case for Conservatism* for Penguin. As Butler recalled, 'these books were written at an early stage under the aegis of the Research Department so as to restore the whole faith and philosophy of the Conservative Party'.[14]

When the Research Department set to work on future policy at the end of the Summer of 1946, Butler selected taxation and industrial policy as the first tasks, but still on an informal and tentative basis. In all of this Butler had the support of Churchill, but the Leader's own policy interests were predominantly defence and foreign policy and he regarded policy in the domestic sphere as something for Governments rather than for Oppositions. He did not intend to sanction any more policy work than was strictly necessary and above all he did not wish to publish policies that would commit a future Conservative Government. As he told Butler, 'when an Opposition spells out its policy in detail, the Government becomes the Opposition and attacks the Opposition which becomes the Government. So, having failed to win the sweets of office, it fails equally to enjoy the benefits of being out of office'. Such attitudes are of course rather a matter of degree, and as time passed both Butler and Churchill took a great interest in the detailed policy. Butler recalled that 'Churchill took very little interest in the early stages of the Research Department and very little interest in the production of the Charters, but when it came to *The Right Road for Britain*, which was published prior to the 1950 election, he took an interest in every line and comma of the document'. Even then, Churchill's commitment was only partial, and it proved difficult to interest him in the major speech at Wolverhampton which was intended to launch the document. For his own part, Butler thought that it had been rather fortunate that the Party had not possessed the means of issuing a policy statement before 1947, for it was only then, in the middle year of the Parliament, that it would have been appropriate to do so anyway.[15]

However, Butler's reluctance to rush headlong into detailed policy making was by no means matched by all of his colleagues, and Conservative meetings and Conferences in 1946 were marked by the extent to which the Party rank and file called on their leaders for a clearer statement of what the Party stood for. This tide of opinion persuaded Churchill into a more amenable attitude and, although he did not make any formal concessions at the Party Conference at Blackpool in October 1946, he moved soon afterwards to set up a high-powered committee to consider industrial policy. J. D. Hoffman has noted that although the subsequent *Industrial Charter* claimed to have been 'drawn up by a Committee appointed as a result of a resolution moved at the Blackpool Conference', it had actually been based on much earlier foundations.[16] The Research Department, early in its new life, had begun work on taxation and on industrial policy for the ACPPE, taking these as the two areas where Party policy most needed redefinition. The work on taxation did not get very far, for there was a general agreement on the Conservative side as to the need to reduce taxes, but there was also a lack of information available to the Opposition as to how this could be done; it did though contribute something to later work on economic policy. Industrial policy was however, both more contentious and more central to the political debate between the Parties in the years when Labour's nationalisation plans were being put into effect. The work done by the Research Department during 1946 was therefore adopted by the Industrial Policy Committee when it was appointed in the Autumn, and continuity was ensured by the appointment of Butler as Chairman of the new Committee. The other members were Macmillan, Maxwell-Fyfe, Stanley and Lyttelton from the front-bench, Derrick Heathcoat-Amory, David Eccles, Sir Peter Bennett and James Hutchison from the back-benches. David Clarke acted as secretary, assisted by Maudling and Fraser, thus drawing on the Secretariat as well as the Research Department. Butler's appointment as Chairman, in preference to Oliver Stanley who was senior to him in the Party, was notice of the line that the Committee might be expected to take and the composition of the Committee as a whole ensured that things would move in a progressive direction.

Butler wished to produce from the Industrial Policy Committee a generalised document that would show that the Conservative Party was aware of the direction in which social currents had moved since 1939; what was needed in his view was a new Tamworth Manifesto, for the War marked as complete a break with the past as the 1832 Reform Act had done. From the beginning then, the political implications were uppermost, and it seems clear that they carried more weight in the minds of the members of the Committee than did any detail of industrial policy.

The Committee met regularly through the Winter of 1946–7 around the 'battered mahogany conference table' in the Chairman's room at Old Queen Street, and a great deal of paper was circulated to the members by the secretaries. Evidence was taken from leading industrialists, in addition to the direct experience of industry that could be called on from several Committee members; later in the Winter, the Committee was broken into smaller groups for visits to the provincial industrial centres, where businessmen and trades unionists were asked for their views. For example, Fraser went with Macmillan and Hutchinson to Newcastle and Leeds, with Lyttleton and Heathcoat Amory to Liverpool and Manchester, and with Maxwell-Fyfe, Eccles and Bennett to Cardiff; other sub-groups serviced by Clarke and Maudling went to Edinburgh, Glasgow, Birmingham and Leicester.[17] This widespread canvassing of opinion by the Committee members themselves demonstrates the extent to which they saw themselves as not just devising a new policy but also selling it to the Party and its industrial supporters. It proved easier to convince the leaders of industry in London, than to put across the same ideas to small businessmen in the provinces, a difference of reaction that had also been noted in the investigations that preceded the Beveridge Report three years earlier. The same care was taken with soundings made in the 1922 Committee, conducted for Butler by Oliver Poole.

The Committee's final proposals were influenced by all of the results of all these various soundings. The Committee itself represented many different backgrounds in the Party, from Macmillan's past career as a rebel to Butler's experience as a member of the Party establishment, but they differed little in their political philosophy. The extreme care that was taken in the drafting of the report, in which Maxwell-Fyfe and Stanley both played important parts, was occasioned by the need to secure acceptance not in the Committee but outside. Several drafts were produced in the Spring of 1947, culminating with much activity in the Easter recess, and the final version showed 'Butler's hand clearly revealed in the wording'.[18] Butler's intentions were also to be seen in the form that the final report took, for the Committee produced not just a report on future policy but an *Industrial Charter*. The very name suggested something that was intended to be of historic importance, a new Tamworth Manifesto.

The *Industrial Charter* sought to weld together the Liberal tradition of free enterprise with the equally-traditional Tory concept of interventionism. Its rhetoric concentrated mostly on the former (surely a result of all the soundings taken during the Winter) while its substantive promises veered rather more to the latter. There was thus a promise that a Conservative Government would 'free industry from unnecessary controls and restrictions', but there was also a recognition that at least part of the nationalisation process could not be put into reverse. Explicit commitments were made in acceptance of Keynesian policies of demand-management so as to implement the commitment to full-employment (which the Party had accepted as part of Churchill's wartime Government in any case). Restrictive practices were attacked on both sides of industry and commitments were given against both monopoly practices and the closed shop, though the assertion that public opinion – when properly informed – ought to be sufficient to remove the worst abuses left some doubt as to whether a Conservative Government would legislate in either field. Finally, the *Charter* sought in its final section to establish a 'Workers' Charter' to give effect to the Party's wish 'to humanise, not to nationalise' industry. Consultation precedures in firms should be promoted and codes of practice would be submitted to Parliament for approval; firms that did not conform to these proposals would experience Government disapproval and might be unable to bid for Government contracts.[19]

As a statement of policy, the *Industrial Charter* was very much a product of its time – the Workers' Charter ideas, for example, drew heavily on wartime experience and the hopes of continuing it in peacetime – and as a result, many of its provisions were politically impracticable by the time that the Party had a chance to carry them out in the 1950s. It has therefore been customary to write off the *Industrial Charter* as mere words, a propaganda prelude to the making of real policy that came when the next election was in sight. But this is to miss the real point of the whole exercise, which was anyway political rather than economic or industrial. In 1947, the Industrial Policy Committee placed the Conservative Party back on the middle course in politics, away from the political fringe where it had seemed to be since Beveridge. As in 1934, it was hoped to steer that middle course between extreme interventionism (represented now by the realities of Labour Government rather than by the abstract ideas of Macmillan) and laissez faire. The middle course was certainly not in the same place in 1947 as it had been in 1934, for all the political landmarks had been shifted in the meantime by the War and the Labour victory of 1945, but the determination to steer for the centre was much the same. The *Industrial Charter* therefore takes its place along with the Tamworth Manifesto, with Disraeli's Crystal Palace speech of 1872, and with Baldwin's speeches of 1924, as a pointer to the way in which Party policy would develop at a time when this was by no means clear; in that sense, it was indeed a propaganda effort, though the propaganda was directed at least as much at Conservatives as at the uncommitted electorate. As Butler later recalled, 'Peel's Tamworth Manifesto made a rallying point for Conservatism in much the same way as our Charters made a rallying point. And I was definitely aware of the need to copy the Tamworth Manifesto not in its content which dated but in the type of document it was'.[20] It was for this reason that the six months *after* the *Industrial Charter* was produced were as important as the six months while it was being compiled, for it was by no means certain that Churchill and his Party would accept what had been done on their behalf.

Butler was kept in doubt of Churchill's views, and though Churchill subsequently announced that the *Industrial Charter* had been 'officially approved by me at what we call a Consultative Committee', things were not quite so straightforward. Meetings of Shadow Ministers were usually held by Churchill over luncheon or dinner, and on this occasion Butler and his colleagues were given no indication of the Leader's view before the dinner itself. However, the penultimate draft had been approved in advance by a meeting of the Shadow Cabinet under Eden, and there is little doubt that Eden had helped to persuade Churchill that the final document should now be approved. At dinner at the Savoy, Churchill invited Butler to the place of honour on his right, 'plied me with cognac, and said several agreeable and no disagreeable things about my work'. From this, Butler deduced that Churchill had given his approval (though there was no sign that he had actually read the document himself, and subsequent events suggested not – 'it was not well designed to captivate his attention'). Butler therefore decided to go ahead himself and publish it.[21] Publication followed a press conference on 12 May 1947, and the document was given a reasonably warm welcome in the press, though both the Labour papers and those of the extreme right were dubious to the point of hostility. Whatever had really happened at the Savoy, the document was still an unofficial one, and its critics in the Party and press were determined that it should remain so. Over the following six months, the proposals were systematically expounded in speeches by Butler and Macmillan, and especially by Eden who delivered the imprimatur of the Deputy Leader in a number of speeches produced for him by Reginald Maudling. Churchill though remained silent on the subject and in default of any ruling from him, both supporters and opponents prepared to have it out at the Party Conference at Brighton in October. In the meantime, the research apparatus was used to give publicity to what was intended, not only in speeches, but also in leaflets, Party magazines, and through the CPC's two-way contact programme. As well as actually expounding the policy, supporters of the *Industrial Charter* sought to give the impression that it was already virtually an official policy and that to oppose it was to rock the Party boat and to play into the hands of the Socialists.[22]

Although opinion was certainly heavily in favour of the *Industrial Charter* as the Party Conference approached, the Party managers were taking no chances on an embarrassing split at Brighton and had as usual prepared for debates only on fairly non-committal resolutions. At the first session, Peter Thorneycroft and Hugh Molson intervened in a general debate on economic policy to explain the new policy and to assert that it was supported by Churchill. When the document itself came on for discussion, the resolution that was proposed merely gave a welcome to the *Charter* as a basis for further discussion, but the supporters wanted to go rather further. An amendment was therefore proposed by Reginald Maudling (in his capacity as prospective candidate for Barnet, not as a member of the Secretariat or as one of the assistant secretaries to the Industrial Policy Committee, though the overlap of roles was scarcely coincidental). This would commit the Party to acceptance of the *Industrial Charter* as 'a clear statement of the general principles of Conservative economic policy' and would be the basis for all future policy work and for the election manifesto. Although the diehards mounted a last-ditch effort to stop it, the Conference would hardly give them a hearing, and Maudling's amendment was eventually carried with only three votes cast against it. Hoffman has pointed out how fortunate it was that the progressive Conservatives had to meet an attack only from the extreme right, from proponents of laissez faire like Sir Waldron Smithers, for it would have been far more difficult to head off a more reasoned response from more moderate critics.[23] Furthermore, events at the Conference itself were as carefully stage-managed as the previous months of publicity had been, and it was no accident that Maudling was called to put his critical amendment, by the President of the National Union for the year, Harold Macmillan.

The final stage was to secure the Leader's recognition of what had been done on the floor of the Conference, and although Churchill congratulated Butler on his success he was by no means so keen on the policy, as Maudling has recounted:

I was working for Winston on his concluding speech to the Conference and we came to the topic of the Industrial Charter. 'Give me five lines, Maudling,' he said, 'explaining what the Industrial Charter says.' This I did. He read it with care, and then said, 'But I do not agree with a word of this.' 'Well, sir,' I said, 'this is what the Conference adopted.' 'Oh well,' he said, 'leave it in,' and he duly read it out in the course of his speech, with the calculated coolness which he always accorded to those passages in his speeches, rare as they were, which had been drafted by other people, before he went back to the real meat of his own dictation.[24]

This done, the *Industrial Charter* was indisputably official policy and served as the basis for all that Butler and his staff did later.

The sequel was the attempt to repeat this success on a more limited scale in the following year with a report on agriculture, for the Party was as anxious as ever to demonstrate to its many rural supporters that an interest in industrial policy was not exclusive of other interests too. Butler was again the chairman of the committee, with Harry Crookshank, Thomas Dugdale and Anthony Hurd as members, and with Michael Fraser as secretary. Once again meetings were mainly at Old Queen Street, with outside experts from the NFU and the CLA invited to give evidence, and with Professor Engledow of Cambridge again involved in the exercise. According to press reports, the Agricultural Policy Committee consulted no less than two hundred advisers and experts in the course of its work, and both Dugdale and Hurd could be considered to be experts on farming in their own right. Once again, the Committee's proposals took account of opinions in the Party through the CPC as well as through more informal soundings. When first published, Butler made it clear that he expected – and would welcome – criticisms, and that changes in the policy could still be made. The *Agricultural Charter*, published in June 1948 and approved by Conference in October, made a rather smaller impact, though it contained more detailed policy suggestions than the *Industrial Charter* had done; its policies and output targets provided the basis of the Party's policy in the 1950s when Dugdale was Minister of Agriculture.[25] Other later 'charters' were on Imperial affairs, Wales, Scotland and women's affairs but there was a gradual diminution of interest in each of these as they appeared. In part this is a tribute to the psychological impact that had been planned for the *Industrial Charter* and achieved by it, an impact that could not in the nature of things be endlessly repeated, but it also reflected a change of emphasis. By 1948, the Party faithful were calling for rather more meaty explanations of policy, going on from the philosophical level of the charters to a rather more definite spelling out of policies and priorities.

However, the cumulative effect of these efforts was not only to secure a policy advance, but also to enhance the position in the Party of those Conservatives most identified with it, and this was the firmest guarantee that the policy advance would not be put into reverse, as the *Observer*'s political correspondent noted in June 1948:

> The Agricultural Charter, like the Industrial Charter, is a composite document, but a large part of the credit must go to Mr. R. A. Butler. For the last three years, Mr. Butler has been in retirement in the Tory Research Offices, that building which looks out demurely on one side at an adjunct to the Board of Trade and on the other has a view of grass, flaming flowers, growling cats and courting couples. As a consequence Mr. Butler may seem to have faded a little in the political sense, to be too academic, too intellectual even, for higher things.

But this was far from the case, for,

> the really solid work of plotting the Party's future course has been largely done by two men – Mr. Butler and Mr. Harold Macmillan. While the immediate succession would fall automatically to Mr. Eden, the influence of Mr. Butler and Mr. Macmillan will remain a highly important factor.[26]

In this sense, the appointment of Butler as the first Conservative Chancellor of the Exchequer after the return to power in 1951 (and of Macmillan, Thorneycroft, Heathcoat-Amory and Maudling after him) was a clear pledge to the country that the spirit of the *Industrial Charter* remained central to Party policy. But for the death of Oliver Stanley and the disappointing parliamentary performances of Oliver Lyttleton, Butler might well have become Minister of Labour rather than Chancellor, in which case a different side of the *Industrial Charter* might well have come to the fore; in any case, he had clearly earned the right to a senior post and the implications of his appointment would be unmistakable.

Notes

1   CRD file, 'Finance and National Revenue'.
2   PWPCC, correspondence file.
3   *Ibid.*
4   PWPCC, minutes; Hoffman, *Conservative Party*, 38–40.
5   PWPCC, minutes.
6   PWPCC, minutes; Hoffman, *Conservative Party*, 40–2.
7   PWPCC, minutes and correspondence file.
8   Fraser, 'The Conservative Research Department', II, 4–5.
9   CRD file, 'General Election 1945, Emergency Business Committee'.
10 Butler, *Art of the Possible*, 133–4; CRD (N) file, 'Notes for Lord Butler's Memoirs', 21.
11 CRD (N) file, 'Notes for Lord Butler's Memoirs', 23.
12 Butler, *Art of the Possible*, 139–40; CRD file, ACPPE reports for 1946–7.
13 CRD file, ACPPE reports for 1946–47; PWPCC minutes.
14 CRD (N) file, 'Notes for Lord Butler's Memoirs', 13.
15 *Ibid*, 14.
16 Hoffman, *Conservative Party*, 137–43.
17 Fraser, 'Conservative Research Department', III, 1–2; Butler, *Art of the Possible*, 143–5.
18 Hoffman, *Conservative Party*, 147.
19 *Ibid*, 148–52.
20 CRD (N) file, 'Notes for Lord Butler's Memoirs', 13.
21 Butler, *Art of the Possible*, 145.
22 Hoffman, *Conservative Party*, 158–62.
23 *Ibid*, 162–6.
24 Maudling, *Memoirs*, 45–6.
25 Fraser, 'The Conservative Research Department', III, 2–3; CRD file, 'Agricultural Committee'.
26 *Observer*, 27 June 1948.

Chapter 6

Finding 'the right road' (1947–1951)

Although the Secretariat was in principle quite separate from the Research Department, it shared offices, worked on combined projects and did much that officers of Ball's Department had done before 1939; it also made a contribution to the settled form of Research Department that emerged in the 1950s. It will therefore be instructive to look at the Secretariat operating independently in the years after the War. Its main work was for Parliamentary Committees, which had resumed operation by December 1945, and which were co-ordinated by a committee of all the chairmen under Eden's chairmanship. David Clarke was secretary to this Committee of Chairmen, handing over to Henry Hopkinson in May 1946 after a brief overlap. The principal business at its weekly meetings was to discuss tactics for debates, what form of whip should be imposed, and what should be the Conservatives' initial reaction to Government proposals. Problems arose regularly from the difficulty of divining what Churchill's attitude might be and the impossibility of finding out well in advance of any debate; so in April 1946 two separate lists of speakers were drawn up for the budget debate, so that Churchill could then decide whether or not to speak without disrupting the Party's preparations. In the following July, Churchill was urged to speak in the debate on Palestine but Eden was lined up to take his place if necessary, and in October the Committee had to be told by the Chief Whip that Churchill had just decided he would speak on defence in the following week. At times the Committee could express fairly sharp divergence from Churchill's method of running the Opposition, as in March 1947, when it was agreed that the Party's broadcast on the coming budget must be entrusted to somebody who was a *Conservative* and not to Churchill's choice, Sir John Anderson. The same jealousy was shown on the question of the National Liberals, who were only to attend Conservative Parliamentary Committees by special invitation, though there were elaborate schemes to ensure agreement with the National Liberals on the allocation of supply days and on tactics for debate.[1]

From October 1946, the Committee of Chairmen was almost a Shadow Cabinet without the Leader, for from that time each Parliamentary Committee had a chairman who was a front-bencher appointed by the Leader, only the Vice-chairman being elected by the members. (Some committees were run like this before October 1946, all of them from then on.) It came to be known as the Business Committee and became an even more general clearing house for discussion of Party affairs. So in December 1946, criticisms were made of the poor attendance of Conservative MPs in the House, and chairmen were asked to avoid holding unnecessary meetings of their committees since they were draining the Party of its scarce manpower. This criticism had been made in the press, which had commented on the scarcity even of front-benchers at question time; the Business Committee therefore instituted a rota, so that the Party would be properly represented. More aggressive were the regular attempts to embarrass the Government by calling for the restoration of the full measure of private members' time; it was decided to press for this in October 1946 'although it was realised that this request would not be agreed to', and the issue was kept alive throughout the next year by repeated requests. In part, this was also linked with the wish to disrupt the Government's legislation by depriving them of time; it was decided in April 1947 that the Party would use the Conscription Bill to try to wreck the Government's programme for the session, and the Secretariat was instructed to draw up as many amendments to it as possible. Delay could be of use on the Conservative side too. A fundamental disagreement on the tactics to be followed on the Second Reading of the National Health Service Bill was followed by a softening of the Party line, and further disagreements led to only a two-line whip being imposed for the Third Reading. A proposal to hold a debate on Palestine was shelved altogether in May 1946 because of the impossibility of avoiding a split.[2]

Party tactics on particular issues involved the co-ordination of forces inside and outside the House, as the cases of iron and steel, and of transport make clear. In May 1946 the Business Committee was told that Sir Andrew Duncan, a Conservative MP and also chairman of the Iron and Steel Federation, had placed at the Party's disposal a Mr Willis who would keep them informed on matters affecting the industry and liaise between the Party and the industry. Three weeks later, arrangements were reported for a two-day debate on iron and steel with a straight vote against the Government's motion and a three-line whip. But iron and steel was well down the Government's agenda of industries to nationalise, and opportunities for joint action were not to come until later; transport was already a lively issue in 1946 and 1947. A special sub-committee was set up under Thomas Galbraith in January 1946 to deal with the nationalisation of transport, but its report suggesting a reasoned Party response proved to be unacceptable when presented in April, and a further group was set up under W. S. Morrison. By June, the balance of opinion had moved even further from 'reasoned opposition' or the preparation of an alternative scheme (based on fixed-rate control of transport services rather than actual nationalisation) and it was decided instead to place all the emphasis on opposition to the Government's plans. Harold Macmillan reported that an agreed programme of opposition was being worked out by the various road and rail committees in collaboration with the companies involved.

When the Transport Bill was published it was reviewed by the Business Committee, and it was agreed that there would be a three-line whip and all-out opposition. By this time, at the end of 1946, officers of the Research Department and Secretariat were in close touch with the various transport interests to co-ordinate their defence against nationalisation, relations channelled through Peter Goldman on the Party side. Then in January 1947, Central Office tried to take this collaboration a stage further when Woolton suggested that groups of Conservative MPs should be publicly associated with the campaign of the Road Haulage Federation in the country, addressing meetings and speaking at rallies. Woolton no doubt felt that such a public connection would show industry how far the Conservatives cared for its interests, and the raising of industrial subscriptions might thus become easier, but others felt that there were political dangers in the public association of the Party with a threatened industry. It would also threaten the middle position that was being worked out at the time by the Industrial Policy Committee. It was decided that the industry was making a good job of its own defence in the country and that the question of collaboration should be left to individual MPs. Two months later, Woolton returned to the attack and again the suggestion was turned down, though Eden promised to raise it with Churchill. And here it was left, with the Party maintaining close organisational contacts with the road hauliers but remaining separate from them in public. After unfortunate experiences over coal, it was felt necessary to keep industrial pressure groups outside the Party organisation: at least, no industry was allowed to pay directly for research or a research officer in the Department.

Finally in April 1947, the Business Committee resolved that it would continue to delay the Transport Bill for as long as possible in the Commons, even though the Government had imposed a guillotine, and the Secretariat was once again instructed to prepare special ammunition for the debate. Indeed in all of this manoeuvring the Secretariat played its part, maintaining liaison with all the extra-parliamentary groups, framing amendments to Bills and Questions to Ministers, and providing option papers to the Business Committee when tactical decisions had to be taken. There was also an informal relationship with the lobby correspondents, though usually through the politicians; in December 1946, officers and committee members were all invited by Butler to a party where they would meet the correspondents of 'friendly' papers, and in the following months Robert Hudson was deputed to see the correspondents to explain the reasons for the Conservative opposition to the Electricity Bill. So much had the Secretariat become an important part of the work of the Parliamentary Party, that a room in the Palace of Westminster had been set aside for its work. The introduction of Party advisers had though to be done indirectly, and for Parliamentary purposes it had to be known as 'Mr Eden's personal secretariat'. In order to get passes to the Palace for the officers, they had to be described as personal secretaries to Members; each officer was therefore assigned to a front-bencher with whom he worked closely, as his 'secretary', Clarke to Butler, Hopkinson to Eden, Powell to Morrison and so on.[3] An even bigger advance came when the Department was allowed seats 'below the gallery' in the Commons, opposite the position from which civil servants waited to brief Ministers. The gain was worth even more in those early post-war years when bomb-damage forced the House of Commons to sit in the Lords' Chamber, for in the Lords' Chamber the advisers' seats are much nearer to the front benches. Messages could be passed and advice given with greater facility than in the Commons' Chamber.

Something of the flavour of the Secretariat's ordinary work can be gathered from the writings and correspondence of its most illustrious members, and from the memories of those who knew them at the time. There is perhaps no time in the Research Department's history that has been so much reminisced about as the years when Maudling, Powell and Macleod worked there. Readers should beware of regarding this phase as typical of the longer story, for with three such men working together it could hardly have been so, but it nevertheless gives a clear account of what was being done. Butler recalled that

Maudling from the very earliest day showed a great ability in economics especially and even in those earlier times he had his own contacts with the City such as he has now. These of course were very useful to the Conservative Party because . . . he did most of our economic briefs and speeches. Oliver Stanley . . . once said that the Conservative Party was all Eton and Magdalene, or Eden and Maudling, because Maudling used to write Eden's speeches and Eden used to find them extremely good. Maudling perhaps was the most worldly of the members of the Research Department in keeping contact with the outside world, and I think in many ways he was the ablest . . . Maudling gave the impression of being much more at ease and not straining himself as much as the others.

Maudling himself wrote of the excitement for a young would-be politician of working in close proximity to such historic figures as Eden and Churchill, providing the background material for their speeches, producing facts and checking references. It was with Maudling's assistance that Eden's speeches developed the idea of 'the property-owning democracy'; when Eden's speeches on domestic affairs were published in 1947, he chose as his title *Freedom and Order*, taking it from an article written by Maudling in the *Spectator*.

Maudling's main task, as a non-economist, was to interpret ideas about the economy, current among economists and financial pundits, for men who were considerably less informed on the subject than he was himself. In this sense, the advice did not need to be at a particularly high level of specialisation, though the analysis on which it was based needed to be as sound of that of any professional economist. This contrast came out when Maudling was asked to advise 'a distinguished Back-bench MP of long standing' who had to move a motion on economic matters for the Party:

> He asked me for help and suggestions, which I gladly gave him, but as our conversation continued he seemed to grow more uneasy. Finally, he burst out, 'That is all very well, Reggie, I am sure, but answer me this one. I am told that the National Debt is more than £2,000 million. When on earth are we going to pay it back?

Servicing Churchill was rather more straightforward, for he explained precisely what he needed for his speeches, and made it clear that although he had been Chancellor of the Exchequer for five years, 'I never understood that bucket-shop side of the Treasury'. (A story that is curiously reminiscent of his father's time at the Treasury and his inability to master decimal points – 'all those damned dots'.)[4]

Maudling remembered Enoch Powell as the most formidable of his colleagues in the Secretariat, and he was in a good position to judge since they shared a room at Old Queen Street for two years. Whereas

Maudling covered economic and financial affairs and Macleod looked after domestic and especially social policy, Powell ranged more widely, specialising in defence but tackling other areas too as the need arose.

> At one stage when Enoch was detailed to become the expert on town and country planning, he acquired the standard textbook and read it from page to page, as an ordinary mortal would read a novel. Within a matter of weeks he had fully grasped both the principles of the problem and the details of the legal situation. Within a matter of a few months he was writing to the author of the textbook, pointing out the errors that he had made.

Similarly, it was Powell who was turned to the task of developing a Conservative policy for Wales, a subject on which he had no previous experience. He was also given responsibility for covering the Government's Representation of the People Bill, and at a Central Office meeting on the Bill he greatly impressed the Party's election experts with the range of his knowledge. This reliability and thoroughness was achieved at a price though, for Powell also won the reputation of being humourless and difficult to work with; he drove himself extremely hard, but he expected the same commitment from everyone else in the Party, and he made no concessions to the more junior employees who had a less single-minded approach. In this too he was actually rather more flexible than he allowed himself to appear, for he eventually became one of the Research Department officers to marry a wife from within the Department.

Powell already had the reputation of being unusually theoretical in his attitude to politics and of being well to the right of the Party, both in his attitudes to the role of Government in domestic affairs and in relation to the Empire; the story that he sought to persuade the Party of the possibility of a military reconquest of India is wide of the mark, but there is no doubt that the British withdrawal from India did upset him deeply. For the same reason he was strongly opposed to the new British Nationality Bill with its distinction between Commonwealth and UK citizens, and he provided the briefs with which Maxwell-Fyfe led the Party's attack on the Bill.[5] Nor can it be doubted that Powell already saw himself as a politician in his own right, not merely as a backroom boy employed to service others. He fought a hopeless contest in the Normanton by-election in February 1947 and, after a vigorous search he was adopted for a winnable seat before the end of 1948. His correspondence as secretary to the Party's Army Committee makes clear the extent to which he expected MPs to treat him as an equal, but it also demonstrates how valuable such a research officer could be to the Party. He wrote in very strong terms to C. H. Gage MP in July 1947, explaining that he had been unable to supply a brief for a recent debate because Gage's request had only been posted on Friday for a debate on the following Monday, and Powell expected rather more notice. Two days later, he sent to Harry Legge-Bourke a draft for a Parliamentary Question 'which you thought of putting down'. Most of his work at this stage was done through Antony Head, who was chairman of the Army Committee, though he was also providing material on the army for Eden's speeches. In August he sent Head a paper on army numbers, based on figures that had been drawn from the Government in Parliamentary Questions and showing that it would be necessary for a run-down to take place if the Government were to avoid lengthening the term for National Service; in September and October, reductions is the size of overseas garrisons were duly announced by the Government, and Head was ready and prepared with an Opposition reply. The same motive prompted Head to put down a question on recruiting, suggested and drafted by Powell in October, so that material would be available in advance for a debate in the Lords. When the Army Committee was reorganised at the end of 1947, Head wrote to thank Powell 'for all the hard work you've put in for the old Army Cttee. You have been its main prop and stay and I am grateful and I'm sure the others are too. As a Parliamentary spiv I salute the workers of Old Queen Street and hope they don't start a union'.

The Spring of 1948 brought a series of briefs and papers from Powell on the army estimates and on the Army and Air Force Bill, circulated to a number of MPs and peers who specialised in the subject. It also brought a skirmish with Conservative Peers when a Party spokesman, Lord Mancroft, made a speech on recruiting without Powell's advice. We wrote to Lord Bridgeman, sending a marked extract from Mancroft's speech and deprecating its references to the trades unions: 'the suggestion that compulsion to stimulate recruiting should be put upon the trades unions by the Government is presumably not one that could possibly commend itself to the Party'. Two days later, Bridgeman wrote to 'agree with you that the words underlined are not well chosen' and to say that he had talked it over with Mancroft; on the same day, Mancroft wrote to Powell to ask for a brief for his next speech. In May, Powell drafted for Head a question on the Lewis Report on Court Martials which had been with the Secretary of State for rather too long without publication, and in July (writing by this time to 'Dear Head') he sent him a comprehensive report on officers' pay. Pay and allowances in the army was one of the topics most often submitted to Powell for his comments, no doubt because these extremely technical questions were beyond the powers of most back-benchers, but they demonstrated Powell's tough attitude; he did not use these approaches merely as opportunities to score points off the Government, and indeed he usually took the side of the Government – or rather of the army authorities. So for example, when asked to provide Churchill's staff with a draft reply to one of the Leader's constituents on the lack of married quarters, Powell replied as follows:[6]

> It is public policy that there should be no inducement to a Regular Officer to marry in the early twenties, and I have no reason to suppose that the Party is in disagreement with this policy. Nobody obliged Lieutenant . . . of the King's Dragoon Guards to marry at the age of twenty or less when he was perfectly aware of the financial consequences and was intending a career as a Regular Officer. He has therefore no complaint.

Macleod like Powell regarded his time in the Secretariat as the prelude to a political career of his own. As the Secretariat's expert on social questions, he was on the receiving end of many enquiries about the working of the new National Health Service, directed to him because neither Conservative MPs nor their constituents could easily find their way through the new labyrinth of regulations. Macleod could be extremely forceful when necessary and did not trouble to conceal his low opinion of those with whom he had to deal. When F. W. Harris MP sent him a list of ideas for Parliamentary Questions, put to him by a constituent, Macleod replied that 'the questions that you forwarded to me are all ridiculous ones and I am certain nothing can be based on them. I suspect that your constituent is a little touched'. When asked to draft a reply to complicated questions from a Mr Rose, Macleod suggested sending only a formal acknowledgement; 'I should not say more than this because I have had some correspondence with him before and he writes interminable letters on the slightest provocation'. When forwarding to Ralph Assheton the Party's draft policy statement on health in December, 1948, Macleod added the comment that 'a great deal of work is still to be done before we have any sort of clear-cut policy'.

Macleod was reluctant to engage in the popular Conservative pastime of spotting flaws in the Health Service, arguing that it was essential to give it time to settle down and that Conservatives should make sure they had a policy of their own before criticising that of the Government. He sent to Butler in January 1949 a projection of the future costs of the NHS, showing that its cost to the Exchequer would rise by at least £100 million by 1952–3, but urging that this should be accepted. He wrote to David Eccles in February, enclosing a brief on supplementary estimates for the Health Service and suggesting that he should speak in favour of increased remuneration for GPs in view of his support for the BMA during its dispute with Bevan. However, the lack of a clear Conservative line made his position difficult. To Gerald Williams MP in June 1949 he could only suggest delaying a reply to a constituent until the Party's policy document came out. To Malcolm McCorquodale he suggested a more temporising line: 'There is, of course, no official Party line on this matter and perhaps you might say that you are in general sympathy with his suggestion, but that it is perhaps early in the workings of the scheme to take a definite decision, particularly as we have no access to ministerial sources of information'. Finally, at the end of 1949, he bemoaned to Hugh Lucas-Tooth the effect of his Party's indecision: 'there is no subject on which we have in fact been more consistently right than health, but unfortunately at the same time there is no subject on which it is believed we have been more consistently wrong'.[7]

A more routine task for Macleod, from his earliest days in the Secretariat, was his responsibility for Scottish affairs, a responsibility that placed him in an awkwardly-exposed position because of the constitutional separation of the Conservative Party in Scotland. Working for the Scottish MPs at Westminster was not especially difficult, and since Macleod was himself a Scot it might have seemed a natural choice, but it did not work out that way, for Macleod's loyalties lay not to the Scottish Conservatives but with his employers in the Party organisation for England and Wales. Routine business, framing the amendments to bills and Questions to the Government worked smoothly enough, for he could work well with the Scottish MPs and their chairman, J. R. Hutchison. The problem was that a research officer based in London was necessarily at least as distanced from the sources of advice and information as those MPs that he was trying to service. In December 1948, he wrote to Hutchison to explain that the progress of the Scottish Legal Aid Bill had shown up a defect in the service that the Secretariat could give:

> I did not know and I have no means of knowing that there was any agitation in Scotland against this Bill. My only real contact with opinion in Scotland is provided by the 'Scotsman' which I get one day late. It would be impossible to get all the Scottish papers here and I am not able, as in the case of an English Bill, to go and see the societies concerned in Scotland.

He anticipated that the same difficulty would arise with the Scottish Criminal Justice Bill, and suggested that he should receive a copy of all briefs sent to MPs from Colonel Blair in Scottish Central Office, that he should establish contact with someone in Blair's staff, and that he should visit Edinburgh from time to time himself. This sensible idea failed because of the resistance of the Scottish Party organisers, scenting an attempt to put them under English control; 'I think perhaps Blair feels I have some connection with Central Office – as you know, we are quite distinct'. Macleod therefore carried on as before but giving Scotland and its affairs a lower priority. When there was a clash of commitments, he asked Michael Fraser to stand in for him with the Scottish Members and went himself to a meeting on health. He wrote to Hopkinson in March 1949, requesting on behalf of the Scottish Members that there should be statutory representation for Scotland on any new air board that might be set up, but the form of the letter made it clear that he was acting only as the Committee's mouthpiece and that he did not support the idea himself. On at least one occasion he showed which way his real loyalty lay; when asked to frame a letter for the Scottish Members' Committee to send to Butler on the general trend of policy towards Scotland, he sent a copy of the draft to Butler so that he could prepare his reply before the Committee even sent him its request.

Macleod was indeed the most Departmentally-minded of the Secretariat's three famous officers of the 1940s, and he retained the closest links with the Research Department in the years after he ceased to work there. He was well known both for the reliability of his work and the clarity of his thinking. Michael Fraser, who shared a room with him for some time, recalled that

> Iain used to sit, almost lie, with his feet on the desk, gazing abstractedly out of the window. He had the telephone switched off and his concentration was complete. He was constructing the memorandum in his head. He then rang for a secretary and dictated it lucidly and without hesitation in its final form. Corrections were seldom necessary. It was a way of working which perfectly illustrated his quick, clear mind and his brilliant memory.

He was a complete contrast to Powell, for he was an officer who did not like working long hours; 'he liked to start late and finish early, and he and Reggie Maudling often had convivial lunches together at Crockford's, where he was still playing bridge in his spare time'. But there were long hours of argument between Powell and Macleod, sometimes long into the night at Powell's bachelor flat in Earls Court

Square, arguments in which 'Powell would usually take a rather doctrinaire Right-wing position, while Macleod jumped about in the Centre of Tory politics'.[8]

Despite the value of a spell at Old Queen Street to the future careers of Party celebrities, it should not be thought that this was anything like typical of the rest of the staff. An alternative view is given by Ursula Branston, who joined the Secretariat in 1946 after a time with the BBC European Service and as a foreign correspondent. She rapidly rose in the hierarchy and became Head of the Foreign Affairs Section in the 1950s, and she certainly had a considerable influence on policy through a close working relationship with Anthony Eden, but all did not start so confidently. Her recollection of what it was like to be new at Old Queen Street, and in such august company gives both an interesting picture of the office as it was at that time and something of the sense of wonderment that all new research officers feel at their sudden proximity to the great names of the land:

Nothing could be less like an office than the room in Old Queen Street that formed my introduction to the Parliamentary Secretariat (later Research Department) in the Winter of 1946. An eccentric, push-button, brass and mahogany lift – supreme comfort for one, hell for two – took me to the top floor of No. 34. There in a large and lofty room a coal fire burned in an early 19th century grate, and the windows looked out on an unfailingly lovely prospect of St. James' Park, the Horse Guards and the pinnacles of Whitehall. The furnishings were austere: a table, a chair, bookshelf, fender, and a set of fire-irons, used by the commissionaire who, twice daily 'mended' my fire and renewed the coal scuttle. Twice daily, too, a cheerful tea-lady brought refreshment. Unorthodox, but ideal conditions, from my point of view, in which to start a new job from scratch. . . . There was nothing in the nature of what is now called a 'job description', and I soon discovered that freedom to initiate was the hallmark of the Department's style of working; the example was set by my idiosyncratic colleagues, Iain Macleod, Reggie Maudling and Enoch Powell. Side by side with this freedom was acceptance of wholly flexible hours, and a total readiness to drop everything if summoned by any member of the Front Bench.

. . . The Commons sat in the Lords' debating chamber and the peers in the Robing Room. My male colleagues were privileged to sit behind the bar on the floor of the Chamber, together with the Government's civil service advisers. There was no precedent, however, to admit a female to this privilege, and I had to be escorted instead to a Peeresses' Gallery or one reserved for the wives of Ambassadors. This distinction between the sexes was a considerable handicap in my job, and it was due to the personal intervention of Rab, and much pressure of correspondence, that the barrier was lifted after the re-opening of the Commons Chamber.

The passage from Old Queen Street to the St. Stephen's entrance could be accomplished in haste in three minutes, but the geography of the Palace of Westminster was an altogether greater hazard. The first time I was summoned by Anthony Eden, I made the crossing in good time in spite of pouring rain, then lost my way in the labyrinth *en route* to his room, reached by a turret staircase as dark and forbidding as a Gothick novel by Mrs. Radclyffe. When I appeared, wet and exhausted, AE took one glance, led me to a sofa, and said 'Sit down and don't say anything until you've recovered yourself,' then went to his desk and wrote for the next five minutes. Thus I survived what might have been a disaster and a lasting *rapport* was soon established.

It will already have become clear that there was never as complete a separation of Research Department and Secretariat as had been intended at first. The two had been housed together in 24 Old Queen Street, with number thirty-four leased as well as twenty-four to allow for expansion of staff; a close relationship had resulted. The fact that David Clarke had recruited the staff of both organisations helped to pull them together. Indeed, in the memoirs of officers and in other accounts of the Party organisation after the War, the exact relationship has become so blurred that it is not easy to tell what precisely was done by each side.

Relations with Central Office were less cordial (perhaps in part because Butler and Woolton were not particularly close) though not so bad as before 1939, when contact was almost non-existent and when legal action had once been threatened. Butler did not think that Central Office was doing enough to publicise the Charters; when this subject was raised at the ACPPE in July 1948, Butler replied with obvious exasperation 'that he, as Chairman of the Research Department, had not the time nor the ability to produce popular propaganda. This must remain the responsibility of the Chairman of the Party'.[9] At the same time, there was some resentment in the Research Department at the extent to which Central Office drew on their services; so in April 1948, a letter submitted to Central Office asking for an explanation of what was meant by 'the property-owning democracy' was sent on to the Research Department for an answer. These frustrations came to a head in 1948 with the declining impact made by policy reports after the *Industrial Charter*, and by the seeming inability of the Party to make much electoral impact in the country. In the Conservative Party itself, Woolton was achieving great things in both membership and finance, but there was as yet no evidence that it had won back the votes of the uncommitted. No by-election had been won from Labour, and the failure to win either Edmonton or Hammersmith South in the Winter of 1948–9 produced continuing gloom about the Party's future. By this time though, two steps had been taken in the reorganisation of the research and policy apparatus, in an attempt to meet all of these problems.

Firstly, the policy making and information services were to be brought together, and the Secretariat and Research Department were to be united into one new organisation, together with the Library and Information Department from Central Office. The development began with a minute from Churchill calling for closer integration of long and short-term policy machinery, was taken up by Clarke with a draft amalgamation scheme in March 1948, and followed by lengthy negotiations. The new structure was announced in a circular issued over Butler's name, following a meeting of Butler, Woolton and Churchill in November 1948:

> The Conservative Research Department will be a self-contained unit within the framework of the Party Headquarters and will thus be under the general administrative control of the Chairman of the Party Organisation. The Research Department in its various forms has always had a Chairman appointed by the Leader of the Party and responsible to him for matters affecting Party policy, and I have been asked to continue in this capacity in the newly combined organisation.

Butler therefore assumed a wider responsibility than before in areas of policy, but gave up to Woolton overall administrative control of the Department; from 1946 the Research Department had anyway ceased to be separately financed and now came under the Party Treasurers. In effect though, 'general administrative control' might mean very little when the Chairman of the Research Department was a senior member of the Shadow Cabinet; henceforth, the Research Department would work *with* Central Office but would enjoy almost all the independence that it needed.

The different responsibilities of the three units that made up the new Department were not at first entirely submerged: three joint Directors were appointed in November 1948, David Clarke, Henry Hopkinson and Percy Cohen (who had been in charge of the staff now transferred from Central Office), and they each continued to specialise in the fields that they had been previously responsible for. Later, when Henry Hopkinson entered the House of Commons in 1950, Clarke took over two of the three shares; Clarke was succeeded by Michael Fraser in 1951, so that Fraser and Cohen were joint Directors through the 1950s; only when Cohen retired in 1959 and Fraser became sole Director of the Research Department did all

Departmental business again come under one head. Lower down, integration went ahead at once; four sections were set up in 1948:

1 External and Defence, under Brigadier Blunt.
2 Economic, under Reginald Maudling.
3 Home Affairs, under Enoch Powell and Iain Macleod.
4 General, under Oliver Stebbings.

The only major change of this pattern was the sub-division of the General section into two in 1950, concentrating respectively on political matters and publications. Other changes took place only after 1959, but the basic pattern, whereby all 'desk officers' who cover a single policy area are grouped in sections each under a Head of Section, has remained as set up in 1948.[10]

The new organisation absorbed all of the duties formerly carried out by its constituent parts, and these were set down as:

(a) *Between Elections*
    1 To undertake long-term research and to assist in the formulation of Party Policy.
    2 To provide official secretaries for the Parliamentary Committees of the Party and to prepare briefs on issues coming before Parliament.
    3 To provide Members, candidates, speakers and all Party workers with information and guidance on current political affairs.
    4 To assist all departments of the Central Office with factual information.

(b) *At Elections*
    1 To service and assist the Questions of Policy Committee in giving policy guidance.
    2 To assist in drafting of the policy statement and of its short popular version.
    3 To assist in the preparation of broadcasts, both TV and Sound, and of speeches and articles.
    4 To check publicity material for policy and factual accuracy.
    5 To prepare special information publications of which the chief are 'The Campaign Guide' and 'Daily Notes'.
    6 To supply information of all kinds to all parts of the Party Organisation.

The structure of the new Department therefore came close to the all-embracing information and research organisation that Chamberlain had envisaged in 1930 but which had never come into existence before the War. It was also possible, in the buoyant state of the Party's finances at the time, to envisage a Department on much bigger lines than had been possible before 1939. By 1950, the Research Department, which never numbered as many as a dozen before the War and only four at the 1945 election, had a staff of over fifty; of these, about half were research officers and half secretaries. These numbers have since fluctuated, with a tendency for the Department to be larger when the party is in Opposition, but the scale of the operation has remained much the same ever since 1948.[11].

The second organisational change was less welcome to Butler at the time, although it has proved its worth in the long run. As part of the Maxwell-Fyfe reforms of the Party organisation, the old Advisory Committee on Policy and Political Education was wound up and replaced by two new Advisory Committees specialising respectively in Policy and in Political Education. In part this reflected the belief that each department in the Party should have a single line of responsibility to one National Union Committee, so that henceforth the CPC would be responsible to the Advisory Committee on Political Education and the Research Department would work with the Advisory Committee on Policy (ACP).[12] It was a different relationship though, for the ACP was not a National Union Committee (like the CPC) but a committee on which the National Union was represented; both ACP and Research Department were responsible directly to the Leader through their Chairman (Butler in both cases). The new system reflected too the success already achieved by the CPC, for its local groups were so numerous as to need careful handling within the Party organisation if they were not to become a disruptive force in the constituency parties. But most of all, on the policy side, it was felt that a different and more formal method of testing the views of the Party on evolving policies was needed. Thus, although Butler was made chairman of the new Advisory Committee on Policy (ACP) when set up in 1949, it was very different from the old ACPPE; it was a larger group, its members were chosen by the National Union and by MPs and Peers, rather than by the chairman, and they were chosen specifically because they represented different elements in the Organisation. Butler's regret at the separation of policy making from political education is understandable, not least because it distanced him from the CPC which he had created, but he found the new ACP a useful mechanism nonetheless and remained its Chairman until 1964. Liaison with the Research Department was ensured by the provision that the secretary of the ACP should be the Director of the Department (first Clarke and then subsequent Directors); it proved to be a useful sounding board against which policy ideas could be tested before publication. At the very least, the existence of the ACP in this form ensured that representatives of the National Union, of the Young Conservatives, the Conservative Trades Unionists and Conservative women would all feel that they were involved in the making of policy; at its most negative, this made it unlikely that policies would be disowned by any of these sections of the Party after adoption. The ACP was precisely what its name implied, an *advisory* committee (and hence not to be compared with its nearest equivalents in the Labour Party, the policy sub-committees of the National Executive); it did not claim to take away from the Leadership the right to 'make' policy, but it guaranteed that policy would not be made without its broad lines being discussed with the Party in advance.[13]

After a meeting with Eden, Stanley and the leaders of the 1922 Committee in December 1947, Butler wrote to Clarke to lay down the method by which research and policy making should now proceed:

> Research Department should be left to work up subjects on the research side. When these are ready for further public contact and/or advice, a small committee of enquiry should be set up under a member of the Front Bench to carry the work further, either with a view to publication or in order to have material ready for insertion in the Party's final policy. Mr. Stanley insisted, and I think rightly, that subjects to be remitted to sub-committees should be as broad as possible owing to the shortage of manpower among the Front Opposition Bench.

An example of this method of working was housing. After much preliminary work in the Department, mainly by Enoch Powell and Geoffrey Block, a committee was set up by Butler in July 1948 'to draw up a broad statement of Conservative policy on housing . . . with particular reference to (a) the provision of new houses for let and for sale, and (b) the purchase of houses by tenants'. The chairman was Thomas Galbraith and the other members were all back-benchers, with Powell as Secretary and Block as Assistant Secretary. The committee took advice and evidence from about forty firms in the housing industry over the next few months and concluded that the root of the problem was a sharp fall in productivity, mainly due to the precarious nature of the industry and the impossibility of planning ahead for a steady building programme. Principles were established for a Party housing policy which would increase output by encouraging the private builder (largely by reducing controls, the need for building licences and so on) and by cutting costs. The recommendations were made in two groups, a confidential list for the Shadow Cabinet and another list for publication. This procedure was not as sinister as it may appear; it was not possible to say in public precisely what a Conservative Government would do to building plans and regulations without causing even more uncertainty in the industry – and hence a further fall in output – in the run up to the election. This report was sent to Butler in March 1949.

The reports of such sub-committees were then submitted to a Policy Committee of the Leader's Consultative Committee – in effect to a meeting of Shadow Ministers with Eden in the chair. The reorganisation of 1948–9 keyed a wider range of opinions into this system; the amalgamation of the Research Department with the Secretariat ensured that the views of Conservative MPs would be taken on board at the earliest stage in the evolution of policy ideas (since the official secretary of the relevant Parliamentary Committee would also be the desk officer covering the subject in the Research Department and the secretary of the sub-committee of enquiry) and the ACP would be asked for its advice at about the same time as the Policy Committee.[14]

However, the reorganisation was not yet completed when the Party was plunged in 1949 into its most intensive piece of policy making during the 1945 Parliament. Party activists were unhappy with the Party's electoral showing, but they were not alone in seeing the need for more positive action. Iain Macleod, by then an adopted candidate was outspoken in his demands for action when the Party failed to win the by-election in Edmonton; Michael Fraser wrote to Butler in December 1948 to support the case for a more positive policy to win back votes in the industrial areas; evidence from Central Office surveys showed that many voters were not convinced of the sincerity of the Party's commitment to the *Industrial Charter* and that a special effort would be needed if the Party was to live down the memories of the 1930s, and especially of the attitudes of its industrial supporters then. These doubts reached a climax after the Party did not win in Hammersmith in February 1949, when demands from the Party for a clearer statement of where Conservative policy was leading became unstoppable.

A meeting of the Policy Sub-Committee of the Shadow Cabinet on 18 February, with Woolton in the chair in Eden's absence, had pointed to the unsatisfactory state of Party policy on unemployment and had commissioned Butler to get together a committee urgently to work out some proposals. Woolton agreed that 'there could be no question of seeking to upset the complacency by dishonest bidding in the matter of social benefits' although he admitted that this was precisely what the Party activists were demanding. When Butler reported back on 4 March, the Hammersmith result was known; Woolton 'expressed disappointment at the lack of positive action suggested by the proposals' and successfully moved that they be referred back to Butler to be redrafted 'in most precise terms' and 'giving where possible concrete instances'. This represented a complete reversal of all previous instructions from Churchill, who had insisted that policy should *not* be made in detail. Butler's letter to Woolton on 7 March set down the frustration that he undoubtedly felt, the sense that he and his staff were being made scapegoats:

> We have published endless books and booklets and with the aid of my colleagues and the reorganised Research Department have issued general reports, including the Industrial and Agricultural Charters. The Leader gave the strictest injunctions that no detailed policy was to be published, hence the general form and conception of the Charters ... I have, on repeated occasions, stated that I am not attempting to produce propaganda or simple factual statements on the Party attitude. I have always been informed that this was the task of the Party organisation. Endless and day-to-day work has been done by the Research Department answering queries, briefing Front and Back Benchers and interviewing National deputations. I have never been satisfied with the progress made, since I have always wanted to produce a simple but consecutive Party 'line' on which speakers could get to work. Nevertheless, I have been agreeably surprised by the real success – however you look at it – of the Industrial Charter. This has placed the Party on the fairway of modern economic and political thought. ... Despite limited satisfaction, I must register our intense disappointment that the Charters have been followed up by inadequate publicising and propaganda .... We now find, as a result of losing a bye-election, which we never had a great chance of winning, that 'Policy in clear and simple terms' is suddenly imperative. Indeed, Private Members have volunteered the view that we should consider our attitude towards unemployment and the housing question. Fortunately, we have material available on most vital subjects. This has been partially collected. We are, with the invaluable aid of the Policy Committee of the Consultative Committee, pressing ahead to produce a Party line. This cannot be an Election programme, but will be useful and should, in my view, be *published this summer.*

Butler's advice on the question of publishing a policy statement now conformed closely to the wishes of most of his colleagues, but the initiation of the process was taken out of his hands. When the Policy Committee met again on 1 April, it was agreed that a full statement of Conservative policy should be issued, but 'in view of the need for a political slant', Woolton suggested that 'the writing of the draft should be entrusted entirely to Mr Quintin Hogg. It would, of course, be based entirely on the briefs already considered by the Committee or to be considered by them later. There would be no publicity as to authorship. The proposal was accepted.'[15]

The processes by which this decision of April 1949 eventually saw the light of day as *The Right Road for Britain* in July are worth describing at length; this was the first full-length policy document to be published by the Party since the War, the first document of any great range to be published since the Research Department was re-formed, and though it was not initially entrusted to the Department it was there that most of the work on it was actually done. It was no doubt hoped that Hogg would produce for the Party a document that was as stylish as his *The Case for Conservatism* had been, but he swiftly found out that drafting for a Party was not at all the same as putting forward his own views. Most of the first draft was sent to Butler on 26 April, with a covering note explaining how it had been arrived at, for the information of the Policy Committee:

> I have used their documents, or summaries, and the two Charters very extensively, without even a verbal alteration, but in order that, when they come to look at my document, they will look at it as a whole, I have had the whole thing typed out as a connected whole without giving any indication at all where the words are mine and where they are not mine. They must not, therefore, assume either (i) That I have not made verbal alterations in their text right through; or (ii) That I necessarily agree with individual sentiments. What I have tried to do is to cast into a single document within a framework which I have constructed for myself the main conclusions which they have arrived at.

Several gaps remained to be filled, although most of these were supplied in paragraphs sent by Hogg on 3 May, but it remained the case that 'certain parts have been left omitted. This is because there is no Economic policy and I shall have to be told what it is before I can fill up the gaps'. Slightly different problems had affected the draft as regards trades unions, education and housing. Hogg made no attempt to hide his disagreement with the Party's commitment to restore the Trades Disputes Act of 1927 (repealed by the Labour Government) and hence he had written a rather more ambiguous statement into his draft. He could find no reference to universities in the Party's brief on education, 'which I think was a mistake, since these have some concern with Education, and are in receipt of rather considerable Government grants'. Most seriously, he was against any promise to end control of rents in a single Parliament, which he regarded as impracticable in any case. The Party's housing sub-committee had made things rather more difficult by framing their report in two halves, one open for publication and one to be kept secret – 'which rather puts a strain on the honesty of the draftsman'.

By 4 May, Hogg's draft was complete, though he was already dissatisfied with the changes in it which he had been asked to make. As he told Butler, 'We have hardly said a word about liberty in the revised draft. Originally I put it in on p. 19 of the introduction; one of the effects of concentrating this into the text is that liberty does not fit into Economic Policy, Industrial Policy, Agricultural Policy, Housing, or Social Services, and has therefore been omitted. We should never be allowed to get away with this'.[16] By this time too, Hogg's drafting was coming in for criticism by those who had seen it: Oliver Poole wrote to Clarke to urge him to set aside Hogg's paragraphs on economic policy and produce an alternative draft of his own. Poole was concerned that Hogg had placed little emphasis on rising costs under the Labour Government, and he disliked the extent to which Hogg implied that Conservatives accepted that nationalisation had come to stay – 'I do not think we can agree that we are in any way committed to the Socialist experiment'. Thus, the Research Department worked on the text and submitted it to a few selected Conservative MPs for their opinions during May. Most of the internal work was concentrated on detail and accuracy; Macleod asked for time on a detail of hospital policy while he had a parliamentary question asked, and Blunt rewrote a paragraph to remove the impression that the Party was under the influence of the British Legion. Powell argued for substantial revisions, marking one paragraph 'delete as fluff'.

Harold Macmillan concentrated rather on the substance of the argument, taking exactly the opposite line from Poole; he was keen not to over-emphasise the possibility of competition in the modern world and called for a policy of partnership in industry rather than a merely negative opposition to nationalisation. These various comments, together with those of the Policy Committee which discussed the draft on 24 May, led to substantial changes. The Policy Committee removed the pledge that there would be no cuts in social services spending, since Shadow Ministers could not see that such a promise could definitely be honoured; a new chapter was to be added, giving the reasons for the decision not to denationalise all the industries taken into public ownership by the Attlee Government, but also defending the decision to return road haulage to private ownership. The general emphasis was shifted towards the reduction of industrial costs as a means of reducing unemployment – very much along the lines of the idea that had started off the whole exercise back in February.[17]

These changes were made by Clarke, and his revised draft was then circulated to the ACP at the end of May, but by this time the document bore all the signs of having been drafted by several committees and the battle had only just begun. Quintin Hogg was deeply hurt by what had been done to his text, and his resulting letter to Butler had all the verve and style that had been hoped for from the main text:

> My poor Rab. Your friends are beyond human aid, and I am tempted to conclude that it is impossible to assist them. They may be tigers at policy; but the language in which they frame their thoughts is, unfortunately, not the English tongue of our forefathers, and when they write in their queer, pidgin-English jargon, they make no real effort to sustain a coherent or even intelligible argument.
>
> Your document is now as full of solecisms as a colander of holes, and as impregnated with bromides as a mothball with naphtha. I think it is past saving. The 'stern realities of the hour' ('dark hours', of course, the present) are 'faced' once more and we 'set our course' again for new and 'wider horizons'. (May I suggest here a brilliant reference to the 'ship of state' which is inexplicably omitted?) Communism is once more described as 'godless' . . . and when we do not know how to begin a sentence we gaily write 'Thus it is' to conceal our incompetence at writing. Debates in committee have once more resulted in the insertion of flaccid and meaningless paragraphs in improbable and unsuitable places.

He gave a long list of specific examples, together with suggested improvements, and sometimes with cries of despair ('Rewrite this farrago of nonsense') but he had given up hope of the document ever proving of any use:

> What is the use of tinkering with the unmendable? It is the train of reasoning that you have allowed to be broken, not merely the prose. Even the bourgeois gentilhomme spoke something more like his native tongue than your friends . . . Oh dear why ask me to write at all if you are going to turn my prose into unreadable heartbreaking jargon like this? I will do all I can to help your friends; but it seems to me that there is nothing that

can be done, except to start again with a clean sheet. This exercise fails to satisfy the examiners. Yours Q.

Butler sent this trenchant letter on to Clarke, 'thinking you will be amused. We all receive shafts, but I am not sure that Lord Salisbury does not come out of it worst'. (Salisbury had been responsible for the insertion of 'Godless' Communism and so on.) However, the Research Department was instructed to improve the document wherever possible to meet Hogg's strictures, but not to spend too long on the rest of his suggestions; where Hogg had minuted that a pledge to reduce taxation as first priority was 'bad politics', Butler merely added the phrase 'but agreed'.[18]

As before, other critics were more concerned with content, with the protagonists sticking to their earlier positions. Oliver Poole again argued for a more positive commitment against Labour's policies, and David Eccles argued that 'it is too easy to conclude that the main difference between us and Labour is that we will do the same job more efficiently'. From the other side, Harold Macmillan still found the document too negative and too old-fashioned; he objected to 'the system of free enterprise which we wish to see restored' as 'far too Manchester School' and suggested instead a reference to 'that balanced system which we wish to see established where all the virtues of private initiatives and free enterprise will have fair play. We recognise the truth of the traditional Conservative position that government has its own important part to play in the economic and industrial life of the nation'. As in the case of the *Industrial Charter* more was at stake than mere words; to talk of 'restoring' would imply a backward-looking policy, while to talk of 'establishing' would look forward, and the effect would once again be more political than economic. With these conflicting views, Clarke retired to Dartmoor and put together a third draft in the first week of June; a paragraph on women's affairs was provided by the Women's Department at Central Office, one on food by the Research Department and a paragraph on Scotland by Sir Basil Neven-Spence, these filling the last gaps. Clarke then drafted an introduction and sent the material off to Butler in his constituency: 'If you think it is not right feed it to a pig at the show. But if you want it done again I think somebody else will have to have a shot at it, because my head is completely empty now'. Butler returned the introduction, 'slightly revised. I approve Food and Women. Now good luck to the whole'. This draft was then circulated to the Shadow Cabinet, with a covering note from Eden as chairman of the Policy Committee (also written by Clarke), and discussed on 22 June.[19]

By this stage, the document was beginning to attract rather more complimentary responses, and from some there was enthusiastic approval; Mark Chapman-Walker of the Publicity Department at Central Office wrote to Clarke to welcome 'it as an excellent document and I congratulate you on it. If I can't sell it, I will eat my hat'. Eden reported to Butler that 'I saw Winston on Sunday and I am sure that he is kindly disposed towards the policy document'. Woolton was more guarded, now doubting the wisdom of issuing policy in such detail so long before an election, but he admitted that 'if the candidates get this document, they will not be able to say that we have not given them any policy'. After seeing Churchill himself, Butler reported a host of drafting amendments which the Leader had marked on his copy of the text, but he was also able to report acceptance of the substance of what was proposed. In the same letter, he sent Clarke 'Mr Hogg's latest amusing letter (keep all of his for me!)' Hogg was now much more friendly towards the document:

> My dear Rab. I shall undoubtedly go to Heaven. I have picked a painful and laborious way through the thicket of mixed metaphors and clichés once more. I congratulate you. The document is greatly improved.

There was some doubt about the desirability of what was being promised on taxation and on housing (both of which Hogg had criticised before), but

> my general feeling is one of relief. It is much better than I had thought from the last draft.
> P.S. But on my knees I beg:
> (1) Do alter the sentence about strengthening the fighting teeth of the defence services by reducing their swollen tail.
> (2) When the hayseeds say 'The contribution of British Agriculture to the nation's food ought to be raised' explain to them that Shakespeare, who was also a country man, might have been content to say that we should produce more food.
> (3) Many sentences bear unmistakeable signs of having been written either by a German or by a Hyde Park Orator.

This insistence on literary standards was important, for the document of 1949, as it finally emerged, set the standard for a whole series of Party statements in which fluency and style was an essential ingredient. For this, Hogg's contribution in 1949 must take at least some of the credit.[20]

The final stage of preparation involved the circulation of the document in proof to a wider group of Conservatives, and its final submission in page proof to the Shadow Cabinet. The response was now unanimously warm; Henry Brooke, wrote that he 'knew so well the difficulties (and the tedium!) of producing such a document' and concluded that 'there is more substance in this policy statement than in any other I can remember'. Quintin Hogg now admitted to Butler that 'you have improved the formal style out of all knowledge'.[21] The document thus went ahead and was passed for printing early in July. Two problems only remained, a name and the question of whether or not to include an appendix. None of the drafts circulated had had any title at all, and only at the last moment did Butler ask for suggestions. Woolton suggested 'This is what the Conservatives will do' and Chapman-Walker 'The Right Way Forward' – which came close to the final choice of The Right Road for Britain. Churchill had demanded that there should be an appendix which would list all the social reforms carried by Conservative Governments in the past, and so refute the Labour charge that Conservatives could not be trusted with the National Health Service. Macleod's Home Affairs section was set to compiling this list, but when this was produced by Charles Bellairs of the Research Department it proved to be so comprehensive as to threaten that the appendix on the past would dwarf the proposals for the future. Macleod passed it on to Clarke, expressing the hope that the appendix should not be included, and it was eventually decided to publish it separately as Conservative Industrial and Social Reform.

Churchill wrote his own foreword to the document, ignoring drafts submitted by the Research Department, and taking the opportunity to link future policy with the legacy of Disraeli and Lord Randolph Churchill, and also with 'the spirit of liberalism'. This last was probably linked in his mind with the negotiations going on to secure official approval of the document from the National Liberals (who had played no part in its formulation), the policy side of the Woolton-Teviot pact which had begun to bring the constituency organisations of the two Parties together. The Right Road for Britain was finally launched on 23 July with speeches by Churchill at Wolverhampton, Macmillan at Saffron Walden and Eden on the BBC, all of which were drafted or vetted in the Research Department. An intensive campaign of publicity was begun at the same time, starting with a press conference and continuing with signed articles in various magazines by Churchill, Macmillan and Butler; for example, a lengthy analysis of the new document for the Political Quarterly by Butler was based on a draft by David Clarke.[22] The policy was thus completed more than half a year before the election, and this was probably the most difficult exercise of the whole of the post-war years, at least until 1965; henceforth, a solid body of Party policy was in existence which could be modified, refined and kept up to date with changing circumstances. A method had also been evolved which was to be used for a whole family of manifestoes and policy statements in the future.

By the Autumn of 1949, the Party could approach the coming General Election with at least the knowledge that its policy preparations had been made. The demands for Party policy were muted as fewer and fewer gaps remained to be filled; so the number of briefs issued by the Research Department, which had reached a record of 319 in 1947, fell to 243 in 1949, to 184 in 1950 and to only 158 in 1951. More than a thousand briefs had been prepared over five years, well over one brief for each day on which Parliament was sitting, and this in addition to the drafting of speeches, work on policy documents, vetting of minutes and papers for Parliamentary Committees. From 1948, the Department was also responsible for a larger share of the Party's regular publications, especially the fortnightly *Notes on Current Politics*. Of longer-term value was the compilation by David Clarke in 1950 of *Conservatism 1945–1950*, an anthology that drew on all the official and unofficial work done since the 1945 election, a period already seen as that of a historic recovery. Not everyone was quite so confident, even among Party sympathisers, and there was felt to be a need to make a special appeal to the opinion-formers. Hence, Clarke's anthology, which he described to Geoffrey Lloyd as 'a Third Programme effort, and we are anxious to get it into the hands of people who are fairly intelligent and who do not perhaps pay much regard to small leaflets'. One such person was the historian G. M. Young who, when writing to thank Clarke for a complimentary copy, expressed his own scepticism in curiously modern tones: 'So you think that you can live with the Trade Unions? S. B. used to say the greatest error his Party ever made was in not redressing the Taff Vale situation by reaffirming the Cross legislation of 1875. I thought in 1927 that his Trades Disputes Act was an equally grave error. And Trades Unions have long memories. Will they believe you?'[23]

By the time that the 1950 General Election was called, there was already need to revise what had been agreed less than a year earlier, and the evolution of the Party manifesto was as tortuous a process as had produced *The Right Road for Britain*. The first draft, entrusted to David Clarke, was circulated to the Policy Committee on 1 December 1949 with a covering note from Butler which explained its form. 'It will be noted that there are a good many "try-outs" in possible policy, e.g. abolition of certain Ministries, cuts in food subsidies both on home-produced and imported food, reforms in the Health Service etc. These are all included for purposes of discussion. It will further be noted that certain detailed proposals of the Right Road, e.g. pensions increase, equal pay etc. are included subject to a caveat about the financial position'. Many of those 'try-outs' became Party policy, many like food subsidies implemented by 1955. The longstanding Conservative promise to reduce taxation, combined with the country's deteriorating financial position and the antici- pated costs of rearmament made the Research Department much less sanguine about other areas of possible expenditure. This caution was by no means welcome to all of those about to enter an election campaign; Lord Swinton wrote to congratulate Butler on his restraint, but Oliver Stanley urged a much more positive statement on taxation, for 'we must take some risks'.

Churchill now demanded that he be consulted at every stage; David Clarke went down to Chartwell to test his views on various issues needing a decision and sent on to Butler the Leader's ideas on war pensions, conscription and education, 'which will almost certainly give you a fit'. This problem was solved only by a visit to Chartwell by Butler himself (described in full in an appendix to this chapter), but Churchill contributed in substance and in detail to each of the successive drafts. Even after six drafts had been passed around and the final shape had been generally agreed, Butler had to inform Clarke that 'he desires to see a proof at Chartwell, and nothing will stop him'. The decision to build the manifesto around *The Right Road for Britain* was underlined by the choice of *This is the Road* as its title, but this only emphasised the extent to which the Party had been compelled to pull back from its position of the previous year. Reginald Maudling was unhappy that fewer promises were being made, since many of the promises were no more than any good Government would do anyway if it had the chance. During the evolution of the document, the number of specific pledges was whittled down even further, in some cases by straightforward omission, in others by the promise of Royal Commissions or further enquiries. This did not do much to satisfy those in the Party who wanted clear promises, but it helped to ensure a favourable press reaction when the manifesto was published on 24 January 1950. The Party fought the election on the basis that the Labour Government had led Britain into a severe economic and financial crisis, and anything but an extremely cautious Conservative manifesto would certainly have undermined this entire stance.[24]

During the campaign itself, the Department was short of staff since five of its research officers were candidates themselves, but those who remained played an active part. Since the Party was out of office, there were no problems of liaison with Government departments or with the Cabinet Office. The usual Questions of Policy Committee was set up to answer requests for policy information, with Lord Swinton as Chairman, with Lord Margesson, Oliver Poole, Marjorie Maxse (Central Office) and David Clarke as members, and with Gerald Sayers of the Research Department as secretary. Since none of these were candidates and only Swinton had speaking engagements, the Committee was able to meet almost daily; eighty-three rulings on policy were circulated to Conservative candidates, and other minor questions were given individual replies.[25] The *Campaign Guide* had been published well before the election in October 1949, as a co-operative venture which drew on almost all the Department's officers, but a supplement was issued in January 1950 for the actual campaign. *Daily Notes* were issued on each day of the campaign, copies being sent to agents and candidates in the daily mailing, and the Department was used, as before, to check other leaflets and publications for accuracy. For all these publications, the Department's work came under Percy Cohen who had previously done much the same job while housed at Central Office.

Clarke was also made a member of the Tactical Committee which met each day at Central Office under the chairmanship of the General Director. This body reviewed the progress of the campaign, nationally and in the constituencies, co-ordinated the speeches of front-benchers and arranged replies to those of Labour Ministers. So, Clarke presented on 6 February a paper on 'the Labour line' as it had so far emerged, and as a result the Research Department was commissioned to provide material on fishing, for Churchill to use at Tavistock, and on Road Transport, for Eden to use at Newcastle. Special notes on Labour and Liberal proposals were prepared for Conservative candidates in Wales, and Michael Fraser was asked to draw up a reply to a speech by Jennie Lee on housing and to send it to all the Conservative candidates for their use. The Tactical Committee tried to steer a middle path between damning all Liberals and wooing the Liberal voter, for the number of Liberal candidates was the largest since 1929. The advice circulated to Conservative candidates reflected this tactical dilemma. Where the Liberal was the main opponent, he should be identified with Socialism by reminding the electors of what had happened between 1929 and 1931. Where the intervention of a Liberal would help Labour, the Conservative candidate should be polite to Liberals in general but attack the Liberal candidate strongly, concentrating on the need not to split the anti-socialist vote and the 'wasted vote' argument. Where the inter-vention of a Liberal would help the Conservative, he should be ignored altogether, so that the hostility of the Labour candidate would antagonise 'responsible Liberal opinion'. Where there was no Liberal candidate, there should be a great emphasis on the extent to which Conservatives and Liberals agreed on policy matters. To facilitate this, no candidate should actually 'attack Liberal *principles*. All that are worthwhile have long been endorsed by the Conservative Party'. This tortuous advice paid few dividends in 1950, but probably helped the Party greatly when it was faced with a much reduced slate of Liberal candidates in 1951.

In framing its decisions, the Tactical Committee drew on the advice of a Public Opinion Research Department at Central Office, a unit established in 1948 but which had only very limited resources. Its surveys demonstrated the extent to which Churchill and especially Eden were electoral assets; Eden was widely admired even by Labour voters and his election broadcasts drew by far the most favourable response from the electorate. For the Party as a whole, the surveys showed that a large proportion of the electorate were still unwilling to trust the Conservatives and that memories of the 1930s still ran very deep. Finally, as the campaign drew to a halt, the Committee considered the novel question of what effect the published opinion polls were likely to have on the result. It was widely believed in 1950 that opinion polls would produce a bandwaggon effect – that a Party shown to be in the lead would receive the support of waverers – and this was especially important as polls would be published on polling day by both the *News Chronicle* and the *Daily Express*, the two papers whose readership included the largest proportion of Liberals and doubtful voters. In those primitive days of public-opinion polling, it generally took at least a week for a full-scale survey to be processed and published, and contact between the pollsters and the Parties was already close; the Tactical Committee thus received a paper on the probable final predictions three days before they were published:

> The Daily Express will almost certainly forecast a Conservative win, though perhaps a small one. The News Chronicle will forecast a victory for whichever Party the Gallup Poll expects to win. Gallup will spare no pains to get this right, as it would be almost fatal to him to pick the wrong side after his fiasco in the U.S.A. two years ago. His people will have plenty of good evidence to go on, including probably all that of Transport House. On which side they will come down in the end, it is impossible to

say; if on ours, then so much the better; if on the Socialist side, they may at least scare off some potential Liberal voters.

. . . If we take no action, the Mail will probably not compete directly with the other two. There are ways, however, in which the Mail might be enabled to weigh in with a last minute poll favourable to the Conservatives. It is a matter for decision as to whether this would be desirable.

The *Daily Express* did indeed publish a final poll that showed the Conservatives narrowly ahead, but the Gallup Poll in the *News Chronicle* showed a small Labour lead, and the *Daily Mail* did not publish any poll findings at all. Nevertheless, the whole tone of the discussion paper casts a fascinating light on those early election predictions based on opinion polls; if it normally took between a week and ten days to set up a poll and report its results, how could the *Daily Mail* be persuaded on a Monday to publish on the following Thursday figures for a poll that had not yet started? And in 1951, the *Daily Mail* did in fact publish its own poll findings on polling day, showing a very large – and very misleading – Conservative lead. (This speculation should of course be clearly distinguished from the work done for the *Daily Mail* later by National Opinion Polls, an organisation that was not founded until 1957.)[26]

These discussions in the last days of the campaign reflect the anticipated closeness of the result, a view that was more than confirmed by the reports from the constituencies. In the event, Labour held on by just five seats with a result very close to that which Gallup had predicted. For Conservatives there was some understandable frustration, to have made such a considerable comeback and to miss by so little. For the Research Department, there was a mixture of triumph and disappointment. Hopkinson, Maudling, Powell and Macleod had all been elected MPs and three of the four became founder members of the 'One Nation Group' along with other MPs who had been associated with the Department. There could be little doubt that the scale of the Party's recovery from the disaster of 1945 had owed a great deal to the solid work on policy and research done in Old Queen Street. The *Right Road* had not led to Downing Street, but there was good reason to expect a short parliament and a tired Government that might be pushed out at the second try. But in any case, the making of detailed policy, the taking of decisions that would affect the exact way in which a Conservative government would work, had really begun less than a year before the 1950 election. A little longer to test those policies and refine those decisions would do a subsequent Conservative Government no harm at all.

Appendix: Churchill and Policy

The following memorandum was dictated by R. A. Butler in March 1950, as 'a description of policy-making with WSC.' It was paraphrased and quoted in part in Lord Butler's *The Art of the Possible*, but deserves to be reproduced in full.

A theory has been put about, and is given daily airing by the 'Daily Express', that Mr. Churchill has always been against policy-making and has never wanted to see a policy made for the Conservative Party. He has latterly gone out of his way to express his gratitude to me for what I have been able to do in organising the preparation of a policy statement for the Party. He has further said that it has had a considerable effect in bringing us to the happy position in which we find ourselves in 1950.

This is not an entirely new 'flash in the pan', since when discussing policy questions with him privately, particularly at Westerham, he has been the reverse of uncooperative and has brought to the preparation of our Election Statement all that skill as a writer and proof-corrector, which he proudly says is his primary trade.

Of course he has been animated by the same anxiety that he felt at the time of the Second Front, lest the preparation should not be sufficient and lest too much surface should be exposed to the enemy at the wrong time. He has also been animated by his principle not to promise to carry out more than he can perform. Further, he has been so passionately keen to resume power that he has not wanted to tie himself to any statement which might make that objective more distant. Latterly he has frequently said that the Liberal Party copied their policy from mine and he has told me that he thinks little of the Daily Express view that I am no more than a Socialist.

During the period immediately after his return from Madeira and prior to the Election, I was asked to go to Westerham with the latest draft. He was, needless to say, asleep when I arrived, and we started work on the paper itself full strong at the dinner table. At 1 a.m. he raised his eyes from the task and said 'It must be nearly 11, so we must think of moving'. This brought this particular session to an end, but it was followed up by several other sessions in London and one again at Westerham.

The form in which Eden and three or four others wanted our policy to appear was statatum, with the document arranged in paragraphs. This was speedily killed by Winston who wished the whole document reduced to narrative. He let the whole weight of his mind fall upon the paragraphs prepared, shredding to bits discrepancies or ellipsis. For instance, paragraph 40 or our original draft ran:

> 'We shall drastically reorganise the structure of the Coal Industry and the Railways as public undertakings. By decentralising their activities we shall give greater responsibility to the men on the spot and create again local loyalties and enthusiasm.'

He pointed out that the same argument could not be used for coal and for the railways and that a railway being in perpetual motion was not 'on the spot'. I use this as one instance only.

During the course of the evening his reminiscences were more entertaining than his valuable corrections of style. He warned me in policy statements not to postulate premises into single lines or to generalise on vital issues. He reminded me that in 1905 Lord Spencer had said in a statement 'nor must we forget Ireland'. He had brought down devastating redicule upon his head, from which he never recovered.

On the subject of the Social Services, he said that Edward Grey told him that Gladstone believed that there were no politics in Social Reform and that the old Liberalism which had torn the shackles from the slaves was petering out. (I reminded him of Wilberforce!)

'Lloyd George taught me', said W.S.C., 'what politics there were in the social reform which he instituted, not so much in his Limehouse speeches as in his insurance proposals. Now this policy is wearing a bit thin because the worker has to pay. There will, in future be less politics in social reform though much perhaps in economic break-down. Parish has now been put on the Parish.'

The real difficulty about finishing or rounding off our policy statement arose from the man's determination to write the English of it himself. This issue was actually resolved at a luncheon party a week later attended by Eden and Bracken. I said that if he wrote part and I wrote part the contrast would be so awful that the public would make fun of the effort. He said that he supposed I wished to replace him as Leader of the Party. There was no need to answer this fortunately, since he had to go out to a telephone call. When he finally returned he was singing a different tune and said I was to produce a completely revised version without style and without paragraphs by lunchtime next day. This was achieved thanks to the efficiency of three or four people in the Research Department, and my colleagues Woolton and Oliver Lyttleton stayed behind to help.[27]

Notes

1   CRD file; 'Minutes of Business Committee, 1946–7'.
2   *Ibid.*
3   *Ibid*; Beichman.
4   CRD (N) file, 'Notes for Lord Butler's Memoirs'; Maudling, *Memoirs*, 43–4
5   Roth, *Enoch Powell*, 47–50; Maudling, *Memoirs*, 42.
6   CRD (N) file, 'Brigadier Powell's Army File, 1947–8'.
7   CRD (N) file, 'Mr Macleod's Parliamentary Correspondence, 1948–50'.
8   *Ibid*; Fisher, *Macleod*, 61–3; Roth, *Enoch Powell*, 49.
9   ACPPE minutes, 6 July 1948.
10 CRD (N) file, 'Notes for Lord Butler's Memoirs'; Fraser, 'The Conservative Research Department', II, 7–8.
11 CRD (N) file, 'Notes for Lord Butler's Memoirs'; Fraser, 'The Conservative Research Department', II, 9.
12 *Final Report of the Committee on Party Organisation* (National Union), 40–41.
13 *Ibid*; 37–9.
14 CRD (N) file, 'Notes for Lord Butler's Memoirs'; CRD file, 'Housing Policy Committee, 1948–9'.
15 CRD file, 'Minutes of Policy Committee, 1948–9'; Fraser, 'The Conservative Research Department' III, 4–5.
16 CRD file, '1949 Policy Document – Mr Hogg's First Draft'.
17 CRD files, '1949 Policy Document – Comments on First Draft' and 'Minutes of Policy Committee, 1949'.
18 CRD file, '1949 Policy Document – Comments on Second Draft'.
19 *Ibid*; 'Minutes of Policy Committee, 1949'.
20 CRD file, '1949 Policy Document – Comments on Third Draft'.
21 CRD file, '1949 Policy Document – Comments on Galley Proofs'.
22 CRD files, '1949 Policy Document – Foreword and Appendix', '. . . Cooperation with Liberals' and '. . . Speeches'.
23 Fraser, 'The Conservative Research Department', III, 10; CRD file, 'Publications 1945–50'.
24 CRD files, '1950 Election – Election Manifesto'.
25 CRD file, '1950 Election – Questions of Policy Committee'.
26 CRD file, '1950 Election – Tactical Committee'.
27 CRD (N) file, 'Notes for Lord Butler's Memoirs'.

Chapter 7

'Setting Britain free' (1950–1957)

It is customary to regard the period between the General Elections of 1950 and 1951 as a mere interval during which the ailing Labour Government was harried from office by a Conservative Party confident of victory next time. The reality was much more complex, for the Conservative Party was much less single-minded in its attack on the Labour Government than this might suggest, much less confident in its approach to power. The last eighteen months of opposition were therefore an important time in their own right. The Party rank and file, disappointed by the 1950 result, wanted yet more detail of policy in order to show that their Party meant business. Meanwhile, the international situation continued to deteriorate and the consequent restraints on future public spending became even greater. Between these millstones, policy was further refined and with good effect, so that by the Autumn of 1951, the Conservatives were more ready not only with a policy to put before the electorate but also with a programme that could be carried out in office. In policy terms, it proved to be no bad thing for the Conservatives that their return to power was delayed until 1951.

In the meantime, the problems of Party management and tactics went on as before. The much publicised campaign to harry the Government into all-night sittings, snap votes and other forms of Parliamentary ambush was mainly the work of enthusiastic backbenchers like Robert Boothby, but the official Party was involved from time to time. So in March 1951 it was agreed by the Business Committee that 'it would be desirable to have a division on a prayer in the near future'; the Cheese Order was chosen, not because it was of any great importance in itself, but because its very typicality would make it difficult for the Government to estimate the purpose of the ambush or the chance of it recurring. However, the keynote of Parliamentary business was an increased cordiality between the two front benches, in part because the Labour Government was now being harried from the left as well as from the right. The Business Committee decided in November 1950 that it must support the

Government in the forthcoming foreign policy debate, against a Labour amendment, and it had already agreed in March 1950 to the suspension of Private Members' Bills 'for the special circumstances of the present session'. Similar agreement was reached to suspend sittings of Parliament for the opening of the Festival of Britain and for a Speaker's Dinner for Princess Elizabeth.[1]

All was not quite so smooth within the Conservative machine. The Advisory Committee on Policy had only been set up on its new representative basis in October 1949, so that it had hardly got into its stride by the time of the 1950 election. It had been carefully constructed to reflect the views of all sections of the Party, but this had been thrown out of gear by the election, for several of the representatives of the National Union had now become MPs, thus unbalancing the carefully-balanced structure. Not until April 1950 did it really begin to function, and the Research Department was not at all keen to work with it, for it seemed to present the danger of a divided allegiance – to the Leader *and* to the ACP. David Clarke was reluctant to take over the secretaryship of the ACP, even when he was also offered the more prestigious position of becoming an ex-officio member of the National Union Executive. As he told Butler, he was not much impressed by the new offer:

> It has been open to the Central Council and the National Union Executive to coopt the Director of the Conservative Research Department at any time during the last twenty years. They have not done so and presumably felt no need to do so. I am bound to admit that the Department has also got on without any apparent disability from this cause. If they do not want me in my major capacity, I feel no temptation to sneak in by the servants' door.

He was then made a member of the Executive as Director of the Research Department.

Fears of a loss of independence were probably reinforced by arguments that followed the publication of Michael Fraser's *The Worker in Industry* in September 1950. This was a follow-up to the ideas of the *Industrial Charter* and reflected Fraser's view that the Party had still got a lot to do if it was to win back the confidence of the industrial worker, but the 'hawks' on the Party's Labour Committee were not convinced of this and seized on the fact that the book had not been submitted to the ACP before it was published.[2]

Two other issues that emerged during 1950 also illustrated the difficulty for the Research Department in picking a course between its responsibility to the Party Leader and the need to report to the ACP. On both proportional representation and on relations with the

Liberals, the ACP was more militant than the leadership could afford to be. After a narrow defeat there was a natural casting about for means to make up the deficit, and it was equally natural that greedy eyes should be cast on the two and a half million Liberal votes polled in 1950; there would be far fewer Liberal candidates next time, and so the second preference of Liberal voters would probably decide the outcome of the election. Hence, Churchill asked Butler to prepare an 'Overlap Prospectus' which would show how far Conservative and Liberal ideas coincided. With the help of the Research Department, and later of Harold Macmillan too, this document was drawn up and sent to Churchill in June 1950. Thereafter the Party was always conscious of the need to win Liberal votes and after it did win the lion's share of them at the 1951 election, Churchill demonstrated his gratitude by inviting the Liberal Leader, Clement Davies, to join the Government. Proportional representation was central to this strategy, not only because it was the Liberal Party's main policy objective but also because proportional representation might provide a means for permanent Conservative-Liberal co-operation against Labour – even for the gradual absorption of the Liberals into the Conservative Party. If the Conservatives wished for good relations with the Liberals, then they must at least appear to take proportional representation seriously.

Not everyone thought that way though, and Sir Herbert Williams (representing the National Union on the ACP) wrote to Clarke to express his outright opposition: 'all the chat about proportional representation merely encourages the Liberals to go on, and I think in some way or another we have got to take steps to prevent the present nonsense on the subject in certain high quarters'. Butler reported to Churchill that there was stiff opposition to even discussion of the subject, in both the ACP and 1922 Committee. It was reluctantly agreed that Central Office should be asked for its professional advice on the effect of proportional representation in the cities, but it was also unanimously agreed that no statement should be issued about the investigation. Butler reported to Churchill that 'I am ready to see Lady Violet [Bonham-Carter] and explain the situation'. He then wrote to Pierssené at Central Office on 15 June 1950, offering Peter Goldman's assistance for the enquiry and reporting that 'Mr Churchill is . . . pleased to hear that the Conservative Party is going into this matter and . . . attaches great importance to a careful examination of this proposal'. The idea of adopting proportional representation in the cities (where the Conservatives were weakest) but not in the rest of country was not entirely original; this had been one of the options considered during the debates of 1918, and it was not far from the electoral system adopted in Fourth Republic France to keep the Communists out of power. However, investigations did not convince those who still hoped for the return of a majority Conservative Government, nor those who felt that Churchill was already bipartisan enough in his approach – without proportional representation and enhanced co-operation with the Liberals to encourage him. No commitment to proportional representation was made, and no reference to the subject appeared in the Party's manifesto. Conversely, the idea of restoring the university constituencies, which was universally popular among Conservatives, remained a Party pledge (though one which the Churchill Government made no attempt to implement). From these arguments, and many others in 1950–51, a rough-and-ready concordat emerged; the Research Department should be free to work on policy ideas, often in secret, so that the Party could be prepared even for eventualities that few Conservatives wished to see; publications could be produced through the CPC without the approval of the ACP, providing that it was made clear that no positive commitment was involved; but, when policymaking moved on from preparatory work and the flying of kites to the evolution of definite objectives, then the ACP should be consulted.[3] Thereafter, relations were more harmonious and the ACP far less significant than the ACPPE had been.

Most areas of policy were less contentious and followed the pattern of advisory committees that had evolved before 1950. So for example, Butler wrote to Geoffrey Hutchinson, chairman of the Local Government Advisory Committee on 15 June 1950: 'We have been reviewing the whole field of our policy. I am relying on you and your committee to advise us on Local Government matters. I am trying to have a line on everything ready by the time we adjourn at the end of July owing to the uncertainty of the date of the General Election'. Hutchinson sent off a paper that had been completed in the previous Autumn, this being updated in the Research Department before going to the ACP for approval. More unofficially, proposals for the reform of the Local Government structure were commissioned for Sir Malcolm Trustram Eve and given an airing in the Central Office magazine *The Councillor*.

A year later, Hutchinson resigned as chairman because of parliamentary commitments, and Eve was asked to succeed him. Woolton reported that 'Eve came to see me on Thursday last and said that whilst he would be glad to do the work he must tell me that his election would cause people to conclude that the Party had adopted his views on the construction of the Local Government machine. I did not tell him how vaguely I remembered his views, but I said I would consider the point'. David Clarke was very keen to have a Chairman as knowledgeable as Trustram Eve and saw no great difficulty: 'this committee is an advisory one, and is concerned mainly with what local authorities are doing. The question of structure is a matter of national policy on which the Leader and his colleagues will have the last word'.[4] The committees were thus looking at policies which a Conservative Government might adopt, but there was no supposition that it would in fact do so. On the same basis, a committee under Maxwell-Fyfe looked at the 'Control of the Executive Power', one under Colonel Lancaster produced a detailed plan for the coal industry, and a group under Assheton produced the report on broadcasting that called for a second television service independent of the BBC. When Woolton told Butler that 'on many sides I am being pressed for a clearer definition of the Party's policy for care of the aged', he was told that a Parliamentary group under Angus Maude were already at work on it. The preparation for power went on in other ways too; the Party had decided to abolish the Government machinery for bulk purchase as part of the policy of encouraging free enterprise, and Swinton was commissioned to explain these ideas to some of those who would be affected. Before seeing Sir Robert Menzies, he drafted an explanatory paper and asked the Research Department whether it 'puts what we want to say to him clearly and not too offensively?' A week later he reported to Butler that Menzies accepted the policy, but that his support could not be quoted 'as that would put him wrong with his Country Party who want the earth'.[5]

Three areas of policy that required definition were not so easy: denationalisation, the handling of the National Health Service, and housing. There was general agreement that it was practically impossible to return either coal or the railways to free enterprise, and an equal unanimity on denationalising road haulage and the iron and steel industry, but this left electricity and gas in a middle position. The 1950 manifesto had ducked this issue by stating merely that 'we shall hold ourselves free to decide the future of the Gas and Electricity Boards when we have had more experience of their working'. After the election, it was clear that something more definite would have to be done, at least to prepare for the reorganisation of the industries. A committee on electricity was therefore set up, as Arnold Gridley reported, 'which consists of Lord

Swinton and myself and two other former top leaders in the industry. Under us there is a working committee of four other men formerly occupying positions of high responsibility in the industry'. Gridley and Swinton both felt that time was needed to assess the effectiveness of the structures recently set up, but the news that a committee was in being threatened to force their hands. Proposals were submitted by Aims of Industry, but these were never even circulated to the committee for, as Swinton noted, 'the lines we are working on are more realistic and politically possible'. Herbert Williams though wrote to express his delight 'to learn yesterday that the problem of how to denationalise the Electric Supply Industry was now under consideration. I have always felt that the Industrial Charter was a most defeatist document on the subject'. It soon became clear that the industrialists who made up the committee were out of their political depth, and Swinton therefore intervened directly, asking that the Research Department should be put in touch with 'the working committee'. Swinton had hoped for a report that would localise control of the industries without any change of ownership, and Clarke told him that 'whether we denationalise or not, I think that the central feature must be to restore something very like the local Boards of Directors who really knew the areas'. However, the political pressures tended to submerge these good intentions. When an interim report was produced in October 1950 Oliver Poole (himself an exponent of denationalisation) sent it to a friend who knew the industry well and was surprised to learn that the proposals were impracticable – especially as his adviser 'is also a rather extreme right wing Conservative, so that I do not think Herbert Williams could accuse him of being a pink socialist'. The problem was balancing practicality (both industrial and political) against the demands of ideology; almost all Conservatives would have *liked* to denationalise both gas and electricity, but many Conservatives of all shades of Party opinion were convinced that it just could not be done. When another Conservative industrialist wrote to argue that denationalisation was too difficult on financial grounds, Swinton replied sadly that 'politically it would be more difficult *not* to do anything about denationalisation'. The inevitable result was another compromise, and neither gas nor electricity received even a mention in the 1951 manifesto. The subsequent Conservative Government took the pragmatic step of promoting reorganisations within the industries rather than denationalisation. Many Conservatives had been convinced like Oliver Poole by 1951 that denationalisation was 'unworkable and unrealistic'.[6]

In contrast, work on the National Health Service was done entirely behind the scenes by a small Research Department group whose findings were never published. Conservatives had accepted the principle of a National Health Service before the end of the War, but there was grave concern in the Party both over the form that it had eventually taken under Bevan's guidance, and over its mounting cost. The problem in 1950–51 was to find a Conservative line of policy that would be distinctive, that would keep costs under control, but would at the same time not expose the Party to charges that they would undo Labour's achievement. A committee was set up in January 1951 with Hugh Lucas-Tooth as chairman, Dr Charles Hill and Mrs Evelyn Emmet as its other members, and Michael Fraser as secretary; it was given a wide brief, to investigate the NHS with regard to its efficiency, the areas in which Conservative principles could be applied, and places where economies could be made. In the prevailing political climate, it is not surprising that the main emphasis was on the third of these aims. It was agreed at the very first meeting that the basic administrative structure should not be changed, pending the expected reform of local government (though the committee certainly did not expect that this would be 'pending' for twenty years), that it would be desirable nevertheless to encourage more local control, and that there must be a reform of budgetary methods. The committee met weekly at the House of Commons, with a brief circulated by Fraser in advance of each meeting. By March, the committee had recognised that possible economies could only be small, and was looking for them in the same areas that the Labour Government had already investigated.

It was eventually decided to lay down two alternative economy schemes. Plan One would save £25 million a year and would not go beyond savings that were already a matter of political debate – charges for prescriptions, teeth and spectacles, together with a small saving on the hospital budget. Plan Two had to be much more drastic in order to save £50 million a year – involving a large cut in hospital spending and the imposition of charges for residence in hospitals as well as charges for dental treatment. The committee made no recommendation between these two plans, but pointed out that Plan Two would constitute the largest possible saving that could be made 'without seriously limiting the services provided and destroying the valuable principle of universal access to examination and diagnosis, without direct payment, upon which the NHS was based'.[7] It was perhaps just as well that neither plan was published, and that the Churchill Government did not even feel obliged to implement the cuts of Plan One in full, for Labour continued to argue that the NHS would never be safe 'under the Tories'. In a time of financial stringency, any incoming Government needed plans for economies it might make in the fastest growing area of expenditure, and the Labour Government was making contingency plans rather like those of the Conservative Opposition, but this was an area where the existence of policy was best kept quiet.

When asked by a Bristol Conservative why the Party did not spell out precisely how it meant to apply the means test, Michael Fraser referred to an item already included in the *Campaign Guide* but resisted the suggestion that a prominent place should be found for the means test in the Party manifesto. When asked by Bernard Braine to provide for one of his constituents an analysis of the defects in the NHS, Fraser referred to an American report that was entirely critical, but also to 'a more sober and unbiassed account' in *The Practitioner*; Braine should be careful to point out 'the essential fact that the Conservatives are not in any way opposed to the principle of the National Health Service, but are merely critical of the present administration of that Service'. It may be noted in passing that the Department was becoming expert in the art of deflecting enquiries from constituents, so much so that it occasionally dictated terms to others in the Party. Copies of letters sent out by Churchill's secretaries were submitted to the Department for policy clearance on matters of detail, and a number of these attracted Peter Goldman's attention: 'I notice in reading through them that Mrs Cowper appears to be adopting the practice of saying that the matter is being referred to the appropriate Parliamentary Committee and that she will write again in due course. I wonder if you would be so good as to advise her that the promise to write again is ill-advised. If, in fact, there is a point of substance, we shall naturally write again, but the formula "I will refer this to the appropriate Parliamentary Committee who will consider it", is most useful very often for attempting to shelve the problems of particularly tiresome pressure groups, and I think that we should be careful not to abandon it in its pure form'.[8]

Despite the public arguments over denationalisation and the detailed work on health, it was undoubtedly housing that occasioned both the greatest publicity and the greatest amount of work. Housing had after all been one of the Labour Government's most conspicuous failures in an area that it had promised in 1945 to make 'one of the greatest and one of the earliest tests of a Government's real determination'. It had been an area on which Conservative candidates had found a very real response from the public at the 1950 election; a post-election survey by the Research Department indicated that although three-quarters of the Party's candidates had gone no further than the cautious proposals of the manifesto, every single Conservative candidate had made housing a main priority in his own election address.[9] The Research Department therefore put up to Butler in June 1950 an options paper which asked 'Do we wish to state a numerical target?' At that stage, the view of the ACP was that the political risks were too great to make a stated target desirable, but work went on with this in mind. A paper by Henry Brooke which urged a series of changes in the licensing system was criticised in the Department, and by other housing specialists in the Party, who all argued that what was needed was abolition of licensing – even though the local authorities could be expected to oppose such a radical step.[10] Things changed dramatically at the Party conference at Blackpool in October, when the delegates were outspoken in their demands for a clear pledge to build 300,000 houses a year. Butler has described the result:

> Lord Woolton, who was sitting beside me as the figure began to be picked up by representatives with the mounting excitement one customarily associates with an auction, whispered, '*Could* we build 300,000?' I replied, 'The question is *should* we? And the answer is: it will make it that much more difficult to restore the economy. But if you want to know if its technically feasible, ask David Clarke'. So the Director of the Research Department was consulted behind the scenes and opined (correctly) that the thing could be done, and Lord Woolton stepped forward to the front of the platform to declare in beaming surrender, 'This is magnificent.' And so in a sense it was.[11]

It would be fair to add that Clarke reinforced Butler's doubts as well as saying that 'the thing could be done'. The pledge was repeated *ex cathedra* by Churchill in his closing speech, though with the proviso that the implementation of the pledge must be subject to the rearmament programme, a proviso on which he of all people could scarcely be gainsaid. But now that the promise had been made, the Research Department set to work to prove its Director right. Butler knew at Blackpool, from a document recently sent to him, that the main difficulty in expanding the housebuilding programme would be in scarcity of resources, and it was this problem that now had to be quantified.

Nevertheless, it was clear that the pledge itself had made a considerable impact with the public. The Business Committee decided a fortnight after the Conference that housing would be its main ground for attack on the Government debate on the King's Speech; 'it was agreed that the Party's tactics in the debate should be to avoid cross-examination and to attempt to drive the Government into a position where they would claim that it was impossible to build more houses.'[12] In effect, the success of this tactic doubled the stakes, for it left clear water between the Parties on a purely technocratic question of competence; a great deal was now riding on David Clarke's advice. Since this was largely a technical matter, a group of research officers was set to work on the feasibility of the housing pledge, and reported in March 1951. It was probably only on reading this report that the Party leaders realised to what they had committed themselves; it was estimated that a programme to push the number of completions up to 300,000 would require (annually) an additional 200,000 standards of softwood (probably available, but requiring a large reallocation of shipping resources and foreign currency), 900,000 tons of cement (or a special increase of 9 per cent in the industry's total output), almost a million tons of coal (for making the cement and the bricks) a large but incalculable quantity of non-ferrous metals (in heavy demand for rearmament), and about 2,000 million bricks. The main problem was anticipated to be bricks, for what was needed was a rapid expansion back to the levels of output that the industry had achieved at the end of a prolonged boom in 1938, and there would need to be considerable capital investment and an increase in the labour force by at least 6,000.

The committee recommended the cutting of few corners (though it did suggest reducing the standard size of a three-bedroom house by about ten per cent, putting it back to pre-war levels) and they could suggest few sweeping changes in the role of government. They estimated that it would take at least fifteen years to end rent control and they did not accept the practicality of ending the system of building licences except by phasing it out over a period. However, 'after hearing the views of the leaders of the building industry', they were convinced that sufficient improvements in productivity could be achieved, both in construction and in the supply of resources, to make the target a real possibility, provided always that rearmament did not get in the way. Above all, they were convinced that private builders, given a chance to show what they could do and sufficient freedom to get on with it, would do most of the job for the Party. In the meantime, more work should be done on the problems of the brick industry, since the supply of bricks was likely to be the bottleneck in the whole plan.[13]

By no means all Conservatives were convinced of the wisdom of the housing pledge. Hugh Molson wrote to Butler in the summer of 1951 to urge that the target of 300,000 should be dropped, since it 'is not likely ever to be reached' and because it would use too much of the nation's resources. Butler shared Molson's doubts on the second ground, but he was comforted by the caveat about rearmament that Churchill had introduced at Blackpool. In February 1951, a paper on future economic prospects was prepared by the Research Department for the ACP: it pointed to the shortage of raw materials due to rearmament and to the consequent need to divert resources away from the home market since they could not be spared from export industries. This might necessitate an increase in taxation, but it would certainly make it difficult to fulfil the housing pledge early in the life of the next government. Alarmed by these gloomy tidings, Lord Salisbury wrote to urge that the electorate should be prepared in advance for the non-fulfilment of the housing pledge, and the Party's speakers should be warned not to give too many hostages to fortune:

> No doubt the postponement should only be for two or three years, if all goes as the writer of the paper hopes. During the last two years of our period of office we should be able to go ahead both with housing and with reduction of taxation; but the first three years inevitably will be pretty bleak. That can no doubt be defended owing to the needs of rearmament; but voters ought to be warned of the severe prospects ahead.

Butler accepted the reasoning behind this view, but insisted that 'we should certainly stick to our aim of building 300,000 houses a year; but we should consider this in terms of a target to be reached as soon as the rearmament programme permits'. The pledge, in the form in which Churchill had accepted it, made it clear that the target was definite, but the timing must remain flexible.[14] The ACP accepted this view, and the manifesto of 1951 stated that the Party would 'give housing a priority second only to national defence'. In the event, of course, the end of the Korean War and the improved economic situation provided a little more room for manoeuvre than was anticipated in 1951, and the target was achieved in the third year. There is no doubt though that the detailed preparations for the housing drive, carried out in the main before the Party returned to power, provided the basis on which the successful policy rested. In 1955, the manifesto proclaimed triumphantly that 'our Party's pledge to build 300,000 houses a year was derided by our opponents as impossible to fulfil. In fact nearly 350,000 were built last year, and at least as many are likely to be built this year'.[15] It was a policy success that did much to establish the reputation for competence on which Conservative electioneering in the 1950s rested.

However, back in 1951, the housing pledge still seemed to be a considerable gamble, and the Party's policy makers did not wish to see anything similar happen in other fields. As a result, the Research Department began to produce notes on policy in the spring of 1951, with a view to the urgent preparation of an election manifesto, but also with a view to providing the Party Conference in the autumn with clearer recommendations than had been forthcoming in 1950. Various drafts, entitled *Britain Strong and Free*, were produced by Clarke in May–June, with the approval of Butler, Eden and Macmillan. Salisbury, Crookshank, and Woolton were then consulted and approved the idea of publishing a document even if there should not be an election and Butler therefore circulated it to the Consultative Committee 'at Mr Eden's suggestion'. On the same day, he wrote to Churchill, who was abroad, in order to explain what was being done and why, a letter that obviously anticipated the Leader's reluctance to publish:

> You may well ask why we need publish a paper at all. It was the view of Mr. Eden, Lord Woolton, Sir David Maxwell-Fyfe, Mr. Harold Macmillan and Captain Crookshank . . . that a general statement on the lines of the enclosed would help guide the Party Conference which meets in the first week of October at Scarborough. After discussion, Lord Woolton felt it would be unwise to let the Conference go this year without any guidance at all. You will remember that last year we published nothing and the Conference made its own policy by acclamation. Though this latter method is hallowed by having been used in the Greek city states, I think it would lead to irresponsibility if proceeded with for a second year in succession.

On this basis, the agreement of Churchill was secured, and although the document bore on every draft the legend 'this is not an election programme', it was in fact constructed with a general election or a Party Conference as alternatives. The document was hammered into shape during July and August by Michael Fraser (who had just taken over from David Clarke) and Peter Goldman, and by Selwyn Lloyd (in Butler's absence on holiday).

The final draft was complete and sent to the printers early in September, for publication at the beginning of October, but at this stage the Party was overtaken by the Government's unexpected decision to call an election for late October. Churchill, who had taken no part in the drafting of the policy document, was anxious that the manifesto should be short, forceful and cautious about the future. He therefore issued as the Party manifesto an entirely new document, much shorter than usual, and very much his own work; the *Sunday Dispatch* noted that 'the imprint of Mr Churchill's most admirable style and thought are unmistakeable', the *Sunday Times* detected 'Churchillian prose' in the manifesto, and *Reynolds News* wrote of 'Mr Churchill's manifesto. I say 'his' because when it comes to deciding policy there is no nonsense about democracy in the Tory Party. The 'Leader', i.e. Mr Churchill, has the sole power to decide'. In practice though, the policy points in Churchill's manifesto were all drawn from the lengthier document that had been drawn up by his subordinates, and it was made abundantly clear that the full statement of policy would be published in due course. *Britain Strong and Free* was thus published as intended in early October, but had now become the main policy statement for the election, for the press had tended to dismiss Churchill's manifesto as a mere prelude to the real thing. As a policy statement, it differed little from *This is the Road* or *The Right Road for Britain*, though as the third full length statement in three years, it was hardly to be expected that it would contain many novelties. Its tone was certainly more libertarian than earlier statements, though this reflected more a change of public mood than of Party policy. At the Board of Trade and the Treasury, Harold Wilson and Hugh Gaitskell had already begun the wholesale scrapping of controls that was to be a feature of the first years of Conservative Government after 1951; Conservatives campaigned with the slogan 'Set the People Free', but this reflected more a change of rhetoric than of policy; there was certainly no chance in 1951 (as in 1949) that liberty would be inadvertently left out of the manifesto.[16]

During the election campaign of 1951, the Research Department built on the experience of 1950, improving methods where problems had arisen. The Questions of Policy Committee was made up of exactly the same people, except that Fraser replaced Clarke; this time 103 rulings on policy were made at nineteen meetings. Further detailed preparations were made for election broadcasts, with an advance programme mapped out for the whole series, and through Fraser the Department advised on the content of all the broadcasts. Strict rules were also laid down in advance, so that the office would not be swamped with requests for information as had happened in 1950. No press enquiries would be dealt with by the Research Department, and all press telephone calls would be referred directly to the press department at Central Office. Other enquiries would only be accepted from candidates, agents and constituency officers, unless what was involved was only a simple question that could be answered at once from a Party publication. Steps had already been taken to route many of these routine enquiries to the Area Offices in the first instance, and Area Publicity Officers had been appointed to filter out the routine questions from those which had points of real substance. Nevertheless, something like four thousand requests for information were dealt with in the three weeks of the campaign, most of these involving special work to find the information that was required. For this purpose, the office was manned in each section from 8.30 am until late in the evening, daily, with skeleton staffs in the office even on Sundays. One innovation that made these hours acceptable and which has been repeated at elections since 1951, was the employment of caterers to provide meals in the office for those working late. Just one officer and one secretary would be in the Department on polling day, by which time the Party's need for policy advice was at an end and so officers could be better engaged in more traditional electioneering in the constituencies; the Department then re-opened at its normal hours from the Monday after polling day, with all officers given two additional days leave to compensate for the extra effort involved in the campaign. This pattern too has remained largely unchanged since 1951. The thoroughness of Fraser's administrative preparations may be gauged from the letters that he provided for the Party Chairman to send out to those who had helped in Central Office and the Research Department; four different drafts were produced covering all the possible results of the election from a large Labour win to a big Conservative majority. In the event, the third draft which celebrated a narrow Conservative victory was used.[17]

When the Party returned to office in October 1951, there were no officers of the Research Department who had experience of working with a Conservative Government, and indeed few officers had more than a year or two's experience of the Research Department itself. The pattern established in 1950 and 1951 has been followed ever since: the majority of desk officers work in the Department for only a few years and terms of service tend to coincide with the timetable of Parliaments. The average period for which desk officers have worked for the Department cannot be more than four or five years, and resignations have always tended to be concentrated in the aftermath of an election. Thus, in the early 1950s for the first, but by no means the last time, it became necessary to rebuild the Department for a new Parliament. The short period of service was in part a tribute to the Department's success in recruiting as officers men who were destined for higher things, but the other side of this coin was that they tended to move to those higher things fairly quickly. Another reason was undoubtedly the rate of pay. Officers when first appointed in the early 1950s were paid about £500 a year, not an unreasonable salary for a first job. If the officer proved suitable, this could rise quickly enough to something like £1,000, but there were only three tiers in the hierarchy and little prospect of promotion beyond the first. It therefore made sense for an aspiring politician to spend a few years in the Department while relatively young, to buy his experience at a relatively low rate of remuneration; but it could not offer good career prospects in the long term for more than a few. Nevertheless, for some who were unable to find a seat in Parliament or had never wanted one, the Department also offered a chance to make contacts in the political, literary or industrial worlds on which a subsequent career could be built.

Another attraction the Department offered to its predominantly young staff was a highly enjoyable way to spend their first years in employment; something of the atmosphere of a University existed in Old Queen Street, not only because of methods of work which were akin to those of academic research, but also because the juxtaposition of so many clever young men recreated the style of a graduate common room. When one aspiring officer was asked at his interview by Peter Goldman whether he would prefer to save his mother or the most brilliant philosopher of the age if both were trapped in the burning house, he replied that he had known too many brilliant philosophers in his undergraduate days and that he would save his mother every time: 'I was offered a job in the Department at once'. At the same interview the candidate said that he was not entirely sure that he was a Conservative, and he was told by Michael Fraser that a year or two in the Research Department would be a good way of making up his mind. Methods of recruitment varied widely; some came straight from university, including the one mentioned above who was invited to apply for a job by Lord Woolton when he met him at the Oxford Union; others were recommended by sympathetic university dons and a few merely answered advertisements; a few came into the Department after service abroad in the Colonial or Indian Civil Service; and one transferred his employment from Swinton Conservative College because the monastic conditions of Swinton did not allow for staff tutors who were married.[18] The turnover of staff was accepted as part of the way in which the Department must work, but it reached disturbing proportions at times in the 1950s; insofar as this depended on the salary structure, little could be done, for the Department was always short of money. The reorganisation of 1948 had greatly enlarged the Department, and it had left it entirely dependent on the Party Treasurers for support. With the Party back in power, the Department naturally enjoyed a lower priority in the calculations of the Treasurers.

The Department's budget fell by ten per cent between 1950 and 1953, despite increasing costs; although it then began to rise again, it barely kept pace with inflation. In 1957, it was calculated that the budget had fallen from £59,000 in 1949 to about £55,000, despite a rise of fifty per cent in the retail price index. The effect of this was economies in staff and other expenses. Jobs could not always be filled when they became vacant, and the number of officers therefore fell from thirty-one at the time of the 1951 election, to twenty-five in 1955. This was planned to be the 'peace-time' establishment but numbers actually fell as low as twenty-two in 1957. The number of publications bought for the library was drastically cut back, fees for literary work could no longer be paid to outsiders, and publications had to be more carefully scrutinised to avoid losses.[19] Nevertheless, the Department still managed to attract bright young men to its service, and still managed to pick those who were destined for policital careers of their own. Among those who joined at this stage were Lord Balniel, John Biggs-Davison, Peter Tapsell, Richard Sharples, Anothony Berry, Paul Dean and Gordon Campbell, as well as James Douglas and Brendon Sewill who became Directors in due course.

The need at the end of 1951 was not just to weld a lot of bright but inexperienced recruits into a working team, but also to find a working relationship with the Churchill Government. The issue which required immediate decision was whether or not the Department should continue to service Parliamentary Committees, now that they were composed entirely of back-benchers and might be expected on occasion to be critical of Conservative Ministers. Fraser wrote to the Chief Whip a fortnight after the election, sending as requested a list of the back-benchers who would make suitable chairmen, and also asking for a ruling on the role that the Department should play. The matter was urgent 'as the Scottish and Agriculture Committees have already been getting in touch with their previous secretaries here. As I mentioned when we spoke, while there are certain advantages in providing secretaries from here, such secretaries will have to be given very careful terms of reference, since, though they can clearly provide members of the committees with factual information for debates, there must be no briefing from the point of view of policy or comment'. It was decided that officers should continue as secretaries, except that they should no longer take any part in drafting amendments to Bills. Fraser recalled that 'the only change otherwise was one of emphasis. Parliamentary briefing became a less onerous aspect of the Department's work, while on the other hand publications and information and general help to Ministers and the Central Office in putting over the Government line became more important and time-consuming'. The number of briefs provided thus fell sharply, to well under a hundred a year (compared with over two hundred when the Party had been in opposition), while there was an equivalent increase in publications and drafts for speeches.[20]

On policy, the Department had to feel its way towards a *modus vivendi* with the Government and this actually became more difficult as time went on, for with time the Department was more and more distanced from the thinking of Ministers. In the first months, relations were close: Butler asked for suggestions from Fraser on items to be included in the King's Speech of 1951, and detailed plans on housing were sent to Harold Macmillan in November to carry over the work of opposition into a policy in power. In January 1952, Fraser promised to send Woolton detailed plans on state trading and on town and country planning, 'in a form suitable for circulation to a Cabinet Committee'. In March, a list of Conservative commitments on labour policy were sent to Monckton at the Ministry of Labour, together with a request that he should keep the Department in touch with his thinking. One of the Ministers who was most helpful was Harold Macmillan, who appreciated the Department's new position. In April, Fraser wrote to him for advice on requests for briefs by Conservative Peers on housing; 'we must of course avoid putting into such a brief matter that might be at all embarrassing to the Government'. Macmillan replied specifying which lines should and which should not be pursued, giving Fraser 'just the guidance we need', and the Peers thus got a brief that was already cleared with the Ministry of Housing. A month later, the Department was quick to warn Macmillan of an error of detail in one of his Parliamentary speeches; he had wrongly attributed the idea of the 'People's House' standard to Bevan, instead of to Dalton, and he should take care to see that the error was corrected before the bound volume of *Hansard* went to press.

In February 1954, Macmillan agreed to make a statement on the progress of the housing drive in a speech at Lowestoft, and arranged for collaboration between the Department and his Ministry to secure maximum publicity. Two months later, he wrote to Fraser to warn of possible political difficulties that would come when the Repairs and Rents Bill became law in a few weeks time:

> There are sure to be some rascally landlords who will try to get away with parts of the Bill, and frighten their tenants into doing things they cannot make them do. All the black sheep will be our black sheep, unless we are careful. So I think our Members and Candidates and Agents should be given a short explanatory memorandum to keep, properly printed and clear.

Other Ministers used the Department too: when Butler wanted a detailed costing of Labour's new social programme in 1954, it was to the Research Department rather than to the Treasury that he turned, and he also asked for a political brief on possible tax changes before the preparation of his budgets; when Iain Macleod wanted to oppose the suggestion of differential housing subsidies, he decided that the matter was too politically sensitive to be handled through the normal Ministerial or Cabinet channels and circulated a paper to his colleagues from Old Queen Street instead. Of course, not all Ministers were so co-operative and some interpreted their role as leaving no room for collaboration with the Party machine. After Peter Goldman had worked up a brief on the options open to the Government on broadcasting policy, a copy was sent on to Butler with a note explaining that it had 'been written without any knowledge of the Government's decision, and will not be issued until the Government statement has been made and will be amended in the light of it'. As it turned out, the decision of the Government to launch an experiment with commercial television was closely in accord with Goldman's advice, and so his draft did not have to be substantially revised before it was published in defence of the Government's decision, but the agreement was somewhat fortuitous. When he was asked to comment on Ernest Marples' paper on *Research and a Five Year Parliament*, in January 1955, Fraser noted that all the necessary machinery existed; the problem was that the Government was reluctant to use it, either for working out the detail of agreed policy, or for throwing up ideas to fill policy gaps in the Government's programme.[21]

In these rather trying circumstances, the Research Department could only indulge in research in limited areas: in a general programme drawn up by Fraser in December 1952, it was laid down that there should be no work on items covered in the 1951 manifesto, except at the specific request of Ministers or where there were good reasons to believe that the proposal in question would not have been implemented by the next election. The Department should not duplicate the work done by Government departments, but it should fix its attention on more distant horizons, looking at broad themes with a view to the policies that would be needed in the future.[22] The difficulty with this approach was that the amalgamation of secretariat and research duties in 1948 had ended the existence of the only group committed solely to long-term thinking; with the reduction of staff after 1951, the immediate demands of Parliament and publications had to take precedence and long-term research tended to be forgotten. The Department was also heavily burdened with its routine work for the Party. The ACP met about four times a year and needed a number of papers for each meeting, and the Research Department continued to write a lot of the words published by the CPC, though less than before 1951.

There was also a responsibility to the Treasurers at Central Office, helping them explain to the Party's industrial contributors how and why policy was developing. This task fell largely to David Dear and the economic section in general, taking up a lot of their time and their correspondence. It was not always easy to explain policy while having no hand in shaping it, and the Party's industrial supporters were not always understanding, as Dear suggested when asked to draft a reply to complaints (of the lack of businessmen in Government) from an industrial subscriber in February 1956:

> First, may I make a candid comment, which of course should not be passed on. We suffer quite enough as a Party by being branded as the Party of the capitalists and big business without having a number of business men in important cabinet posts. Moreover, there is nothing to prevent business men from reaching the highest posts in Government, provided they are willing to go through the hard school of political life. It is understandable that they should prefer to make their careers in business with its much greater financial rewards, but they cannot expect to have it both ways. As you cannot very well say this, I suggest a soft answer on the following lines . . .[23]

Two examples may be cited to illustrate the Department's sensitive position between the Government and the Party. In July 1954, breaking new ground, Reginald Maudling went on BBC television to answer questions sent in by viewers on Government policy. Inevitably, more questions were sent in than could be answered on the air, and it was therefore decided that the Research Department should draft replies to all of the remaining six hundred questions and send them to the Treasury for Maudling to sign. This mammoth task was completed in four days as an exercise in good public relations; a few days later the Treasury sent round a bill for £2.15.0 for the headed stationery used for the letters.

Peter Tapsell's experience with the Parliamentary Committee on social services was rather different. He was instructed, as Secretary to the Committee, to write a letter to the press to make a case against increased remuneration for doctors in the National Health Service, to which the Conservative MPs on the committee were opposed but which the Conservative Government was thought to be considering. When he refused, the Chairman made an official complaint to the Chief Whip who passed it on to Fraser, and Tapsell was duly 'carpeted' by his boss. He pointed out that there were three reasons to justify his refusal to sign the letter: as the desk officer working on social services, it was his responsibility to keep up good relations with the BMA, which would not be helped by a public repudiation of their case; it was more than likely that the Government were going to give way to the doctors anyway, so little would be gained by backing the losing side; and as a man who had political ambitions of his own, Tapsell should not be expected to make a public pronouncement that went wholly against his own views. It was perfectly reasonable to expect a desk officer to accept instructions and write to order when acting anonymously, but it was a wholly different thing when he was asked to 'break surface' in the press. Fraser accepted these reasons, though he also made it clear that with the little more tact the whole problem might well have been avoided.[24]

The most continuous and comprehensive work on policy proceeded from the need to present the Party's and Government's collective view, and for this a major innovation was the Liaison Committee set up when the Party returned to power. This originated in a suggestion from John Wyndham to Michael Fraser, passed on to Butler and then pressed on the Party leaders by Fraser. Butler suggested that Lord Swinton should be Chairman of this 'clearing house' committee, since he was the Minister responsible for the Government's own information services, and he was eventually persuaded to accept the job. The terms of reference were simply 'to give guidance to Members of Parliament, candidates and others on the interpretation of Government policy and to take such action as, in their opinion, is necessary to sustain public confidence in the Conservative Administration'. For the Research Department, its purpose was more specific, as a letter from Fraser to Butler in November 1951 suggests:

Both Central Office and the Research Department are now unable to deal expeditiously with Socialist propaganda, and the questions from our own supporters which inevitably result from it, because no regular channel exists, as it did before the General Election, between our own Front Bench and ourselves. As a result, there is an inevitable time lag during which the Socialists are able to make the whole of their case in the Press and elsewhere unchallenged. I am sure that this is doing us a great deal of harm in the constituencies, and that if allowed to continue it will adversely affect by-election results and the municipal elections in the Spring.

As well as Swinton, the Committee included Heathcoat-Amory as Deputy Chairman, John Hare (or Lady Maxwell-Fyfe as an alternate – they were joint Vice-chairmen of the Party), Angus Maude (Director, CPC), Mark Chapman-Walker (Chief Publicity Officer, Central Office), Richard Greville (PA to the Party Chairman), Michael Fraser (Director, CRD), Edward Heath (Whips' Office) and John Wyndham (secretary). It met weekly while Parliament was sitting, so that 374 meetings were held during the first ten years, pulling together all the Party's publicity and information services; Swinton was succeeded as Chairman by Heathcoat-Amory and later by Butler.

A good start, carrying over the close relationship between politicians and Party organisers that had existed in opposition, was followed by a gradual drifting apart, not because Ministers became more secretive, but because they – as always – found it increasingly difficult to remember that everyone in the Party hierarchy did not know what they knew themselves. By 1955, the usefulness of the Committee had declined so far as to make a general shake-up necessary. David Dear, as secretary, wrote to Heathcoat-Amory, now Chairman, urging that he write to Ministers to remind them of Lord Swinton's original intentions and their subsequent neglect:

On 2nd January 1952, Lord Swinton wrote to Ministers announcing the setting up of the Liaison Committee. In his letter he suggested ways in which Ministers could help the Committee to ensure that Government policy was effectively interpreted through the Party Organisation, and that Socialist attacks on Government policy were speedily countered.

In particular, he suggested that it would be a great help to the Committee, and sometimes useful to Ministers, if when a Minister was going to issue to the Press an announcement on a matter of policy or on a subject likely to have political reactions . . . liaison could be effected through Ministers' private secretaries (or P.P.S.s) and the secretary of the Liaison Committee. This system worked well in the difficult period of

> 1952, but with easier conditions it has tended to lapse. . . . Early information of this kind would also enable us to keep prominently before us the need to ensure that, whenever possible, minor measures with some popular appeal should be timed to coincide with any hard measures that the Government may have to take.

It will be clear from this that the Liaison Committee was working less well by 1955–6, that its effectiveness depended very much on the influence and publicity-consciousness of its Chairman, and on the degree of Ministerial co-operation.[25]

The same pattern can be traced in the Party's weightier publications, moving from an easy position in the aftermath of the 1951 election to an impossible one by the middle of the same Parliament. The first task of the Research Department was to report on the transfer of power and to reassure those who had expected that a Conservative Government would fulfil its pledges in weeks. A weighty brief was circulated to Conservative MPs in April 1952 on 'The First Six Months', stressing the problems facing the Government and the need for time before judging its performance. This was based on a 'Black Book' compiled in the Department over the previous winter and showing a 'survey of the situation at the time the Socialists were defeated'.[26] By the summer of 1952, it was felt desirable to press ahead with a pamphlet for wider circulation, and Butler urged Swinton to agree that it should be done 'through our own political, rather than the Government machine' for material provided by Government departments tended to be 'contradictory, voluminous and not always convincing'. This was duly approved by Churchill on Swinton's proposition, and the Research Department set to work to produce it in time for the Party conference of October 1952. After discussion at the Liaison Committee on 31 July, it was agreed that the document should become 'a general statement of what we found, what we have done about it, and what immediately lies ahead'; it should be about the same length as *Britain Strong and Free* (about 10,000 words) 'though it will not of course be a policy statement', as Fraser reported.

Both the Cabinet and the ACP saw a first draft in August, produced by Dear and Goldman and entitled *We Shall Win Through* – with a subtitle 'The Frist Year'. After extensive revisions, Dear wrote to Central Office to urge the very careful preparation of the press for the sort of document being produced:

> I do not know what arrangements you are considering for publicity. We feel here that it would do harm if the document were presented as in any

sense a statement of policy or represented as new Conservative thinking. As a Progress Report it may well get quite a favourable reception from economists and political commentators. But they will be very disappointed if they are given the impression that it is anything more than a Progress Report.

Butler hoped to meet these anticipated press critics by giving the document a concluding section that would emphasise the philosophical difference between Conservative and Socialism as shown by the evidence of both in Government: 'I really attach importance to summarizing the philosophy at the end, and I imagine I shall see a draft of that (Realism, Encouragement of Success, Help to those in need)'. After talking it over with Swinton, Butler reported that 'we both agree that the document needs a summarised ending which brings the whole together . . . You cannot foreshadow the next Queen's Speech and you only need one or 1½ pages. You can tie the tendencies together'.From a very different viewpoint, Henry Brooke argued that 'my criticism of practically all Conservative documents is that their language is quite remote from the way in which ordinary people, whom we have to win to our side, think about these questions in so far as they affect them', though he accepted that this was of less importance in a document for the Party at its Conference. The difficulties of putting into the same document elements of political philosophy and language understood by the man in the street were probably insuperable, but *We Shall Win Through* was reasonably well accepted by Conference at Scarborough. A few later criticisms were indignantly refuted by Fraser; when complaints were made about the lack of consultation over the Scottish section of the document. Fraser was able to show that the Scottish Office had been asked for advice in detail on several points and that the whole draft had been approved by the Secretary of State; when Lord Lytton complained about the lack of content in the document, Fraser wrote to Cohen that 'We certainly should make no apologies for this publication, which was personally approved by the Prime Minister, which had a good press and satisfactory sales, (53,000)'.[27]

The Party had thus produced a major document for four successive years, but in 1953 the sequence came to a sudden and expensive halt. In January 1953, the ACP decided on Butler's proposal that there should be a publication for the next Party Conference, based this time on 'the return to freedom and hence on the differences between the parties'. Fraser clearly anticipated difficulties this time, for he wrote to Butler to ask for a ruling on the exact relationship between

Government policy and that of the Party, 'as we do not have the clear distinction between Government policy and Party policy which the Labour Party have'. By early March, the timetable and outline of the document were ready. It would be produced in three parts:

(a) a review of the Government's record – diffused authorship in the Research Department;

(b) 'a statement of the fundamental cleavage between Conservatism and Socialism' – to be drafted by Goldman;

(c) outline of the Government's future plans – 'will require the cooperation of Ministers'.

Various preliminary drafts, entitled *On with the Job* were succeeded by a first draft of *Onward in Freedom*, very different from the original plan, and sent to Butler early in May. Section (b) had now been abandoned altogether, though a philosophical introduction would be provided for (c), and (c) had become far more general; it could only be 'tighter' with much more help from Government departments.

This whole plan was then abandoned and a new document, still called *Onward in Freedom* was scheduled for publication in September, after the Labour Party had published its expected document; this would now be organised in three sections on home affairs, economics and foreign policy, with the record, the philosophy and the future all written into each section. It is perhaps not entirely coincidental that in the years when commentators were detecting 'Butskellism' as both Labour and Conservative policy, the Research Department showed a marked reluctance to write at length on 'the fundamental cleavage' between the Parties. The new document went out to the ACP, to the Cabinet and to other Conservatives early in June, with a disappointing response that may be typified in the reaction of Enoch Powell:

> The title is the most sick-making thing I have seen for a long time. Of the various sections, I regard 'Home Affairs' as on the whole good and sound. On the other hand, 'Economic Progress' and 'The World Scene' seem to me so weak that unless they can be considerably toughened, they are worth very little. This is the inevitable result of attempting to treat each of the three parts with approximately equal weight. In Home Affairs it is quite easy to make a record of achievement sound as though it is a policy for the future; this is not so easy in foreign and economic affairs. . . . You cannot write on this sort of subject without giving hostages to fortune. Why need we?

There was general dissatisfaction with the title *Onward in Freedom*, but the ACP decided to press on with preparations for publication. When the second main draft was circulated early in August, the tide of opinion swung more heavily against publication. Heathcoat-Amory, Swinton, Thorneycroft, Stuart, and Poole all wrote to urge that there should be no document at all published, for it seemed impossible to write one that included very much of a future programme; as Oliver Poole wrote, 'if it is decided to publish this pamphlet, the public will assume that it is an alternative statement to the Labour Party policy, and I think that we will be much criticised for the lack of future intentions'. Swinton also argued that it 'would be a mistake to commit ourselves to having a paper of policy every year, and I think if we have another this year we really are almost committed to it as a regular habit'. Iain Macleod merely wrote 'Include me with the Ministers who doubt if we should publish at all'.

Throughout July and August, while the issue was being discussed, the detailed work of drafting and other preparations for publication went on; Butler told Goldman on 3 August that if asked questions by members of the ACP 'You should say to *all*, no decision yet taken finally to publish. One or two ministers have expressed doubts, but I (RAB) think it may be useful to workers etc. – it may not break new ground, but it helps consolidate'. But Butler's position was not quite so clear as this suggests and he naturally did not want to go too far out on a limb; when Fraser put to him an options paper, outlining all the arguments both for and against publication, Butler merely noted on it 'I approve yr. views, RAB'. To Goldman on 4 August he wrote 'I confess I am in two minds about the value of publishing. I feel certain that this question ought to be put squarely to Woolton . . . He ought to give the opinion of Central Office to Sir Winston Churchill'. In the meantime, Goldman could tell Ministers and ACP members who asked that the issue would be settled by the Cabinet at the end of August. It was eventually decided *not* to publish by the Cabinet on 25 August, and Butler then wrote both to ACP and to the junior Ministers to give them the news; on behalf of 'my cabinet colleagues' and in words that made it clear that he was not entirely convinced of the wisdom of the decision, he explained that it was felt that the Government's record was self-explanatory, that the Labour Party's policy statement had been 'a damp squib' which did not need an answer, that there was no chance of producing a policy statement and yet it would have to be more than a progress report so there was a danger of failing to produce either, and finally that the Party should not come to rely on publishing every year. The decision meant a loss of several thousand pounds, which could hardly be spared when the Research Department budget was so stretched, and it also meant the waste of a great deal of work and time; nevertheless, as Fraser wrote to Woolton, 'we all felt that the decision taken was the right one in the circumstances'.[28] In 1953 Butler was in a difficult position, member of a Cabinet which did not want a policy statement published and of a Government whose members would not provide the information to make one viable, and at the same time Chairman of the Advisory Committee on Policy that was demanding publication. 1953 demonstrated that when a Conservative Government was in office, not only did the Cabinet have the final say in what went out as Party policy, but only the Cabinet could decide whether to publish anything at all. But essentially, when in office, Government action and the Queen's speech each November is enough to carry things along; in opposition, the Party must publish from time to time to show that it exists and can provide an alternative.

The decision to interrupt the annual series of publications in 1953 made sense at the time, but it also interrupted the sequence of policy preparations that would have led on to the next General Election. Hence, a few weeks after the cancellation of *Onward in Freedom*, Butler decided to set up a small group of Ministers and Research Department officers to plan for the next election. This body began entirely as an in-house group at the Research Department but was then widened to include Henry Brooke and Iain Macleod (the most research-conscious of Ministers and the most faithful of the Department's old boys). It was decided to call them the Research Study Group; Brooke would take the chair, Macleod would be the main link with Ministers, and the other members would be Fraser, Goldman, and Dear, with Michael Graham of the Research Department as Secretary. It was agreed at the first meeting that the election would not be before October 1954 and more probably later, but that if no election were called in 1954 the RSG would save its material for the coming manifesto rather than use it in a policy document for the Party Conference. Butler would be asked to write to Ministers asking for cooperation, but it was later felt that this would be too formal an introduction for what was after all an entirely informal body; instead, Macleod would write to Ministers to ask them what Bills they expected to present over the next two years. Between October 1953 and April 1955 the RSG held thirty-two meetings, approximately once a fortnight while Parliament was sitting. Themes for a manifesto were discussed in February 1954 and a skeleton draft was in preparation in May; this was kept up to date over the Autumn and provided the first draft of the Party's actual manifesto in the following January. The RSG was kept in touch with the progress of policy work at occasional dinners at the House of Commons, to which all chairman of Parliamentary Committees were invited, and Macleod reported regularly on what was happening within the Government.

In February 1954 the existence of the RSG was revealed to the ACP, which asked it to make a special study of local government, fuel policy and industrial relations; as ordinary research reports came up from the Department, they were referred first to the RSG and only afterwards to the ACP for approval. Finally, in September 1954, Sir Derek Walker-Smith, chairman of the 1922 Committee, was coopted onto the RSG for the run up to the election, so as to keep it in touch with opinion on the back bench. By these means, the RSG kept in touch with all the groups in the Party and developed a manifesto that was more than just a celebration of what had been done already, but still in touch with what the Government was doing. With Macleod present there was no danger that the electoral implications of the RSG's work would ever be forgotten. After a discussion on women's issues, Macleod stressed the importance of woman's votes to the Party, and suggested that a sample survey should be commissioned from a professional organisation 'to discover what women really wanted from an election statement'. In October 1954 Macleod urged the need 'to become increasingly selective in our policy and do more to help the middle classes' and the next meeting was entirely devoted to the discussion of tax reliefs, site values, private medical care and other issues of interest to upper middle-class voters. When the skeleton manifesto was discussed, Macleod submitted a paper questioning the 'E-value' of some of its ideas, and this search for electoral value remained a criterion of the RSG's work throughout.[29]

On 16 March 1955, Fraser suggested that it was time to move the organisation over to an election footing: 'We cannot afford to exclude the possibility of an early election, and the manifesto *must* go to press 5½ weeks before polling day'. This suggestion was no doubt encouraged by a directive received from Central Office a few days earlier, instructing all parts of the Organisation to take part in an 'Election Exercise' with hypothetical polling dates on 19 or 26 May. The Research Department had argued the case for delaying the election until the Autumn, but Fraser recognised the signal from Woolton and all preparations went ahead on the assumption that the election would be on 19 May; it was in fact on 26 May[30]. A great rush was involved to get the *Campaign Guide* out in time, but its publication was brought forward by a fortnight to 21 April as a result of the advance notice of the election. Butler was too heavily involved in the preparation of his fourth budget to take his usual part in the completion of the manifesto. The document went through the usual process of intensive re-drafting in March and April, being edited by Fraser and Goldman, and with Macleod putting some very specific questions to Ministers on their Departments' future plans in order to fill gaps that had been left to this late stage. Finally, Macleod stood in for Butler at meetings with Committee Chairmen and with non-Cabinet Ministers to outline the manifesto to them before it was published. A strange hiatus occurred over the name, when it was alleged that 'For Peace and Prosperity' would be used as a slogan by the Labour Party at the election; the title was therefore changed only a few days before it was published as *United for Peace and Progress* on 21 April. The thoroughness of the Party's preparations showed in another way too. A copy of Labour's manifesto (approved but not yet published) was annotated and provided for Eden's use at the press conference that launched the Tory one.

The 1955 General Election was probably the easiest of all the post-war elections for the Conservative Party, in that the Opposition was neither ready for the dissolution nor able to make any impact with its policies when it came, while the Conservatives (as an official Party report to Eden put it) 'took the initiative at the beginning of the campaign and held it throughout'. At one of the earliest meetings of the RSG it had been noted that there was a distinct decline in the electorate's interest in 'political matters' and a corresponding increase in their interest in material ones, an assumption that informed all of the Party's electoral preparations. Hence, as Brendon Sewill reported for the economic section after the election, 'the main division between the Parties in the field of economics was between prosperity and fair shares. Neither side denied the other's accusations. Socialists said prosperity is not being fairly shared, while Conservatives just said that people were better off and left it at that'. This winning position was rammed home through all of the Party's publicity machinery. It was the theme of Eden's election broadcast, which was drafted in the Research Department and hardly changed by the Prime Minister, and the theme of most of the thirty-eight leaflets drafted or checked by the Department for Central Office.[32] Other work on speeches, newspaper articles and notes for candidates went on much as in 1951, but the letters received after the campaign suggest that the general level was rather better. John Biggs-Davison, who had recently left the Department to become a candidate himself wrote to Fraser to say that 'Speaking as regimental to Staff Officer of the campaign, I should say that the Research Department was even more the master of events than in the last General Election. *Daily Notes* had the answers before the questions were asked!' Edward Heath wrote that he 'thought it an improvement on '50 and '51. I liked having so many points of policy sent to me in addition to answers to questionnaires as such. Its contents were admirable and the machine delivered them unfailingly. I'm sure it makes an enormous difference to candidates knowing that they are backed up by this sort of service'. When the dust had settled, Butler wrote to all the officers of the Department: he had heard nothing but praise for the Department and he wanted them to realise the scale of what had been done – 'By winning the election with an increased majority, the Party has made history, and destroyed for ever the myth that 1945 represented the beginning of some irreversible revolution.'[33]

These optimistic words rang true enough in the Summer of 1955 but they did not encourage any resting on laurels. The Department was perhaps more conscious than most in the Party of the fragility of success and the problems that loomed ahead. For example, one issue that had not really played any part in the campaign was immigration, a case that perfectly illustrates some of the frustrations of being a Party research officer. In November 1954, Fraser had written to Swinton for the information of the Liaison Committee to tell him that 'letters which reach this office show that many people are becoming increasingly worried about the constant influx of coloured immigrants, mainly from the West Indies'; similar letters were reaching Conservative MPs, and the parliamentary committees on labour and on commonwealth affairs had recently discussed the issue. However, none of the drafts of the manifesto suggested any change of policy – or indeed the need for a policy at all. When the manifesto was launched, the Department produced as usual comprehensive notes for the Leader to use in answering questions. Amongst the section on foreign policy was hidden a note on immigration, with advice on how Eden should answer a question on the subject if it arose:

COLOURED IMMIGRATION
This should not be treated as a colour problem since an influx of people from any country could give rise to similar difficulties in both employment and housing.

If questions continued, Eden could announce that the law allowing equal entry to the UK for British subjects was one that 'we would not lightly change', but that there must be a ceiling on total numbers and so the Government would 'keep an eye on immigration'. Thus the notes insisted on regarding the problem as one of jobs and houses, even though it was an issue that was always handled in the Department by the officer specialising in Commonwealth affairs, not by an officer from the home affairs section. The officer in question wrote in his report on the election that coloured immigration was the topic that raised the most interest among those that he covered. When the Liaison Committee met in July 1955 to review the issues thrown up by the campaign, with Heathcoat-Amory now in the chair, immigration was mentioned repeatedly as a topic forced on candidates by the electorate. David Dear drafted for Heathcoat-Amory a letter to Alan Lennox-Boyd, the Colonial Secretary:

> As a result of the discussion I was asked to draw your attention to the considerable feeling that still exists about colonial immigration and the apparent uneven operation of the immigration laws. I have no doubt that this is all old history to you and very much in your mind, but as it is clearly still exercising the minds of our people we thought it worthwhile reminding you of it.

The Department had thus come full circle in less than a year. In July 1955 as in November 1954 it was seeking to draw the Government's attention to the problem that was coming, while in the Spring of 1955 it had to break off to assist the Government in explaining to the press and the electorate that no problem really existed.[34] It was of course a regular feature of Departmental life, warning the Government and defending it on the same issue against outside attackers.

The Department's cautious approach to the Parliament elected in 1955 emerged from early plans for long-term Party publicity. Central Office put forward a 'Three Year Plan for Propaganda Policy' in June 1955, hoping thereby that the impetus of success could be carried on. On behalf of the Research Department, Fraser welcomed the idea but argued that plans should be made on the assumption that the next four years would not be easy ones; Labour had received a shock in the 1955 election and were likely to be a more effective Opposition as a result, there might well be restiveness among Conservative supporters once the 'honeymoon period' after Eden's succession to the leadership was over, and some of the legislation in prospect would certainly make enemies for the Party. And, 'an unsatisfactory outcome from the "Summit" talks and some deterioration in the economic situation – both of which are possible as the public has great expectations in both directions – would give the Labour Party something to bite on and the public something to grumble about'. This assessment was a remarkably accurate prediction of what was actually to happen in the next two years, made at a time when few Conservatives were so gloomy.[35] Other officers of the Department who had worked with the Prime Minister during the strain of the election campaign were already full of similar forebodings on a personal level, forebodings that were equally justified by events.

In the meantime, the Department had to get on with its normal research activities, and now that a whole Parliament separated them from the experience of opposition, rather more effort was put into the work of policy committees set up for special purposes. As Fraser noted in 1961:

> These committees, whose membership is normally drawn half from Conservative Members of Parliament and half from outside experts, are set up by Mr. Butler and serviced by the Research Department. They report to Mr. Butler and their reports are seen by the Advisory Committee on Policy, copies being sent to the Ministers concerned. In the period 1951–59 it was very unusual for such reports to be published.

There were many papers published all the same, sometimes coming indirectly from the policy committees, but more usually originating from individual officers or from internal Research Department groups. These included *Co-partnership* (1955), *Wages and Inflation, The Mechanism of Monetary Policy* and *Labour Restrictive Practices* (1956), *Education Policy* and *Defence* (1957). Fraser considered that advisory committees served 'at least three useful purposes: to produce new ideas for incorporation in the Party's policy; to fly kites for discussion; and to keep involved people occupied and convince them that problems are not quite so easily solved as they think'.[36]

By the mid-fifties, the Research Department no longer had a monopoly of research initiatives in the Party, though Fraser was keen to use the Department to co-ordinate all research whether official or unofficial. Working relations were established with the Bow Group as soon as it came into operation, and several officers of the Department were active members, but the Group published its findings directly through the CPC (and later through its own publishing organisation). When the political committee of the Junior Carlton Club wished to do some research work for the Party in December 1955, it was suggested that the problem of rents would be a suitable topic; terms of reference were framed for them by Fraser, an officer of the Department was provided as secretary, and Enoch Powell as Parliamentary Secretary to the Ministry of Housing was kept in touch with the operation throughout. Something similar occurred with a discussion group that had been set up back in the Winter of 1953 by Reginald Northam, Principal of Swinton College. This had taken some time to get going, and invitations were not sent out until the summer of 1954, with the organisation being done by the Research Department. A long period of work, changing conditions and a fluctuating membership (for Swinton College was rather remote for members to wish to go there very regularly) did not promise well, and the outcome was disappointing; in November 1956, Fraser passed on the report to Butler, describing it as 'an odd mixture. A modicum of common sense and some good points are surrounded by blinding glimpses of the obvious and a good deal of muddle . . . I have agreed that it should go to you in its present form, as I can see nothing else that can be done about it short of rewriting it myself, which I think is hardly called for'. This was not one of the reports that were published.[37]

More typical was the work on occupational pensions, on agriculture and on industrial policy, run by committees serviced by the Department. The occupational pensions group was a sub-committee of the 1922 Committee under Sir Lionel Heald and hence made up entirely of MPs. After several meetings had produced amicable discussions but no firm proposals, the secretary was taken aside by Vice-Admiral Hughes-Hallett and told that unless he wrote the report for them nothing would be achieved at all. Hughes-Hallett suggested the lines that the report should take, the secretary duly drafted it on those lines, and with a few amendments it was approved. This report suggested a substantial change in the way in which public sector pensions were handled, urging the equalisation of pensions for each rank or grade irrespective of the date of retirement, a change accepted by the Government.[38] It was not at all unknown for the secretary of such committees to exercise an influence out of all proportion to his seniority and experience, for he provided all the briefs and background papers, he wrote the minutes of meetings, he drafted and when necessary re-drafted the report, and he alone worked full-time to get up the technical details of the subject. Much depended on the composition of the committee and the way in which it was handled by the chairman; in the case of occupational pensions, the moving force was clearly Hughes-Hallett rather than Heald, but in some cases where the Research Department officer was more experienced it could be the secretary himself.

When things went astray, the Department could call on its Chairman to right the balance, as in the case of agriculture. The Agricultural Policy Committee was set up in the autumn of 1956 with six MPs and four outside experts, and with the highly-experienced Anthony Hurd as its chairman – Hurd had been agricultural correspondent for *The Times* since 1932, an MP for a farming seat since 1945, and a leading member of the NFU, the Farmers' Club and the Royal Agricultural Society. Nevertheless, after a good start, the committee became bogged down, probably through the inexperience of its secretary and its impossibly wide terms of reference. Fraser therefore called in Butler to help in February 1957:

> I had a word with Anthony Hurd recently, and got the impression that the committee is now a little at sea and requires a rather clearer directive with regard to its future work than is given by its present terms of reference, which are very widely drawn. I therefore had a short meeting with the Minister on Thursday, and he has suggested to me the lines on which the committee should proceed . . . . It would, I think, be very helpful and would get the Committee working purposefully again if you were to appear at 10.30 on the 14th and in a few words give them a directive on these lines, suggesting that they might prepare a report for you and the Minister before the summer recess.

This was duly done, a new secretary was appointed when the original officer left the Department, and a report was submitted in the following July.[39] It has indeed usually been accepted that agriculture is a special case, like foreign affairs and defence, in which it is helpful for a recruit to the Department to have background knowledge, and this would probably have remained the case in 1956 but for the squeeze on the Department's budget. In normal circumstances, the defence desk(s) are filled with ex-soldier(s) and the agriculture desk by a man with personal experience of farming. The distinction seems to go back to a time when most Parliamentary Committees were made up of those with an interest in the field in question but who did not necessarily have personal knowledge of it; even at that time, the Party's Agriculture Committee was filled with farmers and the Defence Committee full of soldiers and admirals, so that the Research Department needed specialists if it was to do its job properly.

The work on industrial policy was entrusted to a body called the Industrial Research Committee, 'so as not unduly to restrict the field of enquiry', and this was made up only of Research Department staff. David Dear acted as chairman, James Douglas of the Economic Section as secretary, and the other members were Fraser, Goldman and Block. Its purpose was explained by Fraser at the first meeting:

> Mr. Butler had told him that the Government intended to make a general

enquiry into industrial relations and had asked him, in this connection, to set up a committee in the Research Department to look at certain aspects of the problem, in particular Co-partnership. The Government had itself set up a Cabinet Committee to study the problem.

The Committee rapidly dispensed with co-partnership (on which Block had written a CPC publication and Dear a policy brief, both some years earlier), and passed on to the topical question of strikes. The ACP received an interim report in November 1955 and agreed that no further action was possible on co-partnership, but was anxious for more information on 'the economic effects of collective bargaining'. Informal meetings were held with civil servants and the committee as a whole dined with Lionel Robbins; evidence submitted on the system of industrial relations in other countries suggested the need for a change of the law, but a legal adviser who was consulted argued the need for public opinion first to be educated 'to the idea of an industrial division of the High Court'. The core of the problem was inflation, but the Committee was in substantial disagreement on the means that should be adopted to involve the Trades Unions in fighting inflation. James Douglas suggested that the Party should support a more interventionist policy, but recognised that this could only work if the TUC and the employers' organisations both claimed greater control over their members, an eventuality to which Goldman was strongly opposed. It was a dichotomy that was to recur in the Department and the Party over the next decade and beyond, along lines that Douglas described to Harold Watkinson, Parliamentary Secretary to the Minister of Labour:

> We all agree that any form of Government control à la Hinchingbrooke is out. We also broadly agree that there is not much hope of getting the Unions as at present organised to exercise much greater restraint than they have done so far. . . . Some of us believe that better control could be achieved by strengthening the central bodies both on the TUC side and the BEC side, but others of us are quite as appalled by the thought of creating mammoth collectivist organisations of producers (on both management and labour sides) as by continued inflation.

On 8 December, Watkinson met the committee and poured a douche of cold water on its ideas. Any proposal to change the law on trades unions, supported by 'most members of the Committee', was resisted by Watkinson as contrary to the sacred principle of the 1871 Act. When it was pointed out that most other countries had proper laws on trades unionism, Watkinson replied that it could only be introduced gradually if at all, for the Government's good relations with the Unions must not be put at risk: 'The policy of the Ministry of Labour was to "divide and rule". They only had clashes of opinion with one Union, not with the TUC'. There was no point in referring the matter to a Royal Commission as a means of attracting public support, since a Royal Commission would be filled with lawyers and would inevitably antagonise the TUC. 'He felt it would be impossible for any Conservative Government to introduce legal enforcement unless there was an approach from the T.U.C.' After Watkinson had left, Fraser tried to restore the morale of his staff, saying that 'the committee should not cease discussing things that Mr Watkinson felt were not possible. Conditions might change and there might be a reversal of public opinion'. Occasional meetings therefore continued and the Department sought means of influencing opinion; it was hoped to get PEP to commission a full-scale report on restrictive trades union practices, but this fell through on grounds of cost. In February 1956, a discussion of a Treasury paper on *Wages and Inflation* showed that the Department was still adrift from Government thinking. When Parliament rose for the Summer recess in 1956, the committee was seeking a meeting with Macleod and Robert Carr (by then Minister of Labour and Parliamentary Secretary) to press its views; the meeting does not seem to have taken place, and the Committee drifted into oblivion. In the meantime, the Research Department had to assist the Government to resist the loud demands from Conservatives for immediate action against strikes and strikers.[40] In August 1956, a letter drafted in the Department and arguing the case against strike ballots was 'placed' with a Conservative MP for publication in the *Daily Telegraph*. A week later, Dear was writing to Kenneth Pickthorn MP to put the case against the amendment of the tax laws to discourage wildcat strikes:

> My own view . . . is that this proposal is quite unsound and untenable. One really cannot have the precedent of altering the income tax law to discriminate against people whose activities the Government may happen to disapprove of. Incidentally, as far as I know, arson, rape and manslaughter do not incur this type of penalty.

As in the case of immigration, the Government had rejected any new policy for the medium term in order to avoid difficulties in the present; the Research Department was left with the negative task of defending a decision of which they did not much approve.

Many of these difficulties reflected the general malaise that affected the Eden Government in 1956, intensifying with the onset of inflation and reaching a climax with the Suez invasion and withdrawal. Increasingly, the Department was placed on the defensive, writing merely to protect the Government from the rising tide of criticism. Dear was on the receiving end of a great deal of this, for as often when a Conservative Government was in trouble, the criticism focussed on its ability to communicate – a duty that the Liaison Committee was supposed to take care of. When asked to frame replies to the many Conservatives who wrote to express the concern of middle class families in the time of inflation, he could only write that 'we at Party headquarters, and the Government, are fully aware of the need to stop inflation and rising prices – and of the difficulty of many of those in the middle classes whose incomes are fixed'; he could only plead for time, arguing that Government action already taken would reverse the trend in due course. When confronted with criticism of the Government's timing of unpopular announcements, he could only reply that announcements had to be made sooner or later; a decision to halve the milk subsidy had been taken in February 1956, but the price-rise had not come until July, and such decisions could not be delayed endlessly. In exasperation, he expressed the same view when Central Office made a similar complaint in October:

> This is a very natural complaint, and we have on several occasions raised this question ourselves. In most cases there has proved to be a valid reason why Government announcements are made at a particular time, and it is clear that in many cases, such as the date when a rise in the price of milk must be announced, the date is dictated by administrative necessity. One cannot, unfortunately, have a close season for Government announcements in the month before the local government elections.[41]

The low state of morale was one reason for the decision to produce once again a Party Conference document for Autumn 1956, and this was worked on during the Spring. Mindful of the events of 1953, this was done entirely within the Research Department, and the first draft, circulated to the ACP on 30 July was marked 'no part of this draft had at the time of writing been officially approved by a Minister'. In any case it was swiftly overtaken by the Middle Eastern crisis. Late in August, Fraser told Goldman that 'the decision lies between producing something on these lines – with a new piece on Suez – or producing nothing at all', and it was decided to abandon the whole thing.[42]

On the merits of the Suez crisis itself, officers in the Department were as divided as every other group or organisation in the country; when passing on to John Hare a speech drafted for him in the

Department, Dear noted 'I hardly think it appropriate that you should take this strong line in attacking Nasser and Egypt. But you may find something useful in it'. When the crisis really broke in November, the Department was right in the thick of things. Notes and drafts were provided in defence of the Government's actions, and publicity was gained for the evidence from opinion polls in support of the Government's stand. A 'Week-end talking point' gave a favourable analysis of the economic effects of the crisis and stressed the need for sacrifice 'for Britain's sake'. Only at this last moment then, did the Department enter the crisis that destroyed Eden's Government and his career, but that brief experience gave some insight into the whole business. Comment and information could not be easily supplied even to Ministers, for the Department was not in a position to know exactly what was happening. Oliver Poole informed Macleod in late November that

> It will not be possible to produce any new material on the Suez Crisis for weekend speeches until after the Foreign Secretary's statement on Thursday afternoon. Material will, however, be available at the Research Department on Friday morning. If you wish to make use of this, I should be grateful if you would get in touch direct with Fraser.[43]

When an issue of *Notes on Current Politics* was to be published on Suez, details had to be checked with the Foreign Office and then re-checked with Downing Street. Finally, the Prime Minister insisted that he should see the document himself before it went to the printer; it seemed odd to some that a Prime Minister in the midst of such a crisis should have the time or the inclination to re-write a Party leaflet, a reflection of the extent to which he felt unsure even of the extent to which his own Party could be trusted to express his views accurately. It was in that sense an appropriate climax to the difficult, disorganised and defensive months that had followed the Party's triumph in 1955.[44]

Appendix: The family tree of committees

In order to avoid confusion, it may be as well to set out here the various Party Committees on policy matters that have flourished since the return to power in 1951.[45] The following notes set out the basic features of each committee and the accompanying table puts them in their proper relationship to each other.

1 *Cabinet and Shadow Cabinet*. Continuously in existence with a membership that was always made public. Formally called the 'Leader's Consultative Committee' when the Party is in opposition, and membership is always by invitation from the Leader. Secretary usually the Director of the Research Department when the Party has been in opposition. The supreme decision-making body.

2 *Steering Committee*. First constituted formally in 1957 but following on from other similar bodies in previous Parliaments. The success achieved between 1957 and 1959 has led to the Steering Committee becoming a permanent Party institution, though it has generally been called together only at longish intervals (about twice a year). This is in effect an inner-cabinet of Ministers meeting together, without their civil servants, to look ahead politically (in opposition an inner Shadow-Cabinet). Later Steering Committees have not quite lived up to the example of 1957–1959, though the Committee of 1967–1970 was quite successful in drawing together the threads of the policy review before the return to office.

3 *Research Study Group/Policy Study Group/Official Group*. This has existed under various names, and was also known as the 'Chairman's Committee' while headed by Iain Macleod as Party Chairman. It is a gathering of MPs professionals from the Research Department and Central Office, mainly brought together for the purposes of assembling and drafting a manifesto but advising on other matters too. Usually chaired by a Minister who thus provided access to the Government side when in office, the Secretary coming from the Research Department.

4 *Liaison Committee.* The chief tactical body and more recently called the 'Tactical Committee'. Made up partly of Ministers/Shadow Ministers and partly of professionals, under the chairmanship of the Minister responsible for information services when the Party is in office. A very effective body when first set up in 1951 because it was so economically constituted, with every member present representing a separate Party group.[46] The main coordinating body.

5 *Advisory Committee on Policy.* The main forum for the consultation of extra-Parliamentary opinion in the Party. The Chairman has often been the same senior Party figure who has been Chairman of the Research Department and the Secretary has usually been Director of the CRD. (See also Chapter 1).

The family tree of committees

	Cabinet or Shadow Cabinet	Policy		Tactical	Party Link
		Top Level	Support		
1951–55	Cabinet	'The Intimates'	Research Study Group (Brooke)	Liaison Committee (Swinton)	ACP (Butler)
1957–59	Cabinet	Steering Committee (Macmillan)	Policy Study Group (Macleod)	Liaison Committee (Hill)	ACP (Butler)
1959–64	Cabinet	Steering Committee (Macmillan/Home)	Policy Study Group (Macleod)	Liaison Committee (Hill/Deedes)	ACP (Butler)
1964–70	Shadow Cabinet	Steering Committee (Heath)	Official Group (Fraser)	Policy Initiatives and Methods (Fraser)	ACP (Heath/Maudling/Boyle)
1970–74	Cabinet	Steering Committee (Heath)	Official Group (Fraser)	Liaison (Whitelaw/Prior) / Tactical (Fraser)	ACP (Barber)
Feb 1974–Oct 1974	Shadow Cabinet	Steering Committee (Heath)	Official Group (Fraser)	Tactical (Fraser)	ACP (Heath)

Notes

1 CRD file, 'Business Committee, 1949–51'.
2 CRD file, 'ACP correspondence, 1949–51'.
3 *Ibid.*
4 CRD file, 'AC Local Government, 1950–51'.
5 CRD files, 'ACP correspondence, 1949–51', 'AC Control of the Executive Power', 'AC Broadcasting, 1950–51'.
6 CRD file, 'AC Electricity and Gas, 1950–51'.
7 CRD file, 'Health Policy Papers, 1951'.
8 CRD (N) files, 'Area Agents Correspondence, 1949–50', 'Mr Cohen's correspondence with Churchill Secretariat, 1949–51'.
9 Survey dated 27 July 1950, in CRD file, 'Policy Document Papers, 1951'.
10 CRD file, 'AC Housing, 1950'.
11 Butler, *Art of the Possible*, 155.
12 CRD file, 'Business Committee, 1949–51'.
13 CRD file, 'Housing Policy sub-committees, 1951'.
14 ACP(51)9, 'Economic Policy 1951–1955' and CRD file, 'ACP Correspondence, 1949–51'.
15 Quotations from election manifestoes are taken from F. W. S. Craig (ed), *British General Election Manifestoes, 1918–1966*, Chichester 1970.
16 CRD files, 'Election Manifesto, 1951' and '1951 Policy Document'.
17 CRD files, '1951 Election, General Administration' and '1951 Election – Reports'.
18 Based on interviews.
19 CRD file, '1957 Budget'.
20 CRD file, 'Government Correspondence, 1951–55'; Fraser 'Conservative Research Department' IV, 11.
21 CRD file, 'Government Correspondence, 1951–55'.
22 CRD file, 'Research in 1953 and after'.
23 CRD (N) file, 'Letter Books of David Dear, 1955–6'.
24 CRD file, 'Mr Maudling's TV broadcast'; interview with Mr Peter Tapsell.
25 Fraser, 'Conservative Research Department', IV, 1–2; CRD (N) file, 'Letter Books of David Dear, 1955–6'.
26 CRD files, 'Black Book' and 'The First Six Months'.
27 CRD files, '1952 Policy Document' (drafts and correspondence).
28 CRD files, '1953 Policy Document' (drafts and correspondence).

29 CRD file, 'Research Study Group'; Fraser, 'Conservative Research Department', IV, 4.
30 CRD file, '1955 Election, General Arrangements'.
31 CRD file, '1955 Election, Policy Document'.
32 CRD file, '1955 Election, Reports'.
33 CRD file, '1955 Election, Bouquets'.
34 CRD files, 'Government correspondence, 1951–55' and '1955 Election, Press Conference'; CRD (N) file, 'Letter Books of David Dear 1955–6'.
35 CRD file, 'Three Year Plan for Propaganda Policy'.
36 Fraser, 'Conservative Research Department', IV, 8–9.
37 CRD files, 'Junior Carlton Club, Study of Rents' and 'Northam's Swinton Group'.
38 CRD file, 'Occupational Pensions Sub-committee, 1955'.
39 CRD file, 'Agricultural Policy Committee, 1956–57'.
40 CRD file, 'Industrial Research Committee, 1955–56'.
41 CRD (N) file, 'Letter Books of David Dear, 1955–6'.
42 CRD file, '1956 Policy Document'.
43 CRD file, '1959 Election – Speeches'.
44 CRD (N) file, 'Letter Books of David Dear, 1955–6'; Interviews with Officers.
45 I am grateful to Lord Fraser for clarifying the relationship and function of these various committees, and for supplying the accompanying table.
46 Windlesham, *Communication and Political Power*, 48–49.

Chapter 8

Macmillan and after (1957–1964)

In theory, there was no reason why the retirement of Sir Anthony Eden and the succession of Harold Macmillan to the premiership should have made any real difference to Conservative policy and policymaking. Eden and Macmillan were men of the same First World War generation and from a similar educational background; both had played important parts in the Party's recovery from the disaster of 1945 and no substantial policy difference separated them. Indeed it might well have appeared that the succession of Macmillan would be a setback to the Research Department – since the most likely alternative to him would have been R. A. Butler, to whom the Party's policy makers had worked for more than ten years. But for all this, the six and a half years of Macmillan's leadership marked something of a pinnacle for the Department, a time when it was closer to the centre of Party communications than ever and perhaps the time when it contributed most to the Party's success. Macmillan's feat in bringing his Party back from the dead between 1957 and 1959 has been often described, but it has been insufficiently appreciated how far that success was built on solid work behind the scenes – as important in its way as the vital, bell-ringing confidence exhibited by the Prime Minister and his Cabinet colleagues. After 1959, as after 1955, things did not go well, but it was largely due to decisions taken soon after the 1959 election that long-term preparations were put in hand which almost enabled the Party to pull off a fourth successive win in 1964, under Macmillan's successor.

These successes relied in part on Macmillan's personal attitude to policy, in part on personalities and contacts, and in part on new structures (or new life breathed into old structures) created in the first year of Macmillan's premiership. Despite appearances, Macmillan had always been a very different politician from Eden and he now intended to be a very different Prime Minister. Throughout his career, Macmillan had been a politician who burned with enthusiasm to *do* things with power, not just to occupy office and deny it to the Party's opponents – by no means a unanimous attitude among

Conservatives of the time. In the 1930s he had written the most substantial and original political tract by a Conservative this century, and he had worked with several non-Party research groups like PEP and the 'Next Five Years Group' to foster research on policy planning. As a Shadow Minister he had been as active as any other than Butler in work on the Party's policy in opposition, and as a Minister he showed that he recognised the importance of two-way contact by maintaining a close relationship with the Research Department. Indeed, as Minister of Housing he had benefitted greatly from the Party's preparation for office, and his housing drive of 1951–5 was probably the political success that had made him Prime Minister. The effect of all this was that Macmillan was by far the most policy-orientated Leader with whom the Research Department had had to work since Neville Chamberlain (who was, anyway, too distracted with foreign problems during his premiership to make a fair comparison possible). From 1957, the Research Department could be sure that policy briefs sent to Downing Street would reach the desk of the Prime Minister himself, and they could also call on Macmillan's personal help to bring his Ministers into line. Policy work when the Party is in office depends heavily on the willingness of Ministers to supply the Party with information (since Conservative Ministers could hardly be forced to disgorge it through questions planted on Conservative back-benchers by the Conservative Research Department) and Macmillan was always ready to remind his subordinates that the Party rather than the Civil Service was the basis of their tenure of office. In preparing his important political speeches as Prime Minister, Macmillan called for drafts not only from Government departments, but also from the Research Department, and John Wyndham (his Political Secretary at Number Ten), Michael Fraser, and George Christ (Central Office) worked with him on them. This must in itself have kept a two-way flow of ideas going.

Much depended on the personal relations of Macmillan and Butler, who differed little in their attitudes to policy but who might not have been expected to get on well after their contest for the Leadership in January 1957. In the event they formed a close working relationship, for though Macmillan made it quite clear that he did not envisage Butler as his successor, he demonstrated both by word and by action that he was prepared to give Butler important responsibilities in his Government. For the good of the Party, Butler swallowed his disappointment and accepted the second place that Macmillan offered him, becoming *de facto* Deputy Prime Minister in 1957 and taking the office by name in 1962 – after two years in which he had also been Party Chairman. It had been no secret that Butler had felt dissatisfied with Eden as Prime Minister, and his standing had never been entirely secure in Churchill's time, but from 1957 the Chairman of the Research Department was again the Prime Minister's right hand man. The same enhancement of the Department's standing was to be seen at lower levels of the Government and among the Party professionals. During Macmillan's premiership, Maudling and Powell joined Macleod in the Cabinet to form a group that remained loyal to Old Queen Street and which provided the basis for Butler's campaign for the Leadership in 1963. Most importantly, there was also the enhancement of Michael Fraser's position in the Party. Fraser was sole Director of the Research Department from 1959 but he had already headed the research and Parliamentary side of the Department for eight years by then, and he had established contacts in every corner of Whitehall. Equally important, he had the ear of the Prime Minister and of several other senior Ministers who rightly regarded him as one of the most sagacious political advisers available to them; in the view of at least one colleague, he exercised from the outside an influence as great as most Cabinet Ministers could do from within. Something of the ease with which Fraser was able to come and go in Whitehall may be inferred from the early preparations for the 1963 progress report, *Acceleration*. On 6 December 1962 he informed Dear that 'I am proposing to do one of my periodic rounds of the key Ministries to discuss with Ministers their present problems and future plans. I should like, while doing this to use the opportunity also for clarifying any points where we feel the need in the Department for more information or a stronger publicity line'. The notes provided for Fraser for these meetings indicate that his talks with Ministers would be fairly frank, as the following extracts demonstrate:

> BOARD OF TRADE: *Resale Price Maintenance.* The dilemma here is well known, but we cannot go on hedging much longer. Will the report of the departmental enquiry be published?

> TREASURY: *Nicky* [N.I.C.] What is to be the future of 'Nicky' and how much emphasis do we put in our publicity on the need for an incomes policy? . . . *Neddy.* How soon can we expect anything to come out of 'Neddy'?[1]

Finally, if more contacts were needed, the Prime Minister's secretary was John Wyndham who had spent some time in the Research Department himself and was now available as a direct channel of communication from Old Queen Street to Number Ten. Party management and policy formulation is very much a matter of communication and delegation, but there have been few occasions when it has worked as well, in a Government as a whole and within the Department.

To keep the channels of communication open, it was necessary not only to provide the appropriate personal contacts but also to look at the structures. One such means was the restoration to the Liaison Committee of the powers that had been envisaged for it in 1952. Under the chairmanship of Charles Hill, who as Chancellor of the Duchy had full-time responsibility for information services, it found a leader who well understood the problems of modern communications from personal experience. An analysis of 'The Communication of Conservative Policy, 1957–58' by David Hennessy (Lord Windlesham) identified the Liaison Committee as the 'one committee which had effective power and which met regularly to exercise it'. Made up as before of the representatives of the Government, Central Office, CPC, the Whips, the Party Chairman and his deputies, it had Fraser as a member and Dear as Secretary (Sewill from 1959).

> It was the job of the Liaison Committee to identify what was likely to be controversial in the reception of Government policy, to advise on timing in the execution of policy, and to consider what forms of Party propaganda could be used to ease its communication. It was, for example, this committee, meeting every Wednesday, which chose the subject for a 'Weekend Talking Point'.

This last idea had existed before, but only from 1957 was it brought to really effective use. An outline for a speech was prepared by an officer in the Research Department in the latter half of each week, according to the decision of the Liaison Committee and to detailed instructions from Fraser. This was then sent off on Thursday or Friday to all candidates, MPs, agents, constituency chairmen and Party speakers in time to be used at the weekend. When working well, this ensured that several hundred speeches could be delivered in the half-week after a Liaison Committee meeting, emphasising some point of Government policy and giving the best arguments in defence of it. In short, through this machinery, the Party and the Government could be heard speaking with the same voice and stressing the same issues. No doubt most of the speeches delivered were to audiences of the faithful, but they were no less important for that; explaining its policies to its own supporters is one of any Government's most difficult tasks, and many of the explanations would find their way sooner or later to the world at large through the local press.[2]

The Liaison Committee thus made possible a real communications policy that covered everything from a candidate's weekend speech in a village hall to a full scale policy document. It was nevertheless a fire-brigade organisation, called in to put out the fires of policy dispute when things had gone wrong; in good times it might achieve fire prevention by advance warning of decisions that needed careful handling, but the most that could be done was delay or the sweetening of the pill by timing bad news to coincide with good. The Liaison Committee, in other words, was a body of Party professionals who met to make the best of the policy material with which Ministers now had to provide it. From the summer of 1957 until the summer of 1960, it sailed with a favourable wind, for the balance of popularity was steadily tilting in the Government's favour. Thereafter, it was reminded that there were limits to what could be achieved through communication.

More original was the second structural change, hardly known about at the time, for the existence of the Steering Committee was itself a closely-guarded secret. This operated at a much higher level, with the intention not of making the best of policy matters, but of directing them into a coherent pattern. It seems to have originated in talks between Fraser, Macmillan and Edward Heath, who as Chief Whip was anxious about the range and variety of policy work going on and the lack of organisational coherence. The first paper to be discussed when the Steering Committee met for the first time on 23 December 1957 was one by Heath on 'Organisations at Present Considering Policy'. Apart from internal work in the Research Department, he listed special groups working on agriculture, defence and the nationalised industries, the usual Parliamentary Committees, the ACP, the PSG (which had just been revived under Macleod to repeat for the next election its successful exercise of 1953–55), and lots more unofficial groups. Heath called for some overall plan to be worked out, for priorities on policy work to be decided, and for the programme to be kept under constant supervision.[3] An integrated and permanent programme of Party research could only be carried on outside the Government with the supervision of at least the most senior Ministers; hence the Steering Committee, which was in effect an inner Cabinet group which met without the Cabinet Office staff in order to think out its strategy in a consciously party frame of mind, and without the tyranny of an overweight or immediate agenda to inhibit discussion. The Prime Minister normally took the chair, with

Butler acting for him in his absence, and the other original members were Hailsham, Macleod and Heath, with Fraser as secretary. Home became a member in 1958, and other Cabinet Ministers were invited for particular meetings when appropriate; Oliver Poole as Deputy Chairman of the Party, became a regular attender at later meetings. Peter Goldman was brought in by Fraser when the drafting of the Manifesto itself began. Reports were submitted to the Steering Committee (usually before going to the ACP, and always before a decision was made about publication), and themes of Party strategy emerged from its meetings. It was here that the strands of policy-making at the Government level, research in the Party, and publicity through the Party machine, were brought together, for the membership was carefully chosen to interlock; Fraser was a member of the Liaison Committee as well as the Steering Committee, and Macleod was chairman of the PSG. All these bodies were serviced by the Research Department, and all their papers crossed Michael Fraser's desk. After meetings, verbatim notes on what had actually been said at the Steering Committee were knocked into rather more guarded minutes, which were then circulated together with reminders to members who had agreed to take action at the meeting. However, something of the flavour of the meetings may be gauged from the original rough notes of the meetings where these have survived.

In January 1958, the discussion was mainly on the need to widen the membership of the PSG in order to throw up the original ideas that would be needed for the next manifesto:

Mr. Heath: Marples? Full of ideas – and different ones. Might be the grain of sand that produces the pearl.
Mr. Macleod: Can't have a Manifesto about widening letterboxes.
Mr. Heath: Do seriously suggest him. Also good against cry that too much 'clique' work.

In March, Butler urged the preparation of a document for the Party Conference, in the form of a 'Child's guide to Conservatism' with the emphasis on foreign policy as 'the main and only political issue of the day'. Doubtless remembering the wasted efforts of 1953 and 1956, Fraser suggested that the need might be better met by a series of weighty speeches from Ministers, but Butler's idea was adopted. The same meeting reviewed progress on research in general and discussed replies sent by Ministers to a circular from the Prime Minister inviting their co-operation; the few recalcitrant Ministers who had either not replied or given no usable information would each be seen by a member of the Steering Committee. It was obviously a useful asset to any policymaking organisation to have such a powerful supervising committee that it could call the Chancellor of the Exchequer and the Foreign Secretary to book for the secrecy of their departments. Butler was clearly unhappy at the direction that Treasury policy was taking, and he urged that someone other than the Chancellor (who was too busy just before a budget) should look at overall strategy: 'whether you have a Bolingbroke or really free as had under Winston. Who is going to produce that – steering orders for the economy? Needn't be long but must be damn good'. This prompted an apparently long musing from Macmillan on the way in which power changed perspectives:

> When you are in power of course you are conscious of the weakness of the instrument. Main item I think ought to be that we don't want a socialist state, we don't want a purely laissez-faire state (impossible to run): just as, how do you combine full employment and reasonable stability of prices, how do you combine necessary strategic control in hands of the Government leaving maximum amount of freedom for saving etc. Old problem. We want to summarise that as a result of our experience. Many things we didn't have between the Wars, such as statistics, we now have, but really still not strong enough. What things should the Government settle and what machinery should the Government have to make things settle?

It was decided to ask Edward Boyle and David Clarke to draft a paper on this somewhat large theme, an idea that fell through when Clarke replied that seven years away from Whitehall had left him too out of touch to attempt it. Some of the ideas finally surfaced through in the Prime Minister's own CPC lecture given at Blackpool in the following October, on 'The Middle Way, Twenty Years On'.[4]

In May and July 1958, meetings concentrated on whether or not to publish a policy document and on early drafts for one, but the problem of trades union reform had also surfaced. Macleod, Minister of Labour, conceded that the Party demand for action created a dilemma, since such action would be popular and yet difficult to carry out with success. The same topic arose at the next meeting, in November 1958, and was dismissed by Macmillan, who could see no point in attacking the trades unions by legal means:

> But aren't you more worried about the weakness of the trade unions? Poor old Trade Union man who comes along at £750 a year and gets laughed out of court by the bummarees. But really the role of the Minister of Labour is to strengthen the trade unions to keep control of those chaps. Discussion was again adjourned inconclusively.

Discussion was again adjourned inconclusively.

Meetings in 1959 were mainly taken up with the discussion of the themes that should dominate the manifesto ('*Hailsham*: all themes subordinate to need to keep up our momentum, to keep Labour out. *Heath*: anti-socialism not enough.') and to discussion of drafts as they appeared. Two other issues that surfaced in preparing for the election were nationalised industries and Suez. On nationalisation, it was decided in January 1959 that the manifesto should 'give room for manoeuvre', but that it should 'give something to work on'. In April, Macleod suggested a deal with Labour whereby the Conservatives should promise not to denationalise any more of the steel industry if Labour would promise not to renationalise what had been done already, but this was turned down – the Party needed the issue of nationalisation as a clear issue between the Parties for the coming election. Suez cropped up when the Steering Committee in April 1959 discussed a paper from the Research Department on 'Suez as an issue at the General Election'. It was contended that there would be far less mileage in the issue than Labour had hoped back in 1956–7, but that the Party must be ready with an answer if Labour should raise it; it was even suggested that the Government might want to raise the issue themselves, in order to choose the ground on which it was discussed. Various Foreign Office statements had been made available for the preparation of the paper, but none of them dealt with the questions that Labour was likely to ask, which were the charge that Britain had ignored the UN and that Britain and France had been in collusion with Israel. None of the Ministers present knew the answers (or none were letting on if they did) and so the issue was referred to the Foreign Secretary, Selwyn Lloyd. When the Steering Committee met for the last time before the election, it was pointed out that the Foreign Office had not replied to the request for information, and the Prime Minister undertook to 'chivvy' the Foreign Secretary himself; no reply was ever circulated. It seems that there were some doors that even the Steering Committee could not unlock.[5]

Under the aegis of the Steering Committee, a great deal of detailed policy work was done to fill gaps in the corpus of Party doctrine, updating as well as creation from scratch. In November 1958, Fraser reported on 'Policy – a Summary of Work in Progress' and listed eleven areas where significant work was being done or had already been presented to the Steering Committee itself. These ranged from work on the machinery of Government which was being carried on entirely within the Government itself under Sir Norman Brook, to nationalised industries which were being looked at by a joint group from Ministers and Party, to tax problems which were being considered by a group of officers within the Research Department. It will be worth looking at some of these investigations.[6]

Anthony Hurd's Agricultural Policy Committee had been kept in being after presenting its report in July 1957 in order to take account of the changing circumstances of international trade. In January 1958, it was asked by the ACP to consider the effect of Britain's joining EFTA on British agriculture. It met regularly to watch a situation that was changing rapidly, and received reports from Reginald Maudling on his negotiations with the EFTA countries. Butler wrote to Hurd in June 1958 to express his thanks for the work that had been done in keeping the Government in touch with Party and farming opinion while its new policy for international trade was being developed. This then was a group whose main duty was the monitoring of opinion rather than the evolution of ideas.[7] The group under Robin Turton which investigated the care of the old had a more positive purpose in framing new ideas, though few of these ever saw the light of day. In October 1958, Fraser forwarded its report to Butler:

> The Report, without being in any way revolutionary or exciting, is a workmanlike job with a number of sensible recommendations. You will in particular have noted recommendation No. 2 in the summary [proposing the creation of a single Ministry for Social Services] which could well fit in with the sort of ideas for a rearrangement of Social Service Ministries which we have already discussed in the Steering Committee.

This proposal ran foul of Norman Brook's work on the machinery of Government and it was therefore left to Labour to carry out after 1964.[8] Something similar happened to delay the appointment of a Minister of Science, but this idea did find its way into the manifesto and Hailsham was duly appointed as the first Minister of Science immediately after the 1959 election. It would appear that the Steering Committee was rather less cavalier in enforcing its views on senior Civil Servants than on fellow Ministers.

The Committee on Nationalised Industries had been set up under Butler himself in October 1956, with a brief to consider the questions of restoring accountability and introducing more competition into the public sector. It was soon apparent that the committee was not agreed on its general approach. When it met in May 1957 to discuss possible items for the next Queen's Speech, there was a strong appeal from Sir Gerald Nabarro for the denationalisation of 'the rest of lorries', together with buses, railway hotels, retail outlets of the National Coal Board and the Carlisle pubs. This idea was side-stepped by the rest of the Committee on the ground that it would be inappropriate to decide on matters of detail before a general approach had been agreed; but there was a clear difference of approach between those who wanted to reorganise all the industries to make them profitable and those who wanted to hive off all the profitable parts and let the rest go hang. Inevitably, the final report savoured of compromise; more should be done to decentralise the industries in the public sector and to diffuse responsibility in them, since it would be impossible to denationalise those still in public hands, but further thought should be given to hiving off. After the election, the Macmillan Government tried hard to carry out the first half of this plan, but the second half was quietly shelved.[9]

The work on tax policy consisted in the main of meetings of research officers in the Autumn of each year to provide a brief for the Chancellor before he set to work on the following year's budget. The recurrent message from the Research Department was the need to press on with the reduction of taxes, and when possible to give it a political edge. In September 1957, Brendon Sewill outlined a target for the Party of 'two budgets, each reducing tax by £100 million' before the next election; these cuts should be made in income and purchase tax. The final brief, drafted by Gordon Campbell, called for two budgets cutting tax by £150 million each. In the following year, especial care was taken with the brief, and the final version bore the initials of Fraser, Dear and Sewill:

1. This memorandum is based on the assumption that the next Budget will be the last before a General Election. It is therefore important that any tax reductions should *both*:
   (a) deserve clear priority on economic grounds and on grounds of equity and social justice.
   (b) have the widest appeal to potential supporters.

2. In the view of the Research Department, those considerations rule out reductions in beer, tobacco or petrol duty, and also any costly concessions to business, subject to reviewing the position of initial allowances at a later date. We adhere to our view that investment allowances, being a subsidy to private industry from the general taxpayer, are undesirable.

3. The tax reliefs should not be too complicated or subtle. If possible they should consist of a few, simple, straightforward measures which can be easily understood by the public. It is essential that, as a result of

the tax changes, no one should be left worse off than they were before.

4. In our view, the arguments are overwhelmingly in favour of reductions in income tax and in purchase tax.

This gives a clear indication of the level at which these briefs were aimed, the level of economic advice at which the Research Department concentrated. There was no attempt to tell the Chancellor what his economic policy or his monetary strategy should be – no attempt to compete with the Treasury in forming the 'budget judgement'. The Research Department did not have the resources or the trained economists to enter into that sort of competition, but it did have the determination not to let the Chancellor forget the political implications of what he was deciding. So, speaking as political advisers to a politician, they suggested a number of ways in which the distribution of tax cuts could be made advantageous, once their size and timing had been decided on economic grounds. In 1959, three alternative sets of proposals were submitted, allowing for total tax reductions of £100, £200 and £300 million. If the lowest figure were available, income tax allowances should be increased by £10 a head and purchase tax rates should be lowered to save £45 million; if £200 million were available, then the standard rate of income tax should be reduced by 6d and purchase tax reduced by £70 million. If £300 million were available, all of these things should be done, to- gether with a halving of stamp duty on shares and the announcement of the progressive repayment of post-war credits. It is impossible to tell what weight such advice would have, coming at a time when the Chancellor was deluged with opinions both invited and unsolicited; and it no doubt varied between Chancellors; in 1959, the budget did allocate most of the concessions to income and purchase tax, though it also went directly against the Department's advice by introducing investment allowances for industry.[10]

Concern not to tie the Party's public image too closely to industry was also reflected in the setting up of a committee on share- ownership in 1958, with the intention of linking the ownership of industry to a wider sector of the population. This was set up under Toby Low in April 1958, with the invitations to its ten other members (five MPs, five men from the City) sent out by Butler on 9 May; after its existence had been reported to the Steering Committee, Butler wrote around to the Ministers involved, requisitioning their assistance for the new committee and claiming that it had been started by a decision of the Steering Committee on 21 May. Low's aim was summarised in a paper discussed at the first meeting, in which he called for a commitment from the Party to encourage a 'share-owning democracy'. Subsequent meetings were held with a number of bankers, industrialists and other City experts; a great deal of information on the relatively novel idea of unit trusts being provided for the Committee by Edward du Cann. It was decided not to pursue the first idea of setting up a National Unit Trust to harness the complementary aims of unit trusts and national savings, but agreed instead that the Party should give all encouragement to the existing unit trust system run under free enterprise. This was duly incorporated in the Party's progress report of 1958, *Onward in Freedom*, and was the proposal that received the most general approval in the press, a good example of a policy kite that paid off. When the final report of the committee reached the Steering Committee in January 1959, it received unanimous support, but it proved to be necessary to delay its publication by several months in order not to pre-empt the 1959 budget – or to raise unjustified expectations of the budget in the City, which would be even worse. It was eventually published by the CPC in April 1959 as *Everyman a Capitalist*, for which purpose the report was re-drafted in layman's terms.[11]

Onward in Freedom proved to be a rather more successful publication than the experience of 1953 and 1956 might have indicated, and the early objections to another major document were soon set aside. It was deliberately beamed at the Party and at Conservative sympathisers rather than at a wider public, and linked to the national membership campaign scheduled for the Autumn of 1958. Intensive press briefing in advance made sure that expectations were not raised too high and the document was well received at the Party Conference, as well as providing a useful opportunity to test out some policy ideas in advance of the drafting of a manifesto.[12]

Behind the scenes, work on the preparation of an election programme had been going on ever since the change of leadership. The Policy Study Group was revived after a meeting of Fraser and Macleod on 7 February 1957 and met for the first time a week later; Macleod was chairman, with Powell, Maudling, Ormsby-Gore, Simon, Fraser and Goldman as members, joined later by Brooke and Low. It was decided at that first meeting that the PSG would work on the assumption that the election would be in October 1959, but that the possible alternative dates would be between Spring 1959 and Spring 1960. A manifesto would not therefore be needed before the beginning of 1959, but the PSG would in the meantime meet twice each month, once for a business meeting and once over dinner with a

Ministerial guest. It would range from urgent discussions on matters where Government action was imminent to 'matters involving the long-term re-education of the Party'. Meetings were held throughout 1957 and all areas of Government policy were reviewed one by one in the light of their electoral implications. One such case involved a discussion with John Hare, the new Minister of Agriculture, early in 1958, a discussion summed up by Macleod (according to the rough preliminary notes of the meeting):

> *Macleod*: excellent document. We are considering it almost entirely as politicians and with an eye cocked to the Manifesto. Main things we want to know are whether you are happy (Mr. Hare), or will be with agriculture done this way, direct from you to this committee, or whether you want to use other committees or the Parliamentary Committee in the House.
>
> General Comment: rough conclusion this comes to is ought to go on as we are doing. No reason to contradict this, but isn't really an electorally popular one and need some gimmicks or something to put in Manifesto to appeal to a disgruntled farming vote.

Such plain speaking was all very well behind the closed doors of the Committee, but it was better not to communicate it in exactly this form even to the few people who saw the PSG minutes. The final version of the minutes therefore introduced order into what had been a fairly random summing up of the discussion, interpolating at this point a report on work being done by Hurd's Agricultural Policy Committee that actually occurred later in the meeting. The final minutes described the same part of the meeting as follows, an object lesson to historians who seek to use such minutes as historical sources;

> Mr. Macleod, asking Mr. Hare to introduce his paper, explained the relationship between the various groups working on future policy, and that the Agricultural Policy Committee was now studying the implications of the Free Trade Area. Considering the paper with an eye to the next Election Manifesto, its conclusions seemed to be that the present agricultural policy should continue. Without contradicting this, he wondered if it were possible to find some electorally attractive points which would appeal to the farming vote at the next Election.

Before readers leap to the conclusion that the PSG was adopting an unduly cynical attitude to the question of policy making, it should be emphasised how difficult a problem they faced. Few political tasks can be so awkward as the presentation of policy by a Government after two terms of office, and especially when those terms have been on the whole a success. New departures can hardly be entertained on a grand scale without inviting the question 'Why has this not been done before?' but the lack of new departures may well lead the electorate to conclude that the Government has nothing left to offer. What was at stake was not the content of policy, which was bound to remain largely the same after the election as before, but the way in which that policy was presented. As Macmillan himself observed to the Steering Committee a few months later, after a review of policy in general: 'Problem is, how to present what is in fact "Safety First" into a policy which looks as if it is moving forward'. And his answer was 'On the basis of what has been done, move on'. This was the task that the PSG and the Steering Committee set themselves and which characterised the manifesto of 1959; without fighting the election on the wholly negative defence of its record, the Government managed to present a picture of a developing policy and thus to give the electorate an apparent choice between moderate change and radical change, rather than a choice between Labour change and Conservative inertia. In the meetings of both committees in 1959, great care was taken over successive drafts of the manifesto in order to get this delicate mixture right.[13]

The manifesto for the 1959 election was first drafted in March 1959 by Peter Goldman, and circulated as 'a consecutive statement of some of the likely candidates for inclusion in the forward programme, excluding Foreign Affairs and Defence'. After discussion and the interpolation of more detailed material by several Ministers on their specialist fields, it was felt that the document was still too backward-looking. In May, Macmillan wrote to all his Ministers (the letter drafted by Fraser) and asked them to furnish information on all action that their departments intended to take in the five years from 1960: 'I am much taken with the idea of a Five-Year Plan' – as indeed he had been ever since the 1930s. However, the material that was forthcoming was 'meagre' and especially on the economic side; the Chancellor was not at all keen on promises to encourage share-ownership, and he was becoming worried about the cumulative cost of the plans that were emerging. Butler warned Fraser of this before the next draft was produced:

> Our mutual friend Heathcoat-Amory is very anxious that the manifesto should not make too many promises. This is for reasons of the forward outlook of the Exchequer. It may well be, therefore, that this part should be drafted even less definitely than before. I mention this only because I know from the P.M. that this will come up if we do not face it ahead. I do not suggest absolute negation but I do suggest caution in drafting.

The third draft, circulated early in July was called *The Next Five Years*, and was thought to be complete except for the section on Foreign Affairs, which the Foreign Secretary was drafting himself, with help from the Research Department. Most of the changes made at this stage were the result of bilateral agreements between Ministers to settle disputes; a pledge not to introduce any further rent decontrol was thus inserted after Henry Brooke as the Minister of Housing became concerned about the electoral impact of the issue; a pledge to continue agricultural guarantees was negotiated between the Minister of Agriculture and the Chancellor.

The most generally contentious issue in the last phase of drafting was that of immigration, ignored in 1955 and raised this time only after the manifesto was in its fifth draft. The Lord Chancellor asked for a ruling on the future of immigration controls, pointing out the ambiguity of previous statements; some Ministers had given definite pledges against controls, but others had promised action at least to the extent of introducing deportation powers. Macmillan referred this to the Steering Committee, and asked for a draft: Goldman and Butler conferred together and produced the formula 'We are proud that discrimination on grounds of race or colour has never in this country been part of our life and law, and we intend to uphold this principle'. This did not meet with general agreement, for some Ministers did not like such a definite commitment and all of them felt that it would give the issue undue prominence in the campaign. It was decided to tack it on to the section on law and order and to make no reference to immigration as such; in the seventh draft the same pledge ran 'It will continue to be our policy to protect the citizen, irrespective of creed or colour, against lawlessness and against abuses of power that may limit his liberty under the law'. This could of course be interpreted to mean exactly what the first pledge had said more specifically, and further changes were needed to secure approval. The phrase 'irrespective of creed or colour' was deleted altogether and, after Macleod had canvassed opinion on the subject, so was the final section from 'and against abuses . . .' Finally, it was agreed to restore 'irrespective of creed or colour', now that the pledge excluded anything about the limiting of liberty. As printed, the manifesto committed the Party as follows: 'It will continue to be our policy to protect the citizen, irrespective of creed or colour, against lawlessness'. This was of course a policy that really had nothing to do with immigration at all.

The drafting thus reduced the positive elements considerably, with a corresponding increase in the merely defensive. A useful find therefore was the question of the arts, which arose at the last moment when Sir Hamilton Kerr's Committee on Recreation, the Arts and Sport produced a timely report in July 1959. In January, Macmillan had suggested 'a policy for sport' and Goldman had replied that a departmental committee under Wolfenden was at work on the subject; the Prime Minister instructed 'find out what he is going to say, and if it is good pinch it'. Kerr's committee therefore offered the chance to widen this into a more general approach, and the Chancellor's question 'Do we *need* to have a policy on the arts?' was easily brushed aside. This whole topic fitted in well enough with the theme of the manifesto and it was especially well-suited to presentation along the lines of 'On the basis of what has been done, move on'. *The Next Five Years* therefore included three paragraphs on the subject, one on the past, a longer one on the future, and a linking sentence (as was very appropriate in 1959) stating that Conservatism was not solely about material things:

THE USE OF LEISURE. Two out of three families in the country now own TV, one in three has a car or motorcycle, twice as many are taking their holidays away from home – these are welcome signs of the increasing enjoyment of leisure. They are the fruits of our policies.

But at the same time all this represents a challenge to make the growth of leisure more purposeful and creative, especially for young people.

Our policy of opportunity will therefore be extended. In particular, we propose to reorganise and expand the Youth Service. Measures will be taken to encourage Youth Leadership and the provision of attractive youth clubs, more playing fields and better facilities for sport. We shall do more to support the arts including the living theatre. Improvements will be made in museums and galleries and in the public library service. Particular attention will be given to the needs of provincial centres.

This relatively restrained series of promises was the fruit of a compromise between Sir Hamilton Kerr's more ambitious plans and the understandable wish of the Chancellor not to promise anything that would be expensive. By comparison, Labour's specific pledges on the same subjects did not actually promise any more (no more than the Conservatives did over the next five years anyway); but by attaching expenditure figures to its promises Labour gave the appearance of far greater extravagance. This small example, in an area of policy that none of the Parties had even mentioned in their 1955 manifestoes, stands as representative of the different ways in which the Labour and Conservative parties approached the 1959 election. The Conservatives were for once able to capitalise on their position as the Government despite having had two terms of office already; for the most part, the record was left to speak for itself, while the limited promises for the future were presented as the natural consequences of the record even when they were actually entirely new departures.[14]

Early preparations also ensured that the structure of the Party's campaign had been finalised long before it was needed. The composition of the Emergency Business Committee and the Questions of Policy Committee was decided in November 1958, with the Lord Chancellor to chair both so as to maintain close liaison; the Research Department was therefore able to make its preparations through the Spring of 1959, seeking rulings from Government departments where necessary, in order to have much of its work on policy questions ready in advance of the dissolution. Similar advance work was done on the rest of the campaign; most of the Party literature, the outline of the Prime Minister's major election speeches, the allocation of officers to Research Department duties, the content of the Party's broadcasts, and the manifesto itself, were all complete by July for an election campaign that was not due to begin until October. As Macmillan noted on one such outline plan on 20 July, 'Have to be done by end of the month, or everyone will be in Monaco'.[15] There was a good deal of comment in 1959 on the extent to which a long and warm Summer helped the Government; it was not so well known how far early preparations enabled everyone from the Prime Minister to the humblest Research Department officer to take advantage of the Summer too, and to return in September ready for the fray.

When the election was over, the general view was that rather too much had been planned in advance and that the campaign had therefore rather lacked spontaneity. George Christ, the Prime Minister's main speech-writer for the campaign, argued that Macmillan had been unduly restricted by the plans made in advance; he had had too much work to do before the election and too many of his speech topics were untopical when they came to be delivered. Henry Brooke drew the same conclusion about the campaign as a whole, and about the Questions of Policy procedure in particular, suggesting that more preparation meant less initiative. From within the Department, James Douglas reached the same conclusion about broadcasts; it was agreed that Labour's broadcasts had been better than those of the Conservatives, partly because Labour had been more prepared to trust the professional broadcasters, but partly because the Conservatives had 'put too much in the can' before the election. He wondered indeed if the Research Department was not becoming rather 'remote from the battle' and whether it would be a good idea in future to send officers to by-elections to keep them in touch with the front line. However, there was another side to this entire argument, which is that with limited resources a Party can have flexibility only after the basic work has been done. Thus, while the Conservative *Campaign Guide* was published long before the campaign started, and provided as usual the backbone of the Party's speaking campaign in the constituencies, Labour's equivalent (the *Speakers' Handbook*) ran so late that its publication was eventually abandoned altogether.[16] The early preparations meant that, whatever happened in the campaign, Conservative candidates and speakers had all the raw materials with which to construct their speeches and letters to the press. The Research Department was therefore free to construct tailor-made speeches for the big occasions if it should prove necessary. Indeed, the characteristic of the campaign that most attracted attention from the outside was that, although the Conservatives were somewhat jolted by the way in which the campaign started, they had the necessary flexibility to respond with a devastating counter-attack in the last week. Macmillan's reply to Gaitskell and his promise to make it rain on polling day were both indications of how far the Conservatives *were* able to respond to the events of the campaign, but the counter-attack was more carefully-organised than these surface examples would suggest.

A whole series of major speeches were written in the middle of the campaign, precisely to react to it, one such being Kilmuir's Brighton speech on 5 October. On 22 September, Dear circulated a memorandum to all the Department's Heads of Section as follows:

1. Lord Kilmuir will be making a major speech at Brighton, and full speech material is required by the evening of Thursday 25th September, as it will have to be linked and coordinated in this office.

2. Please lay on sections of this speech as follows:-
   Mr. *Stebbings* – general opening, including section on Nationalisation – 4 quarto pages.
   Mr. *Douglas* – Economic Section – 8 quarto pages.
   Mr. *Block* – Home Affairs Section – 8 quarto pages.
   Mr. *Hadley* – Foreign Affairs – 4 quarto pages.

3. I think this can be a fairly hard-hitting and forceful speech.

Without careful preparations to get a lot of routine work out of the way, it would have been impossible to call on the time of the five most senior officers in the Department, and on several desk officers presumably, to frame a speech for one Cabinet Minister. And Kilmuir's speech was only one of many that were produced in the same few days.[17] Similarly, advance preparations did not preclude broadcasts from being updated before transmission. The first television broadcast, consisting of a discussion between the Prime Minister and senior colleagues really was recorded in the previous July, but the short introduction by Christopher Chataway and the concluding statement by Macmillan were both filmed just before the broadcast went out. The radio talk by Butler was recorded on 17 September and then edited over the following fortnight, with an additional section put on tape only on the day of the broadcast itself.[18] The Department also played the main part in the destructive exercise during the campaign on the cost of the Labour policies; this eventually forced Gaitskell to give a pledge not to raise income tax, so undermining his own credibility. The reaction to the campaign from the Party at large was not as unfavourable as that of Party professionals, and Butler reported to Fraser that 'The Prime Minister had told me that he has never known the briefing and documentation better. Candidates and organisations have been supplied and an atmosphere of confidence has been created'.

Michael Fraser's own conclusion from the Party's victory in the 1959 election was aimed more at the future than the past. His official report stressed the wisdom of delaying the election until the Autumn, for it was clear to him that elections should not be called until the Government had a clear lead in the opinion polls – a view that was to be very relevant when the next election approached in 1964. He also stressed a view that was unfashionable among politicians and Party professionals who had just fought a hard battle, but which was to be accepted as conventional electoral wisdom in the 1960s, that 'elections are won between elections and not during the campaign'. The logic of this view led him to look forward to the next election as soon as the 1959 campaign was over; as he told a correspondent, 'It has certainly been a very satisfactory result which we must now use as a spring-board and not as a sofa'.[19]

Fraser had a very realistic attitude to his Party's prospects; in a two-party system, neither could expect to win every time, but it was his job to try to ensure that next time was not the one that the Conservatives would lose. There was also a rather unusual opportunity created by the disarray in Labour ranks after their party's third defeat in succession; internal dissension and frustrated ambition reduced the Labour Party to near impotence in 1960–61, and there seemed to be a real possibility that if the Conservatives could by some means prolong their winning run to a fourth success, then the Labour Party would break up and a permanent shift in the party system would be achieved.[20] The stakes were therefore unusually high in the Parliament of 1959, and Fraser now had a little more room for manoeuvre in Old Queen Street with which to grasp the opportunity. From the low point of 1956–7, the Research Department had recovered both in staff and in financial position. At the time of the 1959 election there were once again twenty-six research officers, more than at any time since the Party had come into office in 1951, and the number of secretaries was also unusually high at eighteen. Only one officer had left to fight the election this time and in a hopeless seat from which he was due to return, though two former desk officers had been elected MPs – Peter Tapsell and Gordon Campbell. This expansion had been made possible by an easing of the financial restraints; the Department's expenditure rose from £52,789 in 1955 to £78,437 in 1959, an increase well ahead of rises in the cost of living. Thereafter, it marked time for a couple of years and then rose again from 1962, reaching £110,000 in 1964.[21] This made possible a restoration of some of the cuts imposed in the mid-fifties, particularly in the purchase of outside publications, and it also improved the remuneration of officers. The intention was that a desk officer, after a probationary year, should receive an income equivalent to that of a Principal in the Civil Service, while a Head of Section should receive pay equivalent to an Assistant Secretary; this level had been more or less reached in 1960, and the subsequent falling away was due more to the rapid advances of civil service salaries than to the reduction in Research Department pay. In the aftermath of the 1959 election, Fraser intended to use this situation to carry out the research intentions that had been frustrated earlier, and in this he had the full support of Butler, who had always rather regretted the integration of research and information services in 1948.

After consultations with Butler, Fraser wrote to James Douglas and Geoffrey Block, perhaps the officers whose approach to research work could be considered most academic, on 2 November 1959, barely a month after the election:

> Mr. Butler has asked me to prepare for him over the next few weeks our suggestions for a programme for long-term work to be carried out by this Department in conjunction with a network of ad hoc policy committees, making use of the talent on the back-benches in the House and any outside experts whom we may think suitable to bring in from the universities, the Bow Group etc.

The main aim would be to look forward to the five years beginning in 1964 – after the next election – though without duplicating the work being done by the various Royal Commissions which the Government had appointed for the same purpose. Research ideas should build on current policies ('new variations of existing aims should be the aim') and should be carried on with a view to publication by the CPC. Above all it should be remembered that 'We are a Party Research Department and therefore, as we have limited resources, we should concentrate on lines of research that are likely to be of political benefit'. Some sort of internal rearrangement was necessary in any case in 1959 because of the retirement of Percy Cohen after more than forty years in the Party's service. Fraser became the sole Director of the Department and a general reorganisation was put into effect. By the end of November, it had been decided that Oliver Stebbings would take general responsibility under Fraser for publications (especially the regular *Notes on Current Politics* and the *Campaign Guide*), that Douglas and Block would be designated as 'Research Organisers' specialising respectively in economic and in home and constitutional affairs, and that Paul Dean and Brendon Sewill would be promoted to succeed them as Heads of Section. The intention, according to a note from Fraser to Butler, was 'to provide some separation within the Department of those working on forward planning from those carrying out the servicing duties'. At the same time, it was intended to widen the Department's contacts through what was called 'the octopus' (which would spread its tentacles into the Parliamentary Party, the CPC, the Bow Group, the university Conservatives, Swinton College, and such unofficial bodies as the Inns of Court Conservative Association). After a canvassing of opinions, in which Edward Heath and the Chief Whip took a leading part, a list of research topics was evolved before the end of 1959, with the working out of a youth policy as the most urgent. It is significant that Edward Heath took a leading part in the setting up of these new departures, as he had with the beginning of the Steering Committee, for he was rapidly emerging as the Party's main political policy impresario, already destined to play the policy making role that Neville Chamberlain and R. A. Butler had played in the two previous generations.

Work on a youth policy was under way in the early months of 1960, with a committee that included representatives of the Conservative students, Young Conservatives, Bow Group and the Under-35 Group, serviced from the Research Department. Its early findings provided the basis for a discussion at the National Union's Central

Council Meeting in March 1960, and its final report was published by the CPC as *Youth in the Sixties*. A similar group set up in 1962 to consider a policy for Voluntary Service Overseas included Nicholas Scott representing the Young Conservatives and Timothy Raison representing the Bow Group. By the summer of 1960, Fraser reported to Butler that 'We have now had six months of the new regime without Percy Cohen and with the new research arrangements. In general I think they are working well'. By that time, eight research committees were at work and other changes had been made to facilitate their efforts.

It was decided to increase co-ordination with the CPC, so that the two-way contact programme could be used to provide information on the attitudes of the Party rank and file, and Fraser intervened personally to persuade Ministers to take a more active interest in this side of its work. At the other end of the research process, it was decided that most issues of *Notes on Current Politics* should be devoted to one topic, rather than including whatever material happened to come to hand; there were occasional issues which pulled together minor themes that would not justify separate treatment, but for the most part all information on agriculture (for example) could be found in one issue. This made it possible to plan the publishing programme for some months in advance, so that desk officers would know at what date they would be expected to produce a substantial volume of material on their subject, and could arrange their other work around it. By the end of 1960, Fraser was encouraging his staff to think out new topics for research in the new year, so that the momentum should not slacken, and two major topics were begun, into ways of encouraging economic growth and into the reform of local government finance. By the summer of 1961 though the impetus had clearly fallen away somewhat; enough work was in hand to absorb the time and energy of the Department's staff and there were few new policy ideas that could be floated that deserved investigation.[22] Thereafter, as after 1955, more and more of the Department's time was taken up with the defensive tasks of protecting a Government under pressure, so that little new research work was begun in 1962 or 1963. During these years, there was plenty to be done in moving forward projects already begun. Of these, the most important were probably the committees on agriculture, Commonwealth affairs, industrial relations, London government, local government finance, monopolies, science and technology, social services, and town and country planning. Each illustrates a different facet of the problems of research in government.

The problem of agriculture was dominated throughout these years by the future of British trade policy, and especially by the question of the Common Market, for no plans could have any claim to permanence until the outcome was known; as Iain Macleod remarked in November 1962, 'We really are on a painted ocean until Ted Heath comes back from Brussels'. As with the previous committee, Anthony Hurd was chairman, and on this occasion Fraser attended the first meeting to urge a quick report, as Butler had done in 1957. After discussions with Ministers and other advisers, the committee asked its secretary, Peter Minoprio of the Research Department, to submit a draft interim report containing its advice to the Government on the central issue of the day. This draft restated the need for urgency, 'knowing that Ministers must be considering early action' (though if so, it was rather more than they had so far admitted to the House of Commons in June 1960). It presented a rather optimistic picture and concluded that 'we have little doubt that arrangements could be made to accommodate British agriculture within the Common Market framework'. The committee however were not so sanguine, and where Minoprio (a European enthusiast) had stated that agriculture was not a barrier to Britain joining the Common Market, the committee decided that agriculture was not an *impossible* barrier – providing various safeguards were obtained first. Over the following winter, the committee laboured to define what these safeguards should be, while the Government continued to deny that the Common Market was on its mind, but in April 1961, a meeting with Joseph Godber (Under Secretary at the Foreign Office) indicated the trend of events. He explained that the Government was now seriously considering making concessions in order to get Britain into the EEC (or rather to link the EEC and EFTA together). 'Most recently the Prime Minister had received every encouragement from the US President to seek a closer relationship with the Community.' Finally, Godber told the committee that the matter was inherently a political one ('France was the key to the whole problem') and that the main responsibility had therefore been transferred from the Board of Trade to the Foreign Office. By July, the committee was ready to present the Government with its 'stiff terms' for the acceptance of entry to the EEC, though not all members agreed with this view. Somewhat unhelpfully, Hurd told Butler that 'the division of opinion in the Committee on the major long-term question reflects views and uncertainties held in the Conservative Party in the House and in the Country'. By that time too, the Research Department was at work on a 'Plan B' – the option that would remain for Britain if the

negotiations failed – and was helping Conservative MPs to stave off
the attacks of their angry constituents, especially farmers. There is
little doubt that the committee and the Party in general welcomed
the failure of the negotiations, on the grounds that a serious source of
friction could thereby be avoided or postponed.[23]

The future of the Commonwealth was a closely-related issue on
which no amount of research could disguise a real difference of
opinion. It was clear enough in the aftermath of the Suez crisis that
things would never be quite the same again, but the nature of the
change or its timing was not so clear. Enoch Powell had no doubt that
what was needed was a clean cut, as he wrote in February 1957:

> The Tory Party must be cured of the British Empire, of the pitiful
> yearning to cling to relics of a bygone system (and fight for them if
> necessary at the barricades and in other division lobbies) while at the
> same time proclaiming the wonders of a new system whose foster parents
> were Attlee and Nehru. Economically and Politically, we need what the
> Younger Pitt of 1784 stands for: what (and why) the Empire was and
> what (if anything) the Commonwealth is, must be made clear to
> ourselves till it hurts no longer. The courage to act rationally will flow
> from the courage to see things as they are. The Tory Party has to find its
> patriotism again, and to find it, as of old, in 'this England'. This too will
> be a salve to the wound of Suez.[24]

Something of this clear-thinking, though without the same note of
drama, appeared in the work done for the Committee on Commonwealth and Colonies, set up under Lord Colyton in 1958. The Research
Department's drafts expressed great doubts over such experiments as
the Central African Federation, but this was not a view that the
committee accepted. It resolved that such initiatives *must* be made to
work if the multi-racial Commonwealth were to be given time to
develop, and suggested the merging of the Colonial and Commonwealth Relations Offices as a step in the same direction. However,
disagreements persisted, and it was felt wiser to delay the report's
publication until after the 1959 election; it did not appear until 1960.[25]
By the time that its administrative suggestions were put into effect in
1962, the Central African Federation was about to be dissolved. The
extent of disagreement was reflected in the Commonwealth Council,
set up in the early 1950s to encourage Conservatives to identify with
the new Commonwealth idea. In 1961, Gerald Sayers described for
Fraser the effect that subsequent policy had had:

> When the Council was formed – over eight years ago – we envisaged the
> *steady* progress of colonial territories towards self-government – an aim
> to which 99 per cent of Party members subscribed. But, swept along by

the flood tide of nationalism, we have gone at the gallop, and in doing so have upset many of our supporters. As a result, the Party is divided over Colonial policy into (a) the progressives (mainly the younger members) who endorse it, (b) the great majority, who accept it, with regret, as inevitable, as, of course, it is, and (c) the right wing (mainly the older members . . .) who are frankly critical.

The composition of the Commonwealth Council was reconstituted in 1962 and it was then given the go-ahead to publish its views through the CPC, on the strict understanding that they were unofficial.[26] The real basis of the change of policy was given without disguise in a letter drafted by David Dear for the Prime Minister to send to one of his constituents in April 1962:

> Our problem . . . is the wave of nationalism and pressure for independence, which have already brought disastrous complications for other European countries. It would perhaps be possible to hold down this movement by force. But in the Government's view this is not a practical solution, the country would not support such a policy, nor provide the men and the arms to carry it out. The only thing the Government can do is to try to bring about conditions in which black and white can work together peaceably. This raises difficult problems of timing: if we go too fast, we risk having a Congo on our hands; if we go too slow, we risk having an Algeria on our hands. No one can guarantee that our policy will succeed, but at least we can claim that compared to other countries it has been relatively successful.[27]

Divested of ideology and conviction, the Government's policy could be given a strong defence, but this was difficult to put across to the Party faithful, and it did nothing about the gap in Britain's world role that Powell had identified. For Fraser and his staff, the Common Market was earmarked to fill that gap, a policy dashed by De Gaulle's veto.

Industrial relations and monopolies were both cases where disagreement was only on timing and practicality, not on the direction of policy. By the early 1960s, most Conservatives favoured intervention to restrain trades unions in some way, but it was as usual difficult to persuade the Government to act. In 1962, the Committee on Industrial Relations, meeting under the Chairmanship of a Conservative trade unionist, Sir Edward Brown, resolved that legislation was needed before the next election, and that it should include compulsory strike ballots, compulsory registration of unions and compulsory arbitration. The final report was rather less ambitious, stressing the need for reform rather than the form that changes should take, but its impact was reduced by the simultaneous production of a leaflet on the subject by the Monday Club. This presented a difficulty for Goldman at the CPC, for he had been looking for some time for a Monday Club leaflet that he could publish, in order to draw this new body into the Party orbit – to attach it to a tentacle of the octopus; the Monday Club report therefore had priority and stole the headlines.[28] Monopolies illustrated the same difficulty and an opposite result. The committee was under Lord Poole, with its membership and terms of reference cleared with the President of the Board of Trade in advance. According to Poole, the committee relied heavily on the work of James Douglas who acted as secretary: 'he really did the whole thing, and I could not possibly exaggerate all that he did'. The recommendations of the committee proved to be controversial, since they called for stronger action against monopolies (including resale price maintenance, not on the Government's agenda in February 1963), but this time the coincidence of another report actually helped to get the official one out. Since the Bow Group were known to be on the point of publishing very similar recommendations, there could be no point in refusing to publish the views of 'a powerful group of Party figures'. As Fraser reminded the Chief Whip, a decision not to publish would make 'it increasingly difficult thereafter to get people of proper standard to serve on these committees . . . I think this pamphlet should be published, and some members of the committee are sure to make a row if it is not'. The report was thus published in March 1963; in order that it should not be pre-empted by the Bow Group, who were ready to publish late in February, a press release was timed for the same day as the Bow Group leaflet appeared. Sometimes the tentacles of the octopus appeared to get tangled.[29]

Work on science showed the difficulty of keeping up with changing Government policy. When the Committee on Science and Technology first met, with Robert Carr as chairman, in July 1960, the first Minister for Science had been only recently appointed. But the application of technology was an idea that became increasingly popular as the Committee worked. By the time that a report was in draft, the Government had appointed a Minister for Technical Cooperation and soon after the Committee finished its work, Robert Carr became the second Minister to head that new department.[30] Local Government finance was an issue forced on the Government by the escalation of rating bills, but it proved to be *too* sensitive for a research committee. A representative group of MPs, councillors and other experts worked for over a year, but could suggest only minor changes and it was eventually decided that it would be wiser not to publish at all than to offer very little. London Government was worked over only after the new local government system for the capital had become law; Paul Dean from the Research Department was assigned the task of shepherding the Conservative campaign for the new GLC with assistance on the manifesto and other publications. Research Department contacts eased some problems in the run-up to the first GLC election; for example, the South East Plan which had been commissioned by the Minister of Housing was not due to be published until March 1964, but some of its contents were made available while the manifesto was being drafted so that the two documents did not conflict.[31]

Social policy was an area in which research work was continuous, but the project in question had begun with an internal Departmental group set up in 1958 under Geoffrey Block. With Block assigned to long-term research, Fraser took over the Chairmanship of the group in 1960 and it was re-named the Policy Committee for Social Services. Discussions ranged widely and meetings were held with most of the Ministers involved during 1961. The main topic of disagreement was the idea of introducing a voucher system to reduce the cost of education to the Exchequer, an idea pressed by Brendon Sewill but strongly opposed by David Dear as 'in effect the abolition of universal free education in this country'. It was eventually turned down on grounds of its impracticality, but an alternative suggestion of direct contributions from parents was turned down flat. The committee's interim report on financial implications of future policy in all the social services was submitted in May 1961 and was followed by the appointment of an Inter-departmental Group to consider its ideas within the Government. Later meetings looked at structural rather than financial matters and the work was completed in 1963; the final report was approved by the ACP but was never published, being merely circulated to the Ministers concerned. Its character was indicated in the letter from Fraser that went to Butler along with the report itself in September 1963:

> The present report is concerned with the development of the services in the 1960s and beyond. It is not dramatic – as the closer we looked at the more dramatic proposals for the social services the less we liked them – but I think it does contain some useful detailed suggestions under most of the headings.

Policy research was as much about rejecting new solutions as it was about finding them.[32]

Finally in this group of policy reviews, the work on town and country planning ran into a storm of Party protest. This committee was set up under Colin Thornton-Kemsley in March 1960, with Enoch Powell as a member; Geoffrey Block acted as Secretary 'in addition to being a member of the committee'. That reflected his personal knowledge of the subject as an active member of the Town and Country Planning Association. Early meetings were bedevilled by the fundamental disagreement between Powell and the rest as to whether planning should take place at all. Powell presented a number of papers, resisting the assumption that 'planning has now become a necessity' and above all arguing that the Government should plan only on *non*-economic matters (amenities, environment and so forth) and not on such things as the location of industry. Other members were more dubious, but it was agreed that intervention in economic matters should be minimised, which was as far as the committee had got by the Summer recess. When business resumed in the Winter of 1960–61, Powell had become Minister of Health and had therefore resigned from the committee (Ministers never served as actual members). The way was therefore clear for swifter progress towards a more interventionist report, which was duly completed during the Summer of 1961. However, at this point the Committee's ideas met a great deal of Party opposition, based not on a Powellite adherence to free enterprise, but on the protection of local vested interests and on fears that enhanced planning powers would imply the subordination of country interests to those of the towns. Thornton-Kemsley perhaps anticipated the likely response to his Committee's proposal of a local government structure based around city regions and planning by regional authorities, for the later meetings of the Committee were shrouded in secrecy. One man kept in the dark was Henry Brooke, who as Minister of Housing and Local Government might have been thought to have an interest in the matter. Fraser therefore sent Brooke a copy of the report, 'on an entirely personal basis and without anyone on the committee, including Thornton-Kemsley knowing I have done so'. He was not at all happy with what he read, and neither was the ACP when it considered the proposals later in October 1961; Sir Eric Edwards, John Morrison and Lady Davidson were appointed as a sub-committee of the ACP to meet Thornton-Kemsley's Committee and talk the matter over with them.

In order to avoid a pitched battle, it was arranged that Butler would meet both groups over lunch, *before* their negotiations began; Butler was convinced that a great deal of re-writing would be needed, and he asked Fraser to 'put Block fully in charge and warn him that any redrafting must be done by him in the interests of the

Party . . . I agree that the report is a noble document. It certainly wants handling with care'. The note which Fraser provided for Butler's speech to the two committees indicates the line that he meant to take, and it also provided a justification for the whole process of policy research:

> Congratulate committee on providing us with reassessment both fresh and authoritative . . . All agree – myself, the Minister, the ACP and your committee itself – that this report should be published. No fundamental reason why you should in any way alter your view prior to publication. But would hope that your aim is for impact rather than explosion, so hope you may give good hearing both to views of Minister and of representative sub-committee of ACP under Sir Eric Edwards. Also to any minor editorial points of presentation which CPC may raise at later stage. Conscious that time important and never on side of any of us. . . . Would particularly ask you to bear in mind tricky administrative problems, disquiet on the part of many about preservation of the countryside and reservations about compulsory acquisition.
>
> In the twenty years or so in which I have been closely associated with forward policy thinking in the party, I have often been warned of the dangers of thought. Have always been prepared to accept these myself, and believe Party had increasingly done so. Part of secret of success in last decade, and in rapid defeat of socialist revolution of '45 to '51. What is required is not major change in your report but minor tidying up to meet genuine fears. If these reasonably met, believe impact will be greater not less.

After these soothing words, Butler retired and left the two Committees to their task, which proved to be harmonious – 'no head-on collisions or under-water explosions'. Block reported that Sir Eric Edwards 'opened the committee's eyes to one or two unexpected phrases that might offend countrymen, and, when dealing with the proposed regional set-up, he and Sir Eric Brown spoke up for the role of the local authorities'. Block then set to work to draft amendments which were put to the original committee, with variable success, early in December: 'The Committee threw out 35 per cent of my proposed amendments, but accepted the remainder. . . . As I had purposely made my original list of amendments a numerous one, there still remains a list of some fourteen amendments'. On the following day he told Fraser that 'the beating-up on Tuesday was not too bad. An impressive list of changes made still stands, and I shall send these to each member of the Edwards sub-committee. I am sure that these will convince them that they have significantly rewritten the report'. By this means, harmony was preserved, and the opposition of the Minister was reduced by Brooke's transfer to the Home Office on 9 October. The report finally went to press on 20 December and, after further amendments in proof, was published as *Change and Challenge* in February 1962. As on most occasions when local government reform was in the air, it had proved necessary to pitch the opening bid high in order that the final agreement could be at all challenging.[33]

All these investigations had been initiated with a view to the next election, and, as in the two previous Parliaments, it was felt half way through this one that it was time to start pulling themes together. A Policy Study Group was again set up under Macleod, though since he had recently become Chairman of the Party, it was to be called the Chairman's Committee, and it was linked more closely to the Central Office and the Research Department in December 1961. Its aims, as put by the Chairman and recorded in notes of one of its meetings in 1962 were to 'chase ideas around in the hope that even one in ten will come to something'. Ministers were invited to meetings in rotation to discuss their plans, one of the most successful meetings being that with Enoch Powell (then Minister of Health) on social policy; Macleod introduced Powell's discussion paper with the words, 'This shows how you do produce, after ten years of office, new policies in a field. Health, welfare and the old. This is exactly the sort of contribution that I think we hoped for'. Rather more surprisingly, in the general discussion that followed, Powell emerged as a strong supporter of the Chancellor's pay policy, largely because it had already attracted unpopularity and could now expect to pay off in return: 'I am all for the Chancellor's policy. I have just antagonised all the nurses in the country, and all those who go to the physiotherapists, and all the doctors and civil servants throughout the country, and the universities'. At another meeting, Peter Goldman voiced similar opinions when he argued that details of the next manifesto would be far less vital than the success or failure of the Government in economic affairs. Uncertainty on the economy and on the Common Market inhibited all future policy planning, as Macmillan himself made clear in one of his discursive after-dinner reviews. This one was noted in July 1962:

> What have we failed to do? Have made the affluent society for the young, but haven't got them onto the moral basis they should have. . . . Vital to be 'on today's ball'. Enormous decisions to be taken in international affairs from day to day, and these are what turn your hair white, not the income tax. . . . Then we have Europe. That will come along, probably not as quickly as we think, but it will come along. (Socialists in my youth

were an internationalist party. Now they shout about 'horrid foreigners'. Harold Wilson particularly. We fought them and we can work with them; he didn't fight them and he can't work with them.) We can't say we must *definitely* go in or they will all say Yah!, so for the moment the 'antis' can go drip, drip, drip.

> *Housing*: that was great fun because you marked up the score. Not so easy now. . . . Get the European thing into a great thing. And get something on the home front that is a bit more concrete. Some facts – 'slums are being pulled down' – 'universities are being built'. And a general theme of efficiency. If in the Common Market will have to fight; and if out, will fight hard, won't just sink back depressed.

This gives a good indication of the Prime Minister's thinking, less than a week after he had savagely reconstructed his Government on the 'night of the long knives'. As Macleod sadly reflected at the same meeting, '"Conservatives care" – somehow the impression has gone. We haven't changed, but the people think we have become Cotton and Clore men'.[34]

The Research Department sought to deal with these problems, and with the others that beset the Party in 1962–3 by a number of initiatives of its own. An auxillary committee of officers was set up under Paul Dean to examine the political consequences of the Common Market on election prospects and to plan the Party's publications on various assumptions about the outcome of the negotiations. When the Brussels negotiations went wrong, this group was turned over to the task of evolving a different set of themes around which to frame a manifesto. Work was done with a panel of industrialists on future economic policy and the improvement of Britain's rate of growth; their report called for the steadying of levels of demand by the use of monetary controls to 'trim' peaks and troughs, but in general it rejected further intervention and called for a cutting back of Government expenditure. The report was never published because many of the industrialists involved did not wish to be publicly associated with the Party, but again it was circulated to Ministers. Several meetings were also held in 1961 and 1962 to evolve an agreed Departmental line on the policy that the Government should follow 'after the pause', that is after Selwyn Lloyd's first experiment in an incomes policy. It was agreed that the new National Economic Development Council should be encouraged as a means of involving the unions in the Government's policy. For the same reason the Research Department approved of the idea of a National Incomes Commission, provided that it avoided two dangers, '(a) of appearing to be a bit of political camouflage behind which the policy is abandoned, and (b) . . . being effectively sterilised by being boycotted by the unions'. The Department had thus come round to a more interventionist line, but it also recognised that 'if this fails, we shall have to break the Trades Unions' monopoly power and/or work for a more centralised system'. It was not a recipe that was likely to appeal to a Government in a trough of unpopularity, but the unions did sterilise the National Incomes Commission and so the debate went on.[35]

On tax policy, the Department enjoyed good relations with both Selwyn Lloyd and Reginald Maudling, so that their advice on budgetary policy may well have carried more weight than usual. For the 1962 budget, the Department offered the iconoclastic view that it was time to review the 'assumption that . . . taxes must always come down. . . . We realise that for many people the urgency has gone out of tax reductions. Indeed, there are some who would advocate other priorities'. This reflected disagreement in the Department between James Douglas, who was concerned about the level of services and of overall expenditure, and Brendon Sewill who was still looking for tax reductions. But both were agreed that the Government needed to keep its increased expenditure within the rise of National Income. Selwyn Lloyd wrote to express his thanks for the advice received and especially for suggestions about savings, which he had asked his Treasury advisers to evaluate for him. For the 1963 budget, the Department was more definite in its view, for this might be an election budget and would be represented as such if tax cuts were too lavish: 'propaganda about Election Budget and "stop-go" policies, however unjustified, has had an increasing impact on a section of the public'. Much of the urgency had now gone from the tax question, 'and many people now attach more importance to increasing expenditure in one field or another. In particular, if the process of limiting the Estimates involves any unpopular moves, subsequent tax reductions are liable to look unjust or frivolous'. Shortly after presenting his budget, Maudling wrote to Fraser to 'hope you will have observed that the main feature of the income tax changes was based upon the very sound advice of the Research Department'. For the 1964 budget, similar advice was proffered, suggesting moderate cuts to continue our 'success story', but also insisting that 'tax reduction is now fairly low on most people's order of priorities'. At Maudling's request, detailed suggestions were made about savings, personal allowances, and taxes on gambling. Thus, the chickens of the 1959 manifesto came home to roost, and Derrick Heathcoat-

Amory's caution at that time was justified; unless economic growth could be accelerated (and the Research Department could see little chance of this without taking on board the question of industrial reorganisation or trade union law), tax reductions and expansion of Government expenditure were bound to come into conflict.[36] It was a moral full of significance for the future. It was indeed precisely the dilemma that made trades union reformers out of Barbara Castle and Harold Wilson in 1968–9.

Behind the scenes, the Department was also working for the first time on underlying political attitudes and political partisanship. Back in March 1960, James Douglas had put forward the idea of 'a little technical study group' on opinion polls, and this was agreed with the formation of the Psephology Group, made up of Research Department and Central Office staff and with Fraser in the chair. The sort of work that was envisaged for it can be seen from the first meeting, when Douglas introduced a paper on Anthony Crosland's *Can Labour Win?* as 'a first rate piece of work . . . the sort of thing which . . . I would like to see emerging from the Psephology Group'. Nevertheless, Douglas was extremely sceptical about Crosland's 'determinist' argument about voting habits and he argued that what was needed by a successful Party was not just a clear image as Crosland argued, but also an image that was clearly different from the other side. Later meetings were held with academic psephologists and with people from all the opinion polling organisations; special surveys were commissioned from NOP, not on immediate voting intentions but on deep-lying attitudes and on class influences on voting. The group's final report contained some home truths for the Conservative Party in 1963: it was clear that the Party had lost the label of 'competence' which it had been able to claim in the 1950s, and it was unlikely that a return to prosperity would repair this loss (since a rapid boom would confirm rather than refute charges of 'stop-go'). What was needed was a concentrated effort to win back Conservative supporters in the 'marginal' social classes, the C2 and D non-manual groups, many of whom had defected to the Liberals; if won back, these must be made to feel that they were not passengers in the Conservative boat but full members of the crew.[37]

The investigation of causes of the Party's unpopularity indeed became a near obsession during 1962; the Chairman's Committee asked Peter Goldman to give them direct evidence on what had gone wrong in his by-election at Orpington (which he attributed partly to local factors and partly to the protests of 'true-blue Tories' about Government policies on Africa, the economy and the trades unions).

MPs were so concerned by the state of the Party that the back-benchers convened their own Committee on By-Election Results in April 1962, with Sir Richard Nugent as Chairman and Paul Dean as Secretary. The first meeting showed that the back-benchers were very critical of their Government, many calling for an immediate re-shuffle to remove the Ministers who were too 'official' – too immune from Party advice. Sir Gerald Nabarro struck an important and topical note when he said flatly that Conservatives in the country resented the number of old Etonians in the Government. Later meetings were held with Michael Fraser and with several Central Office officials, all of whom were loyal to the Government and all of whom came under severe attack as a result. When Dean asked members to send him papers to help him in framing his report, he received some that he can scarcely have expected; many criticised the patronage policy of the Government, and one merely totted up the number of the Prime Minister's relatives in office. The final report, put to the Party Chairman on 16 May 1962, concluded that 'the present state of the Party is serious' – more serious than in 1957–8. This they blamed on unpopular policies which had created an impression of vacillation, weakness and incompetence. Party disunity had come from the 'weak and blurred' presentation of policy, and they therefore called for a major re-shuffle as soon as possible, with one Minister to be given full-time responsibility for public relations.[38] This trenchant advice undoubtedly helped to push Macmillan into the drastic reorganisation of his team less than two months later; William Deedes, listed second among the back-bench MPs on the committee, was promoted straight into the Cabinet, as Minister without Portfolio and as the man responsible for public relations.

In 1962, the Research Department was being deluged with letters of complaint, sent on by MPs or referred by the Prime Minister's office or the Party Chairman for the drafting of replies; this burden became so heavy that a general brief 'On Current Discontents' was compiled by David Dear in April to furnish MPs with stock answers to the most common lines of criticism. The Department felt constrained to pass on to the Government the full measure of the criticism, however unfair both of them felt it to be, and to urge the Government to draw the right conclusion from it. So on 24 May, Fraser wrote to Butler in remarkably outspoken terms:

Although much current criticism is unfair, the Government must resist the temptation to adopt a martyr complex. They must fight back. If we are to recover public support it must be by our actions between now and the General Election. . . . The Country wants greater change than is appreciated at Westminster. We must bring the country up to date; for example, the rating system, apprenticeships, the structure of taxation, the House of Commons. The Government must put more passion and enthusiasm into their public approach to our affairs. The public cannot be soothed by kindly moderation. The Government must set a lead by a passionate involvement in our affairs, and must show us that they really care.

Nonetheless, something of a Maginot mentality did set in within the Conservative Party in 1963 when the earlier policy difficulties were followed by a public scandal and then by a change of Leader that was unexpected, contentious and unprepared-for. Officers of the Department had to monitor television programmes to see whether charges of undue bias could be made, but this was difficult to sustain, as Dear reported in June 1963: he could find no real grounds for complaint in the broadcasts of the previous three weeks, though 'the general trend of denigration of life in Britain, and therefore by implication of the Government, was continued. . . . It is true that commentators had a field day . . . in discussing the Profumo affair, but this was natural enough in the circumstances'.[39]

When Sir Alec Douglas-Home became Prime Minister, he proved to be a more difficult Leader to service than Macmillan had been, naturally enough since he had such limited experience of many areas of policy and of the policy-making machinery. In October 1963, Dear reported to the Party Chairman that the Research Department was opposed to the idea of publishing an anthology of Douglas-Home's earlier statements on domestic and economic policy (intended to prove that he was *not* a one-sided politician) for many reasons: it was undesirable to run such an obviously defensive exercise and one that might well boomerang if it persuaded the Opposition to go quotation-hunting too; it would be better to fight on future plans than on the past, and the Prime Minister would thus 'rise above Harold Wilson's jibes'; above all, 'the quotations themselves are not very impressive'. The entire Research Department was put to work for the new Prime Minister in order to brief him for what would inevitably be a very tough start and a difficult election campaign thereafter; thirty separate documents were compiled on every subject from the philosophy of economic growth to 'where we stand on the Channel tunnel or bridge'.[40] In retrospect, the succession of Home in October 1963 can be seen as the beginning of the Conservative counter-attack, the time when previous economic decisions began to pay off and when the attempt to restore the image of competence and drive began to get through. But it could only be a partial success and the other side of the economic coin was always visible to the Research Department.

In a sense the Research Department had itself suffered a setback in the succession of Home, for the overwhelming weight of opinion there had favoured Butler, or failing him either Maudling or Heath. All the old boys of the Department in the Government had backed Butler, and some of them (Powell and Macleod) had gone so far in that direction as to make it impossible for them to serve under Home as Leader. Thereafter, Powell kept in touch with the Party and the Department behind the scenes, assisting for example with the 1964 manifesto, for he had resented not Home himself but Macmillan's manoeuvring to make him his successor; but Macleod remained publicly critical and so kept the Party wound open. Macleod's absence from the Government after October 1963 was important, for he symbolised for many the new generation of Conservatives who owed their advancement to merit rather than background, and in this image his Research Department duet with Powell had played an important part. Macmillan's reconstruction of July 1962 had been intended to polish up this face of the Party by putting more such men in the forefront of the Government, but the manner of his own retirement had put it all in jeopardy. It could hardly be denied after October 1963 that the Leadership was open to debate and that the whole style of the Party was linked with it. Letters to the Research Department, sent on by MPs for answering, made this clear enough. It will be worth quoting one of these, not just for the verve of its presentation but because it was typical of many and an indicator of what was to follow the Party's defeat in 1964. The letter was received at Central Office in December 1963 from a senior industrial manager, who described himself as a 44 year-old lifelong Conservative and who said that he and many like him could no longer bring themselves to support the Party. First of all, he emphasised that this had 'nothing to do with Profumo' but was rather the result of 'too many Etonians'. There was too much evidence of

> an 'establishment' and that this establishment would rather lose the election than lose their power in the Party. We are looking for a 1963 leader. Do you remember Kennedy? We liked him. We are sick of seeing old-looking men dressed in flat caps and bedraggled tweeds strolling with a 12 bore. For God's sake, what is your campaign manager doing? These photographs of Macmillan's ghost with Home's face date about 1912.
> The nearest approach to our man is Heath. In every task he performs,

win or lose, he has the facts, figures and knowledge. We don't give a damn if he is a bachelor. He is our age, he is capable, he looks a director (of the Country) and most of all he is quite different from these tired old men, their 19th century appearance and their 18th century platitudes. Capable as we think Mr. Heath is, we don't believe he or his kind will ever be allowed to take the reins from the tired, old men, or the Etonians . . . (This letter) may indicate to you where you are losing your votes – from the younger, thinking management types.[41]

Against such arguments, which became even more outspoken when in 1964 Macleod came into the open with his *Spectator* account of the recent Leadership crisis, the Party could only put up a feeble reply which stressed the need for unity against Labour and the country's gradual economic recovery.

Plans for a counter-attack had been in train before Macmillan retired and were only delayed by the change of Leader, the only change being that they now had to begin in a more defensive mode. A new team of speech-writers had been recruited for Macmillan in the summer of 1963, Nigel Lawson and Eldon Griffiths (later replaced by John Macgregor), and these were inherited by Home when he became Leader, though their appointment made it easier for Labour to caricature Home as a puppet. They had offices in 24 Old Queen Street and were technically employed as Research Department staff, though they were not integrated into the Department; all the same, their presence was a useful means of co-ordinating themes for speeches and of speeding the flow of information. From November 1963, the Research Department was preparing regular *aides memoires* for Ministers, which went out with a strongly-worded letter from the Party Chairman suggesting that they should be used for the Minister's next big speech. Thus, all the Party's main speakers were talking about much the same things, at first defensively about the new Government; then in January 1964 the speaking campaign went onto the offensive with attacks on Labour's plans, and in April confidence returned with a series of speeches celebrating the growing evidence of the Government's economic success. The idea of 'counter-attack' was carried on through an Area Chairmen's Dinner in May, where a regional programme of rallies was announced, all supervised by a single co-ordinating committee.[42]

The return of confidence owed something to the better economic conditions and the perceptible Conservative improvement in opinion polls and by-elections, but it also owed something to the Government's determination to fight its way out of its difficulties. A further cause of the recovery was undoubtedly the fears of Labour's nationalisation plans, highlighted in the Research Department's booklet *Entitled to Know*. By the Spring of 1964, many who had once thought that there was no chance of the Conservatives being re-elected were now debating whether Spring or Autumn would give them the better chance. There was also a feeling among many Conservatives that Harold Wilson might have over-reached himself in his obvious anxiety to win the election, and a real conviction that the Conservatives would be better prepared than Labour to govern after the election. When the *Campaign Guide* came out in February 1964 (timed to be ready for either Spring or Autumn), Brendon Sewill noted one interesting point about it and suggested to William Deedes that much might be made of it:

> The Conservative *Campaign Guide* published this week has a whole chapter on Progress in Science and Technology. The Labour Party's similar document, *Twelve Wasted Years*, only devotes half a page (out of 460 pages) to the same subject. Perhaps this is because their book is dated September 1963, and they did not discover science until their Conference in October.[43]

Wilson had a head start over Home in the battle of images (hence the great success of his 'technological revolution' speech at the Labour Conference) but his Party as a whole was not so well prepared. As the election approached, the Conservatives' patient work of preparation since 1959 began to pay off. But in the long run, it was the lack of a clear focus for the Party's campaign that was to prove the most damaging problem and the most insuperable.

Preparations for the election were not helped by the obvious dilemma about its date. It was widely known that a number of Ministers wanted to fight in the Spring, on the ground that the economic recovery might not be sustained, and it was also known that the Chancellor of the Exchequer, Reginald Maudling, took this view. Evidence to the Research Department from public opinion polls, and from private contacts in the polling organisations, took the opposite view; the Conservative recovery had been proceeding steadily and the election should therefore be delayed to the Autumn if possible. On 25 March, Fraser summed up the case for delay in a letter to the Party Chairman:

> As you know, my own position on timing has always been and remains today that we would be wise to go to the country at the first moment at which it appeared that we had a sporting chance of winning. This does not exist at the moment. . . . We should take our decisions in the next day or two on the basis of the available evidence. This evidence is clear. If we

went to the country now we would lose substantially. There is no sign that we would do better within two months. Indeed, there is no precedent for such a change in so short a space of time in the history of public opinion polling. As of now, therefore, the only sensible decision would be to envisage the possibility of an autumn Election.

It would be dangerous to go to the very end of the Parliament, but it would be far more dangerous to dissolve Parliament with the certainty of losing. The same case was put with even greater force a few days later in a letter to Butler, enclosing the latest poll:

> I believe that this poll means that there is no early option. There seems to me no validity in the kind of thinking that suggests that we should go now because it will be worse in the autumn. All the experience of public opinion over the past decade shows that the governing party tends to gain ground over the summer, particularly once the House is in recess. In any case, it seems to be foolish to go to the country at a time when you appear likely to lose by 100-plus, when there is any alternative.

These arguments, carefully deployed, convinced the Chancellor's allies that the election should be put off; in retrospect he too recognised that delay had been the best policy. Over the next few months, the Research Department carefully plotted the converging lines of party support on graphs showing the trend of published polls. Gradually, the Labour lead declined until in late-September, for the first time since 1961, the Government took the lead; with pardonable satisfaction, Fraser passed on the information to Butler:

> I feel that the meeting of the lines really merits a celebration. Unfortunately it is too soon for that. However, it has at least happened, whatever the future may hold and, as I always said it could, I am naturally mildly pleased.

The final assessment on the eve of poll was that it was 'too close to call' and the Department therefore made no prediction of the outcome; it did however comment on the fact that the Conservative recovery had been much more marked among women than among men, and it reported that the Party had won back the 'competence' label from Labour, but had failed to shift Labour's lead on the question of 'fairness'.[44] The Party had then won the battle on the substantive policy scores, but it had not eroded Wilson's success in image-building.

In part this may have been because the Conservative campaign was so long in preparation that its most positive elements were eroded by critics from inside. The gestation of the 1964 manifesto was marked by a series of radical departures that were discarded one by one. An early draft was sent to Enoch Powell for his comments, but little came of this, as Fraser reported to Goldman: 'My reactions are . . . broadly that most of his drafting suggestions are useful and most of his major suggestions on changes of policy, emphasis and presentation would not commend themselves to the Steering Committee'. The idea of trades union reform, which had been in the air in Party circles for several years and which had a definite public appeal, was gradually scaled down. In February 1964, the Prime Minister asked the Home Secretary to consider setting up a Royal Commission on trades unions; many Conservatives felt that the controversial decision in the case of Rookes *versus* Barnard had provided an excellent reason for a wholesale review. But there were still many who feared antagonising the trades unions, as any reform proposal might do; the manifesto merely promised to make an enquiry of some sort after the election, which was no more than Labour intended to do. Home also asked for consideration of the idea of appointing an Ombudsman, but this too was turned down by his colleagues. When the document was in its third draft, Sewill commented that 'the effect of the whole is rather soporific'. His suggestion of a means to ginger it up was the inclusion of a positive attitude on incomes policy, though the placing of this on the agenda rather increased disagreement, since others were anxious that any initiative should cover more than incomes in the hope of securing trades union adherence to it. Nigel Lawson read the third draft and wondered 'who is the manifesto aimed at?'

> The first thing that strikes the reader about the three main aims of the Conservative and Unionist Party, as declared in the opening of the manifesto, is that they might just as well be the three main aims of the Labour Party, or the Liberal Party. We are all in favour of peace, prosperity and freedom. This points I think to one of the principle currents of thought among people today; the feeling that, since all three parties have the same aims, the party to vote for is obviously that which appears to be the most competent and efficient in execution.[45]

The evidence of the polls suggested that the Party had in fact re-established that point, but that it had not managed to differentiate its policy from Labour's; on the lines that Douglas had diagnosed from Crosland in 1960, the policy was effective but the differentiation of policy was not. In the last weeks of the campaign, with the Parties neck and neck, a brief was sent out to all candidates and Ministers over the Prime Minister's signature, urging them to concentrate on peace, prosperity and modernisation – precisely the themes that

Labour was urging at the same time.[46] The Party surprised most observers by coming so close to winning in 1964, but the fact that it failed convinced many in the Party that it was now necessary to adopt more radical approaches and in this, many of the subordinated themes of 1959–64 were now to become dominant.

Notes

1 CRD file, '1963 Policy Statement'; CRD (N) file, 'Letter Books of David Dear, 1962–4'.
2 Article in the *Political Quarterly*, quoted in Fraser, 'Conservative Research Department', IV, 2–3.
3 CRD file, 'Organisations at present considering policy, 1957'.
4 CRD files, 'Steering Committee, Minutes and Correspondence, 1958–59'.
5 *Ibid.*
6 CRD file, 'Summary of Policy Work in Progress, 1958'.
7 CRD file, 'Agricultural Policy Committee, 1956–58'.
8 CRD file, 'Policy Committee on the Care of the Old, 1958'.
9 CRD file, 'Policy Committee on the Nationalised Industries, 1956–58'.
10 CRD file, 'Office Tax Committee'.
11 CRD files, 'Policy Committee on Share-ownership, 1958–59' and 'Steering Committee, 1959'.
12 CRD file, '1958 Policy Statement'.
13 CRD files, 'Policy Study Group, 1957–59' and 'Steering Committee, 1958'.
14 CRD files, '1959 Election – Manifesto' and 'Committee on Recreation, Sport and the Arts'.
15 CRD files, various files on the 1959 Election.
16 CRD file, '1959 Election – Reports'.
17 CRD file, '1959 Election – Speeches'.
18 CRD file, '1959 Election – Broadcasts'.
19 CRD file, '1959 Election – General'.
20 I have developed this idea further in Lord Butler (ed) *The Conservatives*, 454.
21 CRD files, annual budgets.
22 CRD file, 'Policy Planning'.
23 CRD file, 'Agriculture Committee, 1960–63'; CRD (N) file, 'Peter Minoprio's Letter Books'.
24 CRD file, 'Policy Study Group, 1957'.
25 CRD file, 'Committee on Commonwealth and Colonies, 1958–59'.
26 CRD file, 'Committee on Commonwealth Council, 1961'.
27 CRD (N) file, 'Letter Books of David Dear, 1962–64'.
28 CRD file, 'Committee on Industrial Relations, 1962–63'.
29 CRD file, 'Monopolies'.
30 CRD file, 'Committee on Science and Technology, 1960–62'.

31   CRD files, 'Local Government Finance, 1961–62' and 'London Government, 1963–64'.
32   CRD file, 'Policy Committee on the Social Services, 1958–63'.
33   CRD file, 'Town and Country Planning Policy Committee, 1960–61'.
34   CRD file, 'Chairman's Committee, 1961–62'.
35   CRD files, 'Committee on Economic Growth' and 'After the Pause'.
36   CRD files, 'Office Tax Policy Committee'.
37   CRD file, 'Psephology Group, 1960–63'.
38   CRD file, 'Committee on by-Election Results, 1962'.
39   CRD (N) file, 'Letter Books of David Dear, 1962–64'.
40   *Ibid*; CRD file, 'Briefing 1963'.
41   *Ibid*.
42   CRD files, 'Aides Memoirs, 1963–64' and '1964 Election – General'.
43   CRD file, '1964 Election – Campaign Guide'.
44   CRD files, '1964 Election – Public Opinion' and '1964 Election – Tactics'.
45   CRD file, '1964 Election – Manifesto'.
46   CRD file, '1964 Election – Speeches'.

Chapter 9

The policy exercise of 1964–1970

In November 1968, Douglas Hurd who was then part of the Leader's private office, wrote to Edward Heath about the progress of policy making since the Party had lost office four years earlier:

> This is the first serious attempt by a political party in Britain (? the world) to prepare itself not simply for winning an election but for the real business of government. The frontiers of opposition have been enormously expanded since 1964. At the right moment before the election the fullest possible account of the policy groups and projects should be given to someone like Robert Blake or Rhodes James, who should be encouraged to draw in public the conclusion that this is a historic event in British political history.

Nevertheless, he went on to suggest also that a time had come for recognising that resources were scarce, and that 'there is somewhere a frontier beyond which it is not possible to prepare for government while in opposition'. It was vital, he argued, to remember that the Civil Service would need to be consulted on the outlines of policy as well as on matters of detail, and it was also vital to keep in mind the question of timing – 'when is it all for?'. This was typical of much of the thinking about the making of policy that went on during the six years of opposition; typical both in its recognition of the unique, historic scale of the enterprise and in its self-conscious uncertainty about the end product, uncertain as to just how detailed preparations ought to be.[1]

Much in politics is determined by reaction to previous personalities and events, sometimes by progressive over-reaction, and in this sense the roots of the Conservatives' reaction to the loss of power in 1964 can be found in their explanation of why they had lost and in their low opinion of Harold Wilson's Government. For Michael Fraser, the underlying answer was simply that in thirteen years the electorate had become bored and had come to take rising living standards for granted. The cry of 'time for a change' had become irresistible, a mood that had been underlined by the gulf between the two Parties' public images in 1963–4. Others felt that the matters might go deeper than mere images, but they drew the same conclusion, that the Party should use the period of opposition to show its vigour and its ability to throw up new ideas. A topical theory that also pointed in the same direction, and which attracted many of the younger Tories was the idea that the Party had somehow lost touch with younger management types, men who believed in a merito-cratic, efficiency-orientated approach and who had found Wilson's newly-acquired technology attractive. This was something of a red-herring because such a group of voters, if they ever existed at all (and surveys persistently failed to find them in 1964–5), were certainly statistically insignificant. Many of them were in any case people who would always vote Conservative in a tight corner. Much more important, and much less often discussed in Party circles, were the traditionally-volatile voters in the non-manual working class. As James Douglas had neatly summed up the problem in advice to the Macmillan Government, it was necessary for the Party of the officers to find a means of appealing to the sergeant's mess. In and after 1964, evidence of this trend of thought in the electorate multiplied into an inescapable feature of the political scene, a situation where the majority of the British electorate were more prepared to identify with Labour even when voting Conservative. In a post-election survey done for the Conservatives in 1966, Gallup marked one particular table for special attention, comparing replies to one question over the past five elections: 'Leaving aside the question of which party you support, which party is best for *people like yourself?*' (%)

	1966	1964	1959	1955	1951
Conservative	34	36	38	42	40
Labour	45	40	41	44½	43
Liberal	5	8	7	8	8
Others and Don't Knows	16	16	14	7½	9
Labour Lead	11	4	4	2½	3

The trend was alarming, and it was confirmed by other published surveys and by such work as David Butler and Donald Stokes's *Political Change in Britain*. So, however Conservatives explained their loss of support, they came to a conclusion that they would have to do things differently if they were to reverse the trend. However, it was one thing to agree to change but quite another to agree on a new direction; so in January 1969, Heath told a meeting of Shadow Ministers that 'the present mood of the country was much more willing to accept change than it had been a year or two ago. Indeed, it was interesting to see that much of the present informed criticism of the thirteen Conservative years was that there had not been enough change carried out . . . Mr Maudling, while agreeing, said that the real problem was that whereas there was general acceptance of the need for change there was not general agreement about the nature of the change that was needed'.[2]

The second influence that prompted a new approach was a reaction against the way in which Labour took over office in 1964 and a determination that a Conservative return to power should not be marked by similar indecision and hesitation. Several Conservatives made speeches to this effect, and James Douglas summarised the argument in a brief in May 1967:

> It is almost impossible to think of a single new policy which the Labour Party worked out during its thirteen years of opposition and was able to implement when returned to office. Almost every idea they put forward in opposition had to be either abandoned or thought out again when they took office. The Conservative Party ever since it went into opposition has been determined not to fall into the same pitfall.

A few months later, Brendon Sewill developed the same argument to explain the form that the Conservative reaction had taken:

> The Labour Party won the 1964 election by promising results; faster and steadier growth, more houses, lower interest rates, better social services etc. etc. this produced a natural reaction against talking about broad objectives. This was reinforced in the Conservative Party by the feeling that we had lost the confidence of the public because we had run out of ideas. Thus our natural reaction in recent years has been to seek 'Action not words', policies not aspirations, and to talk about means not ends.

So the way in which the Conservatives left office and the way in which Labour entered it both contributed to the new direction. Both also contributed to the third major influence, the leadership and style of Edward Heath, who directed the policy review from the start and took over as Party Leader in the Summer of 1965.[3]

Heath was an almost perfect symbol of the direction that many Conservatives wanted their Party to take, for his background suited the image of classless meritocracy and his style was that of a man who would get things done. The modernisation and acceleration programme that had been launched by the Macmillan-Home Governments had been centred first on Europe (for which Heath was a natural anchorman as a convinced European) and later on domestic reform for which Heath also gained much of the kudos. The battle with opponents of his tough policy on Resale Price Maintenance in

1964 had been a keystone of the impression that the Home Government had tried to create on the country, and he had become a major force in the Government by the time of its fall in October 1964. Behind the scenes, two other events had underlined this approach of Heath in the policy making area. On the question of RPM, the Research Department had been appalled by the decision to take up such a divisive issue in what had to be an election year, and although the Department had urged the abolition of RPM on successive Presidents of the Board of Trade for several years, they now urged that it be deferred; this advice, like much on the same lines from the back-benchers, had no effect on Heath. When the 1964 manifesto was being prepared, Heath was abroad recovering from the effects of the prolonged battle over RPM. When he was sufficiently recovered to read the manifesto, by this stage in its fifth draft, he sent off a furious salvo to Michael Fraser: in Heath's view, what was needed was less of the lowest common denominator and more positive thinking, even at the risk of alienating some colleagues. This could be done only by leaving the task to a small drafting group. A meeting was therefore held with Heath after his return from Spain and several of his ideas were put into the next draft, though he did not then have sufficient weight to overrule his Cabinet colleagues. The RPM fight was almost a disaster for both Heath and the Party, and the 1964 manifesto as it finally emerged owed rather more to the Lowest Common Denominator principle than to Heath's approach. Nevertheless, by the time of the defeat, and above all *because* of the defeat, Heath's alternative approach of 'Full Steam Ahead and Damn the Torpedoes' was precisely what the Party sought.[4]

Within a few days of the Party's losing office, a reorganisation took place which set the scene for the next six years. In Sir Alec Douglas-Home's Shadow Cabinet, Heath became Shadow Chancellor (in February 1965), a key post when economic difficulties were expected and one for which Heath won great Party applause in his attack on the 1965 Finance Bill. Heath also took over from Butler the control of the Party's thinking machinery, a result of Butler's approaching retirement from politics, of his indiscretions during the recent campaign, and of Heath's increasing importance in the Party. He was made chairman of the ACP a week after the Party went into opposition and, though he did not also succeed Butler as Chairman of the Research Department (for that post was not filled at all), he took over the entire policy apparatus. Although in 1965 Reginald Maudling was Deputy Leader of the Party, he did not have access to the reports on policy that were produced for the ACP under Heath's chairmanship; whatever the titles, Heath had by his energy made himself the second man in the Party by the beginning of 1965 (and arguably on policy matters he was already number one). From July he was Leader of the Party, but he also retained the chairmanship of the ACP until 1968 and did not appoint a Chairman for the Research Department until 1970, so that while the main work of policy planning was going on, Heath had a more personal monopoly of authority in the Party than any Leader since Neville Chamberlain. Things were also reorganised among the Party officials with the primary purpose of utilising Sir Michael Fraser's abilities more widely than the Research Department. He was therefore made Deputy Chairman of the Party Organisation in October 1964, and Secretary to the Shadow Cabinet, but with a continuing special responsibility for the Research Department and its work. It was a greater combination of powers than any Party official had held before and it was used to good effect in co-ordinating the Party's political, publicity and research activities.[5] However, it was easier to promote Fraser than to replace him and Fraser himself was horrified to learn that the Party leaders were looking for a new Director from outside the Research Department and for a man of Fraser's own age and experience; in his view, what was needed was a man from inside who was familiar with the work and the people involved, and a man of the age that he had been when he first took over – and as David Clarke had been back in 1945. This view prevailed and so at the beginning of 1965 Brendon Sewill was appointed Director. He was only 35 and was by no means the most senior officer in the Department before becoming its Director. As Head of the Economic Section he had established a reputation for being able to cope with the urgent issues of day to day politics as well as having a capability for original ideas. Michael Fraser also found in him a tenacity that would be especially useful in opposition.

The Research Department therefore came directly under the Leader of the Party from 1965 to 1970 with both Sewill and Fraser seeing Heath several times a week. The Leader could be used to squeeze additional resources from the Party Treasurers and the Department could be set to work directly on anything that Heath needed done. This remained the case right up to 1970, although alterations were suggested on occasions; for example, Heath suggested at the end of 1965 that a group of research officers should be seconded directly to himself as a private advisory panel, but this was unpopular in the Department since it was felt that *all* the officers should be working to the Leader and the Shadow Cabinet as a whole, and it fell through. In general relations were harmonious, assisted perhaps by the fact that ex-officers of the Department were always on the Leader's staff (such as John Macgregor, and later Douglas Hurd); when needed, officers were seconded for particular tasks, as when a huge backlog of mail built up in the Leader's office in 1966, or when Christopher Patten worked directly to the Leader for a year, preparing briefs for him on topics down for Prime Ministers' Questions – a task that other officers also undertook for a time.

The outline of the policy review was worked out by Heath and Sewill together with James Douglas, who acted as co-ordinator of the policy groups throughout (except for a sabbatical year in 1968–9 when Barney Hayhoe stood in for him). From the beginning it was conceived on a grand scale and as a task of urgency, for there was always a possibility that an early election might be sprung by a Labour Government with a tiny majority; the Conservatives were, in Lord Blakenham's phrase, 're-forming under fire'. It was therefore decided early that it would be impossible to produce any effective policy review for the Spring of 1965, but that all the studies should aim at least at an interim report by the Summer. The first programme envisaged twenty groups, but others were added to the list as the Winter went on and the total eventually reached thirty-six. Not all of these were working at once, and indeed a few, like the group on the arts, never got started at all during this Parliament, but there were certainly over thirty groups at work in the first half of 1965. The basic pattern was to involve in the exercise as wide a spectrum of opinion as possible; about half of the members of each group were Conservative MPs and the Chairman was usually the Shadow Minister most closely involved with the subject in question, but the other half were drawn from the extra-Parliamentary Conservative Party, from the universities and even (in a few cases) from non-Conservative technical advisers. The average number of members in each group was only about ten (eighteen in the group on economic policy was quite unusual, but this group was intended to work mainly through its sub-committees), and a large number of offers of help that flowed in after Heath had announced the policy excercise to the ACP and the 1922 Committee could not be taken up. There was indeed a good deal of criticism from MPs that they were only allotted a half share in the operation and over the whole of the six years efforts had to be made to keep them satisfied; officers of the appropriate Parliamentary Committees were included or later co-opted on most policy groups, regular reports were made to the Executive of the 1922 Committee, and lists were circulated to MPs of all the

Parliamentary members of the groups. This went only half way to settling the question, for it was the other members in whom the MPs were most interested, and it had been decided at the start that secrecy would be maintained. Several industrialists and academics would only give their help in return for a promise of secrecy, and Heath was convinced that this was a fair bargain. It was indeed part of the thought behind the review that it should be used to educate the Party into a more up-to-date way of thinking, and that it should be used also to make the Conservative Party more intellectually respectable.[6]

Looking back at the experience of opposition in the years after 1945, the Research Department was convinced of the success of such efforts as the *Industrial Charter* in the struggle to convince informed observers that there was a real (and well-thought out) alternative to Labour policy; only at second-hand had these 'third-programme efforts' influenced the public, but they had nonetheless been vital. Looking at the position in 1965, many of them were convinced that some such operation was needed again. Hence, as part of a deliberate decision to open up contacts for the Party with as wide a group of people as possible, a special effort was made to create a Conservative presence in the universities. From the Summer of 1965, Heath regularly visited universities himself to make contact with sympathetic academics and to inform himself about their attitudes and ideas; during 1966 Fraser began an even bigger project, with a systematic series of fifty visits to universities and colleges by Michael Spicer of the Research Department. The response of the academics that Spicer met more than justified the reasoning behind the visits. An economist in Edinburgh suggested to him three reasons 'why the university contacts were needed – to make the Conservative Party 'intellectually respectable', to provide sources of 'expert knowledge' on which the Party could then draw, and to find out what academics were thinking about the future of the universities themselves. David Clarke, the ex-Director of the Department and now at the University of Bristol, told Spicer that 'there is a danger that the Research Department – the thinking mechanism of the Party – might become too civil service minded' and he urged the need for a 'long term planning task force of academics' to help it.

A card-index was evolved to list all academics who were Conservatives or who were prepared to help the Conservative Party on some specific area of policy, and this could be very useful. In March 1968, James Douglas sought to use the scheme to plug one of the Party's main gaps of policy, in a letter to Sir Anthony Meyer, who had taken over from Spicer:

> I am getting worried at the way in which we are putting increasing weight
> in our utterances on modern methods of financial/budgetary control, and
> some people (like David Price) draw sharp distinctions between these and
> the antiquated Gladstonian methods of present Treasury control. I
> certainly do not know what all this really means or how much there is in
> the point, and I have a nagging fear that some of the people who make
> these statements have not either. If you could find me someone who is
> versed in these techniques. . .

An adviser was duly found, as was 'a don who knows about social
security without being extreme', asked for in the same letter. All the
same, expectations were never quite realised and a number of the
academics involved came to feel that they were used for purposes that
had more to do with politics than policy; as a Manchester economist
wrote, 'the Party must show that it takes academics more seriously
and not just *use* them', and as a London sociologist said, 'academics
should not be treated as "taps" to be turned on and off at will'. The
end product sometimes looked like this (especially to those whose
expectations were set too high), but the purpose was certainly
serious; reporting to Michael Fraser, Douglas summarised the first
fifty of Spicer's universtity reports as showing 'a strong impression
from dons of Party spokesmen being out of touch with contemporary
ideas (especially on economics, but also for example on defence)'.
The number of votes involved directly would be minute, but
indirectly it could be enormous, for the universities now contributed
greatly to forming national opinions, and would be vital if the Party
was to regain its reputation for competence. This raised a general
problem, though one to which Douglas could see no answer, for it
was too large to be dealt with by briefs from the Department: 'We
can lead our masters to water. We cannot make them drink'.[7]

The procedure to be followed was laid down in a circular letter
from Douglas to all the secretaries of policy groups, first issued in
January 1965. Invitations to serve on the groups would go out directly
from Heath's secretary and lists of those accepting would come in
from Heath's office to the Department. Files of papers and
correspondence would be kept in the Research Department, and
everything involved in the policy exercise would be classified as
'confidential'; 'every now and again when you are on to something
"hot" you may need to step the security classification up to "secret"'.
As a matter of advice, Douglas suggested that minutes should be kept
in the fullest form to assist the secretary in his main task of writing the
final report, especially as in this case the report could be called for at
any time at short notice. Later circulars drew secretaries' attention to

the availability of legal advice for policy groups which had been arranged through the Inns of Court Conservative and Unionist Society, and to the Economist Intelligence Unit from which special studies could be commissioned for a strictly limited number of topics. Douglas also drafted the letter that Heath sent out at the same time to the policy groups' prospective chairmen, setting out the framework in which they should work:

> The general principle in the choice of subjects has been to make it as specific as possible. There are one or two exceptions to this – e.g. economic policy and foreign affairs – but the idea is that what we need at the moment are new Conservative solutions to the problems that the electorate are worried about – 'What are you going to do about the rising cost of land?' or 'What are you going to do about the increase in crime?' – rather than broad reviews of a particular field of Government activity. Of course in many cases the Groups will have to range wider than this in order to come up with the specific solutions and this is entirely a matter for the Chairman and his Group, but I think we should try to bear in mind that the end product ought to be a specific solution to a specific problem. Later I hope that we may be able to establish rather more scientifically and in their relative electoral importance the problems which the electorate are most worried about.

A few months earlier, Heath himself had written in very similar terms to Lady Davidson (a member of the ACP), and giving a more basic explanation of what he thought it was all about:

> The main difficulty here is that though our basic principles are well known and easily distinguished from the Statist emphasis even of moderate Socialism, I do believe that we have to find new practical ways in which to apply our principles to current problems. Abstract conceptions are extremely difficult to put across to a mass electorate. If one speaks of preserving market forces or the need to diversify the centres of power in society one is understood by only a small minority of the electorate, not because the mass of the electorate dislike the market or want to see power concentrated on the government, but merely because most of the electorate are not used to thinking beyond the immediate questions like 'What are you going to do about the rising price of land?'

The policy exercise of 1964–70 was thus arranged in direct contrast to that of 1945–50, with a concentration on practical proposals and a belief that themes would emerge from these practical proposals as work went on. It was an approach that could be linked easily with the public image of Edward Heath after he became Leader, summed up in the 1966 election slogan 'Action not words'.[8]

The early months of the policy work were difficult ones, as was inevitable when so many people were setting out on investigations in different directions. Some confusion was quite unavoidable, though it was probably enhanced by uncertainty about the Leadership of the Party (until Heath's election in July 1965), and by the reluctance of men who had sat in the Macmillan-Home Cabinets to embark on a wholesale review of policy which might seem to imply dissatisfaction with what they had been doing in office. James Douglas was soon convinced that things had not got off to a very good start and by March 1965 he was questioning the whole approach. In March he told Fraser that 'too many people are doing too many things too superficially' and that the Party was spending far too much time on working out its instant reactions to problems and not enough on thinking out ideas. When asked to develop these fears at greater length, he outlined three reasons for the problem. Firstly, the Party had not taken easily to the work of opposition, for Shadow Ministers still had 'too much sympathy with the Government in the problems it is facing and the solution it is advocating'. This was caused by the fact that 'the Government have inherited our problems and our solutions,' (to use Maudling's incautious phrase of November 1964 at a press conference.) Secondly, it was not enough to have clear policies, but it was also vital to be clear about who they were aimed at. Thirdly, Heath was carrying too heavy a burden for any one man, roughly the equivalent of what two or three men had done collectively after 1945, and as a result nobody had time to think about the presentation of policy as opposed to its content. These arguments were to recur, especially after Heath became Leader in addition to all his other commitments.

A month later, Douglas was lamenting to Fraser that there were now so many groups that 'some group is meeting almost every day and at certain times there may be three or four groups meeting concurrently'.

> From all this ferment of activity it would be extremely bad luck if there was not a certain amount of valuable policy matter to be distilled. Whether this is the most efficient way of evolving policy is a different question and I personally, as I think you know, believe that the whole exercise has got over-extended. The most valuable product of the exercise however will probably not be hard policy proposals but education. In a party such as ours, which is based on consensus rather than dogmatic discipline, the dividing line between political education and policy formation is always thin.

He hinted at the same optimistic view in a background brief provided for the *Yorkshire Post* for an article on the policy review in April; it was important to remember that after 1945 it had taken eighteen months for distinctive themes to emerge, as they had done in the *Industrial Charter*, and those eighteen months had been taken up with details of policy:

> Then quite rapidly all the different lines of thought began to point in the same direction, each part fell into place and the pattern of the new policy emerged, fundamentally based on the same principles for which the Tory Party has always stood but very different in detail, style and technique. On this occasion the process will have to take place much quicker but I think it will have to go through the same stages. At the moment we are still in the phase of intensive study.[9]

The main successes of 1965 are therefore to be found in the evolution of policy in detail rather than in the development of new themes. It will be worth looking at trades union reform, at taxation and at foreign policy as examples of how the early policy groups worked. The Group on Trades Union Law and Practice was constituted under Lord Amory in January 1965, one of the first groups to get started, though it caused some difficulties even before it met; it proved impossible to find an academic specialist in industrial relations who was a Conservative sympathiser, and one or two industrialists who were approached had to refuse even their secret assistance lest the news should get out and poison their relations with their own workforce. This might indeed have been a lesson to the Party at the outset, for over the next decade academic commentators were to be almost unanimously hostile and at the best lukewarm about what the Party intended to do. Liaison with the Conservative Parliamentary Committee on Industrial Relations was ensured by the presence of Aidan Crawley on both, and the other MPs were carefully chosen to represent a cross-section of opinion. They were also highly experienced, for many of them had actually served in the Ministry of Labour. The secretary was Stephen Abbott, who serviced the industrial relations policy right up to 1970, in Sewill's phrase 'very much the lynch-pin of the whole exercise.' However, the early meetings made it clear that this policy group intended to recommend a far tougher policy line even than previous Conservative committees had done. The very first meeting resolved 'that unofficial strikes were the number one problem and that the law should be amended to inhibit breaches of collective agreements'. The same meeting went on to decide to investigate the questions of restrictive labour practices and individual rights in trades unions, despite the politically sensitive nature of both subjects. By March, the Group had decided 'that it was in theory desirable to remove the existing immunity against actions for tort' though it was recognised that 'such a step might well be impracticable and, politically, unwise'. From this point, discussions became more moderate and one member of the Group, Joseph Godber, even circulated a paper arguing against any substantial changes in the trades union law (Godber had been the last Minister of Labour before the 1964 election). By the end of May, the group had agreed to recommend the institution of a new industrial court, to be linked with a new Registrar of Trades Unions; in other words, in four months, the Group decided on the bones of the policy that the Party was to adhere to until 1970 and legislate for afterwards. There was a last-minute flurry of disputes on both detail and principle; the Group met Enoch Powell who recommended a strengthening of their proposals and Lord Blakenham who urged greater caution, but the ACP gave general approval to the report as it stood. Things were diluted a little by the time that the ideas were published, for the balance of opinion in the Shadow Cabinet did not correspond exactly to that of the policy group. So where the policy group had urged that all collective agreements should be made enforceable, the Party's policy statement argued only for enforceability of 'certain types of collective agreements, notably those on procedure'. In the notes provided for Heath when this revised version went to the ACP for approval in September 1965, Brendon Sewill explained that 'the section on trade unions (pages 13-16) is a very careful compromise between Sir Keith Joseph and Mr Godber'.[10]

The Policy Group on Future Economic Policy had Heath himself in the chair and was made up otherwise of a very high-powered team of financial journalists, academic economists, bankers, and MPs with a knowledge of economics or taxation. After a number of general discussions, three sub-committees were set up under Angus Maude, Terence Higgins and Sir John Hall, and it was in these that the real work was done. General meetings went on throughout 1965, with Macleod standing in for Heath as Chairman, but with little emerging from a body so large. By October 1965, one of the academic advisers was circulating a paper that wondered 'whether we have been going round the subject rather than to its heart'; he suggested a new method of working. By that time though, the sub-committee reports were coming in and one of these absorbed most of the Group's time during the Winter. Sub-committee A had been set up to consider the reconstruction of the tax system and it duly came up with a radical scheme for a dramatic reduction of the top rates of income tax; the institution of a wealth tax was to provide the necessary cash to the

Exchequer. The god-parents of this package within the sub-committee were a financial journalist and a businessman. Their reasoning was that 'if we are really to reduce the top rate of surtax and abolish the discrimination against investment income a wealth tax is in practical political terms the only way we have any hope of doing it'. The proposal was conveniently summarised as shifting tax benefits from 'owners to earners' and it was precisely on that basis that it proved to be controversial. Its supporters – and Edward Heath was certainly one of its supporters at this stage – argued that it was perfectly possible to justify the large salaries of captains of industry as the rewards of enterprise; it was the essence of the new meritocratic spirit in the Party to reward work rather than inheritance. Its opponents deployed two arguments; some of the academic economists in the Group argued that a wealth tax had never been proved to be either efficient or fair among the various ways of raising money, while others took the political line that for the Conservative Party to advocate a wealth tax was giving weapons to socialism and would create havoc in the Party such as Peel had done in 1846. It was the clearest example that emerged of the difficulty of making policy in detail before securing general agreement about who the policy was aimed at. The result was that everything was held up while the main group discussed and eventually refused to accept its sub-committee's report; the majority were clearly in favour, but the minority was large and absolutely convinced of their rightness. At what Douglas called 'the grand confrontation' in December 1965, Macleod strove vainly to draw agreement from two groups that were still arguing from entirely different premises; it was decided not to submit a report to the ACP, but to send the proposals directly to the Shadow Cabinet together with a note of the views of dissentients. After this difficult time, the Group did not meet again for almost a year. The question of a wealth tax received no mention in the 1966 manifesto but was regularly discussed when the Economic Policy Group was resumed, with a slightly different membership. When it came up in May 1967, 'Mr Macleod said he thought he himself might be persuaded of its desirability but he was not sure at the moment how far the Party as a whole would be prepared to accept it'; discussion was again inconclusive. It was finally laid to rest in June 1968 when a whole new package was presented for approval, without a wealth tax as part of it.

> Mr. Heath said that his considered conclusion, after discussing the matter with Mr. Maudling and Mr. Macleod, was that the introduction of a wealth tax could not form part of Conservative policy. There were

several reasons for this but the simplest and overwhelming reason was that such a policy would be unacceptable to the Conservative Party.

Members who had survived from the earlier group voiced their discontent with this decision and one asked what would now happen if Labour were to introduce a wealth tax; in that case, said Heath, the Conservatives would have to oppose it. Sir Keith Joseph 'asked whether the position was that the Group had changed its mind or whether the situation was that the Group itself would really have liked to keep the capital tax proposal but thought they could not carry the Party on it'; Macleod told him that the Group had changed its mind, and there the matter dropped. However, the implications of *not* introducing a wealth tax were not so easily disposed of, for it had been an integral part of the whole package, a package that had been carefully balanced for the left and right of the Party and for revenue and tax concessions. Without the wealth tax, the package could be portrayed as unduly favourable to the rich; and without the yield from the wealth tax far less would be available for redistribution elsewhere. The beauty of the original package had been its simplicity, but once it was amended to meet one vested interest it could hardly be maintained. As Sewill wrote to Macleod in 1968, after Group members had expressed doubts about what was now being proposed:

> If one is to adopt this attitude, one would be bound to end up by missing the opportunities for a major reform of the tax system. If we try to devise a tax system in which all sections of the community are little worse off or little better off than at present, then it must follow that we must come back to virtually the present system.

Thus, although a great deal of work was done on tax innovations, notably on VAT (then known as TVA) and negative income tax, and on structures within personal taxation, there were limits to what could be agreed on the overall balance of taxation as a means of social redistribution.[11]

Foreign affairs presents an unusual case of a Policy Group in a very wide field and covering the whole area of an existing Parliamentary Committee. It was set up under Lord Carrington and was once again very carefully balanced between different opinions in the Party. When the Monday Club sought to nominate one of its members to the Committee, it was told that no Policy Group members were in that sense representative of sections of the Party but that in any case its views would be reflected by Paul Williams who was already a member. Williams then wrote to Peter Thomas, Acting Chairman in Carrington's absence, to tell him 'That I was horrified to hear that there was no Commonwealth Affairs Committee. This is typical of the worst of the current attitudes of the Tory Party. . .' Heath himself sent a soothing reply, explaining that policy groups were only being set up where a new line of policy was felt to be needed; Williams replied sarcastically that 'if as you say "the general lines of Commonwealth Policy were firmly established and widely accepted in the Party", it would be very pleasant to know exactly what these general lines are, especially in trade matters'; in May 1965 a Policy Group on the Commonwealth was set up. Meanwhile the Foreign Affairs Froup concentrated its attention on Europe; half of its final report was on 'Britain and Europe' and it reached the unequivocal conclusion that 'the highest interests of Britain and Europe alike demand that we should not be left out' of either economic integration or of the developing political union. This then was a policy group intended not to initiate a new departure but to stabilise an existing policy and renew an existing commitment. The Conservative Party could well have reacted to defeat in 1964 (as Labour did in 1970) with a reversal of its attitude to Europe, and the policy group helped to prevent this from happening. Once it had reported in August 1965, it was safer to keep the political temperature on the question as low as possible; the group was wound up and henceforth all work on foreign policy was done through the Shadow Minister and the Parliamentary Committee. When specific work needed to be done, on Europe or on Rhodesia for example, it was put in hand directly through the Research Department for the Shadow Cabinet.[12] This could sometimes be quite exciting in itself, as when Miles Hudson accompanied Lord Carrington on a dangerous expedition into Biafra during the Nigerian Civil War.

It will be seen that although the first steps were towards detail, the policy work of 1965 inevitably involved some general ideas. On 25 March, Sewill wrote to Heath to urge the need of grouping the emergent policy reports around some recognisable theme. He detected two themes that seemed to be emerging: firstly, 'Europe – exciting, interesting and novel, but unfortunately with not much sign of being immediately practicable'; secondly, 'efficiency and competition – this is obviously right and essential but (like modernisation) seems too technical and cold to be really inspiring. It is clearly a means to an end and not a sufficient end in itself'. Sewill's suggestion was to combine these two themes – 'should our aim be to increase our national efficiency so that we can enter Europe from strength and not from weakness, so that we can hope to lead Europe when we are in?' This chimed in well with Heath's own ideas and Sewill was encouraged to work it out at greater length. A further letter on 13 April argued the case for making 'a fairly fundamental shift' and listed a series of areas where 'we could also today break our links with the past and build a new framework of policies'. The four main areas listed were regional policy and delegation of authority from Westminster, social services where there must be a concentration on needs and where 'we must give up claiming to have made the biggest ever increases in universal benefits', Europe as a central aim of both domestic and foreign policy, and above all reform of the trades unions. The need was,

> to take direct action to limit the power of trade unions to push up wages and costs on an industry-wide basis. If we believe in dealing with monopoly power we should clearly also deal with this. It is this power to strike and put up prices against the consumer that most people mean when they talk about the need to check the power of the unions. There seems a danger that we may talk big about taking a strong line on the unions but only deal with some of the minor tangential problems (such as the closed shop, trades union laws etc.) and miss the main abuse of union power.

This package of ideas was very much to Heath's liking (he minuted on the paper 'an excellent paper. We must discuss this week. I agree with almost all of it – I had no idea that anyone held the same views as myself') and it was this approach that formed the basis of the first general review of Party policy.[13]

Emergency plans for a manifesto had been in hand almost ever since the 1964 election, and a first draft had been produced by David Howell (Director of the CPC in succession to Goldman) by January 1965. Into this the findings of the various policy groups were gradually interpolated as they emerged, and as the performance of the Labour Government provided more and better targets, more attacks on Labour policy also found their way into successive drafts. By June, plans were being made for a full-scale policy document to be published in the Autumn, built around the themes of Europe, modernisation and efficiency that had been evolved in Heath's talks with Fraser, Sewill, Howell and Douglas. At this stage though the Leadership issue continued to cloud the horizon; Howell commented in June that 'if the manifesto is intended to be an up-to-date embodiment of Conservative policy at any one time, it would be helpful to have some idea of the Leader's thinking or what he is going to say next. No wonder the Sunday newspapers describe us as "groping for a formula"'. These problems were solved by Heath becoming Leader and remaining chairman of the ACP in July, and in early August it was decided to produce two draft documents; one of these would be a very short election manifesto, almost wholly on the economic side, and the other would be an 'approach document' for the Party Conference, intended 'to convince a sceptical world that we really have got policies and not just a string of well-meaning ideas'. This approach document was in draft by the end of August, embodying the interim reports of all the policy groups, and it then had a fairly rough ride through the Shadow Cabinet and the ACP – hardly surprising in view of the speed with which the policies had been developed and the radical nature of their content.

The first difficulty was in actually making the policy material, written up individually for each Shadow Minister, fit the themes that had been decided on; a Sunday meeting of all the Party officials involved was held to make the document into 'a weighty essay on the shape of future Tory policy, rather than the hold-all for everybody's pet scheme which it looks like at present'. In this form, *Putting Britain Right* went through the Shadow Cabinet in September. (*Ahead* was added to the end of the title at proof stage when Reginald Maudling pointed out that the original title might invite the question as to who had put Britain wrong?) The usual horse-trading between Shadow Ministers was needed to iron out disagreements and infelicities of style, producing agreement on trades union policy, a more 'human ' language for the section on social services and tougher wording in other sections. *Putting Britain Right Ahead* was published in October 1965 and was well received by the Party and press. Comment centred on the positive proposals that the document made on Europe, trades unions, social services and taxation, and on the document's extreme reticence on the questions of incomes policy and economic planning, of which more later.[14]

The very success of the first year of policymaking in opposition created two problems, firstly how to keep the momentum going until the anticipated election, and how then to keep it going for another entire Parliament of opposition. Sewill had warned Heath that the danger of rapid policy making was that the Party might get stuck with policies that became out of date; once the Party had adopted a self-consciously new policy and expounded it up and down the country in speeches and broadcasts, it would be extremely difficult to pull back and accept that it had been misguided. In any case, some reorganisation of the machinery was needed to meet the new situation, for the concentration of jobs on Edward Heath was too great to be sustained. He therefore appointed Sir Edward Boyle as Shadow Minister in charge of policy formation in November 1965 and made him Deputy Chairman of the ACP. Henceforth, while Heath's approval was needed for the setting up of a policy group and for its terms of reference, Boyle was responsible for arranging its membership and for overseeing its work.

Douglas explained, in a letter to all policy group secretaries, that the first phase was now complete; what was now needed was co-ordination of the work of the different groups, filling in of gaps within and between their fields of study, and a rather clearer attempt to aim the policy work at the Party's target voters. He noted that the interim reports had appealed in the main to 'pacemakers', young executives and so on, which was too narrow a base for a mass appeal; what was now needed was concentration on the wider targets, particularly among women and non-manual workers.[15] This represented indeed a very real difference that emerged after the publication of *Putting Britain Right Ahead*, between those like Howell who wanted to build on its theme of efficiency and enterprise, and those like Douglas and Sewill who had seen this as an image that needed to be fostered but not as an end in itself. A series of working lunches were held but disagreement remained. Howell defined his 'Basic Propositions' as:

(a) need to apply management techniques with more vigour than ever before.

(b) need for greater encouragement of merit, to reverse the collectivist spiral.

(c) National and European destiny are one.

All of these are 'concepts of grandeur' which link well with the present leader, but which can also appeal to the whole of society. Our problem at present is the failure to put (a) to (c) across forcibly enough, and to internal disagreements and fuzziness of detail. Quite a lot of basic decisions not yet made.

After internal correspondence in the Research Department, Douglas and Sewill countered with a joint reply on 25 November 1965:

Our main disagreement concerns the selection of the themes of management, competition and tax incentives as the main themes. These concepts appeal to comparatively few voters. Many voters would regard them with suspicion and they would seem to create the impression that the Conservative Party is a party of the rich or of management . . . [Confirmed by the Party's private poll findings.] Competition would be a disastrous word for us to use to present our policies to the general public. Competition is the method that we want to achieve our greater prosperity and steadier prices. I would therefore suggest that we take as our main themes:

(a) the building of a new prosperity,

(b) the stopping of the rise in the cost of living.

All the polls show that the public regard the cost of living as the most important political issue and all our policies can be related to one or other of these issues.

The result of this was a new line that satisfied very few, and a concentration on action above all.[16]

It was clear in the winter of 1965–6 that the long-awaited election was near, and so the work of manifesto preparation began again, and few of the policy groups did much of substance between the Summer of 1965 and the election in March 1966. The first draft of the new-style manifesto eschewed dramatic themes altogether and Sewill reported to Fraser that 'when I showed it to James Douglas and David Dear, one of them commented that it was very well written but that it could equally well have been put out by the Labour Party, and the other that when he had finished reading it he could not really remember what it had said'. A second try by Howell produced an even more hostile response in the Research Department; Sewill suggested that it should be rewritten from scratch; several officers reiterated comments that had been made about the first draft and one of them waxed indignant about the content, the balance, and especially the technocratic style – 'really, ordinary people do not speak this sort of language, and the sooner we realise it the better'; another officer reported that 'we seem to have substituted the university common room for the grouse-moor'. By this time, in the third week of February, an election was due to be announced within days and the Party was fairly mutinous about the state of things. Several officers in the Research Department commented favourably on speeches and writings of Angus Maude in which he had said 'that a technocratic approach is not sufficient and that we must have some philosophy'.[17]

An urgent meeting was held in Albany on 17 February with Heath himself in the chair, less than a fortnight before the election was announced. Long discussions produced no real agreement on the form or style of the document, but the urgency of the situation eventually dictated the outcome; it was decided that there would be a short personal statement from the Leader and that the rest of the document would consist simply of an action programme of promises which would be listed and numbered. It would be too late to take this through the normal Shadow Cabinet procedure, though Fraser was fortunately able to remember that this had not been done in 1950 or 1951 either. The document had been drafted by Howell and Sewill by the end of the following day and, although the election was then delayed slightly longer than expected, the form did not change thereafter. The meeting to approve the final draft in proof was at the Albany on 25 February, attended by only five Shadow Ministers and four Party officials. As Shadow Chancellor, Iain Macleod was horrified by the promises that his colleagues seemed prepared to make, 131 in all, but he was reminded by Heath that all the poll evidence 'goes to show that people think we have run out of ideas'. (Looking back on it all from the viewpoint of November 1967, Macleod was to remark that 'at the last election the Conservative Party Manifesto had contained 131 distinct specific promises. This was far too much to put across to the electorate, and the net result was that everybody thought that we had no policy'.) Sir Alec Douglas-Home questioned the suitability of *Action not Words* as a title 'and wondered if "Ideas" ought to be brought into it'. Shortness of time dictated the impossibility of making any such major change. Despite the rapidity with which *Putting Britain Right Ahead* was assembled in 1965, the Party had been able to put very little flesh on its skeleton of policy by March 1966.[18]

In the circumstances though, it is doubtful whether any preparations would have made any material difference to the 1966 election. The Party's showing improved during the campaign and Fraser later noted how rare it was for the Conservatives to 'win the campaign' so clearly, but the improvement was slow and from a low base. The Research Department performed its now traditional tasks of servicing the Questions of Policy Committee (this time under Carrington) and generally providing research and information back-up for the campaign. The Department had a total staff of fifty-five during the election, its largest to date, and this was just as well for the amount of policy work was unusually heavy. So many of the Party's policy proposals were new even to Conservative candidates that a great deal of education had to be done in mid-campaign. There were also necessary tunings and adjustments of the recently-evolved policies to meet the presentational needs of the campaign itself. For example, it was felt that the Party was not making sufficient head-way in establishing the impression that it was a force for action, and it was therefore decided to take a somewhat tougher line on industrial relations; this was made a main topic for one of the Leader's press conferences and Stephen Abbott of the Research Department was asked to provide a detailed brief on the subject which went rather further than the manifesto had done. He was also on hand to brief the Leader directly before the conference, as were other officers when their subject came up for discussion.

Morale was never high during the campaign; private Party opinion polls showed throughout that two-thirds of the electorate expected a win by Labour, but a poll in Central Office, the Research Department or the Shadow Cabinet would probably have produced an even higher figure. The same polls showed that the electorate did not blame Labour for the country's economic difficulties and that they had not yet got a clear idea of what the Conservatives were offering. Douglas and Sewill had been arguing through the Autumn that Labour was succeeding in creating a cosy image of moderation (what they called 'Wilson's bid for the centre') and that the Conservatives would be left with the role of advocates of change, the new radicals. The Conservatives *were* indeed advocating radical change and, as we have seen, the Research Department was quite as convinced of the necessity for this as was anyone in the Party, but they were also aware that it would not necessarily be a vote-winner; efficiency was a cold concept to offer to the public and it could all too easily be taken for heartlessness, while modernisation might be linked all too easily to new towns, redundancies, compulsory purchase orders and the like. The new policies had hardly had time to get across by March 1966, but those that were understood were not necessarily electoral assets anyway. The one major victory of the campaign was the publicity that it afforded for the Party's criticisms of Labour's handling of the economy, in response to which the Government made exaggerated claims for its achievements and so provided new lines of attack for the years to come. As Fraser later remarked: 'in losing, we said the right things, we forced Labour on to a number of hooks which were to prove extremely embarrassing to them in the years ahead, and we went a long way towards establishing our credibility for the next battle'. This comment received some justification from the events of the next few years and from the 1970 election.[19]

But in 1966, the hard fact was that after the biggest review of its policy ever carried out, the Conservative Party had suffered its second biggest defeat in half a century. It now had to face a full Parliament during which Labour would dictate the terms of the political debate, as Brendon Sewill noted in his report on the election:

> If the Labour Government now moves to the left, our task of winning the next election should not be too difficult. Our most difficult problem will be if they attempt to continue in control of the centre. It is then likely that they will adopt a number of our policies – for example Europe, trade union reform, housing, and some of our social policies – half-heartedly and belatedly. We need to work out a method for dealing with this.

The Department had already drawn attention to the difficulty for Conservatives in dealing with a Labour Government that proved not to be as socialist as expected, but Sewill's was a very acute analysis of what Harold Wilson was to try in his four years of power after 1966. It is hardly surprising that morale remained low through the summer of 1966 as evidence piled up to the effect that Wilson intended to continue his bid for the centre and that on the whole the electorate rather approved of the idea. In July, Sewill drew up a paper commenting on proposals for an increased use of market research and concluding that 'much of the present boredom with politics comes because people cannot distinguish any question of principle between the two main parties . . . What we need is a Leader who can plot a course for the Party, and storm the masses, and awake the feelings of which people are as yet unaware'. Douglas agreed that there was no sign of general dissatisfaction with Labour or of Wilson being forced into a more interventionist policy by his left wing; 'I am frankly in a rather disheartened mood at the moment'. This mood did not remain for long, for with the economic troubles later in the same month the Labour Government began to face mounting unpopularity, but the nagging doubts remained.[20]

The election ended the time of uncertainty about the policy exercise, and the reorganisation that had been begun in the Autumn of 1965 was now completed. Boyle took charge of the exercise under Heath and the number of groups was reduced considerably; those that remained were invited to take a more leisurely look at the problems that remained in their fields and told that they could think of a time scale of one or two years for their work. The system of having a Shadow Minister in charge did not work particularly well, for it led to divided command; Boyle was not perhaps the ideal man for the job – except in the sense that he had a great interest in matters of policy and the correct academic grounding – for he was so heavily involved in other commitments and he was also under attack from the right for the policy he was advocating as Shadow Minister of Education. So for example, he had to give up the chair of the Policy Group on Machinery of Government in December 1966 because of pressure of work and because he anticipated a possible conflict with his membership of the Fulton Committee on the Civil Service. Nor was Boyle very happy with the constraints that his position placed on him, for he preferred to maintain an academic open-mindedness in his approach that exposed him to criticism, especially on education. In early 1966, he had explained this to Anthony Barber in reply to a criticism from one of Barber's constituents of one of his recent speeches:

> This whole business of 'Shadow Ministers' is becoming too formalised, and being taken a shade too seriously . . . I do think one must occasionally be allowed to do a certain amount of 'thinking aloud' in Opposition, and not all the time be expected to remain on parade as though one were nothing but the alternative Government.[21]

Boyle was however responsible for an important innovation in the whole policy review in April 1967, a result of his growing concern that the policy groups were moving further apart in their work rather than drawing together towards common goals. He therefore called the group chairman together for monthly meetings in the Research Department, so that they could report on their findings and avoid conflicts and overlaps. These meetings went on throughout 1967–8 and more irregularly in 1969 as the whole exercise drew to a close and were very useful in reducing confusion and friction.

The general method that Boyle was trying to pursue was described to the ACP in 1968 as putting rather more flesh on the skeleton of what had been proposed in 1965, and he quoted the case of industrial relations as an example; the main ideas had been embodied in *Putting Britain Right Ahead* and in the 1966 manifesto, but the more detailed work since had led up to Robert Carr's announcements on policy to the Party Conference of 1967 and to the full policy statement, just published as *Fair Deal at Work*. This would have the double effect of convincing informed opinion that the Party now knew exactly where it stood and of making sure that a Conservative Minister of Labour would be ready 'to initiate a Conservative policy', but it was a policy that would need to be constantly revised.[22] At the end of 1968, Maudling took over Boyle's responsibilities for the policy exercise and Maudling also became Chairman of the ACP, rather than being Heath's Deputy Chairman. This appointment was not much more successful, for Maudling was convinced that policy work in opposition was something like shadow-boxing, since no Opposition could ever match the Government's resources or its sources of information. He was constantly urging the need to delay decisions until after the election so that the incoming Government should be better informed about the circumstances surrounding its policies before committing itself. It is perhaps arguable that none of this mattered very much, for whoever was 'Shadow Minister in Charge', the real architect of the policy exercise remained Edward Heath and the Research Department still worked to and for the Leader.[23]

One other structural matter was more significant, for it resulted in a division of the Party's resources and a weakening of co-ordination; since 1966 indeed, the Research Department has never been the single research organisation within the official Conservative organisation. The bodies that co-existed with it between 1966 and 1970 were the Public Sector Review Unit and the Conservative Systems Research Centre, both in effect fruits of the disagreement about aims and methods which had preceded the 1966 election. It all began when Ernest Marples was dropped from the Shadow Cabinet after the 1966 election, for in order to retain his public support as an up-to-date technocratic thinker he was asked to look at ways of tightening up the Party organisation. This linked with the ideas of David Howell at the CPC and with the Research Department's desk officer for science and technology, Mark Schreiber. Their thinking came out in an interview given by Marples and Howell to the BBC in February 1967. He emphasised the necessity of separating research into two wings, separating planning from operations:

> First the short-term research – that's the day to day stuff, what I call the instant politics, which is necessary; and secondly, and quite separately, someone who'd be on long term research – finding out precisely what the Conservative Party will do, when it came into office. . . . We haven't at the moment got one full-time man on research, and unless we do that I think we are sunk.

The result was that the PSRU was set up in March as a separate organisation under Marples, with Howell's assistance promised, and with one officer (Schreiber) and one secretary lent by the Research Department. Reports would be made annually to the Leader and findings should be reported to the Shadow Cabinet and the ACP as from other policy sources. There is no doubt that this arrangement was somewhat resented in the Research Department, for it partially reversed the decision of 1948 to integrate operations and research into one organisation, a decision that almost all who had worked in Old Queen Street felt to be more than justified. The PSRU was difficult to integrate into the rest of the research operation because it came outside the orbit of Fraser and Sewill, but at the same time it absorbed cash from the Department's budget. The PSRU sought to avoid this latter problem by raising their own resources in industry, both in finance and in promises of material research aid, but this actually intensified the discontent, for it was a procedure that the Research Department had never been allowed to adopt itself. It is relatively easy to raise industrial subscriptions for political research, certainly much easier than for other Party activities, because industrialists are easily convinced of the need for research and because they like to see that their money is going directly to useful purposes; what is always feared in Smith Square is that direct fund-raising for research will make it more difficult to raise the equally-necessary funds for Party activities that are less easy to present 'with political sex appeal, such as the provision of an agent for Little Piddlington'. The Research Department had since 1948 practised this self-denying ordinance for the good of the Party, and now scented a danger that its most prestigious activity would be hived off to a new body that was free to raise money as it liked.

What actually happened was a good deal less important all round, for the PSRU chose to work in such a restrictive field that the lack of co-ordination with other policy work was not a serious handicap. The PSRU sought to harness the trend 'on both sides of the Atlantic towards a far more detailed and professional approach to the business of Government' and came in practice under the control of David Howell. Its main contribution to the operations of the Heath Government after 1970 was in the concept of 'Policy and Review', outlined by Howell in a CPC publication called *A New Style of Government*. This had undeniable advantages, as Jock Bruce-Gardyne has shown, but it was a small result to come out of the promised 'War on Waste'. The Research Department remained extremely sceptical about the importance of the work; when the PSRU organised a seminar at Sundridge Park in 1969, the summary of its findings produced from Sewill the comment, 'I have read through it and I am afraid I am not much wiser'. The problems of co-ordination were exemplified by the difficulty that Maudling had in extracting from Howell precise information as to the results of his work. Howell's first appearance at the ACP did not produce much enlightenment and he then pressed ahead to get his views published before his second appearance. Considerable tact was required to avoid giving the impression that the ACP was being ignored, and they were eventually shown *A New Style of Government* in proof and just before it was published; it is doubtful if many ACP members really understood its highly technical administrative language.[24] However, the PSRU and the related schemes to bring businessmen into Government appealed greatly to Heath's own ideas on the working of administration.

The second 'private army' was less of a threat and created less antagonism. The CSRC was set up under Michael Spicer, but he left the Research Department to become its Director and the new organisation was financed entirely outside Party channels. Its function was to work on the application of computing techniques to government, an even narrower field than the PSRU. Opinion in the Research Department was that this represented rather a waste of resources, not because computers were not important, but because they were only one of a whole range of problems needing investigation and not necessarily the one on which so much work should be done. This was naturally a matter of opinion, but the application of the computer was certainly a subject that could not have been studied properly within the Party research organisation, for the amount of money involved was too great.[25]

Feelings about the PSRU and CSRC were probably heightened by the pressure of work that the Research Department itself was coming under as it sustained the huge task of policy research. As a result, Carol Mather was commissioned to conduct an internal 'O and M' survey on the Department's methods of information handling and retrieval. Sewill's recollection of the outcome of this illustrates also the less lasting – but far more time-consuming side of the Department's regular work.

> This volume of research put considerable pressure on desk officers. This came to a head (I think in 1966) when Carol Mather was asked to prepare an 'O and M' report on the methods of information handling and retrieval. But Mather went further and reported that the pressures on officers were so great that many were spending three quarters of their time on day to day Parliamentary briefing and only one quarter on research. Inevitably the requests for briefs from the Shadow Cabinet and from the Parliamentary Party and the deadlines for the production of publications all tended to be more urgent than the research work. Mather recommended that the department should be divided into two parts, one of which would contain officers concentrating solely on research – thus in effect re-creating the pre-1948 division. Sewill and Fraser rejected this recommendation, partly because, given the same number of staff, it would mean less specialisation by subject, partly because they felt that the pressure of day to day work did in some ways provide a more fertile medium for political ideas than the ivory tower approach, partly because Ted Heath's personal interest in the development of policy provided a sufficient counterbalance to the other pressures, and partly because it

would break down the delicate network of co-ordination that had been achieved.

The way this network functioned was as follows. Fraser acted as Secretary to the Shadow Cabinet and Sewill also attended all their meetings (essentially in order that the department could be aware of the right line to take on current issues). Fraser, Sewill and Douglas attended all meetings of the ACP, Sewill and Dear attended the weekly Chairman's meetings (which had succeeded the Liaison Committee) and Sewill and Douglas attended Michael Fraser's meetings on policy initiatives and methods. Sewill, together with Ted Heath's personal team of Wolff, Hurd and Reading, met Ted Heath at least once a week, and often more frequently, to discuss his forthcoming speeches, television appearances and outstanding policy issues. Each Research Department desk officer normally specialising on the work of one Government Department acted as assistant and adviser to the appropriate Shadow Minister, also briefed the Leader on that subject, acted as Secretary to the appropriate Parliamentary Committee (thus becoming aware of currents of back-bench feeling), acted as Secretary to the policy group on that subject, and also wrote the more informative party publications on his own subject, such as the relevant sections in the manifesto and campaign guide, notes on current politics, week-end talking points, and vetted Central Office and CPC literature. This co-ordination helped to prevent the problems and embarrassments that can occur when different sections of the Party speak with different voices, and helped to ensure that the research that was done was attuned to the current concerns.

Despite structural innovations and new competitors, the main work of research went on much as before, though on a less extended front. A few new groups were formed after 1966 and some of the old ones were wound up when their work was done, but for most of the period from 1966 to 1970 there were about a dozen groups at work. The Research Department was constantly badgered by Sewill to look for new ideas (such as, in a single month, the viability of building new canals, the long-term consequences of the medicated survival of the old, the possibility of an Arctic zone of disarmament, and the need for a Party line on World Government); although few of these bore fruit, the occasional plum did emerge from such initiatives. Indeed, although most of the really original *ideas* practised by the Heath Government can be traced back to the hectic policy work of 1965–6, most of those that were actually implemented owed more to the steadier progress made after 1966. Among these were the Policy Groups on the Arts, on Nationalised Industries, Transport, Scotland, Regional Government and Trades Unions.[26]

The Group on Patronage of the Arts was one of the original thirty-six planned in 1965, but it proved exceptionally difficult to get anyone of standing in the Party to take on its Chairmanship. A suitable man was eventually found in Robin Chichester-Clark and so the group finally began work in April 1967; the other members included a conductor, a publisher and several people experienced in the patronage and management of artistic enterprises, with Chris Patten as Secretary. Paul Channon was a member of the group from the start and found himself unexpectedly promoted to the Chair when he was appointed as the Party's Spokesman on the Arts in May 1968. The group received a great quantity of background material from Patten and from Norman Lamont (who acted as secretary in Patten's absence on secondment to Heath's office), and verbal evidence was taken from Arts Council staff and from several Shadow Ministers. The final report emphasised the importance to the promotion of the arts of an encouragement of private patronage and suggested the granting of tax relief on donations to arts projects. This occasioned a considerable delay before the report could be published because although the ACP were very keen on the policy suggestions, the Shadow Cabinet had to be consulted over the financial implications. There were in fact several policy ideas floated in the Winter of 1969–70 that needed tax concessions to finance them and there was no real aggreement on how far the Party could go with such schemes. Patten suggested to Sewill that 'what it comes down to is whether we write nothing but platitudes about the arts and the voluntary social services in our manifesto. Promises to "encourage the private patron" and to "stimulate help for voluntary social service" tend to prompt the question "how?"'. In reply Douglas suggested that it might be best for Patten to write up both the original group's proposals and the rather more restrictive ideas favoured by the Shadow Treasury Ministers, 'as kites worth flying, subject to the usual saving clauses as to when economic circumstances permit and all the rest of it'.[27]

Nationalised industries provided an example of a Group which knew exactly what it wanted to do, but of a Secretary who was out of sympathy with their ideas and of a final report that was distinctly controversial. The original decision not to do separate policy work on the nationalised industries (they were supposed to come under the Economic Policy Group, but they were hardly even discussed there) was reversed in 1967, and a group was then set up under Nicholas Ridley. The chairman was tough-minded in his approach to the subject as well as a strong personality, and he had an ally on the Group in Sir John Eden; these two carried the rest of the members along with them, certainly further than either the academic economists or the secretary (Tony Newton) would have wished to go. After only six weeks of work, Ridley circulated a paper summarising what had been agreed so far, usually a job for the Secretary, and Ridley also drafted the Group's reports. Some revisions were insisted on by more moderate members of the committee, but the final report agreed in July 1968 was fairly sweeping. The Group was then wound up, before any decision had been taken about whether to accept their ideas, or whether even to publish them. Over the following two years, Ridley was stalled by those in the Party who feared that such a tough report would do a great deal of political harm – fears that were justified by the furore that followed the leaking of the report (and of a similar report in 1978). In April 1969, Sewill suggested to Ridley that he should go through Maudling to the ACP, but he hinted also that it might not receive a very favourable reception.

> The paper is at the moment written starting from the assumption that denationalisation is right in principle. While all Conservatives naturally agree with this I feel that the next Conservative Government is going to be faced with so many urgent problems in the economic sphere that there will be a natural desire not to upset more apple carts than strictly necessary.

After a mixed reception from the ACP, more work was done on the technical and financial aspects of Ridley's proposals and things were further confused by the setting up of an 'Action Group' under the PSRU to investigate the same problems. When these findings became available in March 1970, they did not much impress Newton:

> Frankly it does not seem to me to take things much further than the Policy Group Report, which was itself very weak on these financial aspects . . . I would be opposed to us getting committed to such a half-baked proposal. What, by the way, is the Central Capability Unit? It really would be nice to have a short clear statement of precisely what the present drift of PSRU thinking is.

It is quite a commentary on the lack of communication that the Head of the Economic Section should only hear of the PSRU's major proposal for a 'think tank' by accident, and this only three months before the election – by which time the manifesto was already in its third draft. Further negotiations on just how the Policy Group Report should be given publicity followed, As Douglas reported:

> I have finally managed to get hold of Nick Ridley. . . . He tells me he understands from Reggie Maudling that he (RM) does not want a pamphlet but would like a speech from EH which he (NR) has drafted. Wires crossed somewhere.

This was all overtaken by the approach of the election, and the manifesto did not add much to what had already been made known. Previous announcements about the hiving off of small but profitable bits of the public sector were confirmed, but these had largely emanated from the individual Shadow Ministers involved (such as Peter Walker's pledge to sell off Thomas Cook's) and there was no sign of a more general commitment. Ridley was naturally discomfitted by this and complained strongly; Douglas suggested a placatory reply, and the suggestion that the omission should be repaired by a speech during the election itself, to a business audience:

> The language of the Manifesto is, I think best seen as (a) Providing a mandate for the Party to act when returned to power, and (b) providing cues to policies developed at greater length and in fuller detail elsewhere, and without the same degree of commitment, but to which candidates, informed journalists and so on can refer when discussing the policies. So far as the latter is concerned, it is in retrospect perhaps rather a pity that the Ridley/Eden proposals have not yet appeared as a pamphlet, but given the relatively low salience of nationalised industry policy, the choice of priorities was almost certainly right.

The Party did not therefore seek a specific mandate for the Ridley proposals, but neither did it fly them as a kite or offer a 'cue' to them in the election campaign.[28]

Transport policy, like trades unions, illustrated the difficulty of evolving a policy in circumstances that were constantly changed by the Government, but it also illustrates some difficulties imposed from within the Opposition. The Group began work under Peter Walker in July 1966, with Mark Schreiber (later Carol Mather) as Secretary; it was known that Labour was not intending to introduce legislation on transport before 1968, and it was therefore decided to press ahead and publish a policy statement before then. There were also three advisory groups working for Walker directly, outside the main policy network; these were investigating the docks, London Transport, and problems of transport in rural areas, but it was not explained how they would fit into the main Policy Group. However, the Government published a White Paper setting out its own policy in November 1966, and a good deal of the Group's work was dictated by the need to agree on reactions to it, even though legislation was still some way off. A large number of meetings were held with the leaders of British Rail and other transport interests during 1967, but no very firm lines of policy emerged, and the coherence of the Group was not helped by the addition of three new members half way through its discussions. In October 1967, Douglas was not very hopeful about this Group; 'This group has tended to take a rather short-term view of policy. The chairman has used it largely as a means of submitting the Government's proposals (and anticipated proposals) to expert criticism'. He could see no sign that the Group was really tackling 'the more fundamental questions such as "should the use of the motor car be tailored to fit the limitations imposed by our cities, or should the structure of towns be altered to accommodate the motor car?"' In fact, the group had decided at its very first meeting that it was necessary to work *for* the car-owner, rather than to restrict him, even if this meant an increased number of cars; little more was heard of this in detail, but it ran directly contrary to the Research Department's advice to Macleod that he should use the level of the road fund licence to limit the growth of car ownership on environmental grounds. In an attempt to pull things together, Mather was encouraged to circulate 'Conclusions from the proceedings' in November 1968, though this rather underlined how many basic decisions still had to be made.

By this time, Margaret Thatcher had become spokesman on transport; at the first meeting she attended she urged the group to address itself to two main priorities, '(a) on communications for trade, (b) on a policy to win the election'. However, she concluded after reading through the voluminous file of papers that 'whilst a great deal of evidence has been taken and valuable work done, it is clear that the Group had not reached the stage of making specific decisions, nor are any immediate decisions likely on the basis of the present evidence'. She therefore dissolved the Policy Group in January 1969 and set up in its place a Transport Policy Steering Group, with a completely different membership; this was intended to work intensively, first on general principles and then on details, with the aim of producing a report by June. Shortly after it began work, she was promoted to the Shadow Cabinet to look after education. With Michael Heseltine as spokesman on transport, no further policy making through the official Party channels was carried out. Much work was done before the election, but both Walker and Heseltine preferred to keep it under a strictly personal control, with experts reporting to them directly. One of the consequences of a more professional generation of Party spokesmen was that at least some of them had come to interpret policy making in the narrower sense of preparing themselves to be Ministers rather than preparing a policy for the Party as a whole.[29]

Policy on Scotland illustrated another side of the need to react to events. The old antagonism between Scottish Central Office and the main Party organisation had not died away and so a policy for Scotland could not be a priority for the research programme of 1965. A Scottish section of the *Campaign Guide* and a Scottish edition of the manifesto had tended to be compiled after the main job had been done, usually by the Party's spokesman on Scottish affairs; in 1966, Christopher Patten had made his name in the Research Department by the skill with which he had re-worked a potentially-disastrous Scottish chapter of the *Campaign Guide* as his first task after joining the Department. Nothing much was done after the 1966 election until the sudden surge of Scottish Nationalism became too urgent to be ignored after the Hamilton by-election of November 1967. A secret meeting was held at the Albany on 16 November, a fortnight after Hamilton, attended by leading Scottish Conservatives and by the Party managers. It was decided that a public relations campaign should be launched against the SNP and that Heath should make a series of visits to Scotland during 1968, but it was also decided that substantive ideas on devolution should be left to a policy group of Scottish Conservatives, and above all that it should all be *seen* to be done by Scotsmen. After Heath's Edinburgh visit of January 1968, he expressed his dissatisfaction with the policy servicing available, hardly surprising since the Research Department did not have an officer available to assign to the task full-time. Heath argued the need for more material 'of a debating-point nature' so that the case put out by the SNP could be resisted; 'What I was given this week-end were paltry crumbs that fell unnoticed on the floor. This just will not do. Again there must be an analysis of each field of Government activity in Scotland leading to a clear proposition which I can enunciate'.

The Party's disturbed state was hardly improved by a private opinion poll which showed voting intentions in Scotland as: Labour 40 per cent, SNP 40 per cent, Conservative 15 per cent, though this later turned out to be so far out of line with other polls as to be no more than a freak result. (The *Daily Express*, a few days later, showed: Labour 30 per cent, Conservative 30 per cent, SNP 32 per cent – which was bad enough on previous form, but not quite so devastatingly so.) By the end of February, Sewill was ready to reply to Heath's request for assistance: 'You asked me to think about "imaginative" policy proposals that we could put forward, i.e. ones that would have electoral appeal'. Investigations had produced a rather negative response on the social and economic front, 'so one comes back to the key question of what we should say about the future pattern of Government in Scotland'. Since there was likely to be a significant number of SNP Members in the next Parliament, 'we should think very carefully which side of the Home Rule fence we are going to come down on'. Sewill was not at all happy to leave it all to the Scottish Conservative MPs to work out, for their vested interest would make it almost inevitable that they would come down in favour of a slightly modified status quo. It will be recalled that the devolution of power and regional government had been one of the themes that Sewill had put forward in 1966, and he now suggested that the Party should commission from Peter Goldman a special report on the whole question. This was duly done, and proved not to be along the lines of what Heath and the Scottish Tories were thinking; Goldman suggested that a Conservative commitment to a moderate reform might fail to satisfy Scottish aspirations but might lead ultimately to home rule. Heath's speech to the Scottish Conservative Conference at Perth in May 1968 was thus drafted with great care, but was eventually couched in more forthcoming terms than Goldman had suggested, though by no means all of the Shadow Cabinet were so convinced as Heath himself of the need to go so far. Robert Blake argued on behalf of many Conservatives in his comments on Heath's speech at Perth, urging that the commitment to devolution should be to no more than 'the Church Assembly stage', and not move on to 'the Stormont stage'. With this underlying disagreement and with the subsequent falling away of support for the SNP, it is perhaps not surprising that Shadow Cabinet interest in Scottish questions waned after the summer of 1968. A constitutional committee under Sir Alec Douglas-Home was set up and was serviced from Scottish Central Office, but liaison between Edinburgh and London was certainly improved; papers from Scottish policy groups were sent to the Research Department for information and comment, and they were then forwarded to the ACP for general approval before being published, though the intention was always to produce a Scottish manifesto from Edinburgh as a truly independent operation. The result was that the progress of detailed policy for Scotland was kept in step with the equivalent work elsewhere (for example on education), but there was rather less liaison on policy concerning the future of Scotland as a whole.[30]

A similar fate befell the Policy Group on Regional Government, which repeated many of the ideas – and many of the difficulties – of the Group of 1961–2. This Group was set up under Geoffrey Rippon in February 1966, with the aim of reporting by July, though because of the General Election work did not actually begin before the Summer:

> It was thought essential to determine whether we wanted to see the introduction of regional government, and if we did, what form it should take, i.e. the decentralisation of central government or the setting up of regionally elected local authorities.

These were exactly the sort of fundamental decisions that the Group never did take, largely because it became entangled with the question of local government reform and the myriad of vested interests involved. Papers by Arthur Jones MP expounded the idea of the city region, but this both divided the Policy Group down the middle and raised the very important question of whether it was possible to reach any firm conclusions before the existing Royal Commission had reported. It was decided to await the Royal Commission, and since its report was postponed more than once, the Policy Group almost folded up in the meantime. In September 1969, John Barnes wrote to Barney Hayhoe to ask 'whether the Party's policy group still exists, since we do not seem to have met for some time'; Hayhoe replied that 'as far as I know the group is still formally in existence, and Peter Walker is chairman'. The Group did not meet more than three times after the end of 1967 and not at all after 1968, first on the pretext of waiting for the Royal Commission and then because the Chairman did not want a meeting 'until the dust has settled somewhat after the publication of the Maud Report'. Something of the difficulty of working for such a Group may be gauged from Tony Newton's reaction to a request from Geoffrey Rippon for an assessment of Party proposals on London local government:

> On the face of it it seems ridiculous that the Research Department should provide comments in criticism of a report which the Research Department itself prepared – in the shape of Barney Hayhoe.

The result was a short letter pointing out that the Department was 'favourably disposed' to its own report, a letter that was in any case cleared with Hayhoe before being sent off. When Peter Walker became Chairman of the defunct Group in his capacity as Shadow Spokesman, he preferred to run things much as he had done with transport, 'holding a great series of conferences with local government people in various parts of the country'.[31]

It will be clear from all of this that the trend of events throughout the years after 1966 was for policy groups in the orthodox sense to fall out of use, and to be replaced by task forces, steering groups or panels of experts working directly to the Shadow Spokesman and to the Research Department. The Policy Group on Trades Unions provided a clear exception to this trend, keeping its corporate existence under various Chairmen and meeting right up to the spring of 1970. After the 1966 election, with Joseph in the chair, the Group reiterated its demand for the enforceability of all agreements, not just the procedural ones that had been accepted by the Party in 1965, though not all the members agreed with this. The chief area of contention at this stage was how far the Government and the law should be involved, with Joseph and Nicholas Ridley arguing for a major change of emphasis; they wanted to place the onus for invoking the new framework of law on management and to reduce the Government role to a minimum, a proposal that Aidan Crawley resisted as reversing all that the Group had agreed on so painfully over the past two years. However, these ideas did not command majority support, and it was actually decided in February 1967 to increase the powers proposed for the Government by the institution of a compulsory cooling-off period. It was at this point that Robert Carr took over as Shadow Minister and as chairman of the Group, and he made it clear that he did not wish to go over ground that had already been traversed, especially where policy pledges had already been made public. It was at Carr's suggestion that the basic framework of rules by which the new Registrar would work were adopted in April 1967, and his influence was apparent in the wish to preserve a balance in the proposals.

Trades union reform was felt to be an issue where the Party had a good lead over Labour, so it was decided to press on in making the policies public, before the Donovan Royal Commission had reported. They were therefore written up by Stephen Abbott as *Fair Deal at Work* and published in 1968, backed by a battery of supporting fire from speeches and Party publications. When the Royal Commission reported and when the Labour Government published a White Paper, the Policy Group met to discuss these alternative plans, but on each occasion decided that no substantial change was needed in their own ideas. This was an area where the Party made the running and kept its lead; it was also one of the areas where Party leaders would have felt most confident in 1970, for although trades union leaders had made it clear to them (in private soundings) that they would oppose the Conservative plans root and branch, they also admitted in private that they would feel obliged to accept them if they became law. It is possible that this late stage of the evolution of the policy was rather too dominated by the lawyers, though the proposals were now entering stages of great legal complexity. On one occasion, it was pointed out that the trades unions might not accept injunctions made against them by a court that they did not recognise, but the other members of the group did not take this threat very seriously; in a committee that included so many lawyers, it was perhaps difficult to accept that the law might be set aside by naked political and industrial power. In any case, the determination to balance the proposals – in Carr's view intended to strengthen the responsible trades unionist against political militants – remained throughout. As a result of this, the original intention to reform the political levy system, approved unanimously by the Group at the start, was never included in any policy statement and was quietly dropped early in 1970 so as to avoid political antagonism. The over-riding irony of the whole policy on industrial relations was that the framers of the proposals were desperately keen to remove from them any possible source of friction or antagonism, whatever the rest of the Party may have wanted.[32]

Despite all this work during 1967 and 1968, the senior men in the Research Department remained worried about the difficulty of detecting evidence that the Party had really got its new approach across to the electorate. The opinion polls done for the Party by ORC made depressing reading, not in the answers to questions about voting intentions but in their deeper investigations; even where the electorate approved of a Party policy, as on industrial relations, there were few signs that the policy was well known or well understood, and there was definite evidence that it was not the issue about which the electors cared most. The officials therefore tried very hard to establish two points; they sought to isolate dominant themes from the mass of policy work in order to give the Party a clearer identity, and they urged a decision from the Party on the question that the electorate regarded as most important – prices.

It is worth emphasising that public opinion polling was regarded as a tool and not as an indicator of the direction to go. Before 1966, one Conservative leader told David Butler that 'we're very old-fashioned about these things. We decide what the right policy is, and then we look at the research simply to see how best to present it'. Nor was this only the policy admitted in public, for a meeting of party professionals resolved in 1968 that 'the proper purpose of public opinion research was not to lead the public from behind but, having established a policy and an identity, to help in the presentation of it'.[33] The difficulty with this view was that though the policy had been clearly decided in most areas, the identity of the Party remained shadowy to the electorate, and it proved difficult to project individual policies without a strong peg on which to hang them. Insofar as common ground was emerging, it was as likely as not to be directly counter to what the Party intended, as Boyle told Margaret Thatcher in November 1967:

> It is extraordinary and rather disturbing the way in which a lot of Policy Groups are coming up with proposals, all perfectly sound in their own context, which would have the incidental effect of raising prices of something or other, and this is a tendency we must I am sure guard against.

The Party officials sought to remedy this central defect in the whole operation by going back to the earlier arguments about clarifying the Party's philosophy, or at the least of publishing something on Conservative principles that would not relate solely to the domain of one Shadow Minister or any immediate policy debate. In March 1967, this 'Official Group' of senior Research Department officers decided to prepare the outline of a paper for the Party Conference of that year; Boyle was enthusiastically in favour of the proposal and Heath gave the go-ahead, on the understanding that a final decision would have to be made at a later date. Various drafts were circulated among the officials during May, with Hayhoe acting as rapporteur and with Michael Wolff designated to write up the final version. The purpose behind it all was described by Sewill to Maudling:

> My own feeling is that since October 1964 we have produced a large number of new policies and the Party wants to see some sort of purpose running through them more than mere expediency. Our object therefore in producing the draft has been an attempt to demonstrate the practical application of traditional Conservative principles to the new problems of today and also to try to appeal to the under-thirties by getting away from some of the more traditional language of the post-war period.

Responses from Shadow Ministers varied from the guarded welcome given by Douglas-Home to the outright hostility of Macleod. The attempt to introduce a note of idealism was not all that popular either; it was intended to call it *Make Life Better*, but some Shadow Ministers dubbed it 'Blessed are the peacemakers' and Douglas-Home noted that 'I thought the introduction rather reminiscent of an M.R.A. approach!' The 1945 policy exercise had proceeded from a philosophical base to more detailed policies; the 1964–70 exercise had begun with details and it was therefore extremely difficult to establish the common core of ideas afterwards. By August, most Shadow Ministers agreed with Keith Joseph's view that 'Surely we don't *need* such a paper' and even earlier supporters like Boyle had come down against the publication. There was an attempt to bring it out indirectly, 'over the name of some prominent Party figure associated with ideas' such as Angus Maude, but this had the obvious disadvantage that the prominent figure would naturally wish to write it himself – which might be even more divisive. Drafting went on, but early in September the whole thing was abandoned.[34]

The Party's policy makers were naturally rather disheartened by this set-back, but the attempt of 1967 did nevertheless produce positive results. Arguments over the prospective document had certainly revealed the depth of disagreement and the need to pull things together, and from 1967 Michael Fraser took a rather more direct role in the whole policy exercise. As secretary of the Shadow Cabinet and Deputy Chairman of the Party organisation he was a useful ally in persuading Shadow Ministers to take policy preparation more seriously. When a full-scale policy document was finally produced in 1968, the experience of 1967 was helpful in avoiding pitfalls. Fraser and Douglas met in October 1967 and agreed that the general election would not be likely to be held within a year but could come at any time after that, and that the Party should work on these assumptions. The difficulty was that most of the policies that had been evolved would have unpleasant consequences in the short term, however vital they might be in the long term. The priorities were therefore to do two things:

(1) pick out some plums with political attraction

(2) do enough detailed work and no more than will ensure that what we propose in the package is intellectually respectable and can be done, as opposed to trying to tell people how we would do it, which is the job of the civil service once we are elected.

Areas of difference between the parties should be indentified and more work should be done to pull the work of the groups together. Fraser was also a believer in the need to publish, for (as he told a meeting of group chairmen in February 1968), 'it was one thing not to have a policy document in office becuase people could see your activity. In Opposition, if you produced nothing official, nobody could see that you stood for anything at all'. The need for differentiation was a constant theme at which Fraser, Douglas and Sewill hammered away, as in February 1969, when Fraser read to the Policy Initiatives Committee extracts from *Political Change in Britain* by Butler and Stokes. Douglas had pursued this line of thought in a paper on policy differentiation in May 1967, rejecting much fashionable theory on the way:

> For years the responsibilities of government have been growing steadily wider while public affairs have become increasingly technical and complex. These two tendencies have resulted in the business of government being seen more and more in managerial terms – a matter of technical competence rather than representative values. Though now a commonplace, this view is fundamentally illogical. Managerial techniques can tell us how to maximise almost any given factor but they cannot tell us which factor ought to be maximised.

The factors that ought to be emphasised were taxation, social policies, industrial relations and Europe. It was indeed these that emerged in 1968 as the distinctive core of the Party's approach to government.[35]

Work on a document for the 1968 Conference began in May of that year, with a draft circulated by Michael Wolff and a bulky accompanying analysis of all the policy work done so far, compiled by the Official Group. Once again, reactions were mixed, even inside the Party organisation. Carol Mather felt that it did not contain enough of 'what Conservatives worry about' and Charles Bellairs lamented the decline from 'what might be called the Peter Goldman style of Policy Document' into a less literary, more staccato style. When the ACP discussed the third draft in July, 'All members of the Committee were apprehensive about producing a document that begged too many questions. One or two were sceptical about producing any document. The preponderant view of the Committee, however, was that it would be extremely difficult to have no document'. The Official Group was anxious to salvage something from the abandoned document of 1967, and so all the various drafts included a lengthy introduction on the ideas underlying the more specific parts of the document, as Sewill explained when circulating the fifth draft at the end of July:

> I feel that what Conservatives – our normal supporters and the millions more who have come over to us more recently – want to know is what the Party stands for. They want to know not what our policies are but what their purpose is. They want to feel that Conservatism is a cause worth fighting for. They are seeking some sense of idealism to inspire them . . .

However, Shadow Ministers (and Macleod in particular) were arguing that if a document had to be published, then it should concentrate on proposals rather than ideas. The outcome was a compromise, whereby the first section was redrafted along

Macleod's lines and the rest remained as before, a decision that few of
the Party officials approved of. Russell Lewis of the CPC suggested
that 'if the beginning goes out in its present form and falls into the
hands of say Rees-Mogg in one of his hatchet-swinging moods, I can
only fear the worst'. Sewill had more fundamental doubts, for the
sixth draft version that was finally approved had removed most of the
connecting thought that had been the major reason for publishing at
all. He told David Clarke that,

> like you I had thought that the idea at this stage in the Parliament was to
> show where the car was going more than what we were going to do
> inside the engine. But this was apparently not at all the idea of our
> leaders. They firmly gave instructions that we were to be much more
> specific, and have all expressed themselves much more pleased with the
> Sixth draft than with any previous ones . . . Why don't you write to Ted
> Heath some time and tell him that the public want to know where he
> wants to go just as much as how he means to get there?

It was not quite true to say that all the Party's leaders had taken this
line, for both Robert Carr and Margaret Thatcher (at least) had
expressed the opposite view; loyal to the consensus, Sewill could only
remind them what had happened to a different form of document in
the previous year. The final irony came when the title of the 1967
document was appropriated at the last moment for the very different
document of 1968, which duly appeared as *Make Life Better*. It would
also be fair to point out though that fears about its reception were
proved to be exaggerated, for the press and Party were happy to
concentrate on the details of proposals contained in it, (especially on
immigration, which represented an inevitable compromise between
left and right) and made little comment on what was *not* there.[36]
    The effect of this failure to insert a connecting thread of thought
into the policy operation in 1967–8 left a resounding gap in the Party's
preparations, one that could be filled only by picking out 'political
plums' for their electoral appeal and running them for all they were
worth, and by ordering priorities between existing policy commitments at the Shadow Cabinet level. This latter had been a constant
cause of concern among the Party's officials ever since 1964, for the
Shadow Cabinet was run on a tight rein and Shadow Ministers
showed little inclination to accept that a Shadow Cabinet need not
operate in exactly the same way as a real Cabinet. So Sewill noted in
December 1965 that the Shadow Cabinet was still thinking rather too
much about next week's second reading debate, and rather too little
about what they might wish to do three or four years hence. A few

months later, Douglas wrote that 'there is something radically wrong with the way in which the Shadow Cabinet operates. It seems to me that they still go on pretending that they are the Cabinet, discussing the topical question of the day just as if they had to decide what the Government should do about them'.[37] It was hoped that this would be remedied by the setting up of an Economic Policy Group, under Heath's own chairmanship again, for this would include most of the senior Shadow Ministers and would have to impinge on the whole field of policy.

In practice though, things went on much as before; for example, one meeting of the Economic Policy Group in April 1967 was intended to receive a weighty paper from Brian Reading on economic policy but was diverted from this by a suggestion from Macleod that Reading should give an impromptu briefing on the budget, after which the Group had little time for what was on the agenda. More seriously, the very constitution of the Economic Policy Group recognised that there was a deep difference of opinion on basic objectives and methods of economic policy; Nigel Fisher has described this as a divergence between Maudling and Joseph, but it was just as much a divergence between Maudling as the last Conservative Chancellor and Macleod as the Chancellor-elect. Maudling was, not unnaturally, unwilling to abandon the line of policy that he had pursued at the Treasury, most of all the belief in an incomes policy, but Macleod was much closer to Joseph's opposition to such interventionist ideas. Heath had taken the chair of this time-consuming committee himself because of the impossibility of making either Macleod or Maudling chairman and because nobody but himself was senior to them both. The EPG did much useful work on the tax package, in quite remarkable levels of detail, and in 1967–8 it met with most of the policy group chairmen in turn to discuss the financial and economic implications of their proposals. In this sense it acted for a time like an inner Shadow Cabinet, but it was steered well clear of the fundamental matters of economic management that divided its members; when in July 1968, Joseph asked when the Economic Policy Group was actually going to discuss economic policy, as opposed to taxation, it was agreed to start work on other issues in October, but this never actually happened. After the summer of 1969, when the EPG was wound up, the gap in economic policy still remained.[38]

By this time though, the approach of the General Election had begun to concentrate minds, and some of the defects of the Shadow Cabinet approach had ceased to matter much. From the beginning of

1969, the Party had to be ready for an election at any time, and so the dichotomy between short and long-term preparations was rather less important. In January, a Future Legislation Committee was set up under Maudling, with Carrington, Whitelaw and Fraser as its other members; Sewill was co-opted as a member and Hayhoe acted as Secretary. Work centred around a paper on 'Priorities for Government Action' produced by the Official Group. With the approach of actual legislative plans by a future Conservative Government, the discussions assumed an air of greater reality; Maudling summed up the committee's findings after the second meeting with the observation that 'this had been a useful exercise and that the priorities were clear – machinery of government, taxation, immigration and industrial relations'. The Research Department then produced a legislation chart, showing how the incoming Government might time-table its programme in the first year in order to get the drafting, legislation and implementation of its major priorities ahead as quickly as possible. In March 1970, a detailed 'Conservative Government Programme' was in existence and was then kept up to date for the various projected election dates; this was approved with a few amendments at a meeting of senior Shadow Ministers, and a final copy was sent over to Downing Street on 19 June, the day after the election. This was perhaps the most successful of all the policy preparations and was undoubtedly a major factor in the speed with which many of the Government's most contentious Bills were placed on the statute book.[39] (See page 280.)

However, future legislation was precisely the technical, managerial matter which Party officials accepted as important but not as the only matter of importance. There was much greater difficulty in getting straight answers on more substantive questions of policy content which also had to be settled before the election. Autumn conferences had been held at Swinton Conservative College in each year since 1966, and one purpose of these had been to get Shadow Ministers away from the urgent atmosphere of Westminster for a more reflective look at policy trends. In December 1966 and October 1967, successful conferences were held, but on both occasions they tended to be over-weighted by back-bench MPs, since the number of Shadow Ministers was never very high and the other policy group members who attended seemed to be overawed. The remoteness of Swinton from London did not help, and so it was decided to cancel the weekend planned for 1969 and not to plan one for 1970, though the Research Department had hopes of achieving the original purpose by a slightly different method. In September 1969, James Douglas reported to David Clarke on Maudling's view of the idea of a 1970 weekend session:

> His view is 'not'. I think he feels, and I must admit that his would be my own view, that at this stage we do not need to stimulate ideas and discussion – which was the great achievement of the Swinton week-ends – so much as to get agreement, decision and follow-through on the ideas that are already around. Brendon and I have a sinister notion which is to incarcerate the Shadow Cabinet for a week-end where they can really concentrate free from distraction on their policy and strategy for the next Election. Swinton would be the ideal place for this, but as you can imagine it will be far from easy to sell this idea.[40]

Thus was born the idea of the Selsdon Conference, and the preparation of the manifesto proved to be the lever that brought it about.

A manifesto had been in draft, for emergency purposes, ever since February 1968; this was polished up for publication at the Party Conference of 1969 but not eventually published, and work began in earnest in October 1969. It rapidly became clear that a manifesto that would ask for a mandate for what the next Conservative Government actually intended to do would be a pretty harsh document, and that decisions could not be delayed any longer. This was especially true of proposed changes in taxation, and of the shift to selectivity in social policy. Geoffrey Block's reaction in January 1970 was typical of many:

> This is no doubt our policy, but it is not the sort of manifesto with which we can win a General Election. . . . Few people read manifestoes; but those who do have not been accustomed to being told this sort of economic realism at election times for years. One may almost say therefore that we will have to win the next general election in spite of, rather than with the aid of, our manifesto.

This was what the Official Group had been saying for some time, but it was only with the actual appearance of manifesto drafts and the approach of what looked increasingly like a close election that the message got home. A Shadow Cabinet weekend was therefore arranged for the Selsdon Park Hotel (rather less remote than Swinton) on 30 January 1970, and it was decided to use it also as a public relations exercise to demonstrate how far the Party was prepared for office, how far it meant business. In this sense it was, as *The Political Year* put it, 'a brilliant piece of window-dressing', and the Party's private polls showed that it had made a quite unusual impact on the public. Publicity concentrated on the issues of law and order, for the rather accidental reason that it was the only major item from the agenda that had been completed by the time that Heath met the press on the Saturday, but discussion ranged over the whole area of policy, bar one. Little that was discussed at Selsdon was new, and in that sense too it was as much about public relations as about policy, but it did have a deeper significance. The policy ideas had for the most part been floating around for some time, at least behind the scenes, but many of them had not been firmly adopted as Party policy, and they had certainly not been totted up as an overall bill of fare for the electorate. As Brendon Sewill put it, the Shadow Cabinet were confronted with the decisions that they had made piecemeal, shown how tough a package it added up to overall, and asked 'Are you with it?'; when they said yes, the decks could be cleared for the election. It was however rather characteristic that the one substantial paper prepared for Selsdon that was never reached on the agenda was a paper by Sewill himself calling for decisions to be made about an incomes policy.[41]

After Selsdon, the production of the manifesto was probably easier than most such documents have been. There were four more drafts between March and the end of May, written by Hayhoe and Wolff, but in fact compiled through the 'diffused authorship' that was now standard practice in the Research Department. Difficulty was occasioned by the wording of the section on Northern Ireland, and a warning was given that the Party must give the Ulster Unionists 'something on which they can hang a case for a mandate to support the Conservative Party after the election. There is a very real danger that if things move in the direction that they appear to be going the candidates may have to break the link in the course of the election campaign'. A suitable form of words was found and saved the link for one more election. It was also decided, late in the day, to stick to the original commitment to leave a decision on the Common Market to Parliament rather than throwing in the idea of a referendum, on the argument that Parliament would not act directly against public opinion on such a vital issue; the question whether or not to allow a free vote was considered and deferred. (One unusual feature in 1970 was the publication of a special manifesto for the West of England as well as editions for Scotland and Wales, the fruit of a regional policy group that had been sitting since 1966 under John Peyton.) The result of this work was that the Conservatives got their manifesto out first even though Labour had called the election. The final policy gap was closed at the very last moment, in a way that is best described in the Research Department's official report on the election:

For many, many years we had realised that the public considered the cost of living 'the most important political issue'. This was the main theme of our advertising campaign in the year before the election. Nevertheless, due probably to the traumatic experiences of incomes policy in the early 1960s, there was a remarkable reluctance by the Shadow Cabinet during the years of Opposition to discuss any policy for dealing with inflation. The Economic Policy Group did not include this subject in their work. Various papers put up by the Research Department, for example, one on prices policy for Selsdon Park, were dismissed without consideration. A Shadow Cabinet sub-committee set up after Selsdon Park disbanded itself after one inconclusive meeting. The result was that the Research Department had, at the very last moment, to invent a policy for dealing with inflation; and this was spatchcocked into the manifesto after the seventh draft when it was in final proof stage. This did not, however, prevent us from developing the cost of living as our main election issue, although our credibility was always a bit shaky.

If future legislation was the clearest success of the policy exercise (as the most technical) then economic policy (as the most substantive) must be accounted the least successful.[42]

The election campaign was not easy, for Conservatives were desperately anxious not to lose after their commanding lead in public opinion throughout the past four years. The campaign did not revolve much around issues, and the television news editors 'soon turned merely to reporting the style of campaigning, much to the disadvantage of Ted Heath and the advantage of Harold Wilson'. There was an underlying fear that things were going rather like 1966, that the Conservatives were simply not eroding Labour's lead fast enough to win. However, the Party kept its nerve rather well, largely due to the confidence of Heath himself who specifically refused to conduct an exaggerated attack on the state of the economy because of damage that this had done in 1964. Nor did the Party shift its ground as a result of poll findings during the campaign, for private polls remained favourable; the main strategy had in fact been laid down as long ago as 1968 and the detailed planning for the election had laid down exactly what did take place. It had been recognised that the crucial thing was to bang away at issues where the Conservatives had a recognisably different public image from Labour, and to stress prices above all; and it was recognised that this strategy must be pursued single-mindedly even if it did not seem to be working at first. In other words, the Conservatives were banking on winning the campaign whenever it took place because they felt that the concentrated publicity that would be directed at the Government's record would bring about a sufficient demand for a change, if they could only make it clear that the Conservatives really did represent a change. It was a strategy that proved ideal for the circumstances of June 1970, and especially for a campaign where all the bad news for the Government came in the last few days, when it seemed to validate all that the Opposition had been saying. But it was also a strategy that owed something to Labour's decision to portray the Conservatives as a Party of harsh measures after Selsdon, for this succeeded in differentiating the Conservative image more than anything in the previous four years.

However, this question of images carried a more dangerous message too, as Sewill noted in concluding his report, for it underlined the fears that the Department had been expressing ever since the Party had begun psephological investigations in 1960:

> In the historical perspective the surprising thing is not that the Conservatives won the election but that, after five and a half years of Labour Government which even impartial observers would recognise as dogged by failure and unpopularity, we so nearly lost. The root cause of Labour's near success must lie in the public's greater identification with Labour; that to most people, in Harold Wilson's words, Labour is 'your party', and to most people the Conservatives are an alien exterior party; that Labour has a soft heart but also a soft head, that the Conservatives have hard hearts but also hard heads; so that the public turn to the Conservatives in time of trouble, but do not think of us as their party. To put this right must surely be the major task of the Conservative Government and the Conservative Party between now and the next election.[43]

Perhaps this was unduly gloomy, for the election had produced the biggest swing between major parties since 1945, and constituted the only post-war example of a clear majority for one party being transformed directly into a clear majority for the other. Moreover, the detailed working-up of policy – co-ordinated through a Leader who gave policy making a high priority and an effective Steering Committee – played a key part in the recovery of power. Few incoming governments have been so well prepared for office, and all the surveys indicated that the electorate now saw the Conservatives as having a clearly different approach. Such perceptions owed much to the Party's hard work in opposition and were an important factor in the recovery, through two London victories in 1967 and 1970, through countless by-elections to the installation of Edward Heath in Number Ten.

Appendix: The future legislation exercise

This was undertaken in the Winter of 1969–70 when the early return of a Conservative Government seemed likely, and actual decisions about the first items to pursue after the election were taken at the conference of Shadow Ministers at Selsdon. These decisions became the basis for a future legislation chart, produced by the Research Department and sent to Edward Heath on 10 March 1970. This took early October as its starting-point and set out a full programme of legislation (drafting as well as enactment), ministerial announcements, White Papers, and outside events such as decimalisation that might be expected to have political consequences. In the event of course, political circumstances changed quickly after March and the election was, unexpectedly, in June, but the future legislation chart in this form was sent over to Downing Street on the day that Heath moved in, the day after the General Election. Because the election had taken place before rather than immediately after a Summer recess, there was more time than had been expected for preliminary drafting work, but the programme of events over the Winter of 1970–71 conformed very closely to what had been worked out a year earlier.

CONSERVATIVE GOVERNMENT

	OCTOBER	NOVEMBER	DECEMBER
	2 4 6 8 10 12 14 16 18 20 22 24 26 28 30	1 3 5 7 9 11 13 15 17 19 21 23 25 27 29	1 3 5 7 9 11 13 15 17 19

EVENTS

Election
UN special ssn.

PARLIAMENTARY BUSINESS

Queen's Speech
Debate on Queen's Speech
Expiring Laws Continuance

Over-80s Bill
Disability Bill
Mortgage Guarantee Bill
Local Councillor's Bill
Machinery of Government Bill
Widows Bill
Crossman Repeal Bill
Public Service Pensions Bill

GOVERNMENT ANNOUNCEMENTS

Cabinet List
Directive on economy
Sale of Council Houses
Betterment levy statement

DRAFTING LEGISLATION

Industrial Relations Bill
Aliens Bill

Over-80s Bill ⌐P
Disability Bill ⌐P
Mortgage Guarantee ⌐P
Local Councillors Bill ⌐P
Machinery of Government Bill p
Widow's Bill ⌐P
Crossman Repeal Bill ⌐P
Public Service Pensions Bill ⌐P
Company Law Bill ⌐P
Ports Bill ⌐P

PROGRAMME 1970–71

	JANUARY	FEBRUARY

21 23 25 27 29 31 2 4 6 8 10 12 14 16 18 20 22 24 26 28 30 1 3 5 7 9 11 13 15 17 19 21 23 25 27 1 3 5 7 9 11 13

Christmas

Decimal Day

Recess

Industrial Relations Bill

Green Paper on tax

Government off-backs speech

Defence White Paper

Aid for immigration areas

P

P

Finance Bill

Housing Subsidies Bill   P

	MARCH	APRIL	MAY

15 17 19 21 23 25 27 29 31 2 4 6 8 10 12 14 16 18 20 22 24 26 28 30 2 4 6 8 10 12 14 16 18 20 22 24 26 28 30

EVENTS

Easter

PARLIAMENTARY BUSINESS

Aliens Bill

Repatriation Bill

Recess

Budget

Budget debate

Housing Subsidies Bill

Finance Bill

GOVERNMENT ANNOUNCEMENTS

Agricultural price review

DRAFTING LEGISLATION

P

Agricultural Levies Bill

P

Pensions Uprating Bill

P

	JUNE			JULY			AUGUST		
1 3 5 7 9 11 13	15 17 19 21 23 25 27 29	2 4 6 8 10 12 14	16 18 20 22 24 26 28 30	1 3 5 7	9 11 13 15 17				

Finance Bill

Agricultural Levies Bill

Recess   Recess

Pensions Uprating Bill

White Paper on our pensions scheme

White Paper on Local Government

Our Pensions Bill

Notes

1   CRD file, 'General Correspondence'.
2   CRD files, '1966 General Election, Opinion Research' and 'Economic Policy Group'.
3   CRD file, 'General Correspondence'.
4   CRD file, '1964 General Election, Manifesto'.
5   D. E. Butler and A. King, *The British General Election of 1966*, 53–4.
6   CRD files, 'General Correspondence', 'People' and 'Correspondence of the Shadow Minister in Charge'.
7   CRD files, 'University reports' and 'Links with Universities'.
8   CRD files, 'General Correspondence' and 'Correspondence of the Shadow Minister in Charge'.
9   CRD files, 'Party Organisation' and 'Correspondence of the Shadow Minister in Charge'.
10 CRD files, 'P. G. on Trade Union Law and Practice' and '1965 Policy document, correspondence'.
11 Nigel Fisher, *Iain Macleod*, 263–5; CRD files, 'Future Economic Policy' and 'Economic Policy Group'.
12 CRD file, 'Foreign Affairs'.
13 CRD file, 'Policy Ideas'.
14 Butler and King, *General Election of 1966*, 62–4; CRD files, '1965 Policy Document'.
15 CRD file, 'General Correspondence'.
16 CRD files, 'Tactics' and 'Leader's working lunches'.
17 CRD files, '1966 Election manifesto – 1st and 2nd drafts and correspondence'.
18 CRD files, '1966 Election manifesto – 3rd and 4th drafts and correspondence'.
19 CRD files, '1966 Election, Tactics', ' . . . Arrangements'; Robert Rhodes James, *Ambitions and Realities*, 98–9.
20 CRD files, '1966 Election, reports' and '1967 Policy Document'.
21 CRD files, 'Correspondence of the Shadow Minister in Charge'.
22 *Ibid*; CRD file, 'Meetings of Policy Group Chairman'.
23 CRD file, 'Correspondence of the Shadow Minister in Charge'.
24 *Ibid*; CRD file, 'Public Sector Research Unit'; J. Bruce-Gardyne, *Whatever happened to the Quiet Revolution*.
25 CRD file, 'General Correspondence'.

26 CRD files, 'Ideas' and 'Policy Initiatives and Methods Committee'.
27 CRD file, 'Patronage of the Arts'.
28 CRD files, 'Future Economic Policy' and 'Nationalised Industries'.
29 CRD files, 'Transport' and 'General Correspondence'.
30 CRD files, 'Scottish Nationalism' and 'Scottish Policy Groups'.
31 CRD file, 'Regional Government'.
32 CRD file, 'Industrial Relations'.
33 Butler and King, *General Election of 1966*, 65; CRD files, 'Public Opinion Monthly Survey Meetings' and 'Policy Initiatives and Methods Committee'.
34 CRD file, '1967 Policy Document '.
35 CRD files, 'General Correspondence', 'Policy Initiatives and Methods Committee' and 'Policy Differentiation'.
36 CRD file, '1968 Policy Document'.
37 CRD files, '1967 Policy Document' and 'Tactics'.
38 Fisher, *Macleod*, 284; Reginald Maudling, *Memoirs*, 1978, 191–2, 209, 263; D. E. Butler and M. Pinto-Duschinsky, *The British General Election of 1970*, 73–4; CRD file, 'Economic Policy Group'.
39 CRD file, 'Future Legislative Programme'.
40 CRD file, 'Swinton Weekends'.
41 R. Oakley and P. Rose, *The Political Year, 1970*, 141–2; CRD files, '1970 Election Manifesto' and 'Public Opinion Monthly Survey Meetings'.
42 CRD files, '1970 Election Manifesto' and '1970 Election, reports'.
43 CRD file, '1970 Election, reports'.

Chapter 10

Power and opposition in the seventies

As in 1951, the return of the Conservatives to power in 1970 left the Research Department in an uncertain position. Having played the central role in the policy review of 1964–1970, officers now had to adjust once again to having only limited access to the Party leaders, and to competition with the civil service. Newspapers that commented on this after the election also hinted that the Party might be taking an unfair advantage in that competition, for a number of Party professionals moved into Whitehall, either to temporary posts in the civil service or to positions as political advisers to Ministers. Thus, Stephen Abbot moved to the Department of Employment to help draft the Industrial Relations Bill, Miles Hudson went into the Foreign Office, and Christopher Patten to the Cabinet Office; Michael Wolff, Douglas Hurd and Brian Reading all went direct to Downing Street, either to the Cabinet Office or to the Prime Minister's personal staff. Similarly, Mark Schreiber moved from the PSRU to the Civil Service Department to pursue the plans that he had worked on in opposition, and a second wave of political appointments later in the life of the Government included Robert Jackson and John Cope. These moves had been discussed informally before the election but were decided only afterwards. One other move was entirely unexpected: when Iain Macleod died only a few weeks after becoming Chancellor of the Exchequer, Anthony Barber who replaced him (but without the benefit of working on the Party's economic and taxation plans in opposition) summoned Brendon Sewill to assist him at the Treasury. There were therefore Party men in position in several key Ministries, and there were charges from the Opposition that a new network of political patronage was being introduced.

In fact though, there was no real threat of political or constitutional impropriety, and the incoming Labour Government of 1974 took things much further in any case. Between 1970 and 1974, few of the Conservative advisers in Whitehall were either encouraged or allowed to be politicians. Whether they were political advisers or civil servants, they had to keep a low profile within their departments so as not to offend the established departmental order. Some of those who had entered their new departments expecting that they should have to fight tooth and nail for the Party's manifesto pledges found rather that the established civil servants were as keen on the proposals as the Party and had already done some work on them to prepare for the possible return of a Conservative Government. At least one adviser found that he did not get to see his Minister often enough to have any effective influence over him. There was not at first much liaison between the political advisers themselves, although informal contacts and friendships of course remained, and it was not until the Government was fighting for its life at the end of 1973 that they began to meet regularly as a group. Michael Fraser, conscious as ever of the need for communication, organised a series of lunches at the St Stephen's Club to keep Ministers and Party professionals in contact with each other, but there was no systematic means of keeping the political advisers in touch with the Research Department as a whole. The advisers might be used as channels of communication in an emergency, but their role in Whitehall was sufficiently anomalous to make them ever mindful of the terrors of the Official Secrets Act. As Douglas Hurd wrote, 'the Official Secrets Act and (far more important) the entrenched habits of Whitehall turn the familiar friend into an occasional acquaintance.' The Party was thus distanced even from its former employees – even indeed from the political advisers that it continued to employ. Research Department contact with the Government was for the most part a personal contact between desk officers and Ministers (especially junior ministers); liaison on the central areas of political strategy took place as before through the Department's Chairman and Director, acting directly to the Prime Minister. The leadership of the Research Department itself was therefore a matter of great weight.

There had been concern even before the election about the standing of the Research Department in the Party and about its role under a future Government. The Department had not had its own Chairman since 1964, so that its independence seemed to be less clear and its future role more uncertain. Edward Heath retained personal control of the Department in the political field, and it came under Fraser as Deputy Chairman of the Party 'with special responsibility for the Conservative Research Department' in a more general sense. In opposition this had worked well, for it was a positive advantage to have a direct line to the Leader – especially if the Leader was entirely dependant on the Department for briefing. Heath was regularly in the office, and his room there was generally known as 'Mr Heath's room', rather than 'The Chairman's room' as it has been before and since. All of this changed when Heath moved to Downing Street, for he became both more subjected to alternative sources of advice and too busy to make more than occasional visits to the office. He came back as often as possible; when there he held open meetings with the officers to encourage free discussion, but there could never be enough time in a Prime Minister's diary to make this an effective means of communication. The link was to be through Michael Fraser, who not only remained Deputy Chairman of the Party and Deputy Chairman of the ACP (under Barber), but now in 1970 became Chairman of the Research Department in name as well as in fact. The fact that Fraser was not a member of the Government or of either House meant that he was denied access to classified papers and contact with MPs in the Palace of Westminster (where Butler had done such valuable, informal work). Fraser's appointment thus preserved the Department's independence but at the same time distanced it from the centre of Party affairs in Government.

Brendon Sewill had foreseen these problems in a minute sent to Heath in December 1969. He emphasised that he had 'no objection to the present situation, it works well and I do not suggest any change.' But it worked well only because it revolved around Fraser's personal position. As a former Director of the Research Department, Fraser was sensitive to its special needs and realised that it was not just a section of Central Office. Fraser had acted as a buffer and a communication channel between the two departments, and as Party Chairman Anthony Barber had not claimed any greater right to oversee the Research Department than his predecessors. However, Sewill foresaw a danger that if and when Fraser should move on, 'if no specific decision is taken the Research Department will fall into position as one of the departments of Central Office. Most people would think that this was administratively tidy, and merely formalised the present situation.' But Sewill did not think so; such a permanent link with Central Office would inevitably increase demands that the Research Department should work more for the constituencies, rather than for the Parliamentary Party and its leaders; it would also place (from the Leader's viewpoint) a potentially undesirable amount of power in the hands of the Party Chairman. There was, in short, a separate political role that should be assigned to someone of Cabinet rank:

It is important to have some leading member of the Party with a specific responsibility for the forward look in policy as Chairman of the Advisory Committee on Policy. Not only does this confer responsibility for organising policy groups and other research work, but such a person acts as a focal point to whom Members of Parliament, Cabinet colleagues and outside experts can direct ideas and queries about policy. It seems important that the Chairman of the A.C.P. should have a close personal contact with the Research Department, to gain and give advice, to help get decisions on outstanding policy points, and to put some weight behind the policy work of the Department and prevent it getting submerged in day-to-day business.

Sewill insisted that a problem would emerge only if Fraser did not continue in his present role, but much of the point of his argument would remain even if Fraser were to stay on, and so it did after 1970. Because of his position at Central Office, Fraser was receiving a wider range of Party advice than previous Chairmen of the Research Department, and hence he was not the representative only of the Department in his dealings with the Government. Moreover, although Sir Michael Fraser was undoubtedly as able and as influential as any unelected Party figure has been in this century, he could hardly be said to carry the clout of either Neville Chamberlain in the thirties or Rab Butler from 1945 to 1964. He could not sit in on Cabinet meetings (as in opposition he had sat in on the meetings of the Shadow Cabinet) and he could not easily smooth the Department's path in the scores of informal meetings that take place on each parliamentary day in the lobbies and smoking rooms.

It should be emphasised though that Fraser was as aware of these difficulties as anyone, for he shared the general Research Department view that it ought to have as its Chairman a senior Cabinet Minister, one of those like Neville Chamberlain or Rab Butler without whom no important decision could be made. But it was crystal clear to all Party professionals in 1970 that Heath had no intention of giving such a role to any one of his colleagues. There was indeed a somewhat long delay after the 1970 election before the Leader could be persuaded to appoint anyone of Cabinet status to the equally important position of Party Chairman, in succession to Barber; only the insistence of the National Union ensured that a Cabinet Minister was appointed, but nobody was more surprised than Peter Thomas when it turned out to be him. Since there was no powerful body like the National Union to argue its case, the position of the Research Department went by default. Fraser might regret this, but it was a fact of political life of which he and the rest of the Party organisation had to make the best.

Indeed, the real point was that unless Heath had himself held the Chairmanship of the Research Department (as Chamberlain had done as Prime Minister, but which was practically impossible for Heath because of the pressures of work and time), there was in any case nobody who carried enough clout to be the impresario of policy in a Heath Government.

With the benefit of hindsight, it must be clear even to the most sympathetic observer that the Conservative Government of 1970–1974 tackled a programme that was over-ambitious for one Parliament; this becomes clear when we add up the entry into Europe, reform of the machinery of government, the new tax package, industrial relations reforms, reconstruction of the NHS, and the introduction of an entirely new structure of local government – to name only the main areas of activity. This would have been a huge task even in a time when politics were otherwise quiet, but politics after 1970 were anything but quiet. As a result, the programme of work, and the weight of parliamentary activity that it entailed, tended to keep Ministers' noses so firmly to the grindstones of legislation and administration that a group of relatively weak communicators became at times virtual non-comunicators. Too little time and effort by Ministers went into the political presentation of their case, and they became insulated in their Ministries from the real world of opinion outside. Douglas Hurd has shown that there was an uncomfortable awareness even in the Prime Minister's private office that this might be happening, and he attributes some of the shortcomings to the Government's own information services. The death of Iain Macleod right at the start was of course a very severe blow in this sense; he might not have proved to be a great Chancellor of the Exchequer, but he was unquestionably a great Party communicator. With Macleod's death, and with Hailsham's withdrawal into the less-political office of Lord Chancellor, the Party lost its only real trumpeters. Hence, although all the machinery of committees for efficient Government/Party communication was set up in 1970 and worked right up to 1974, it did not produce enough results in the, admittedly very difficult, circumstances.

Thus, although Michael Fraser stayed on, it was in a position that was effectively different from what it had been before 1970. He was also backed up by a new Director of the Research Department, James Douglas, who was appointed when Sewill went to the Treasury. Douglas had come to the Department in 1950 after some time in the Civil Service, and had been Head of the Economic Section and subsequently Research Organiser. He was one of the sharpest intellects that the Department has ever had, with an academic and sometimes an iconoclastic turn of mind; as a specialist in economics and psephology, he seemed an appropriate choice in the circumstances of 1970 when, it must be remembered, the Party was *not* anticipating three-and-a-half years of prolonged crisis ahead. In another way the position of the Department was enhanced in the Parliament of 1970, for the group of former Research Department officers in Government and Parliament was again enlarged. Gordon Campbell joined Maudling and Macleod in the Cabinet, and the Government as a whole included Richard Sharples, Lord Balniel, Michael Alison, Paul Dean, Eldon Griffiths and Keith Speed. The new MPs included Carol Mather, Barney Hayhoe, John Wilkinson and Sir Anthony Meyer (re-elected in 1970 after a spell at Old Queen Street during his short absence from the House).

The bulk of the Department's work in the 1970 Parliament came as always in matters of routine, the thousand little ways in which briefs for Ministers, drafts of speeches, work for Parliamentary Committees, regular publication of *Notes on Current Politics*, suggested replies to letters, and so on, all oiled the wheels of government and kept a reduced staff under heavy pressure at Old Queen Street. At a more elevated level, other routines of the pre-1964 period were restarted. Early work was put in hand, in collaboration with Ministers where possible, for a manifesto and a *Campaign Guide* for next time. Papers on policy and tactics were prepared for the ACP and the Liaison Committee, which was set up straight after the 1970 election, first under Whitelaw and later Prior, with Fraser, Douglas, Hurd, Wolff, and Tucker (later Harker) as members, and with Newton as secretary. Other briefs were sent direct to ministers or to their advisers, with or without requests for them. So for example, an office committee was re-formed for the purpose of considering each budget in advance and making suggestions to the Chancellor; one of the officers involved has estimated that about half of these recommendations were carried out, but that as in all such advice to Governments, 'it was like firing into a fog.' Occasionally, a request for further copies of the brief in question would indicate that the advice had struck home, but more often it was simply a case of blazing away at where the target was thought to be; even if the enemy was killed, you could never be sure that it was your bullet that had hit him. One exception to this general rule was in the implementation of the tax package, for the presence of Brendon Sewill and Arthur Cockfield in government as advisers ensured both continuity from opposition and continued liaison in the present.

The Department's own forward thinking was principally organised around the activities of the Official Group; this had been founded by Fraser in 1967 as a group of officials from inside and outside the Department, with the specific task of supervising the work on the 1968 *Make Life Better* and the subsequent manifesto – the heir of the RSG and PSG of previous years – but it became a more general clearing-house for publicity and research business. During the period of Government after 1970, it consisted of Fraser (in the chair), Clarke, Douglas, Hurd, Wolff, Tucker, and Newton (as Secretary); it thus brought together Party officials from the Research Department, Central Office, Swinton College, the Prime Minister's Office, and the Lord President's Office, and constituted what might be regarded as a collective leadership for the research programme. The original decision to reconstitute the Group after the election envisaged it as 'a piece of machinery to consider the forward-movement of long-term policy thinking in the immediate future and working towards the next General Election'. It was decided however to make a clearer separation, with short- and medium-term issues being left to the Liaison Committee and to Fraser's Tactical Committee at Central Office, and with the Official Group looking further ahead. Hence, the first post-election meeting considered papers on likely developments up to July 1975 as well as the implications of legislation in the coming session. Fraser told Douglas that research on policy should both 'skirmish ahead along the extrapolation of existing policy lines' and 'try to devise one or two entirely new initiatives.' It was also hoped that the Steering Committee would be re-convened in due course, for on the basis of his experience before 1964, Fraser was conscious 'of the value of senior political figures meeting outside the machinery of government itself.' (It was in fact set up in June 1971 and met twice-yearly until July 1973, but then replaced, less satisfactorily, by *ad hoc* meetings of the various Ministers). The Official Group was intended to hold longish meetings at infrequent intervals, and with lengthy papers circulated in advance. It was also fed with regular reports on the opinion surveys commissioned by the Party at the time of the 1970 election.

It was not until 1971 that the Department got on to the task of research for the future, as opposed to routine business. In part, the delay may be attributed to the normal turnover of staff and the consequent need to re-establish the office with its new crew before embarking for more distant waters. In April 1971 though, all officers were invited to indicate areas in their own fields on which detailed research would be needed before the next election, and their replies were embodied in a review paper by David Dear. Some fields were deemed to need very little research, because the problems were those of resources and opportunity rather than the choice of policies (foreign affairs or schools), and many others suggested only the need for further refinement of the work done since 1964. This whole exercise was naturally weakened by the impossibility of finding out just what the Government intended to do. What was to be the future of the Civil Service in the wake of the Fulton Report? What work was being done on regional policy to prepare for entry to the EEC? What was the progress on a policy for Scotland? The Research Department was thus inhibited not only in the advice it could give to Ministers, but in deciding what work to undertake itself.

The distancing between Government and Party should not be exaggerated, real though it was. It was customary for the Department to receive advance notice of major announcements of policy (such as the decision on the future of Rolls Royce in 1972), but this would occur only a few hours before it all became public and had to be restricted to one or two senior men at Old Queen Street anyway. It was usual for a Treasury Minister to spend the evening of Budget Day at the Research Department, in order to explain the reasons that lay behind the Chancellor's announcements of the afternoon. Such briefing from Government to the Research Department was essential if the Government and Party publicity machines were not to get out of step, but it cast the Party in the role of an accessory *after* the fact. All of this was constitutionally correct; it left the Department with a considerable leeway for affecting policy in detail, and with a vital task of explanation and exposition, but it also left it in a somewhat more subordinate position than it had occupied before 1964. To a great extent this change reflected the fact that the Government of 1970 was obliged to react to events, while Conservative governments of the fifties had been more able to control them. But above all, the Research Department without a politician as its Chairman was less able to apply a political lever to the Government's own policy making, and much would therefore depend on how politically Ministers approached their own jobs.

This soon emerged as a real problem when the Official Group sought to lay down a programme of research. In April 1971, it was agreed to work only at a few broad themes, and the Liaison Committee was invited to suggest what these should be – so as to involve Ministers in the very idea of Party research. The nuts and bolts of policy would have to be left to Ministers themselves, or to the Research Department where it had an appropriate relationship with a Minister. This was questioned by David Clarke, who noted that 'the Research Department had traditionally functioned as a check on blinkered Departments and Ministers, and as a sounding board for Ministerial ideas.' Further discussion produced a recommendation from Douglas that the whole approach to research while in office should be low-key, because of the practical impossibility of getting decisions on really radical ideas in those circumstances; in support of his view, he cited the experience of 1951–1964, and asked whether the new policy on industrial relations would ever have come about in 1965 if the Party had not been defeated in 1964. He therefore recommended work on new areas of policy, such as consumerism and the problems of urban decay, since these need not run counter to the preconceived ideas of either civil servants or their Ministers. He suggested that instead of a large programme of policy groups, they should rely on the informal contact of desk officers with Ministers, but it was thought that this would rely too much on Ministers knowing in advance what would be the right questions to ask in three years time. The logical corollary of this, that the Ministers who proved uncooperative should have more political advice thrust on them by 'enlisting Research Department officers for this task', was met by Douglas with the reflection that 'there was little that a Research Department officer could do if the Minister were not willing to use his services.' The problem was identified, and it was agreed that 'it was necessary that Ministers be made more aware of political implications', but no way of achieving this could be seen. There is no escaping the fact that Edward Heath's own predilections made this difficulty greater; he had an understandable wish to be remembered as a statesmanlike Prime Minister rather than merely as a political partisan, no doubt in part an over reaction to his predecessor, and this made him more open to advice from the civil service than from his Party. Douglas Hurd has described the complex and difficult balance that a Prime Minister must strike in the taking of advice, and he has also suggested that this balance was not always achieved after 1970.

This whole argument sharpened in the Autumn of 1971. By then, the Research Department was hard at work in presenting the Government's case to the electorate. The Party Chairman's Conference speech was used as an occasion for a general review of what had been achieved since the election; the Department was keeping up lists of manifesto pledges that had been redeemed and was constructing an agenda of 'plus factors on which we can make the running next year.' All of this was affected by what seemed to be the strange reluctance of Ministers to act like politicians. They were constantly being urged to make greater use of their opportunities to present a Party case – and to attack Labour more often. In November 1971, the Official Group discussed the idea of producing a short 'bible' for ministerial speech-writers, but Michael Wolff 'doubted whether this would be either acceptable or practicable. In any event, there was already too great a tendency to think in terms of hand-outs. The real problem was to get Ministers continuously to present their work within a political framework'. He cited a recent party political broadcast as an example of this, and several ministerial broadcasts that might just as well have been made by civil servants themselves for all the political content that they had had; it may have been this meeting that prompted Douglas Hurd to advise the Prime Minister that 'there is a general impression at all levels within the Party that this administration is in fact less politically conscious than its Conservative predecessor.' Nor should it be thought that this was an ideological divide, with Conservative right wishing to be more partisan than the Conservative left, for both the Party advisers and the Ministers that they criticised came from all sides of the Party. Some positive policy research was done, despite all of these difficulties. For example, work on urban problems resulted in a substantial paper being submitted to the ACP and the Steering Committee, but this research probably had more impact after the party lost office in 1974 than before.

The Party organisation had been heavily committed to opinion polling since 1960, and the Research Department was closely involved with this largely because of the personal interest taken by both Fraser and Douglas in psephology. As a result, the considerable costs of commissioning private polls appeared as part of the Research Department's budget now that the Party accounts were published, and this conveyed an inflated idea of how expensive research operations really were. Conversely though, such market research activities may have encouraged business contributions to Party funds. The chief message of survey results coming in after 1970 was largely to confirm earlier trends. Evidence for the 1970 election showed that the Party had not made any disproportionate gain among women voters (despite much press comment to that effect), and that its improved performance had been mainly in the C2, D and E social groups, with a considerable passive gain (Labour abstentions) in the large C2 group. In the electorate as a whole, actual conversions had had a greater effect than differential abstention, and the survey confirmed recent academic research in pointing up the scale of electoral volatility; the net movement between the parties had been only a little over a million votes, but to produce this net result more than seven million electors had actually changed their minds and voted for different parties. When account was also taken of those who had switched to or from abstention it appeared that, in only five years, about half of the electorate had 'floated'. The second major finding was the disproportionate effect of the young voters, when the 1947 population bulge and the new franchise for 18–year olds both hit the register at the same time in 1970; the evidence suggested that this 'cohort' of voters had the lowest turnout of any group, but that it was overwhelmingly pro-Labour and that its inclusion in the 1970 electorate had done much to hold down the size of the Conservative majority. The consolidated results of panel surveys since 1964 confirmed the view of other researchers that party identity was a better indicator of future voting behaviour than was expressed voting intentions: of those who had said back in 1967–8 that they still considered themselves to be Labour people but who intended to vote Conservative, most had gone back to Labour by 1970, but of those who had actually identified with the Conservatives in 1967–8 most had stayed loyal at the election – whatever their votes in the past. These various findings had three important implications. First, the increased volatility of the electorate would make the prediction of future trends a far more hazardous business, and it would therefore be more difficult for Governments to synchronise their electioneering with their other policies, as Harold Wilson had just discovered; in place of the Party professionals' dictum of the fifties that 'elections are won and lost *between* the campaigns' came a new dictum for the mid-seventies which said that all was to be played for after the dissolution of Parliament. Secondly, the continuing reluctance of voters actually to identify with the Conservative Party, as opposed to saying that they would vote for it, suggested a degree of vulnerability for the Heath Government, a vulnerability that was underlined by the extent to which Labour abstentions had contributed to the recent victory. And thirdly, the young voters would have to enter into all future calculations.

The Research Department was therefore much concerned to impress the results of the pollsters' work on the Party leaders, mainly through presentations of their findings to Ministers by Fraser, for as one of the pollsters put it, 'the survey provides the map, it does not provide the vehicle, the power or the driver.' Research into attitudes demonstrated above all the need to win back both young voters and wavering voters in the C2 group by a demonstration of competence in the central economic sphere. Papers coming forward from the Research Department therefore stressed 'the need to deliver' on economic policy, emphasing that this actually presented a good opening, for it was an area in which neither Party had done very well in the sixties. Douglas Hurd has recorded that 'Sir Michael Fraser, the wise and philosophical Deputy Chairman of the Party, together with the Directors of Organisation, Publicity and the Research Department, used every opportunity open to them to keep inflation at the top of Ministers' minds.' Such promptings were backed up with more specific policy recommendations, especially on the urgent need to take action over both prices and unemployment; Douglas suggested that the minimum policy for winning the next election would be unemployment at under half a million and inflation at under six per cent. These reflections no doubt helped to encourage the Government's changes of course in economic policy during 1972, with the obvious proviso that they can only have reinforced Ministers' own reactions which led them along similar lines.

More specifically, the Department used its survey evidence to recommend changes in the Party's approach to the young. Advertising agents should be used to gear up propaganda in papers and magazines read by the under twenty-fives, greater efforts were needed to explain why the Government was pursuing particular industrial policies in specific cases, and there should be a much greater emphasis on television; within this last area, the Party should make for ITV, watched by a far greater proportion of young and wavering voters than the BBC. As in other fields, these were recommendations that bore more fruit after the loss of office in 1974, not just because defeat concentrated minds on the subject, but because further survey evidence could then be cited in support. The very fact that the Party had won in 1970 may have made it difficult to emphasise arguments that pointed to its electoral vulnerability.

This catalogue of difficulties should not suggest that morale was low in the Research Department during the 1970 Parliament. In part this reflected a calculated optimism about the Party's and the Government's future prospects, in part a natural tendency to believe even in the worst moments that all is not too bad so long as there is a Conservative Government. In general, Research Department morale fluctuates much less in power than in opposition; proximity to the Ministers of the Crown (and hence to real decisions that will actually be carried out) has an effect in keeping up the spirits of the Party professionals, and so long as the Party is in office, then it can control the terms of the future debate and decide both the issues and the timing of the next election. And so it seemed in 1972, even after the humiliation of the Miners' strike and the difficult passage of the European Communities Bill through Parliament. More objectively, the Department's own economic specialists were certainly not predicting in 1972 that the future need be gloomy, except on occasions when they wished to press the Government into greater action on prices. An internal paper on economic prospects up to 1975, written in December 1971, admitted the difficulty of forecasting in existing conditions, but confidently predicted that the measures already taken would lower unemployment and inflation towards acceptable levels in 1972–3. A gloomier paper that was circulated to the Official Group at the same time went out with a covering note from Tony Newton, explaining that he did not really feel such an 'air of pessimism' and that the tone of the paper was to be explained by the fact that it had been commissioned for another committee – the Steering Committee. Optimism about the Party's future prospects was naturally encouraged by the obvious internal divisions of the Labour Party over Europe – and by the fact that nobody could predict in 1971 the dramatic upsurge of the Liberals a year later.

Morale *was* affected though, for some research officers at least, by the way in which the Government seemed to shift its policy during 1972, moving towards interventionism in industry and incomes control. No Government can escape the need to adapt its policy when economic conditions change, and there were few if any in the Department who denied the need for more definite policies on inflation. But all the same, the way in which the shift was handled, and the Department's role in presenting the shift to the electorate, placed a political strain on some loyalties. The Department had certainly seen changes coming, not through direct leaks of secret information but through the informal network of contacts which indicated the direction of the Cabinet's thinking. Party briefs and publicity material had therefore attempted to prepare a fall-back position for the Government in advance, mainly by the negative tactic of omission. From the beginning of 1972, previous commitments against the very idea of an incomes policy were quietly dropped from briefs and from drafts of speeches; work began behind the scenes to devise ways in which the new policy could be grafted on-to the old. Indeed, some officers had argued in favour of such caution from the start, with the seasoned professionals' reluctance to use the word 'never'. To the more cynical, it could even be an interesting intellectual diversion when the change came to justify a change of direction as if it was characterised by absolute consistency: old

speeches were rifled for casual references to incomes policies in order
to demonstrate that the present turn of events had been anticipated
from the start. The change of policy was perhaps greater than any
which the Party has made in office since the Suez crisis of 1956, or the
adoption of indicative planning in the early-sixties. It was of course
far less abrupt than the policy revolution that the Party had carried
out in the first half of 1965, but the British electorate, somewhat
illogically, expects absolute consistency from its Governments and
yet allows great latitude to its Oppositions. What was most difficult
to cope with was the fact that, in order to maximise its flimsy chance
of appearing to be consistent, the Government would not *admit* to
having changed its mind, and that it did not therefore state clearly the
ultimate aim of its policy – except in the most general terms, that it
meant to reduce inflation. Stage One of the incomes policy lasted for
only a few months and Stage Two, though longer, was also presented
as no more than a temporary measure. Planning for future policy was
thus damaged by uncertainty as to how the most central issue would
eventually be handled.

The first discussion of the next manifesto had taken place during
1971, though this was only a preliminary consideration of possible
themes. It was however decided to plan on the assumption that an
election could be as early as 1973, not because anyone wanted to hold
one then, but merely in order to be prepared. The Official Group noted
the need to obtain 'guidance about the broad direction in which the
Party should now move'. With the backing of a letter from the Prime
Minister to his colleagues, the Department set about collecting from
government departments ideas that might emerge in time for the
next election. A paper setting out themes for the manifesto was
drawn up on the basis of these ideas and was approved in March 1972.
From this point, most work in 1972 centred on a policy report that
was to be published for the Party Conference, setting out what had
been done since 1970. Increasing time was also spent from this time
on in defending the Government from attack.

A draft manifesto was produced at the end of 1972, by which time
expectations had at least begun to change. The Government's narrow
survival in 1972 (at the hands both of the miners and the anti-
marketeers) had provoked more serious consideration of the idea of
an early election, and from henceforth election preparations went on
with this option always in mind. The draft was as uneven as any
manifesto must be at that stage, with some policies already worked
out in great detail (such as that on crime) and with others that could
only be left as gaps in the text, such as immigration or incomes policy,

for 'the tone and content of what we say here will inevitably depend largely on developments between now and the election'. The extreme difficulty of thinking ahead was shown up by the postponement of discussions on policy options in January 1973, 'in view of the impending announcements on Prices and Incomes.' When the discussions took place in February, the discussion paper had to be revised to show 'the need for greater flexibility and a continuing search for a jointly-determined policy, rather than the importance of getting away entirely from a statutory policy before the election'. In other words, once the Government had adopted a semi-permanent incomes policy in Stage Two, its Party advisers had to assume that there would be no return to non-interventionism before the election. But this remained an assumption that was never confirmed – until the election itself took both Government and Party by storm in the following Winter.

The Steering Committee considered the timing of the election and the nature of the manifesto in May 1973, and it decided on a programme of further research to fill some of the remaining gaps. A second set of letters was sent out to Ministers by the Prime Minister after they had been drafted in the Research Department, so as to ensure that exactly the right questions were asked. Policy groups were then set up on inner city problems, on housing, government and the citizen, and on women's affairs, mainly under the chairmanship of junior ministers. Work over the following Summer concentrated on the Scottish and Welsh manifestoes and on the need to get a *Campaign Guide* out in the Winter of 1973–4.

This stage of manifesto-making also threw into relief the Research Department's relations with the Central Policy Review Staff, which had been set up in 1970 in order to foster forward-thinking, but for the Government rather than the Party. Lord Rothschild (as head of this 'think tank') and Michael Fraser had held reciprocal lunches in order to keep in touch with what each was doing, but there had been little contact lower down. After a brief altercation earlier in the Parliament, the Research Department had been placed on the circulation for the CPRS's end-of-session reviews of Government policy, but was not invited to the Chequers week-ends for which these reports were prepared. Party professionals tended to be as sceptical of the value of the CPRS as they had been when the idea was evolving before 1970. One professional who did attend the Chequers week-ends felt that their value was greatly reduced by the fact that civil servants also attended; 'with them present, the ministers never relaxed and one felt that they each felt obliged to fight their corner on behalf of their department.' What was needed was something more like the Steering Committee or Seldon Park had allowed. In 1973, the CPRS asked to be allowed to see the replies sent by Ministers to the Prime Minister's letter about the manifesto. Fraser told Douglas Hurd that he had no objection to this, but he clearly sensed that there might be an encroachment; he was quite willing for Rothschild to see the letters and,

> indeed it would seem in some ways stupid that he should not. On the other hand I do not think it would be wise or sensible for the CPRS to take over work on the manifesto which is essentially political and must remain a Party matter. As I understand it, Lord Rothschild has it in mind to turn the next strategy meeting very much in the direction of the manifesto. This would, I think, only be advisable if Party professional representatives were also present, such as myself, James Douglas and Tony Newton.

Things were duly agreed on those lines, though not as an urgent priority. All these long-term plans for an election in the middle distance were overtaken by the events of the Autumn of 1973.

By October 1973, the Party's professional advisers had moved from their earlier insistence that the Government must be seen to deliver the economic goods to win the election to an opposite position; the recent by-election defeats and the economic difficulties stemming from the oil crisis led them instead to recommend that the Party should actually campaign on the extreme nature of the crisis. This would be a 'problem-oriented approach, stressing the irrelevance of Labour nostrums and the inexperience of the Liberals, but without hiding the scale of the difficulties.' Instead of pointing to its success in overcoming difficulties, the Party should point up the difficulties that remained to be dealt with, and use these as an argument against a change of Government. The cause of the crisis to be put before the electorate was at that stage seen as the arabs and the price of oil, rather than the miners and price of coal, but the idea of a problem-oriented approach remained even when the source of the most acute problem changed. By this time, in October 1973, it was also clear that the Government might actually be forced into an election, and it was therefore decided to press on with a manifesto even in a time of by-election defeats, 'for the duty of both Ministers and Party was to keep the Prime Minister's options open by being ready to fight at any time.' From this point though, the bandwaggon towards a snap election gathered pace inexorably.

For this reason, a senior Conservative journalist was recruited to the Research Department in November 1973; he was added to the

Official Group and invited by Fraser to draft a special manifesto for a possible snap election. The first full draft of an ordinary manifesto was circulated by Newton at the end of November (and was in any case rather combative). The 'alternative manifesto' was drafted in December as *An Appeal to the Nation*; this rejected the charge that the Government had deliberately picked a fight with the miners, but it went on in highly-coloured language to attack politically-motivated militants and to argue that the defence of Phase Three was now Britain's last hedge against hyper-inflation. It did not present a general catalogue of proposals for the next Parliament, but after concluding with the words 'This is the moment of truth for the British People', it added an appendix of measures that might possibly be taken after the election to curb excessive trades union power. It should be stressed that the author, as a skilled and highly-experienced journalist, was writing to a brief; his draft did not mean that the Party had already decided on such an approach to the election, merely that it was covering all the options. Nevertheless, when this document was drafted it was less than two months before the Party's actual manifesto went to press for the election, and its circulation sparked off a debate among the Party's tactical advisers that doubtless reflected the tactical discussions going on throughout the Party hierarchy.

James Douglas was the most critical, and he posed three problems raised by the very ideas of a crisis election and a manifesto of the sort that had been drafted. Firstly, the manifesto seemed to be composed 'for the scenario of Sophocles' and yet to make at the same time an appeal for the support of moderates: 'can Oedipus ever be a moderate?' Then he urged the need for the Party to find a better peg on which to hang its appeal for the defence of democracy than something that was merely called Stage Three: 'if we outlive this day and come safe home, will we indeed rouse up and stand atiptoe at the name Stage Three?' Finally, he pointed out the need for a much clearer definition of what would be done *after* the election and doubted whether the public would really support measures as tough as those implied by the manifesto's definition of the scale of the crisis. The author himself countered, most pertinently, by asking what, 'given the premise of the scale of the crisis,' 'is your preferred alternative?' This was indeed the nub of the argument, for most Conservatives shared the sense that the country and Party were at a hinge of fate, but they also shared a reluctance to adopt draconian measures against the unions. Hence, they drifted towards a crisis election without proposals that were of crisis proportions.

When the Official Group met to discuss the drafts in mid-December 1973, the debate continued. Some members expressed their misgivings about the whole idea of pinning all on the defence of Stage Three and hence on a battle with the miners; others pointed out that a snap election could only be justified at all if there was a crisis. It was agreed though to proceed with both drafts, redrafting to meet the points raised at the meeting, and that the Research Department like the civil service would work on possible changes in trades union law. The manifesto came back to the Research Department only after it had been cleared with Ministers in late-January 1974. The process of pushing it through the Cabinet had naturally blurred its message even more, and what was left was a long document that sought to put across the message of the earlier short draft. The Party was laid even more open to the charge of inconsistency, in having an extreme analysis of the situation but only moderate proposals for dealing with it.

Given the suddenness of the decision to hold an election, the Party organisation was surprisingly well-prepared in February 1974. The *Campaign Guide* could not be made ready in time for the dissolution, but it was sent out to candidates and others in page proof and so helped to plug the gap left by a manifesto that concentrated mainly on one subject; like all the series it was primarily a review of past events. The election routines worked well enough at Old Queen Street, and the morale of the whole Party was lifted at least at the start by a conviction that it was fighting for great and historic issues. When things began to go badly wrong during the campaign, it was for most part due to events beyond the Party's control anyway (emanating from the CBI and the Pay Board, for example) and it was largely too late to allow time for a Party reaction to be effectively organised. In so far as the Party made serious mistakes in the February 1974 campaign, it was in its strategy rather than its tactics, for the campaign exposed precisely the flaws in the Party's position that such people as Douglas, Newton and Clarke had pointed out two months earlier.

Defeat at the election called into question many of the policy making arrangements of the past few years. Moreover, the experiments with new methods in power could now be seen to have weakened the policy apparatus on which the Party would have to depend in opposition. The CPRS, the Prime Minister's personal office, and the institution of political advisers to Ministers may or may not have been successful in their own terms, but they had certainly weakened the Research Department; back in opposition from March 1974, only this weakened research Department was left to the Party and it would take time for it to re-establish itself on the old basis. Also as a result of defeat, Edward Heath's Leadership came under more pressure; his closest advisers on policy could no longer feel secure about his future or their own, and 1974–5 therefore represented a period of uncertainty which culminated in a rearrangement both of structures and personnel. Heath had to give ground to the extent of appointing for the first time a single colleague at Cabinet level to supervise all policy work. Ian Gilmour was thus appointed Chairman of the ACP and of the Research Department, though since Gilmour was a colleague close to the Leader's own way of thinking, the appointment did not do much to satisfy the critics. Michael Fraser, who had been made Lord Fraser of Kilmorack in Heath's resignation honours list as a tribute to his thirty years of service, remained Deputy Chairman of the ACP and of the Party organisation; he also retained the chair of the Official Group until it ceased to meet in July 1974, but he gave up his direct responsibility for the Research Department. In the wake of the Party's defeat it was many months before the Department settled down; not only had there been the usual turnover of staff, but it proved difficult to find sufficiently-experienced replacements who could be pitched into the electoral front-line within weeks. Similarly, there were changes of staff at Central Office and in the Leader's office, so that even the Research Department officers who were not new to their jobs found themselves dealing with new men. Above all, there loomed the future of the Director of the Department, a question that was left unsettled until more than half of the 1974 Parliament had passed. There were some who noted that all Directors except Fraser had held office for relatively short periods, and that different talents would be needed for a stormy period of opposition ahead from those looked for in 1970 for a period in power. Others who did not perhaps know of the objections that both Fraser and Douglas had expressed to the strategy on which the Party had just fought the February election, attributed to them a share of the blame for defeat. Heath, Douglas and Fraser had all had severe misgivings about the election, but all three were to be replaced in due course because it had been held and lost; such are the fortunes of politics. However, as previous periods after the defeat had shown, the Conservative Party does not find such decisions easy to take, and hence there were several months of delay before Christopher Patten was appointed Director, with Douglas staying on as Associate Director.

In these circumstances, it is understandable that policy work between the two elections of 1974 was slow to get started. The Official Group met in March, with a slightly-revised membership and with Stephen Sherbourne as secretary in place of Tony Newton (now an MP). It reviewed the election and agreed on the necessity of publishing a defensive document about the 1970–74 Government, in order to 'nail the myths' that had been put about during the campaign. It also agreed to revise the *Campaign Guide* that had been used in the election but not actually published, a decision that indicates that the second election that was expected was seen as the second round of a contest already begun; it was duly published in May. A particular difficulty was that the Party had to be ready for a snap election at any time – one in June 1974 was regarded as a serious possibility – and constant speculation about this deflected both Shadow Ministers and advisers from substantive matters. It was therefore decided to set up only a limited number of policy groups, nothing like the ambitious programme of 1965, and to build them up from ones started before the election. Thus the Housing Group would continue its work, but with the addition of an ex-Minister with Treasury experience, no doubt a reaction to the recent campaign experience which suggested that housing finance was a major problem for the middle-class home-owner. On the other hand, a high-powered group would be set up to work on devolution policy, following the success of the SNP at the election. Later discussions produced a slight increase in the number of groups, but still on a low key. As before 1970, the central Economic Policy Group remained under the Leader's direct control, but this time industrial relations was similarly treated, for it was tacked on as a sub-committee of the EPG. Nonetheless, most of these new groups, like the EPG itself, did not get into their stride before the Summer recess; some of them had not met before the October election was called.

All policy making after the loss of office was also affected to a degree by the Party's bewilderment about the election result itself. There has perhaps been no modern election that Conservatives have so much wanted to win as that of February 1974, none of which the lasting significance seemed so clear. The inconclusive result, by which Conservatives beat Labour in votes but held less seats, was a terrible anti-climax to what had begun as an epic struggle to decide 'Who governs Britain'. Conservatives felt that all too many of the electorate had simply ducked the issue by abstaining or by voting Liberal; as Lord Carrington put it so aptly, 'We were clobbered by the "head-under-the-bedclothes vote".' It was therefore difficult to adjust to defeat or to explain its causes. The Research Department waited impatiently for the results of election surveys and the Party's pollsters were urged to hurry up with the delivery of their findings – lest the results should arrive too late to be of use for the next contest. Hard evidence on the February election began to come in only in May and June. By and large this confirmed trends that had been detected in 1970, the polarisation of society, the reluctance of the majority of electors to think of Conservatives as 'their' party, and especially the exposed position of the Party among the young – it appeared that the Conservatives had got the votes of only a tenth of those who had been entitled to vote for the first time. (Labour and the Liberals had each claimed about a sixth of these new electors, but more than half of them had not voted at all.) The figures showed that the Conservatives had actually gained more votes from Labour than they had lost, but had lost the election because of their disproportionate losses to Liberals and other parties, and because of Labour's net gain from young voters and previous abstainers. The critical factors for the next election would therefore be the views of the young (which seemed to be too fixed to be easily affected) and of those who had defected to the Liberals (a group that seemed more uncertain, and who would thus provide the Conservatives' best chance of bouncing back to power). But the attitude surveys for this last group made gloomy reading, for they showed how far the Conservative Party's reputation for 'competence' had taken a knock from the events of the Winter of 1973–4. The surveys demonstrated that, apart from price levels and mortgage rates (which were issues raised by almost all respondents), a lack of faith in the Conservatives' ability to get on with the trade unions was the greatest deterrent to the floating voter when he considered voting Conservative.

These poll findings were influential not only for what they actually said, but because they reinforced in independent form the advice of newspapers and the view of many in the Party itself. It was therefore with this information in mind that preparations were made for the next election. The Official Group wanted a manifesto that would be short and punchy, as that of February had not been, but it did not get its way. Again it proved difficult to hang a manifesto around a central theme that was as yet unknown; in circulating the first draft, Sherbourne pointed out that 'the central requirement was to provide a satisfactory explanation of how a new Conservative Government would be able to take tough measures to restrain inflation without provoking an industrial conflict. Without a satisfactory answer to this central question, the rest of the manifesto, however powerful, would prove inadequate.' The same dilemma as in the previous

Winter and a much easier question to ask than to answer.

The second draft, circulated in the middle of May, again called for decisions to be made on contentious issues like inflation and devolution, and a third draft which went to the Shadow Cabinet in June included a list of the points that would have to be settled before the parliamentary recess. At the end of June, the new regime began to take over, when the Shadow Cabinet asked Gilmour to draft an introduction to the text; this inspired discussion at the Official Group as to whether the Party intended to make a case for a Conservative or a coalition government, and at least one of the Party's advisers urged that there should be an unequivocal call for coalition. But this went far beyond the Party professionals' terms of reference, and the Official Group was told that there was to be no talk of coalitions until after the election was over; instead, the Party would emphasise the need for a national approach to government, in the hope of stopping waverers from voting Labour. In view of the attempt to make an alliance with the Liberals in the early days of March and the state of the opinion polls in June, this divergence of aims was understandable; the policy adopted was relatively successful in October, for the swing was very small and Labour was very nearly denied a majority. Meanwhile, ordinary preparations for an election went ahead as early as possible. The Questions of Policy Committee was set up especially early, with Lord Windlesham in the chair and David Clarke as Secretary, as in February, because with a short manifesto and a lot of new candidates, the Department anticipated that there might be a lot of policy enquiries. By August, the original idea of a short manifesto had been abandoned anyway, at the insistence of the Steering Committee and the Shadow Cabinet; later drafts were the work of Gilmour and Patten, using material that had come from those policy groups that had started their work, but taking little from the earlier drafts of the manifesto itself. The Official Group was never re-convened after its meeting on 12 July, and hence the more collective leadership of policymaking that had been emerging since 1967 gave way to a new (or rather older) approach. By the end of the Summer, the new regime was fully established.

The October 1974 manifesto received a particularly good press when it appeared, reflecting in part the greater coherence given by its having been drafted by a small rather than a large team. Its policy on central economic issues derived more from the speeches of Robert Carr as Shadow Chancellor than from decisions of the EPG or of the Shadow Cabinet. Other preparations for the election were also well in hand by the time that the manifesto came out in September, and so the machinery worked quite well for the election. The Party's problems, as in February, were political and strategic rather than tactical, and expectations in the Research Department were not pitched very high; in the event, it was felt that a very small swing to Labour was as good a result as could have been hoped for. However, the fact of a second defeat within a year (and the ultimate emergence of a majority Labour government, which the Party's strategy had been designed to prevent), meant that the Conservatives were plunged into a Leadership crisis that was bound to affect the Party organisation and the policy machine. The announcement that Margaret Thatcher would oppose Edward Heath's re-election as Leader opened another time of uncertainty that was ended only with her election as Leader in 1975. However, the Leadership battle had permanent consequences too; Sir Keith Joseph's Centre for Policy Studies, founded as a separate organisation when there was dissatisfaction with Heath's regime in the Party, was kept in being as a personal research organisation even after the candidate that Joseph supported became Party Leader. The victory of Margaret Thatcher led to other changes though; in March 1975 Angus Maude was made Chairman of the Research Department in succession to Gilmour, and he became an additional Deputy Chairman of the Party along with Fraser; Joseph became Chairman of the ACP and took special responsibility for the development of Party policy. This dual-monarchy in the policy machinery might well have led to serious clashes but hardly ever did so at the time, though its longer-term implications were more serious. Maude's appointment in succession to Gilmour confirmed for a time the independence of the Research Department, for though Maude like Fraser had responsibilities to the Party organisation as a whole, he was a senior Shadow Cabinet figure, close to the Leader, and with more past interest in policy than in the details of organisation. Both Joseph and Maude were kept in close touch with the Department through their Party positions, and the link with Joseph at least helped to keep possible conflicts with the Centre for Policy Studies to a minimum.

Policy making since 1975 has certainly been a very different operation from that of the recent past. As their attitudes before 1970 had shown, Margaret Thatcher, Keith Joseph and Angus Maude had not been wholly in sympathy with the problem-solving approach that had characterised all policy making since 1965. All had in their different ways expressed the view that the principles and ideas should be settled before policy was laid down in detail, and Maude had indeed been removed from the Opposition front bench in 1965 for saying it too insistently. This attitude was shared by a number of Party professionals, as Chapter 9 has shown, and 'it was a view that could be held whether one was on the left or the right of the Party'; it may also be true though that the more overtly ideological tone of the new regime has given an added dimension to the point. There is little doubt that all three (and the Party as a whole), had had their natural inclinations strongly reinforced by the experience of the 1970 Government, which had been perhaps over-prepared with policies for power, but under-prepared for the changing circumstances that it might find when it got there. The chief characteristic of policy work since 1975 has thus been to say not what the Party would do when elected, or how it would do it, but how it would approach problems, stressing the unpredictability of events and the necessity of 'seeing the books' after the election before making too many promises. This naturally attracted some unfavourable comment, not least from Labour, but there has rarely been a modern Opposition that has hedged its bets so completely (in terms of actual *pledges*) and still retained a reasonable credibility. In part, this new style was aided by the difficulties and performance of the Government, which lent further credence to the Conservatives' new diffidence about what could actually be promised and redeemed. All the same, the concentration on themes rather than details had certainly paid a dividend before the 1979 election campaign began, for commentators had no difficulty in working out what the Conservative attitude to government would be, long before the manifesto was published; the Party thus succeeded in 1975–9 (as it had not done in 1964–70 until Selsdon) in building for itself a clear identity – and one that was clearly different from that of the Labour Government.

The consequences of this new approach were that there was no imposing array of policy groups as before 1970, and that all the tunes of policy tended to be played in a minor key. Much more attention was paid to the views of back-benchers, as expressed through the 1922 Committee and in the various Parliamentary Committees. More emphasis had to be placed on getting general agreement within the Party's collective leadership, though this change had begun under Edward Heath rather than under the new Leader; Patten has noted that the manifesto of October 1974 'obviously had to be broadly acceptable to both sides, and to that extent may be thought to represent – like later documents – a treaty between those with different points of view.' The first major policy document of the new regime was therefore *The Right Approach*, produced for the 1976 Party Conference and intended to head off those in the Party who were

310 The Making of Conservative Party Policy

demanding a clearer line – as they always do in times of opposition. This was described as a 'strategy document' or as an 'approach document', which is to say that it sought to spell out how a Conservative Government would approach problems rather than to lay down what exactly the solutions would be. In that sense, it was rather like the *Industrial Charter*, and like that it did not satisfy either the Party or the press for long. There was indeed something of a shift of direction in 1976, and a much larger number of policy groups were then set up, but these had a markedly-lower status than their predecessors of 1964–70 and there was a lesser chance of their findings ever being published. Patten suggests that,

> More backbenchers wanted to be involved in policy work and the Shadow Cabinet was wisely disposed to let a hundred flowers bloom. In order to ensure that they could be picked without placing too large a burden on the Shadow Cabinet itself, which must necessarily spend quite a lot of its time determining Parliamentary tactics week by week, a policy sub-committee under Sir Keith Joseph's Chairmanship was established to vet policy proposals before their submission to the Shadow Cabinet.

However, this initial decision to run the exercise on a light rein was gradually replaced by a firmer hand on the controls.

The drift towards more detailed policy making could be seen by 1977 with *The Right Approach to the Economy*, still presented as a strategy document, but coming nearer to definite promises (for example on taxation) as the Party came a year nearer to office. It was edited by Maude but published over the joint signatures of Howe, Howell, Joseph and Prior, so helping to refute claims that there were unbridgeable gulfs within the Shadow Cabinet. The Research Department was closely involved in all the work done in these later years of the Parliament, servicing groups and writing up their reports. Early work was also done for the next manifesto, for an election was possible at any time after the Labour Government lost its parliamentary majority in 1977; when an election was generally expected in the Autumn of 1978, the manifesto was ready for the press.

The Department was changed in a number of ways during the Parliament of 1974–9, but its position in the Party hierarchy made its exact future a matter of some speculation. It was certainly recovering its overall importance to the Party, but it did not occupy the position that it had done in, say, the late-forties. The existence of the Centre for Policy Studies removed its absolute monopoly of research advice to Shadow Ministers and there were a few who, like Peter Walker before 1970, preferred to rely as much on their own contacts to prepare them for office as on the Party apparatus. But the centrality of the Research Department to the work of the Opposition was much as before, in practice if not in appearance, and many desk officers were acting virtually as special assistants to their Shadow Ministers, involved in the evolution of policy on a daily basis. What was different was the inevitable involvement of the Department in the Party's ideological division; with the Conservative Party being led from the right of centre for the first time in the half century of the Research Department's existence, its generally progressive approach to Conservatism seemed out of alignment with the leadership. Work and co-operation continued but sympathy and understanding were less evident than sometimes in the past, and there were certainly some on the right of the Party who detected in Old Queen Street a nest of left-wingers (which was only partly true) and Heathmen (which was entirely untrue, if it implied any disloyalty to Margaret Thatcher). These ideas probably made some impact though, and the Department did not enjoy a very happy coverage in the Conservative press in 1978 and 1979. All of this no doubt contributed to the decisions that were taken after the 1979 election.

Other changes had already been made though. Previous work for by-elections was stepped up and a new service was introduced in 1978 to give policy advice to candidates and agents in marginal seats. Much greater interest was being shown in the European dimension of British politics in the aftermath of Britain's joining the EEC, and especially with the advent of direct elections to the European Parliament. With two separate Conservative Parliamentary Parties to be serviced from the Summer of 1979, the Department had to widen its horizons and to develop a new apparatus to link the two. By 1979 there was already a close cooperation with the Secretariat of the European Conservative Group, which was headed by Peter Minoprio (an ex-CRD officer) and staffed largely by former CRD officers; already other desk officers were crossing and re-crossing the Channel much more frequently than before.

All future developments were though affected by the decision to move the Research Department from Old Queen Street into the Central Office building at Smith Square, announced in May 1979 soon after the General Election. Christopher Patten entered the Commons at the election and Angus Maude became a Cabinet Minister but was not re-appointed Chairman of the Research Department; instead, the functions of the Chairman were added to those of the Party Chairman and the new Director was appointed from the Party Chairman's Central Office staff, the first Director who had not worked for the Research Department himself. This reversal of the 1948 concordat between Butler and Woolton appeared to threaten the independence for which the Department and its various Directors had fought ever since 1929, and Lord Butler made some characteristically trenchant observations on the subject to the BBC. However, the Department's strength has always been in its direct line of responsibility to the Leader and so it could make no real appeal against the decisions of the Leader herself. It was made clear to the press that the 'independence' of the Department would not be materially altered by the change of its location. Indeed, ever since 1929 the relationship between the Research Department and Central Office has been a tenuous one, and there have been regular proposals for an amalgamation; it is a relationship that has constantly changed over the years, and indeed one of the strengths of the Department has been its adapatability throughout, so that it is unlikely that the 1979 solution to the problem will prove any more permanent than previous ones. What is not to be doubted, as the Department enters its second half century is that the need for a substantial research organisation carrying out the tasks that have been done at Old Queen Street since 1929 will assuredly continue to exist. The Department will have to go on adapting to circumstances and to political realities, but its research task will still remain basically the same.

Notes

It would be inappropriate to give detailed footnote references to a chapter that is of necessity based more on private information than on documents or other sources on the public record. It would also be ungracious of the author not to acknowledge the assistance of many former and present research officers who have provided that information. There is also an obvious debt to two published works, both of which appeared during the writing of this book. All quotations from Douglas Hurd are from his *An End to Promises*, all quotations from Christopher Patten are from his 'Policy Making in the Conservative Party' in Z. Layton-Henry (ed), *Conservative Party Politics*.

Select Bibliography

J. Amery, *The Life of Joseph Chamberlain*, vi, London, Macmillan, 1969.

L. S. Amery, *My Political Life*, London, Hutchinson, 1953–55.

A. Barker and M. Rush, *The Member of Parliament and his Information*, London, Allen and Unwin, 1970.

A. Beichman, 'The Conservative Research Department: how an elite subsystem within the British Conservative Party participates in the policy-making process', Ph.D. thesis, Columbia, 1973.

J. Bruce-Gardyne, *Whatever happened to the Quiet Revolution?*, London, Knight, 1974.

D. E. Butler and A. King, *The British General Election of 1966*, London, Macmillan, 1966.

D. E. Butler and M. Pinto-Duschinsky, *The British General Election of 1970*, London, Macmillan, 1971.

Lord Butler of Saffron Walden, *The Art of the Possible*, London, Hamilton, 1971.

Lord Butler of Saffron Walden (ed), *The Conservatives*, London, Allen and Unwin, 1977.

F. W. S. Craig (ed), *British Parliamentary Election Manifestoes, 1918–1966*, Chichester, Political Reference Publications, 1970.

J. C. C. Davidson, *Memoirs of a Conservative*, R. Rhodes James (ed), London, Weidenfield, 1969.

N. Fisher, *Iain Macleod*, London, Deutsch, 1973.

K. Feiling, *The Life of Neville Chamberlain*, London, Macmillan, 1956.

Lord Fraser of Kilmorack, 'The Conservative Research Department and Conservative Recovery after 1945', unpublished paper, 1961.

W. L. Guttsmann, *The British Political Elite*, London, Macgibbon and Kee, 1963.

D. A. Hamer, *The Politics of Electoral Pressure*, Hassocks, Harvester, 1977.

M. Hatfield, *The House the Left Built: inside Labour Policy-making, 1970–1975*, London, Gollancz, 1978.

J. D. Hoffman, *The Conservative Party in Opposition 1945–1951*, London, Macgibbon and Kee, 1964.

D. Hurd, *An End to Promises*, London, Collins, 1979.

A. King, 'How the Conservatives evolve policies', *New Society*, 20 July, 1972.

Z. Layton-Henry, *Conservative Party Politics*, London, Macmillan, 1980.

R. T. McKenzie, *British Political Parties*, London, Heinemann, 1955.

R. T. McKenzie and A. Silver, *Angels in Marble*, London, Heinemann, 1968.

J. P. Mackintosh (ed), *People and Parliament*, London, Saxon House, 1978.

I. S. Macleod, *Neville Chamberlain*, London, Muller, 1961.

H. Macmillan, *Winds of Change*, London, Macmillan, 1966.

R. Maudling, *Memoirs*, London, Sidgwick and Jackson, 1978.

K. Middlemas and A. J. L. Barnes, *Baldwin*, London, Weidenfield, 1969.

R. Oakley and P. Rose, *The Political Year 1970*, London, Pitman, 1970.

Lord Percy of Newcastle, *Some Memories*, London, Eyre and Spottiswoode, 1958.

R. M. Punnett, *Front Bench Opposition*, London, Heinemann, 1973.

J. A. Ramsden, *The Age of Balfour and Baldwin*, London, Longman, 1978.

J. A. Ramsden, 'The Organisation of the Conservative and Unionist Party in Britain, 1910–1930', D.Phil. thesis, Oxford, 1974.

R. Rhodes James, *Ambitions and Strategies 1964–1970*, London, Weidenfield, 1972.

A. Roth, *Enoch Powell*, London, Macdonald, 1970.

G. R. Searle, *The Quest for National Efficiency, 1899–1914*, Oxford, Blackwell, 1971.

R. Skidelsky, *Politicians and the Slump*, London, Macmillan, 1967.

J. A. Smith, *John Buchan*, London, Hart-Davis, 1965.

Lord Windlesham, *Communication and Political Power*, London, Cape, 1966.

J. Wyndham, *Wyndham and Children First*, London, Macmillan, 1965.

Index